NOT PEACE BUT A SWORD

Not Peace But A Sword examines the rise of Puritan radicalism during the English revolution of the 1640s. Based largely on close readings of the sermons preached to the Long Parliament, Stephen Baskerville analyzes the link between Calvinist ideology and the revolutionary zeal which culminated in the Civil War. In the hands of the Puritans the sermon became a source of political understanding and social consciousness which challenged traditional assumptions, appealing to the needs of a people caught up in the problems of rapid social and economic change. The book explores the social psychology behind the rise of Puritanism through textual criticism of the sermons, placing them in the mental context of their time, and offers a new understanding of the link between the language of religion and the act of revolution.

Stephen Baskerville teaches with the Civic Education Project at Palacky University, Olomouc, Czechoslovakia. He was formerly Lecturer in Political Science at Howard University, Washington, from 1987 to 1992.

NOT PEACE
BUT A SWORD

The political theology
of the English revolution

Stephen Baskerville

London and New York

First published 1993
by Routledge
11 New Fetter Lane, London EC4P 4EE

Simultaneously published in the USA and Canada
by Routledge
29 West 35th Street, New York, NY 10001

Typeset in 10 on 12 point Garamond by
Computerset, Harmondsworth, Middlesex
Printed in Great Britain by
T J Press (Padstow) Ltd, Padstow, Cornwall

British Library Cataloguing in Publication Data
A catalogue record for this book is available from the British Library.

Library of Congress Cataloging in Publication Data applied for.
Baskerville, Stephen
Not peace but a sword : the political theology of the English Revolution /
Stephen Baskerville
p. c.m.
Includes bibliographical references and index.
1. Preaching—England—History—17th century. 2. Puritans—England—History—
17th century. 3. Great Britain—History—Puritan Revolution, 1642–1660.
4. Christianity and politics—History—17th century. I. Title.
BV4208.G7B37 1993
274.2′06–dc   92-16630

ISBN 0-415-08520-9

Books published under the joint imprint of LSE/Routledge are works of high
academic merit approved by the Publications Committee of the London School of
Economics and Political Science. These publications are drawn from the wide
range of academic studies in the social sciences for which the LSE has an
international reputation.

To my mother and my sister
and the memory of my father

CONTENTS

ACKNOWLEDGMENTS

Portions of this study have been read at the seminars of the Institute of Historical Research and the Center for the History of British Political Thought at the Folger Shakespeare Library in Washington. To the members of these groups and to others who read parts of previous drafts I am grateful for their comments and suggestions, whether or not they were finally heeded: my dissertation supervisor, Peter Lake, Prof. Barnet Baskerville, Maria Dowling, Joan Henderson, William Lamont, John Morrill, Howard Nenner, J.G.A. Pocock, Phillip Richards, Gordon Schochet, Nicholas Tyacke, and Robert Zaller. I wish to thank the staffs of the Institute of Historical Research, the Folger Library, Dr Williams's Library, and the British Library and extend a special note of gratitude to the men and women of the General Reading Rooms Division of the Library of Congress. This study was paid for largely by the student loan program, to which I owe, as they say, an enormous debt. A fellowship from the Folger Institute assisted in the revision of my thesis. Substantive attributions will be found in the notes, though my students at Howard University probably did more to make me think about the nature of bondage and freedom than any academic writing. To my parents, who always took a keen interest in my education and made many sacrifices for it, I owe the most, and to Linda Weiss Baskerville for both her helpful comments and her patient efforts to humor a Puritan.

Stephen Baskerville
March 1992

INTRODUCTION

The pulpit is ever this earth's foremost part; all the rest comes in the rear; the pulpit leads the world.

Melville

This strange wildfire among the people was not so much and so furiously kindled by the breath of the Parliament as of the clergy, who both administered fuel and blowed the coals in the Houses too. These men . . . infused seditious inclinations into the hearts of men against the present government . . . . They contained themselves within no bounds and as freely and without control inveighed against the person of the King . . . to incense and stir up the people against their most gracious sovereign . . . . And indeed no good Christian can without horror think of those ministers of the church, who, by their function being messengers of peace, are the only trumpets of war and incendiaries towards rebellion.

Clarendon

The purpose of this book is to examine the language the Puritan ministers used to instigate revolution in seventeenth-century England. It is based largely on sermons and in particular the sermons preached to the Long Parliament and other political assemblies on days of public fasting. It is not concerned with the technical tenets of systematic theology or academic political theory, nor with the heated controversies, sacred and secular, that were fought out between the Puritans and their opponents. The aim instead is to understand the popular appeal of religious radicalism and the social conditions that gave rise to it.[1]

Like any radical political movement, revolutionary Puritanism emerged in a time of turbulent change and found sympathizers among those who felt most acutely the confusion and disorientation that accompanied its disruptions. The doctrine of predestination, with its stark portrayal of human weakness before the terrible power of an Almighty God, appealed to feelings of helplessness and powerlessness created by rapid and bewildering change in a people largely unacquainted with it. To appreciate fully the attraction of this ideology it is best to consider it within the context of the mental and material world that produced it.

1

England before the revolution can be described as a traditional society, attached to custom and suspicious of innovation. The very recognition of change was difficult for a people limited in the vocabulary available even to describe let alone cope with it, and change in itself was generally assumed to be for the worse, often for good reason. An overriding concern for order reinforced traditional values of hierarchy, ceremony, local community, and the extended family; political life in particular was dominated by personalities – family connections, patronage, local loyalties in the provinces and factions at court – rather than impersonal rules or abstract ideas. Much of the population was still habituated to the old religion, with its ornate rituals and affinities to popular culture and magic, and the new, more intellectual creed of Protestantism had sometimes met with stubborn resistance. The apex of political authority was the monarchy, whose person was consecrated with a sanctity and who commanded a sacred awe that was as much religious as political: kings and queens were objects of cultic veneration, widely credited with magical powers and accorded a status of almost divine proportions. Challenges to the existing order were not only resisted among all ranks, but virtually inconceivable in terms of moral or political principle. Modern concepts of 'reform' and 'revolution' were rudimentary or nonexistent, and the older notion of the civil war as the design of a confident Parliament seeking to wrest power from an incompetent king and justifying its actions by appeals to liberal theories of natural rights, individual liberty, resistance to tyrants, representative government, and religious toleration has been, if not wholly discredited, at least much too simple. Before the war, it has been written, most members of Parliament were not struggling to achieve increased political responsibilities: 'They were struggling to avoid them.'[2]

At the same time these were precisely the conservative habits and attitudes Puritanism was designed to break down. For in fact the century or so before the revolution was a period of profound change, change that for most of the population was in itself far from benign or propitious. The breakup of the traditional agrarian order and the beginnings of industrial development created severe dislocation and disorder, and some of the consequences should be mentioned at the outset, as they will recur in the rather different idiom of the preachers. The disruptive effects of change – rapid social mobility, fierce competition for status, general feelings of personal and social insecurity at all levels, along with an acute apprehension about the growing problem of poverty – were among the most commented-upon features of the age.[3] While I will argue that these were the fears Puritanism addressed and exploited, in themselves they did not guarantee Puritan sympathies, and I have no desire to represent religious ideas as a simple reflex response to economic phenomena.

Other options for coping with the new stresses besides radical religion were certainly available, as the ministers themselves often observed with dismay; and to the uncertainties and insecurities of change people responded in different ways, and with varying degrees of success, to enhance or at least protect their position, reinforce their self-esteem, or simply survive. Those at the higher social levels developed codes of personal honor and martial valor, learned to exploit the potential of their estates, arranged marriages with newer wealth, took lucrative positions in government service, pursued fashionable occupations and pastimes, and cultivated or affected the arts and culture, education and learning, distinctive styles of speech, dress, manners, and bodily comportment. These in turn were imitated by the urban and entrepreneurial middle classes who, as they prospered (or failed to prosper) by exploiting the new economic opportunities, married into older families, purchased titles of honor, and displayed their new status through consumption and leisure. Any of these private means of securing status, position, and power might coexist with a tendency to Puritanism, at least as some of the gentry saw it, though their rivalry with religion could provoke a response in the ministers ranging from muted contempt to vituperative denunciation.[4] But while social change by its nature blurred distinctions of status, and while no response was specific to any single stratum of society, for the vast majority the options were more limited; and it was the responses available to (though by no means only to) the lower orders that seemed most to disturb the preachers, especially the more destructive and self-destructive outlets for frustration and resentment. This leads to perhaps the most fearful consequences of change: new social problems, especially those associated with poverty.[5] For while some benefited handsomely from the new opportunities, far greater numbers suffered, often being reduced to destitution as the victims of unemployment, inflation, debt, and confiscation.

The resulting proximity of new wealth and new poverty, along with the dilemmas this posed for individuals caught in between, resulted in the perception of a society increasingly polarized between the rich and the poor. This has led some to see Puritanism simply as the religion of the newly affluent aimed at the control of their victims. The reality was much more complex. Problems now familiar as the by-products of economic development and perhaps endemic to modern society were appearing in Europe, if not for the first time, at least in new and disturbing forms, problems that created in people of all social ranks the feeling of being overwhelmed by forces beyond their control – in their terms, acts of 'God': population increase and urbanization, rising prices and falling incomes, dislocations in the markets for goods, land, and labor, the destruction of traditional agricultural methods, manufacturing techniques, economic arrangements, social relations, family ties, local communities, ways of life. With the development of a market economy came new opportunities for various forms of commercial exploitation: enclosures, deforestation, fen drainage, depopulation, rent-racking, wage labor, usury, engrossing and forestalling, hoarding, price fixing, cozenage, forgery, fraud. These in turn were closely associated with the kind of official corruption that arose as new economic pressures placed increased strains on government finance: monopolies, bribery, nepotism, clientage, cronyism, sinecures, factionalism, favoritism, the sale of offices and honors, reversions, litigiousness, impropriations. Perhaps most immediately important, these problems emerged within a traditional system of government and administration, as well as law enforcement and legal justice, that was often ill-equipped to address them, with a ruling elite largely lacking in the kind of basic political habits that in modern societies is usually assumed. A mostly unprofessional administrative system was often strained by inexperience, inefficiency, and indirection, while the diffidence of public officials often made them reluctant to face problems, accept responsibility, or challenge higher authority. The absence of effective bureaucratic procedures, confusion about ethical norms and social values, and inadequately developed mechanisms of legal redress all helped erode confidence in the social and political system. Further, the lack of an organized political opposition meant that criticism of government policy was limited to what has been characterized as a 'disorganized, divided, and undisciplined House of Commons'.[6] Finally, all this must be placed against the wider backdrop of a general population that was itself not only wholly lacking in the political skills necessary for modern citizenship, but still marked by high levels of illiteracy, ignorance, and superstition. Together, all these created or exacerbated or simply failed to alleviate conditions of not just accepted and unavoidable hardship but unaccountable and menacing squalor: urban overcrowding, food shortages and famine, disease, homelessness and vagrancy, crime, riots and popular rebellion, alcohol abuse, family breakdown and domestic violence, illegitimacy, prostitution, social and sexual deviance, suicide, the resort to popular magic. To these may be added the unleashing of less tangible but very real psychic disorders that might go under the names of anxiety, alienation, resentment, frustration, aggression, loneliness, apathy, anomie, cynicism, fantasy, impotence, depression, despair. These were the conditions that bred Calvinism: it was these that convinced the people of England that they were on their way to hell, and it was from these that they sought salvation.

These economic changes and social problems, along with the specific political responses they generated, are not in themselves the subject of this study; a society pervaded by poverty, instability, and violence in the years before the civil war has been described and documented in a host of recent works.[7] The purpose of this essay – like that of the Puritan sermon – is to connect them to the realm of ideas and in particular to that system of revolutionary ideas that produced the movement known as Puritanism. 'A true revolution needs ideas to fuel it; without them there is only a rebellion or a coup d'état,' writes a historian. 'In England the most far-reaching in its influence on men's minds, although very difficult to pin down in precise detail, was Puritanism.'[8] This study is an attempt to pin down Puritan ideas in as precise detail as possible, and not as they were formulated in abstract academic expositions or codified in official doctrinal manifestos, but through a careful examination of the actual words by which they were imparted to sympathetic listeners as agents of political change. Without coming to terms with Puritan ideas and the complex emotions they touched and mobilized, without coming to grips with how people expressed their own perceptions and feelings about their world and their place within it, no depiction of English society or English politics will ever account for revolutionary fervor. What needs to be explained is not only the cleavages that may have been opening up in a rapidly changing society or how the administrative system may have failed to meet new needs, but why under these circumstances people from a wide range of social stations and political positions became susceptible to radical ideas.[9] Why, for example, through what has been termed 'the rhetoric of suffering' – describing themselves and their followers as the 'poor', 'oppressed', 'despised', 'reproached', 'disgraced', 'scorned', 'persecuted', 'hated', 'miserable', 'outcast', 'forlorn', 'wretched', 'mangled', 'contemptible', 'foolish', 'meek', 'humble', 'base', 'weak', 'afflicted', 'neglected', and 'unworthy' – the Puritan preachers could receive a sympathetic hearing from an audience drawn not only from the swarms of uprooted poor who massed to London and the burgeoning towns in the decades before the war but from every social rank up to and including the illustrious members of the House of Lords. 'I speak to a great assembly, to an assembly of gods,' the eminent Stephen Marshall told that chamber early in the decade, 'but I speak in the name of a great God, before whom you are but as so many grasshoppers . . . his poor sinful creatures.' Few of the ministers themselves or their most important followers were the direct victims of problems such as poverty, at least in its most devastating form (though they did complain about it often enough); mostly they were drawn from among those with enough leisure to be involved in the world of ideas. Yet this could not be distinguished sharply in their minds from the world as a whole, and while they were not unmindful of the effects of poverty on the body and the estate, what most captured their attention was its impact on the mind and, as they said, the 'soul'. Thus the use of social conditions as metaphors for mental and 'spiritual' ones, even in those apparently untouched by the material reality: 'spiritual poverty', 'spiritual whoredom', 'spiritual warfare'.[10]

Social change, then, was not an abstraction in some grand historical theory but a phenomenon of frightening proportions that created turmoil not only in the lives of the English people but in their souls as well. Accordingly, Puritan ideas, even at their most 'spiritual', did not confine themselves to an ethereal 'other' world, separate from the problems of this one; neither were they produced simply to divert the attention of the people to another life as a way of diffusing their discontents over the one they had to endure here. Rather, by articulating the problems of their society as ideas the Puritan preachers used their religion to help fearful and troubled people, tormented with rage and sorrow, racked with guilt and self-hate, to transform a confused and often destructive discontent into a new social and political consciousness. This consciousness, apparently so pessimistic in its origins, was in the end marked by a persistent 'cosmic optimism', which, while manifested in the popular stereotype of the grim Puritan personality, the preachers themselves argued was less the cause than the cure. 'It is false that religion breeds melancholy and cuts off all mirth,' William Perkins maintained. 'It doth not abolish mirth, but rectify it; nay, it brings men to true and perfect joy.' The purpose of Puritan religion was not simply to eliminate the anxiety and the bitterness, the sense of loss and rootlessness created by the new social conditions, if that were even possible, but to harness the energy they generated and direct it into a new course, to organize and mobilize people for collective action to face their problems openly and constructively and gain a measure of control over their lives. 'Religion takes not away the earnestness of the affections,' argued the great pastoral divine Richard Sibbes.

> It doth direct them to better things . . . . Religion taketh them not away but turns them that way that they should go . . . . Religion takes nothing away that is good but lifts it up; it elevateth and advanceth it to better objects. There are riches, and honors, and pleasures . . . but . . . they run in a better, in a clearer channel. Whereas before they ran amain to earthly, dirty things below, the same affections, of love, of desire, and zeal, do remain still.

Religion on its own, then, like any system of ideas, neither created nor extinguished human motivations, aspirations, passions, or emotions, so much as it articulated and organized them. And if what follows sometimes appears as a cruel and violent religion, it was because it addressed itself to people who led violent lives; but it was no more so than the society from which it emerged and the material on which it had to work. 'Violence requires the height and strength of the affections,' Sibbes added. 'He that was violent before is as violent still, only the stream is turned.'[11]

In this way it is possible to see Puritan thought as a response to seemingly overwhelming social and economic forces and yet in the face of those a testament to, rather than a denial of, human freedom – much as did its own predestinarian 'determinism', paradoxically perhaps. The Puritans' own view of history as a process led inexorably forward by divine wisdom to a predetermined end was itself essential in bringing about the events in which they were instrumental. While this would seem to conflict with the current view that historical events are 'not foreordained' and 'not inevitable', it was compatible with the corollary position that great political upheavals were often driven by a power very different from what those who seemed to make them might consciously intend. 'I dare say you thought at first only to restrain the exorbitancy of the bishops and reform some faults of the service book, to rectify the irregularity of civil courts,' one minister suggested to the House of Commons in 1644, 'and God hath discovered innumerable abominations unto you and hath led you in paths not intended by you but well pleasing to himself.' Yet to allow our understanding of the civil war to end at that is plainly inadequate. The English revolution happened because, in one sense or another, the people of England wanted it to happen and because enough of them were willing to risk, and in the end sacrifice, their lives to make it happen. Most expressed this willingness in religious terms, and no account which ignores the conscious wills of morally free people or the sincerity – the deadly serious pursuit of sincerity – in their religious commitment will ever explain why people are willing to fight and die for a cause. The bold self-assurance, the indefatigable sense of purpose and mission and righteous zeal that impelled them to defy and eventually execute their king, and the conviction that they performed

God's will in doing so, invested the parliamentary cause with the sense of destiny and authority from heaven that it needed to challenge a monarchy that claimed to rule by divine right. 'This Parliament seems to have been called by God,' Thomas Goodwin declared before the House of Commons in 1642. 'You, Right Honorable, are the anointed of the Lord set apart from your brethren to the great work of the Lord.' Yet those most vocal about their divine inspiration may after all be trying to convince themselves, and this conviction began not as a confident assumption but itself a goal to be chosen and pursued as part of their struggle. 'And if you will not do it,' Goodwin went on to warn the House, 'God will do it without you.'[12]

However tempting it may be to regard religion as a simple exercise in self-deception or a harmless release for pent-up rage, the emotional business in which the Puritans were involved was in fact a fairly desperate one. In analyzing the 'political' theology of the Puritans I have had no intention of arguing what William Ames called 'that Machiavellian blasphemy, that religion is nothing but a politic engine'. Certainly at a time when government repression and censorship made it hazardous to organize an open political opposition, discontent often found its outlet in religious activity that legitimized political grievances within the respectability of the conventional and orthodox; there even came to be an element of the more cynical principles of civil statecraft. Yet religious ideas were not simply a disguise for political or other ideas that were not safe to express; they contained a purpose and a dynamic of their own. Above all, religious hypocrisy (and other kinds too), though a charge leveled against the ministers by both their adversaries and many historians, was among the foremost of their own targets as well and one they attempted to overcome by the most disarming method possible – directing the accusation against themselves. Religion encompassed all of Puritan life, and the fact that it was inseparable from its social and political environment made it more, not less, 'real'. 'Religion is not a chimera or a notion,' Ames added, 'but a real thing in the hearts and lives of good men.'[13]

And yet Puritan religion was different in a number of ways, not least of which was precisely its relation to the world of 'reality' and its own internal imperative to be made a 'real thing' in the hearts and lives of the people. 'Every man can talk of religion, but where is the practice?' asked Sibbes. 'A little obedience is worth all the discourse and contemplation in the world.' Puritan ideas did not claim to set forth a disinterested appraisal of their society. On the contrary, they were designed by their very nature to effect a change in that and those with whom they came in contact. 'Earlier theologians had explained the world,' writes another historian; 'for Puritans the point was to change it.'[14] The precise relationship between thought and society, between the 'ideal' and the 'real', is an endless dilemma in intellectual history, and it is always difficult to devise a single formula for assessing the relationship between what people believe about their world and, if this is a legitimate distinction, the world itself. And yet the very significance of the subject matter of this study is that it offered within itself, possibly for the first time in the history of ideas, precisely such a formula. Protestantism – that complex system of interconnected ideas that reached their nexus in the revolutionary concept of justification by faith – as no other set of beliefs, exalted the idea of belief itself, and the radical Protestantism of the English revolution made it a matter of immediate practical importance as the basis for a program of political action. This more than anything gave to Protestantism and especially Puritanism the claim to be an *ideology:* a system of ideas that creates its own reality, that derives its fulfillment from the very fact that it is believed.[15]

It was here that the Protestant Reformation created not only a new kind of piety but also a new kind of politics, and English Puritanism created a new kind of person: the citizen, the activist, the 'ideologically committed political radical'.[16] The revolutionary impact of Puritan dissent was more than simply an 'accidental by-product' of controversies over abstract and arcane points of the creed. Christianity itself encompasses a rich symbolic structure carrying subtle but far-reaching social and political implications, all of which were thoroughly explored and exploited by the Puritan intellectuals, who used it to develop a complete system of popular psychology, sociology, anthropology, economics, and political thought that has been almost completely ignored by modern historians. While this study will not concern itself with the technicalities of systematic theology, it is worth remarking that Calvinism did constitute a highly schematic religion that organized its tenets into a closely interconnected doctrinal system. For its stark dogmas such as predestination, its denial of human free will, and other apparent rejections of everyday experience (or at least our everyday experience), the preachers claimed with a rigid and doctrinaire intolerance the status of absolute truth. Yet here it is the application of those dogmas in the practical and popular commentary of the sermon with which we will be mostly concerned. For it was from the pulpit that the Puritan ministers would explicate and apply the austere tenets of their demanding doctrine to an impressive range of emotional needs with a delicate and even moving sensitivity. In the process, they brought to politics a passion and an urgency that transformed it for the first time into a matter that could determine the fate of not merely the body and the estate but also the immortal soul.[17] In the end, the case for Puritanism as a radical ideological movement lies not in any originality in its thought (a notion the ministers themselves would have repudiated), nor in incidental differences of opinion with its opponents, but in its uncompromising commitment to the popularization of religious and political ideas themselves. The apparently most conservative ideas become revolutionary once they are made accessible to a mass audience, and the opening of ideas to the people made the Protestant Reformation the first truly popular political movement. 'Truth and doctrine should always be preached openly and firmly, without compromise or concealment,' ran a central tenet of the religion whose 'truth and doctrine' itself taught that 'faith cometh by hearing'. 'It should be preached to all men, at all times and in all places.'[18]

The sermon then was not simply a medium, and the pulpit not simply a platform, for issuing political statements; the promotion of preaching, the very act of delivering a sermon, was itself a political statement. 'Promote preaching of the word of faith which is so powerful,' Thomas Wilson urged the House of Commons, '. . . for faith comes by the word preached.' Without the problems outlined above rendering Calvinist doctrine plausible and appealing to the men and women of the time no amount of Puritan preaching would have made any impact; yet it remains equally true that neither would social conditions by themselves have produced a political revolution without the ideological direction furnished by Puritan ideas and the preaching by which they were broadcast throughout society. 'God doth devise things by way of preparing men,' Samuel Hieron said. 'Such are afflictions, crosses, inward affrightments. But when all is done and spoken that can be, to this we must come at last, that the main work (ordinarily) either by preaching it is wrought or not at all.' Like all intellectuals, the Puritan ministers saw the dissemination of ideas as itself a means of addressing societal problems and promoting social order. 'Human society doth consist in communicating prudent notions one to another for the preservation of the whole society,' Francis Cheynell said, 'and therefore a man cannot be a useful member of the body politic, because he cannot be a sociable man . . . without knowledge and prudence.' And yet such knowledge (and prudence) was intended not merely as a contemplative or academic understanding but to make people 'useful' and 'sociable', to encourage them to become actively involved in practical and political affairs. 'This knowledge . . . is not a mental or speculative understanding of human affairs or things belonging either to church or commonwealth,' Stephen Marshall explained, 'but a practical knowledge, which is a wise ability to manage all the understanding that [you] have in reference to [your] duty.' This emphasis on 'practical knowledge' not only was the ideal expressed by the ministers in their sermons but reached its greatest fulfillment in the very exercise of preaching itself. 'The end of our preaching is not that you should know, but that you should do and practice,' said the influential John Preston. 'Practice is all in all; so much as you practice, so much you know.'[19] If Puritan ideas did not purport to be detached or disinterested theory, they were ideas that were valid, that were 'true', only to the extent that they were expressed and communicated and put to use; for this the sermon was the logical medium, communicating not simply information but what the preachers called 'exhortation'. 'It is not only the minister's office by doctrine to inform the judgment of his people but also to use the words of exhortation,' explained Richard Bernard. 'For a minister is . . . by doctrine to enlighten the understanding and by exhortation to quicken affection.' It was exhortation that applied the doctrine to 'use', that combined theory and practice. 'Let us use words of exhortation, because we are so exhorted,' exhorted Bernard himself. 'It is necessary because it serves for moving and winning the heart, without which understanding will never come to practice.' Exhortation then was by definition exhortation to *do* something, and it translated abstract ideas into concrete actions and events. 'Exhortation is for the exciting and quickening of our affections unto any grace or duty,' John Wilkins said. ''Tis so principal a part of preaching that all that [is] to be spoken is called exhortation.'[20]

If anything was truly distinctive and innovative in Puritan ideas about revolution, therefore, it was not what they said about it but that they did it; they put their theory into practice, their thought into action. This kind of dialectical praxis of theory and practice, thought and action (or as they termed it, faith and works), made preaching itself an expression of what is arguably the central contention of all radicalism: that the popularization of ideas and beliefs offers a more effective, reliable, and permanent alternative to the coercive power of the state in repressing human aggression and enforcing civilized conduct – that 'the word', in the parlance of the Puritans, 'not the sword, reaches the heart': 'The power of the word in the consciences of people binds more strongly to obedience than the power of the sword over the bodies of people.' And 'the word', in the ministers' lexicon, always meant the spoken word, the word preached. 'Men through the preaching of the word conscionably are brought to more even civil humanity than by the laws of man which may bridle somewhat,' Richard Bernard asserted. 'It is the word only which worketh conscience to God, true obedience to men . . . . The word can work such humiliation and subjection, and that to be voluntary . . . as no power of man can bring them unto.' And yet while the principle that the word is mightier than the sword was one of those 'eternal' truths to which the ministers were solemnly dedicated, it was also a difficult one for mortal flesh faced with critical problems in the here and now; that it could be breached by the very vehemence with which it was propounded is a moral paradox typically indicated by the metaphor one preacher used to express it. 'It hath pleased [God] all along in all ages to carry on his great design of changing the hearts of men by an ordinance of spiritual efficacy and not in the way of outward power,' Lazarus Seaman proclaimed. 'It should be done by way of divine oratory . . . the sword that cometh out of the mouth of the Lord.' The result, as Seaman's metaphor also indicates, was that the sword came to be infused with and activated by the purpose of the word. 'Soldiers are gathered together and battles brought on by the sound of a trumpet,' Francis Peck announced. 'So are true believers and worshippers in the Lord's mountain to be brought on to his spiritual warfare by the sound of the Lord's trumpet – that is, the powerful preaching of the gospel.' On this note, perhaps the greatest panegyric to the political power of preaching was provided by the greatest of the political preachers. 'It were an endless task for me to recount unto you what preaching hath done,' declared the infamous Stephen Marshall (himself known as the 'trumpet' of St Margaret's church) in 1646,

> what strong castles have been demolished by preaching, how many thousand enemies have been made friends by preaching, how many kingdoms have been subdued by preaching, how . . . the preaching of the word had gone into all the earth and unto the ends of the world and rent in pieces the kingdom of the devil . . . . In a word, preaching is that whereby Christ destroys the very kingdom of Antichrist. Though it is the devil's

masterpiece laid the deepest in policy and founded not only in states but in men's consciences, yet Christ destroys it by the 'word of his mouth' – that is, the preaching of the gospel in the mouths of his ministers.[21]

A dedication to the power of the 'word', then, and especially the spoken word, must take primacy in any attempt at the elusive task of defining Puritanism. 'What power and efficacy the word hath,' remarked Richard Sibbes. 'It is a word that changeth and altereth the whole man.' The word provided the basis of both piety and power for the Puritan clergy and their sympathizers, and especially so following the tremendous growth in literacy and education in the hundred or so years before the war (itself largely a product of the Puritans' own campaign to eradicate ignorance and introduce mass education). A new demand and interest in ideas, as well as opportunities and pretentions to political influence for those who could demonstrate a command over them, had been combined with an overproduction of clergy and intellectuals beyond the available employment, so that the expectations aroused often met with frustration and disappointment. Even as ideas were assuming a new importance in the social order, therefore, they came to acquire particular force as a means of expressing discontent on the part of those whose place in that order was uneasy. It is this that accounts in part for the strong strain of *anti*-intellectualism in the Puritan clergy, who could use their roles as prophets to denounce the values of a society that had failed to make sufficient use of their talents and those of their followers. When to this is added the aspirations and resentments of those still dependent upon hearing rather than reading for inclusion in the new world of ideas, a preaching ministry can be seen to have possessed a popular influence that could never be matched by the secular intelligentsia.[22]

For all these reasons the ministers developed an intimate identification with their role as expositors of the word and often demanded for their medium that respect and recognition they desperately craved for themselves. 'The exercise of preaching ought to receive from us all esteem,' said Samuel Hieron in a sermon on 'the dignity of preaching'. 'The preaching of God's holy word, though it be meanly esteemed by the world, it is the ministry of the spirit.' The point was, as often as not, directed at themselves and, like their theology generally, was intended to use such a mean estimation as an encouragement to a sense of honor and duty in delivering a messsage that itself was largely devoted to promoting those virtues. 'Honor and esteem is the due of preaching,' Hieron continued. 'It is the life and glory of our profession. To be termed a preacher is the fairest flower in our garland.' In this way the preachers' own self-image and sense of self-respect was to be intertwined with their foremost function. 'Preaching deserves esteem,' Hieron reiterated. 'Take heed how we expose it to contempt. Our diligence in dispensing the word . . . our endeavoring in the eyes of the people to frame our lives according to the word shall uphold the credit of this worthy service.' The connection between thought and action, and the insistence that the very 'truth' of their ideas was dependent upon the practical application to which they were put, was brought out in these injunctions the ministers issued to one another that their

11

precepts would only be respected if they themselves practiced them, both in their sermons and in their own lives as well. 'Because the doctrine of the word is hard both to be understood and to be practiced, therefore the minister ought to express that by his example which he teacheth as it were by a type,' Perkins urged. 'It is a thing execrable in the sight of God that godly speech should be conjoined with an ungodly life.' The imperative to practice what they preached and the close relationship between speech and life were sometimes indicated by the way the preachers described the life of a minister, and by extension of others as well, as itself a kind of sermon. 'The life of a minister preacheth as much as his doctrine,' Edmund Calamy told his colleagues. 'All that a minister doth is a kind of preaching, and if you live a covetous or a careless life you preach these sins to your people by your practice.'[23]

But for a preacher a godly life was almost defined by godly speech, similarly seen in terms of practical utility and an ability to communicate simply and effectively, without affected display or embellishment. 'If the plainness of the style be either questioned or blamed, my answer is ready,' declared Joseph Boden with some defiance. 'It was chosen on purpose, that if any good do issue upon either the preaching or publishing this piece the praise may be of and to God, not the weak and unworthy instrument.' The famous Puritan 'plain style' was devised out of a concern to facilitate understanding, and regardless of the gifts a speaker might seem to possess, no learning was genuine, no idea was said to truly exist until it could be communicated in clear and plain expressions comprehensible by even the least educated listener. 'The phrase must be plain and natural,' John Wilkins enjoined. 'Obscurity in the discourse is an argument of ignorance in the mind. The greatest learning is to be seen in the greatest plainness. The more clearly we understand anything ourselves, the more easily we can expect to expound it to others.' The ministers were suspicious of philosophical speculation and contemptuous of purely academic learning and tried to resist the temptation to delve into the arcana of technical theology or secular political theory. 'It hinders much profitable preaching,' Richard Kentish warned. 'It causes many sermons to be fitter for an academical chair than a popular pulpit.' At their most elegant they placed these problems as well in the marginalia for the specialists. The ministers had a tremendous respect for learning and even style, but these were judged successful to the extent that they were effective without being obtrusive, and practical knowledge was not to be obscured by the frivolous aestheticism and gratuitous exhibitions of wit that characterized much of their adversaries' elocution. 'The minister may, yea and must privately use at his liberty the arts, philosophy, and variety of reading, whilst he is in framing his sermon,' ran a famous passage from an influential preaching manual by William Perkins; 'but he ought in public to conceal all these from the people and not to make the least ostentation. It is also a point of art to conceal art.' The preachers had no illusions that a style that was popular without being vulgar was easy; on the contrary, they were more aware than anyone that clear and precise prose required far more effort and finesse than pedantic obscurity or pretentious jargon. 'What skill is necessary to make the truth plain . . . and . . . suitable to the capacities of our hearers,' remarked Richard Baxter. 'It is no easy matter to speak so plainly that the most ignorant may understand us.' One of the most heinous sins a minister could commit, and what more than anything deprived preaching of the 'esteem' it deserved, was to indulge in a style that failed to provide clear understanding or positively impeded it through affected erudition. 'When men strive to . . . affect terms more than matter, embellishing their sermons with the gleanings of all manner of authors, sacred, profane, anything which may be thought to smell of learning and may raise an opinion of eloquence, profound-ness, variety of reading in the hearers', as Samuel Hieron put it. 'This shall be found to dishonor God's ordinance. For what is that which indeed makes preaching honorable in the hearts of God's people but their understanding it? . . . That therefore which hindereth understanding must needs expose this cause to a kind of disgrace.' The bitterness and resentment in English society on which Puritan ideas thrived were reflected in the scorn with which they themselves resented and despised those who deliberately obscured their rhetoric to confuse the simple for the sake of their own status and power. 'Why do you not speak so as to be understood?' Baxter demanded of his colleagues in exaspera-tion. 'That a man should purposely cloud the matter in strange words . . . is the way to make fools admire his profound learning and wise men his folly, pride, and hypocrisy.' Godly preaching, on the other hand, demanded discourse that could be both widely and deeply understood and make a real and lasting impact on a mass audience. 'All our teaching must be as plain and as simple as possible,' Baxter enjoined. 'He that would be understood must speak to the capacity of his hearers . . . There is no better way to make a good cause prevail than to make it as plain and as generally and thoroughly known as we can.'[24]

At the same time, the preachers did not pander to their audience and bitterly detested those who in their view did. The demands they made on themselves to explain complex concepts with simplicity and clarity and free from pretentious displays of learning were matched by those they made on their listeners to endure long and intensive orations (an expectation that seems to have been enlarged for their readership). 'Preaching and hearing are relatives,' said John Brinsley. 'If there lie a necessity upon us to preach, by the same rule there lieth a necessity upon you to hear.' If the preachers themselves disdained those who affected easy eloquence, those who sought a message delivered in terms from which they would not feel excluded could be under no illusions that it would be without effort on their own part, and both the preaching and hearing of the word were symbolic preparations for even more strenuous demands. 'If God be not weary of speaking, be not you weary of hearing,' Brinsley continued. 'Whatever the world thinks and speaks of it, it is no disgrace to be accounted a frequenter of sermons.' For the Puritans a true understanding of religion required more than simply memorizing the dogmas of a creed or reciting a catechism, and it was in the sermon that they made an apparently dry and dour theology come alive as a source of practical understanding and social awareness. 'Embrace every occasion which the Lord offereth in the public ministry of his word,' Brinsley urged. 'Get something from every sermon, from this which you have this day heard.' That the effort to acquire this understanding, like that of the revolution generally, was not an easy one, and that it met with resistance and varying degrees of success, the preachers themselves were the first to acknowledge. Yet to the arrogant but now apparently fashionable suggestion that partisans remained largely unaware of the spiritual principles for which they contended Francis Cheynell provided perhaps the most succinct rejoinder when he warned his fellow ministers that 'men will not die for a religion which they do not understand'.[25]

For all its insistence on a plain style therefore, Puritan literature has seldom failed to move by its very absence of sophistication. Emerging at a time when the English language itself was undergoing an enormous expansion, Puritan discourse has had an impact on our social and political vocabulary comparable to that of the Elizabethan poets and dramatists on literary style, and it has done so by popularizing and expanding upon the poetry and drama of perhaps the most influential written work in the English language, the King James version of the Bible. Any study of Puritanism presents a temptation to go one step beyond the sources and examine the preachers' understanding and use of the Bible. Scriptural passages are quoted with a frequency roughly similar to that with which I in turn quote the sermons. In fact, while they also cited subsequent Christian authorities (as well as pagan and profane ones), these can be said to have stood to scripture in a relation analogous to that of the historian between a primary and secondary source, and not accidentally, as with all ideologies there was an indispensable historical component to their theology, as, they themselves pointed out, there was in the Bible.[26] Yet while their claim that scripture served as the inspiration for their ideas will be taken seriously, it is these ideas as they were employed in their own time that must take primacy here – not so much a denial of their biblical origins as a tribute to their enduring power in different historical circumstances. 'God never proposed to leave his holy word to be no more but read, either privately in men's houses or publicly in our churches, but appointed there should be men ordained to expand the same by voice and apply it to the occasions and necessities of the people,' said Samuel Hieron. 'This is the soul of prophecying and the very life of preaching. It openeth the scripture to show what it meaneth; it fits to the particular uses and cases of the hearers.' This self-image of the preachers as the 'prophets' of God provides one of the clearest illustrations of how they saw themselves as not simply adhering to the word of God but living it, even re-creating it. 'The prophets of God, the ministers of the word, are God's mouth, whereby he speaks and makes known his will to his people,' said John Brinsley. 'We are criers, heralds from the Lord of Hosts, the king of heaven, from God himself, to declare and proclaim his will to the church.' The term had come to carry connotations of foretelling the future; but its broader meaning was closer to what would now be termed a social critic or dissident, as were the prophets of old. 'In the strictest taking of the word, "prophecying" is to foretell some future thing, and so accordingly they were termed "prophets" to whom God revealed his special purposes touching these after times,' Hieron observed. 'But now . . . we find this term "prophecying" not so much to signify a revealing beforehand by divine inspirement what touching states and common-wealths and particular persons shall ensue, as an expounding the scriptures in such sort as might advance the common benefit . . . . It is even the very same which we term "preaching".'[27]

I have tried to allow the preachers to speak for themselves and not hesitated to follow their practice of extensively quoting what they argued were their own sources and authorities. 'Bring in the prophets . . . speaking in their own words,' Richard Bernard suggested. 'If we would reprehend bribery in great ones, we may say, I will not reprove this sin, but Isaiah he shall tell who they be.' Inevitably this resulted in repetition, though this too was often a deliberate device to provide thorough understanding by attacking the same point from a variety of angles. 'I love to inculcate the same things rather than to abound in variety,' another preacher confessed without apology, 'because I desire more to profit than to please.' I have selected not so much passages addressing public affairs or personal devotion as those which seem to make a connection between the two in some pointed or significant way. While the intention has been to provide a representa-tive sample of themes and utterances from sermons of different preachers at different times, naturally I have favored passages that seem somehow especially revealing to the modern reader, either because something that is usually implicit is made explicit through the use of distinctions or comparisons or because a preacher uses what seems to be a particularly suggestive figure of speech. The latter, however, tend to be mainly social and political. For the sake of space I have tended to omit the many homely illustrations the preachers used to sugar a very bitter pill. These constitute some of the most poetic passages in Puritan literature, and as they remind us that Puritanism was a movement whose prophets used the word to make their ideas felt in the daily lives of plain people this absence is an unfortunate one. Many of the preachers took from everyday life and speech or borrowed from one another, though these borrowings blend into those from biblical passages. 'Use similitudes, which may be taken from persons, things, and actions . . . to win the hearer by so plain and evident demonstrations,' Bernard advised. 'But here beware the similes be from things known, easy to be conceived, and apt; so are all similes made in scripture . . . the scriptures being full of tropes and figures.' This attention to the details of language, occasionally somewhat mechanical, at its best reflected the preachers' keen sensitivity to the power of words and metaphor and the impact of style on content. 'Similes are of excellent use even to teach, move, and delight the hearer,' Bernard insisted, 'and their minister powerful who must use them.' These too, however, again with great reluctance, have been pared to a minimum. One example, illustrating the technique in the process of advocating it, might serve to demonstrate how the ideas and the rhetorical method used to deliver them were inseparable: 'God doth reveal heavenly truths in certain apt similitudes,' explained Francis Cheynell.

God descends to our weak capacity, when he clothes a heavenly truth with an earthly representation . . . . I have represented heavenly truths by comparisons taken from earthly things: I have brought down the bough which was out of your reach and put it into your hand and helped you up, so that you may now climb from earth to heaven by these similitudes.[28]

For reasons wholly consistent with the message of the preachers, their sermons change remarkably little over time, and in keeping with my effort to view the larger phenomenon of Puritanism I have moved freely over the years with little or no attempt to isolate variations according to chronology or the fortunes of either the parliamentary party as a whole or various emerging tendencies within it. The preachers did at times bring current events into their sermons in an effort to 'speak a word in season' and vivify the abstractions of their theology. 'This is to have the tongue of the learned,' said John Wilkins, 'which knows how to speak a word in due season.'[29] Yet such references were usually oblique, and most often the purpose of mentioning them at all was to demonstrate a need to transcend their uncertainty. To try to tie broad religious precepts to short-term fluctuations in the fortunes of particular groups beyond the strictly limited point to which they did so would be, for them and us, to defeat the purpose of the exercise. On the other hand, what did change over time was the composition of the parliamentary 'party', including the clergymen it patronized. I have chosen to present Puritanism as a series of dialectical tensions, ambiguities, and ambivalences upon which differences (orthodox or otherwise) were variations but which must be taken in their entirety in an effort to understand the dynamics of the movement. In this respect the sermons preached to Parliament or printed under its authority reflect at any given moment the boundaries of the collective viewpoint of a shifting coalition: ministers outside this consensus were not invited to preach, and those who overstepped the bounds of acceptable, impersonal criticism or transgressed their own professed principles by engaging in overt polemic from the pulpit (at least outside the consensus of the moment) were not requested to print.[30]

The preachers freely admit to expanding the printed version from what they actually said, but there is little reason to assume they were not faithful in writing to what they knew to be acceptable and therefore effective in speaking. Printed literature too was of vast importance in the transmission of revolutionary ideas, and it is difficult to conceive of the politics of the 1640s without the development of printing. Nevertheless, if mass communication made political revolution possible, the most significant unavoidable limitation of this study will always remain the loss of the chosen medium of all democratic and especially radical and revolutionary politics which is surely public address: 'that one thing throughout the sermons the printer could not find any characters or letters to express – that is, the spirit with which they were delivered with lively voice'. One would like to accept the claim of the great poet John Milton that 'writing is more public than preaching', but the lamentations of the now obscure William Reyner probably capture better the leap of imagination required of a reader in any age:

The notes are not so warm to me now in writing as they were in speaking; nor will they, I fear, be to any in reading as they were, I hope, to some in hearing. Speaking and writing have their several graces and glosses . . . . The same things (experience shows) which while spoken seemed stirring passages, afterwards when read move little.[31]

The academic literature on Puritanism and the English revolution is vast. In the course of this study I have come to acquire a view of the Puritans very different from what most of it conveys.[32] It may be that in the long run Puritanism, like other dissenting movements, was important less for the answers it supplied than the questions it asked, and what many continue to dismiss as the simplistic certitudes of hypocritical bigots I will argue was the manifestation of deep inner conflict, representing the complex moral agony of a profoundly disturbed society. A movement that fundamentally changed the world and continues to exert a strong influence by the straightforward simplicity with which it was able to make its message understood by the common people has now, as in its own day, more difficulty being heard by the educated. 'Thus it was in Christ's time,' Edmund Calamy observed. 'The great men and the great scholars crucified Christ, and the poor received the gospel. The followers of Christ were a company of poor people and silly women . . . . Thus it was in Christ's time, and thus it is in ours.' In a time of conservative intellectual as well as political trends, even ostensibly radical scholars have little time for religious zealots and the mass politics they created and seem to prefer registering their disapproval or distancing themselves with patronizing theories of human behavior rather than simply listening with a measure of sympathy to the simple pleas and tormented cries of the spiritually and materially dispossessed. This is ironic in the study of Puritanism, for if there was one urgent need of Puritan preaching, issued in anguished appeals in sermon after sermon, it was to be heard and understood – not necessarily by the 'great scholars', perhaps, but by the 'poor people and silly women'. 'Great scholars busy themselves about questions and intricacies,' said Richard Sibbes. 'A poor Christian . . . instead of disputing, he believes.'

In recent years it has become fashionable among great scholars to pronounce upon the 'failure' of Puritanism, usually with little thought to how it may have succeeded. My argument is that on another, perhaps more humble level it is now so much a part of us that we seldom notice its impact. The religious convictions of the men and women of seventeenth-century England, when they are not ignored altogether, are too often simply assumed by historians without actually being understood. But they were never assumed by the Puritans. What can be safely assumed does not need to be stated, and for the Puritan preachers religion was to be declaimed at every available opportunity. For decades they cried out from their pulpits, and from their tortured souls, a message of fear and frustration, rage and resentment, bitterness and guilt, blending moving encomiums of love with vicious invectives of hate; they used a severe religious doctrine to repress, but in the process also to give voice to an immense range of often confused and conflicting emotions extending from the deepest sorrow to the most ecstatic joy;

17

they tirelessly explored and developed to the extremes of its potential what is without doubt the most powerful system of ideas the world has ever known and used it to inveigh against the failings and abuses of a social order from which they felt rejected and alienated; and they infused a deceptively simple language with rich meaning capable of conveying a complex social analysis and social commentary, no less sophisticated in its fashion and in some ways more effective than that now found in the more specialized vocabularies of modern social science. An appreciation for 'the power of godliness', as the Puritan ministers tried repeatedly to make clear, does not require access to esoteric learning or arcane mysteries; it does require what they called 'spiritual' knowledge – a sensitivity to the psychic effects of human suffering they often found lacking among the politically powerful and professionally learned of their day. 'The reason why these great politicians and jolly wise men of the world (as they are called) for all their depths and devices, with all their wit and windings cannot understand one tittle of the things of God is because this spiritual knowledge is hid from them,' argued Robert Bolton. 'Worldly men make an idol of their wisdom . . . because they secretly desire to be admired and adored for it, as men of extraordinary endowments [and] with an imperious disdainfulness they scorn the simplicity of the saints.' Those so scorned sought a different outlet for their need to be admired and adored, and this is an account of the torturous and sometimes disturbing paths their quest could take. 'What is the reason that unlettered men many times stand out in their profession to blood, whereas those that are more able and learned yield to anything?' asked Sibbes. 'The knowledge of the one is set fast upon the soul . . . whereas the learning and abilities of the other is only a discursive thing . . . . Their knowledge of truths is not spiritual.' This perhaps gives to religion a quality of mystery and transcendence that does not lend itself easily to scholarly scrutiny, and while the Puritans were dedicated to the proposition that religion could be imparted through 'the word', in the end it is difficult not to commiserate with the frustration expressed by one divine. 'Religion is the greatest mystery in the world,' he remarked.

> Religion it seems is a paradox, a riddle, and that's the reason that so many out-stand, out-sit so many sermons, one after another, and yet are where they were . . . grown more wise for the world, and more provident and more politic for their own secular advantage, but still as great strangers to the power of godliness as ever. How cometh this to pass?[33]

Spelling and punctuation have been modernized, though the latter has been retained freely wherever modern usage permits, especially in longer quotations, in an effort to preserve some of the rhythms and emphases of the originals.

1

PROVIDENCE

I have often told you I thought you would see troublesome times; but, my dear Ned, keep your heart above the world, and then you will not be troubled at the changes in it.

Lady Brilliana Harley, 1642

'Now grant me but these two principles, that there is a God and that scripture is the word of God, and my work is at an end.' Though the second of these two axioms demanded by Francis Cheynell in his sermon to Parliament in 1645 distinguished the Puritans, and finally set them in conflict with their society, the first attached them to it. At least a professed belief in a God who created and governed the world was the starting point for their effort to create a shared understanding of events, and while this might not seem to possess all the excitement of the more transcendent mysteries of redemption, it was at least simpler to understand, requiring no necessary reference to the Bible. 'Had we no other light but that of nature, and no other writings but the book of the world, we might read a God and see his providence,' Edward Corbet told the Long Parliament in 1642. 'But to find a savior, to know a gospel, to understand the mysteries of salvation, is above the art of human learning; the spirit of God must be our tutor therein, and the holy scriptures only can teach us such a lesson.' The metaphor suggests that the two were not always so categorically separated, but despite their preference for the transcendent and the scriptural, the essentially worldly departure point of Puritan religion is evident from the preachers' attention to God's control over the things of this world. 'The most wise God is pleased . . . to make known himself unto the world, and the works of his providence are one of those means by which he letteth in some beams of himself upon the hearts of men,' John Rowe explained.

The word of God indeed is [where] we have the most direct and express representation both of his nature and his will. But because this word of his is not revealed unto all, and because that many of those who have the word laid before them do willfully shut their eyes against it, therefore is the Lord pleased to manifest himself in the works of providence, and these are oftentimes so visible and conspicuous that there is no man but must see some appearance of God in them.

The meaning of God's will derived from the word was often contentious and potentially divisive, and while the preachers did not hesitate to engage in fierce polemic when appropriate, in the pulpit they consistently eschewed doctrinal technicalities and the often arcane disputes they provoked. 'The nature and condition of God's will, with those distinctions and difficulties disputed amongst the schoolmen and betwixt the Arminians and contra-Arminians are either too high for human understanding to reach or else are piously resolved by learned pens already,' Corbet insisted. 'I shall only touch upon the power and providence thereof so far as may conduce the quieting of our thoughts in these distracted times.' The ministers generally avoided open confrontation with the authorities (especially before 1640, when government censorship had forced them to adopt covert strategies), preferring to strengthen their movement from within and build support through the recruitment of souls. 'To gain men to a party before they be gained to God is not so warrantable,' Thomas Manton cautioned, 'and to press zeal in some particular ways doth but produce blind fury, which undoeth all.'[1]

As indicated, the Calvinist God was an inscrutable deity who condescended to reveal himself only on his own terms, and the preachers emphasized the distance between heaven and earth and the inability of human faculties to fully comprehend God and his ways. 'Our God whom we seek is most high,' said Gaspar Hickes. 'We cannot mount to him on our own wings, nor reach him by our own strength; as soon may we scale heaven with ladders.' Nevertheless, in his condescending wisdom God had provided some 'footsteps' by which the ascent might begin. 'God ordereth his good providence upon just and weighty reasons,' said William Gouge, 'and though his counsel be unsearchable, and his ways past finding out . . . yet hath he left some footsteps whereby we may observe some grounds of his wise proceedings.' While the preachers did invoke biblical illustrations of the ways of the Almighty, their most compelling evidence for his existence and authority was simply the created order over which his providence presided. 'He that created all things . . . must have a providence over all things,' argued Richard Sibbes. 'For what is providence but a continuance of creation, a preservation of those things in being that God hath given to have a being.' Socially and politically, even morally neutral in itself, providence in this sense was sufficient in the absence of acute trauma, when the world seemed to be functioning according to plan. 'God's providence is as general as his creation,' Corbet said, in terms that might seem aesthetic for a Puritan. 'This glorious fabric of the world would soon lose its beauty and . . . fall into confusion if the hand of providence did not guide their motions and by a sweet command conduct them to their ends.'[2]

God generally worked his providence through the natural mechanisms he had created, for though the act of creation was by definition without prior cause, once he had created natural causes he tended to use them. 'In the work of creation God did all alone, and in many works of providence God only works,' Joseph Caryl explained. 'But in most of his works . . . he acts (as I may so speak) in consort with the creature.' Yet creatures themselves were simply 'tools' or 'instruments', having no power or will of their own but directly dependent on the immediate will of the creator. 'All the world of creatures are but instruments at the most, such as contribute no assistance to the Almighty God,' Corbet continued. 'They work by his continual influence and receive their ends from his eternal order.' The point was not wholly to deny the efficacy of natural causes, though it did serve to express a sense of disbelief toward prevailing assumptions concerning the processes of nature. 'Atheists of old . . . asked with what tools or instruments . . . the Lord did set up this mighty frame of heaven and earth,' Caryl noted. 'In the works of providence . . . little mention is to be made of instruments. All must be ascribed to him.'[3]

It was not that God would ever entirely forgo the use of mechanisms so much as that he could use or not use a variety of them as he chose. 'God doth not confine himself to one method or way of working.' Occasionally the preachers seemed to suggest that God still intervened across what were thought to be the laws or causes of nature, and they always insisted that he could do so (and they did believe in 'miracles', though how they defined these will be discussed later); but it was more that even when he did employ 'second causes' he continued to keep a direct control over them. 'In the ordinary course of providence, second causes do occur,' Corbet conceded. 'Yet . . . the God of providence . . . can work above means, sometimes he disableth the greatest means, and sometimes he useth no means at all.' In most instances the perceptions of people were such that they tended to focus only on the 'means' and did not see the ends, the hand of God controlling the things of the world. 'We are so locked up in second causes as not to see the first,' said Thomas Hodges. 'Secondary causes indeed can do nothing without him, but he doth in heaven and earth whatsoever he please without them.' And yet sometimes God took steps to make it easier to perceive his presence; since while he seldom abandoned causes altogether, there were times when he seemed to have forsaken the causes through which he customarily worked, and then the world was thrown into a state of disorder and confusion. 'When causes seem confused in their operations,' said Samuel Rutherford, 'God exerciseth his dominion.'[4]

Yet it was not so much that he worked with or without 'means' as that he selected and manipulated the means according to his own ends, while the creatures themselves, considered on their own terms, remained entirely 'free'. 'The eternal purpose and . . . rule of providence . . . doth no way prejudice the liberty of second causes,' said John Owen. 'He . . . by his making, preserving, and guiding of men, hindereth not, yea effectually causeth that they work freely, agreeable to their nature.' The point was most significant with respect to human creatures: they too were under his determination and control, though this did not limit their practical freedom (or moral responsibility) in mundane affairs in their relation to others. 'Those things which be most free and absolute, the hearts and wills of men, follow the influence of divine providence,' Corbet asserted. 'They voluntarily perform what certainly shall come to pass.' Though God tended to use nature for continuing the world and grace for transcending it, both were determined by the same eternal decree. 'We cannot utter one word, think one thought, turn our eye, or move a finger, without the concurrence of his power who giveth life and breath and all things,' Corbet said. 'Much less can we of ourselves . . . tread one step toward heaven.'[5]

God thus worked in the world much as he did on the soul, and to infer that he had no time for the things of the world and thereby 'confine him to heaven' was not piety but heresy. 'Those do err who . . . deny the divine providence because they think it too base for the divine majesty of God to take care in human affairs,' said William Perkins. 'They do err who make chance and fortune, without any wise ordination of the divine providence . . . who imagine that all things are governed by fate or an unresistable and violent necessity.' The distinction between 'temporal' and 'eternal' could be thin, and there were times when a realization of God's command over the most secular of 'human affairs', and his ability to override the powers of 'fate' and 'necessity', seemed especially critical. 'God hath this sovereign power or command over nations – not only particular persons, but over whole nations – to deal with them as he pleases,' John Cardell asserted. 'States and kingdoms are not managed by men only, or according as they please, but they are managed and ordered, and disposed of, by the Lord our God.' The notion that God had the final say in the destinies of not only individuals but nations and states as a whole, often bringing to pass outcomes very different from what people and particularly politicians might intend in their acts of public policy, though by no means new to the 1640s (or anyone versed in the Bible), was perhaps the most significant theme in the sermons of the revolution. 'That the flourishing state of commonwealths springs out rather from the blessing of God's providence than from the best forecast of human prudence,' argued William Pemberton, 'history, the witness of times, and light of truth doth plainly testify.'[6]

What God wrought in the fullness of time was thus as unalterably predestined as that which lay beyond it. 'Every event of providence is managed and preordained by an admirable wisdom,' asserted John Wilkins. 'There is no liberty for causes to operate in a loose and straggling way, but in matters of greatest uncertainty there is a preordained course of effects.' Providence then can be seen as predestination applied to the things of this world, whose 'uncertainty' was determined by the same intelligence as that of the next. 'The wisdom of providence in the government of this lower world hath disposed to everything its particular season,' Wilkins said. 'Every particular event is most beautiful in that time which the providence of God hath allotted to it.' The providential and predestinarian scheme was not merely a resigned or reactionary placebo however; on the contrary, its entire purpose was to encourage people to look forward rather than backward and to provide them with the confidence to approach the problems of their increasingly confusing world on a more sophisticated level than simply longing for lost innocence or a naive nostalgia for the good old days. 'Be not transported with that common humor of censuring and condemning the present state of times and commending the times past,' Wilkins urged, 'as if the course of events were not managed by the same wise providence now which governed the world before.' The wisdom of providence became especially appealing in times of change, helping to mediate the transition to modernity by teaching people that the disruptions they felt in their lives (and their souls) need not necessarily be for the worse, but might be the beginning of something promising, even exciting. 'Though smooth and peaceable times are best for the man that lives in them, yet times that are full of change and vicissitude are best for the historian that writes of them,' Wilkins noted. 'So though quiet seasons may best suit with our desires and outward conditions, yet these disturbed, confused times may be best improved . . . and do most set forth the wisdom of providence.'*[7]

The preachers encouraged their listeners to see this wisdom in both the public affairs of the nation and their own daily lives. 'The providence of God goes through the whole world and extends itself to everything,' said Jeremiah Burroughs. 'Not only that God by his providence doth rule the world and govern all things in general, but that it reaches to every particular. Not only to order the great affairs of kingdoms, but it reaches to every man's family; it reaches to every man in the family. It reaches to . . . everything that falls out concerning thee in every particular.' Providence was as infinitely detailed as it was majestic, and God's presence was to be perceived as subjectively as objectively, by each individual no matter how apparently insignificant. 'There's nothing befalls thee, good or evil, but there is a providence,' Burroughs added. 'It reaches to the least things.' Further, providence tied together these 'particulars' and 'least things' as components of a larger and more comprehensive whole, presided over by a single God whose unity facilitated a kind of holistic understanding of otherwise seemingly haphazard phenomena. 'We indeed look at things by pieces,' Burroughs pointed out. 'We look at one particular and do not consider the reference that one thing hath to another. But God looks at all things at once, and sees the reference that one thing hath to another.' Providence was designed to promote an awareness of the world not as a random assortment of isolated things and discrete events but as an interrelated and interdependent system. 'There is infinite variety of the works of God in an ordinary providence, and yet they all work in an orderly way,' Burroughs said. 'For God in the way of his providence causes a thousand thousand things one to depend upon another.' The point was not to see the

---

*Despite the 'determinism', providence provided a way of coping with the increasing complexity of the seventeenth-century world and described a cosmos with a capacity for infinite expansion. 'As it is in the works of nature, where there are many common things of excellent beauty which for their littleness do not fall under our sense,' Wilkins explained, 'so in the work of providence, there are very many passages of frequent daily occurence whose excellent continuance doth not fall under our sense or observation.' Wilkins's evidence for his observation was taken from recent scientific discoveries: 'They that have experimented the use of microscopes can tell how in the parts of the most minute creatures there may be discerned such gildings and embroideries and such curious variety as another would scarce believe.'

23

'temporal' and 'eternal' as somehow spatially separated from one another, but to discern an eternal and even inexorable purpose behind the contingent and seemingly random events of time. 'All the works of providence that ever God did from all eternity or ever will do . . . all make up but one work,' Burroughs added, 'and . . . have had their orderly motion to attain the end that God from all eternity hath appointed.' The need to know that behind confusing worldly occurrences there was deliberate order was in this way developed into the doctrine that particular events were moved with a purpose or, as the preachers often said, were directed to an appointed 'end'. 'The providence of God it always supposeth an end,' explained John Rowe.

Providence . . . is the disposure of things unto the end. . . . There are several wills or meanings of God in such and such providences of his. Now we must look into these providences of his to find out those wills or meanings of God, and when we have found them out we must labor to comply with them.[8]

This 'end' could imply both a purpose and also a final conclusion to all things, for either the individual or the world at large (or both together); in that providence gave an eternal purpose to temporal occurrences, there was not always a clear distinction between the two, and the 'means' of temporal providence could contribute to the 'end' of eternal election. 'Providence is serviceable to predestination and election,' said Richard Sibbes. 'There is a mystery of providence, not only in great matters as election and predestination but in ordering of the common things of the world.' Precisely how this worked was complex; most obvious was that God used worldly means to call his elect in his own time. 'The sweet providence of God brings those that belong to election under the compass of the means at one time or [an]other.' But the role of providence in directing people to redemption was more than simply ensuring they were in the right place at the right time to hear the message; far more important was how it prepared them to be receptive to the message they heard – the impact it made not so much on the body as on the soul. 'God in election hath a purpose to call us out of the world, to save our souls,' Sibbes explained. 'Providence, that is a general government of all things in the world.' What was essential was how they interacted:

Whom God purposeth to save . . . he directs providence as may serve his purpose. . . . Providence works all things for their good. All things by the overruling providence . . . serve his purpose to bring them to heaven. Thereupon comes the dispensation of riches or poverty, honor or abasement.[9]

A very important connection thus existed between the temporal and the eternal, and even, as Sibbes notes, between the material and the spiritual; yet election was determined not by one's worldly condition alone but by the spiritual disposition that resulted, and the preachers insisted again and again that providence in itself carried no moral authority nor provided any indication whatever of one's final status with God. 'Outward providences at all times are no infallible rules to judge by,' Thomas Palmer warned. 'We cannot say presently that any are in God's favor because they thrive and prosper, nor conclude others under a curse because that misery and trouble doth fill and attend them.' While the conditions created by providence were essential in forcing a choice, moral worth was decided not by any outward objective condition but by the inward subjective attitude. 'The providential concurrence of God to the actions of men makes them not good nor evil morally,' John Warren insisted. 'But the good and evil of them is in their relation to a rule . . . and . . . the demands of conscience.' The point was not that election automatically followed providence, or that the eternal fate of the soul was reflected in the temporal condition of the body, but that the uncertainties of providence, when correctly comprehended, could lead to the certainties of election. 'It cannot but bring strong security to the soul to know that in all variety of changes and intercourse of good and bad events . . . all serves to bring God's electing love and our glorification together,' Sibbes observed.

God's providence serveth his purpose to save us. All sufferings, all blessings . . . further God's good intendment to us . . . . God oft disposeth little occasions to great purposes. And by those very ways whereby proud men have gone about to withstand God's counsels, they have fulfilled them.[10]

While it is easy to dismiss providence as cynically self-serving after the fact (as it was later to become for some), it began as precisely the opposite, describing a moral agony that no conscientious soul could evade; and in fact, far from treating people merely as passive objects, providence operated with special reference to moral and rational beings. 'The providence of God . . . reaches to thee who art a rational creature,' Burroughs said. 'The providence of God is more special towards rational creatures than any others.' This distinction between 'ordinary' or 'common' providence as it controlled the world 'generally' and that which was 'special' and could be seen in 'particular' details by rational creatures was frequently invoked for the purpose of drawing corresponding moral (and eventually political) distinctions. 'Providence is either common or special,' said Nicholas Lockyer. The one governed the 'temporal' world in the strictest sense of the word, without judgmental distinction of rational and non-rational, animate and inanimate, good and evil. 'Common providence is . . . dispensing things commonly: the heavens give their wealth to all, and so do the earth and the sea; the sun lights good and bad,' Lockyer explained. 'Common providence lasts but for a time.' The other was not so limited temporally: it was in motion and expressly teleological; it infused temporal confusion with an eternal purpose. 'Special providence is wisdom ordering all things about man to an eternal good,' Lockyer continued, 'giving and taking away, clothing and stripping to make the soul divine.' Such a providence was more distressing perhaps, but also more instructive. 'A man is not to measure special providence by an external success of action towards him as most do but by an internal success,' Lockyer added. 'How doth poverty or riches, health or sickness, [honor and dishonor] better the heart?' While such changes in personal status and material fortune – 'honor or dishonor', 'poverty or riches' – were the elements of special providence, God was less concerned with one's 'external' success than with the 'internal' disposition of the heart in response, and those who recognized this special providence were, by virtue of that very recognition, those to whom it applied. 'There is a singular and special care and providence that God hath for his people,' William Bridge said. 'Such is . . . the goodness of his providence.'[11]

Yet providence was not always entirely good, at least not immediately; the 'end' might ultimately be benign (in one sense or another), even glorious, but in the meantime there would be sorrow before there could be rejoicing. 'The providence of God hath two sides,' observed Samuel Rutherford, 'one black and sad, the other white and joyful.' To some unspecified extent the two sides constituted a chronological sequence, and the plausibility of providence began with the experience of suffering and misfortune, which would eventually be transformed into its diametrical opposite. 'We do in this world (for the most part) see only the dark side of providence,' John Wilkins said. 'At the last and great day . . . then we shall be able to see the beauty of providence in all the rugged passages of it.' Even in the meantime however, and much like the fate of the soul to which it was closely tied, both the woeful and the joyous would be in constant operation, and God often used the two sides of his providence together, dealing with people in unpredictable and seemingly contradictory ways. 'In the carriage of divine providence . . . he brings his promises to pass strangely above the reach of man,' Sibbes observed. 'God brings his children to heaven by strange ways, yea, by contrary ways.' What seemed like arbitrary and 'contrary' acts were the method behind providence, determining that God's 'ends' would be achieved dialectically through the resolution of apparently contradictory 'means'. 'God's ways seem oft to us full of contradictions, because his course is to bring things to pass by contrary means,' said Sibbes. 'There is a mystery not only in God's decree concerning man's eternal estate, but likewise in his providence . . . though we for the present see not the . . . linking together of one [thing] with another.' This dialectical interaction not only between the bad and the good but also between temporal providence and eternal election, and alongside it between the objective acts of God and the subjective responses of man, made the recognition of eternal providence inextricable from not only one's temporal well-being but even the fate of one's immortal soul. 'Those that honor providence shall be kept by providence,' said William Bridge. 'God's providence and the soul's immortality are so united together that he that denies the one destroyeth the other.'[12]

CHANGE

Providence, then, while it pertained to real events, was largely an attitude of mind, and even as the preachers stressed that there was a point beyond which it was neither pious nor instructive to go in attempting to understand God, they indicated how the space between heaven and earth was as much psychical as physical, beginning with the inability of the human mind to comprehend the infinite mind of heaven. 'To the infiniteness of God's thoughts,' said Nathaniel Holmes, 'our thoughts are finite.' The notion of God having 'thoughts' may seem an odd one, but it did emphasize how far the distance between humanity and divinity was one of ideas. 'God thinks all his thoughts at once,' Holmes said. 'He makes not any rational intellectual discourse to go from one thing to another in his thoughts, but he can and doth comprehend all at once.' That God's thoughts were above temporal succession meant that God was above time itself. 'The Lord be an infinite omniscient essence above time,' said Thomas Carter. 'In God there is no yesterday or tomorrow, he being but one point and act of eternity.' So just as God had determined from before the beginning of the world to whom he would give everlasting life and whom he would condemn to perpetual death, so the uncertainties of this world were all part of his preordained plan, laid out before all time. 'Nothing comes to pass in time but what was decreed from eternity,' said Thomas Hill. 'Then surely armies, cities, countries cannot be lost without his providence.'[13]

This fascination with time at the heart of the providential and predestinarian system, the distinguishing feature of Calvinist theology after all, did not exist simply for the sake of creating metaphysical paradoxes but arose in response to phenomena in the temporal world; and an awareness of time (perhaps even the relativity of time), along with the search for a counterpoise that was absolute and eternal, reflected foremost a perception of change. 'Time goeth not about God as it goeth about creatures,' said Samuel Rutherford. 'And this maketh God free from change, and from ups and downs, from falling and rising that are incident to all created natures, even to men and angels.' The distinction between 'temporal' and 'eternal' after all was one not of place but of time, and yet the two were related within the world since time itself was nothing more than a measurement of change. 'What is time but the measure of motion,' asked another preacher, expressing an increasingly common concept of seventeenth-century physics, '. . . the measure of the creatures in their changes?' In their warnings against perception limited to immediate causation and dependence upon the things of the world, in their distinctions between temporal and eternal, ordinary and special providence, the preachers seem to have been expressing a response to the breakdown of the routine mechanisms of human society, mechanisms through which God worked in the course of his 'ordinary' providence but which at present were, for whatever reason, not working. 'When God seems to . . . forsake the earth by the suspension of the manifest working of his power, then [people] say . . . "There is no God",' according to Thomas Hodges. 'If they grant there is one, they confine him to the heavens.' The urgency therefore with which they sought to instill in their listeners an awareness of the immediate presence of God within this world can be seen as a response to the problems of change. 'Now on the contrary,' Hodges added, 'when God puts forth his power in working any great unexpected change in the world, the notion of God that nature hath planted in men's minds revives, and God recovers his glory.' It is often said that seventeenth-century England was a society where change was not only not welcomed but even not recognized, and yet the preachers recognized it frequently and responded by invoking the authority of a God with whose assistance they could cope with it. 'He changes not,' Hodges asserted. 'Though both heaven and earth wax old . . . and as a vesture he doth change them, yet . . . for all these changes he remains the same.' By contrast, all the world, everything apart from God, was in a state of commotion, continually in agitation, caught up in the endless vicissitudes of time and the perpetual cycles of birth, growth, death, and decay. 'Indeed, there is nothing but change in all things else,' Hodges observed. 'They are full of motion and revolution.'

> There is the wheel of times and seasons. 'Seed time and harvest, cold and heat, summer and winter, day and night.' . . . There is the wheel of generation. One generation passeth away, and another cometh. Some die, and others are born . . . . There is the wheel of state and condition. Look upon bodies politic. What is become of those four monarchies that issued from between the brazen mountains of God's providence, are they not vanished? And may we not say the like of others too? Either their own overgrown greatness or else some hand of violence hath destroyed them, so that except in history we know not where to find them.

Hodges lays special emphasis on the changes of great nations, which he also tries to fit within the framework of recurring cycles or 'revolutions'; but he goes on to explain how anxiety over the larger catastrophes of nations and the more subtle alterations in society leads to an awareness of more irregular change and especially its impact on the individual. 'Let us but cast an eye upon ourselves,' he urged, '. . . children of change.'

> How do we change in all we are and have? From childhood to youth, from youth to man's estate, from thence to age, we never stand at a stay till dust returns to dust. The face of heaven admits not of more changes than our minds. As for our outward estate, how doth it change, and put on several shapes? Today in wealth, tomorrow as poor as Job. Now on the throne, the next day on the pile . . . . Today in honor and reputation, tomorrow . . . begging an alms of passengers. Whether it be from good to bad or contrary, it matters not, for still it is change.

The soul was thus urged to fix its gaze on the ways of God with a special attention in times of irregular change and abrupt dislocation. 'Oh let us be more wise and learn to see our God in all his works,' Hodges added. 'It will make us live more comfortably in all changes.'[14]

In one sense change was the way of all earthly things. 'All things under the sun are mere vanities, fading flowers, and perishing delights.' Change in its most fundamental sense was merely ephemerality, evanescence, and mortality, and not the least of the vanities of the world was life itself. 'The vanity of this life' was pointed out by Jeremiah Whitaker. 'Truly, this life, consider the shortness of it,' he lamented. 'Our lives, alas! What are they?' The realization that all worldly change came together in the mortality of men and women was perhaps the starting point for all religion, and as might be expected the preachers devoted considerable attention to the subject of death, which Sibbes called 'the last change'. 'Let . . . no occasion of grief, of sorrow, of comfort, of joy, of company, of one thing or another, public or private . . . divert our thoughts and turn them aside from thinking upon death.' This was never a morbid preoccupation, however, since part of the fascination was based on the realization that (in a number of ways) only through death was brought forth life. 'Death . . . is a door and passage to life,' Sibbes insisted. 'Death is the death of itself, destroyeth itself. We never truly live till we die, and when we die, we are past fear of death. So that . . . misery dieth, death dieth.' If uncertainty as to what lay beyond the grave and one's ultimate place in the order of things was the life of all religious devotion, it gave a special vitality to the Puritan version. 'Get death into your thoughts,' Richard Vines urged Parliament, 'and it will put life into your actions.' A consciousness of the death inherent in ('this') life – the realization that 'as soon as we begin to live, we begin to die' – made for an energetic, even frantic pursuit of the living, vital, active, along with its corollary, the desperate need to escape or somehow transcend not only the lifeless and dead but, more frighteningly, anything trapped in the inexorable process of dying: decay, putrefaction, corruption. 'We carry our deaths . . . about us; our life is dying and mortal,' said Sibbes. 'It is but mortal flesh we carry . . . . It is a mortal life, that must end in dust and rottenness.' Even in the course of life, many little 'deaths', troubles and miseries and worries, could hasten the end or simply make the allotted time more sad. 'All cares, and fears, and sorrows, and sicknesses, are less[er] and petty deaths,' Sibbes added, 'harbingers to death itself.' While death was often thus used as a metaphor to describe certain conditions of life, the metaphors used to describe death itself were also revealing; sometimes, for example, they were political. 'Death is the great king of kings and the emperor of emperors,' Sibbes declared, 'for no king hath such dominion as death hath.' Ultimately, the most exalted earthly authority could never inspire such fear in the soul as the leviathan Death:

> It spreads its government and victory over all nations. He is equal, though a tyrant. As a tyrant spares none, he is equal in this. He subdueth young and old, poor and rich. He levels sceptres and spades together. He levels all. There is no difference between the dust of an emperor and the meanest man. He is a tyrant that governeth over all.[15]

The image may have been especially vivid, so to speak, among the illustrious members of the gentry and nobility to whom the ministers preached extensively before and during the war and into whom they labored to inculcate the message that before God all human efforts at immortality and all worldly standards of honor were valueless. 'Titles of honor are written in dust,' Vines declared in his funeral sermon for a leading nobleman. 'Princes and great men must fall, their very monuments are mortal and will in time . . . decay and perish.' Social status was perhaps foremost subject to change, if only the last one. 'My Lords,' William Jenkyn told that House, 'the sepulcher and the scripture know no difference 'twixt robes and rags, peers and peasants.' The theme was an old one, often invoked in similar periods of instability and insecurity; what was striking was the attention devoted to it in sermons to Parliament and various bodies of magistrates and how the preachers did not hesitate to press the logic to its conclusion. 'Kings, though in civil respects they differ from other men, yet are they of the same metal and shall end in death,' Sibbes observed. 'All their glory must lie in the dust.'

Perhaps most significant about the Puritan handling of the theme was a willingness to express it not only in private counsels at court but in public declamations before popular audiences, and by the 1640s it was precisely this kind of literal disillusionment that undermined the popular deification of monarchy. 'If he be God enduring forever, what fools are we to place our hope in a King that shall die?' Samuel Rutherford asked in 1644. 'He is but a man and may change.' In the long run, however, what may have been more important than the lengths to which the message could be carried was the willingness, even eagerness of some members of the gentry and nobility – those who otherwise had their own interest in preserving the sanctity of traditional hierarchy – to listen to it. '[Great men] must die as well as others,' Edmund Calamy told the House of Lords, 'and death makes all equal.' Equality then was the final status of all. 'The difference put by God between man and man is but for the time of this life at farthest,' said William Strong. 'At death all these relations shall cease. Death levels all.' Whether the distinctions were social, economic, political, intellectual, even moral, at best they were temporal. 'There is (indeed) in this world a difference between the learned and the unlearned, betwixt the honorable and the base, betwixt the wise and the foolish, betwixt the rich and the poor,' said Jeremiah Whitaker. 'But look but a little beyond the grave, and there the rich and the poor meet together, there the honorable and the base lie down together, and the Lord is found the maker of them both.' By contrast, God put one difference between individuals, and it was not confined to this life. 'But now look upon the difference that grace makes betwixt the sons of men,' Whitaker added. 'The difference that grace maketh is . . . not only for a moment but unto eternity.'*[16]

*The suggestion that the things of this life, especially those that conferred status and rank, were not quite 'real' in comparison to the things of God was conveyed by William Strong in terms that may explain something about the special indignation the Puritans directed against the theater: 'This life is fitly compared to a play . . . where one acts the part of a prince, another of a peasant,' he noted. 'But

How far this contrast between the temporal and the eternal carried implications for 'this' life was unclear, but certainly the things in it were as finite and precarious as life itself. 'There is nothing which you can lose by death,' warned Obadiah Sedgwick, 'but what may be lost, and what (for the most part) must be lost, in life.' The vanity of this life could be highlighted by God's actions in this world and in particular those which he undertook on a large scale against entire societies; for while change was in one sense the natural order of things, it could also manifest itself on a wider and less regular scale, and change and mortality (and the loss of 'honor' too) were endemic to entire societies as well as individuals. 'As it is with particular men, so it is with whole countries,' observed John Whincop. 'Where is now the glory of Athens, the pomp of Macedon?' The political insecurity of the age was reflected in extended accounts of the decline of great nations, eliciting the theories of various writers, both pagan and Christian, on how long states could be expected to last and the causes of their downfalls. 'But these niceties I desire not to insist in or put weight upon,' Whincop said after setting forth his own views. 'It's the general only is my aim to show, how fading the beauty of this world is and how there's nothing permanent here below.' William Greenhill, preaching in 1643, also declined to hazard specific predictions but did venture to bring home the point by suggesting that the many changes God inflicted upon nations were now being wrought on England. 'I might here first show you that all kingdoms have their periods,' he said, 'and learned writers tell us that there are no kingdoms so great, so glorious, so powerful that extend their duration above five or six hundred years at most but are either ruined and fall to ashes or else suffer some great change.' Greenhill similarly cited illustrations from both profane and sacred history and reminded his audience of England's age as a nation. 'I do not desire to prophesy and foretell things to come,' he added. 'But it's thought . . . if we be not ruined altogether, certainly there will be some great alteration in the kingdom.'[17]

---

the play ended, there remains no difference nor impression of any of their former honors.' Richard Sibbes's elaboration further indicated why the ministers developed not only an overt hostility to religious ceremony but a thinly veiled contempt for the civil version as well. 'Learn to conceive aright of the things of this life, that there is no reality in them,' he urged in words also ironically reminiscent of his illustrious contemporary:

> All this is but a pageant, as it were, as a man that acts in a pageant or in a play. . . . While we live here, we act the part, some of a rich man, some of a nobleman, some of a beggar, or poor man; all is but the acting of a part. . . . Considering that this world is but an apparition, but the acting of a part, why should we think ourselves the better for anything here? Doth he that acts the part of a nobleman upon the stage think himself better than another that acts the part of a poor man? No. He knows he shall go off in a short time, and then he shall be as he was before. . . . All is but an apparition. . . . All here is but a pageant. If you talk of reality, it is in the things of religion. . . . The things of this life are all but apparitions and pageants. . . . Pull off the mask, and then you shall see the things of this world. . . . There is emptiness, and not only so, but vexation.

WAR

Greenhill was preaching after several months of civil war, and certainly for both persons and nations the most traumatic change, which more than any other brought together personal and national mortality, was the onset of war. 'God is called a "man of war",' noted Joseph Caryl, 'but nothing shows him more a God than war.' God's own chosen titles thus indicated a special interest in war: 'God is not in vain called THE LORD OF HOSTS.' War more than anything highlighted providence, since war was the final breakdown of human authority, when the potential for disorder and injustice was greatest and God alone was in control. 'I do not know any one thing wherein the providence of God is more fully set out in scripture than in the workings of it about wars,' observed Jeremiah Burroughs. 'God seems to glory much in his workings about warlike affairs.' There was even what Burroughs called a 'special providence of God in the affairs of wars and battles in the world'. 'It is true, the providence of God is over the least things in the world,' he acknowledged, 'but God challengeth a more special and peculiar acknowledgment of his work of providence about warlike affairs in regard whereof he takes the title to himself of Lord of Hosts.' As in the affairs of the world generally, God had a hand in all aspects of war, though the special nature of his providence there led the preachers to address the particularities in some detail:

> God is much seen in the provocations to wars, consultations about them, enclining men's hearts to them, taking them off from peace, etc. . . . . God works in the raising of wars when and how he pleaseth. He is the great general, and all battles are appointed by him . . . . God's providence in wars works in the continuance of them. How long they shall abide in a land, and when they shall cease, is wholly from the appointment of the Lord of Hosts . . . . When God gives commission to the sword it must stay; it must go on devouring till the commission be out.

Such control extended as much to the inward as to the outward aspects of war. 'The work of this Lord of Hosts in war is to give wisdom and counsel for the managing of the affairs of it,' Burroughs added. 'This Lord of Hosts gives all the counsel and wisdom from himself to all under him.' God's power also naturally extended to determining the final outcome. 'The Lord of Hosts hath the absolute power over all weapons in battle, to let them prosper or not prosper as he pleaseth,' according to Burroughs. 'All the success in battles is from the Lord of Hosts.' And when God decided to align himself with one side in war that side was certain to claim the victory. 'Yea, lastly, the whole battle is the Lord's when it is a just cause.' Only when God was satisfied (and only on God's terms) would war come to an end. 'And when God is pleased to give the word, he makes wars to cease.'[18]

God did not necessarily delight in war (though he was said to 'glory' in it) and avoided it as much as possible; but when once he had decided on war it was usually severe and unrelenting, even total in its destructive force. 'God usually is a long time before he draws his sword; he is whetting, preparing, delaying it,' Burroughs said. 'But when it is once drawn, he many times will not put it up again until it be bathed, filled, fatted, satiated, drunk with blood.' The point was not even necessarily who or which side it was that God favored so much as the terms on which war was waged, and every war had some mandate from heaven. 'If God be the Lord of Hosts,' Burroughs said, 'there is no war to be undertaken but for God and according to God's will; it must be by commission from this great general.' Given the existence of war then, the purpose was for the nation as a whole to see that they did indeed fight for God. 'It is a blessed thing for a kingdom when their army may be said to be . . . "a heavenly host",' Burroughs declared. 'This great Lord of Hosts will certainly do great things to such a host.'[19]

Most significant, however, was that war on earth seemed to crystallize cosmic battles throughout the heavens. 'There is never any sword drawn on earth till it be first drawn in heaven,' said Stephen Marshall. 'Never doth war come in any country till God bathes his sword in heaven, draweth it out and brandisheth it in heaven and then saith, "Sword, go into such a land."' God claimed the title of Lord of Hosts with regard not only to the outbreak of actual war but even to his control over the entire creation. 'God is the Lord of Hosts in respect of that absolute command he hath over all creatures,' Burroughs said. 'He hath all creatures in heaven and earth under him, as a general hath his soldiers.' God's tight control over the creation was thus comparable to a well-disciplined army. 'In regard of their ready obedience to their great general,' said Thomas Hill, 'all creatures stand ready in battle array, pressed to do the will of God, as an army set in martial order.' It was difficult to tell sometimes where the metaphorical left off and the literal began, and God's armies were spread throughout heaven and earth. 'He hath multitudes of armies,' Burroughs announced. 'The Lord of Hosts hath armies in the heavens, armies in the air, armies in the seas, armies on the earth dispersed in every country. All the whole world is filled with the multitudes of the armies of the Lord.' This militarization of the universe seems to have expressed a certain confusion about the way the creation was currently operating, as well perhaps as a measure of frustrated enmity against those who were operating it. 'All creatures in heaven and earth are his armies,' Burroughs continued. 'The angels, sun, moon, stars, the dragons, the deep, the fire, hail, snow, wind, the mountains, trees, cedars, the beasts, and all creeping things, the flying fowls, the kings of the earth, and all people are the Hosts of the Lord.' When God so mobilized his creation for war one could be sure he had good reason, and souls were expected to search the ways of God and respond. 'If God be the Lord of Hosts, if he hath such wonderful workings of his providence in wars and battles, hence in all wars and battles there is some special thing of God to be looked at,' Burroughs concluded. 'Whosoever lives to see the issue of these great stirs and warlike commotions amongst us shall see that God had a hand in them to bring great things to pass, that the mercy he intended for us was worth all the trouble these have brought upon us, yea all the blood, the most precious blood that hath been shed amongst us.'[20]

HONOR

War thus seemed to awaken and intensify deeper feelings concerning the relations between the soul and the universe and to bring into this world anxieties and expectations usually thought to pertain to the next. Moreover, war had the potential to politicize religion by crystallizing a more general dissolution of human and especially political society, to describe conditions 'where the bands and sinews of civil government are cut asunder and [there is] no conjunction or associating of a people into or under government'. This 'war' as it pervaded English society resembled a kind of Hobbesian state of nature. 'Politicians say that in such times every man is at war with every man, every man is an enemy to every man,' according to Stephen Marshall. 'So in truth it is with us . . . . Almost every man is divided from every man.' This idea of a 'divided' society, while describing the divisions produced by civil war, also provided a language with which to characterize more subtle but at the same time more long-standing and far-reaching problems of English society – not simply the war of one side against another, but the war of all against all. 'We are a divided people,' Burroughs complained, 'whose hearts are divided, and heads too':

> King and subjects are divided, Parliament is divided, Assembly is divided, armies are divided, church is divided, and state is divided, city is divided, country is divided, towns are divided, families divided, godly people are divided, ministers almost everywhere are divided.

And that which rent society could also tear apart the soul. 'Yea,' Burroughs added, 'and what heart almost is there at this time but is divided within itself?' This last was particularly troubling to the preachers and, they said, to God himself. 'God cannot abide a cloven heart,' another warned, 'a heart parted and divided within itself.'[21]

Division thus extended from the greatest affairs of the nation to the innermost conflicts of the soul, and the two types of instability were closely connected. 'Heart-division will cause emptiness of good,' Burroughs observed, 'both in men's spirits and in church and state.' The division that was to become a polarization of the nation into two opposing camps began as more of an atomization of society into a myriad of 'divided hearts': 'hearts that are at distance one from another, that are alienated and not easily reconciled'. Whether these hearts were divided among or within individuals, the point was the same: alienated hearts were lonely hearts – cut off from one another, from themselves, from 'God'. 'A man alienated from God is cut off from all,' said Nicholas Lockyer. 'An alienated person hath not the shadow of love . . . . He carries the name of the living, and he is dead . . . . He calls himself a man, and he is a carcass . . . . Alienation is a sad condition . . . . Alienation is a condition without hope.' This loss of hope and estrangement of the individual meant lives without purpose or meaning, lives of what one called 'spiritual emptiness': 'Empty lives cause but empty joy.'

The societal pressures making for such empty and joyless lives were difficult to identify precisely, but from the attention they received in the sermons they were both widespread throughout society and deep within the individual. 'They may be so violent as to disturb the whole man in such manner as he hath no joy in anything,' observed Thomas Valentine, 'but may be weary of himself, weary of living, weary of the world, and . . . the weight of such burdens as many do bear and have been long exercised with in this kind . . . cause[s] fainting of the spirits.' The disturbed and restless images that fill virtually every Puritan sermon testify to the pervasiveness of such spirits and such lives in English society: 'filled with perplexity', 'trouble and anxiety of mind', 'many doubts, fears, and mistrustings', 'unsettled', 'confusion, bitterness, disturbance, and vexation', 'dejection of spirit', 'melancholy distempers', 'distracted and discomposed', 'troubled, pensive, and dejected', 'inordinate and extreme sorrow', 'sinkings and despondencies of spirits', 'solitariness', 'anguish of mind', 'drooping spirits', 'continual agitation and tossing', 'sharp spiritual conflicts', 'unstableness of mind', 'fears and doubting', 'bursting with discontent', 'vexing and fretting', 'impotence and inability', 'an unsettled and unstable spirit', 'spiritual poverty and barrenness of soul', 'disconsolate', 'discouraged, cast down, and disquieted', 'disorder and ataxy', 'war in the soul'. At their most severe such spiritual nightmares could press the soul down into the most dreaded condition of all, that of final 'despair'. 'Despair is a soul wracking itself with what is and with what will be,' said Lockyer, 'torturing and tearing all under his apprehension of things.' The self-destructive power of despair was perhaps the most troubling problem confronting the preachers, and sermon after sermon described the condition. 'A despairing soul is a terror to itself,' said Thomas Brooks. 'It cannot rest but . . . is always tossed here and there. It is troubled on every side. It is full of fears and fightings . . . . It is still avexing, terrifying, tormenting, condemning, and perplexing itself.' Such psychic desperation was the product of a society without authority – 'estranged in opinions and affections', as one described it – with nothing solid, nothing dependable to believe in or obey. 'A wonderful disorder and confusion', was how Lazarus Seaman characterized it, where 'those that are under authority cannot be reconciled to them that are in authority' and 'those that govern cannot be reconciled to them that are under government'. This crisis of authority was not limited to civil 'government', but it did extend to it, and the strain of social and political relations was one of the most graphic ways of portraying this social deterioration: 'the fathers being against their children and children against their fathers . . . when inferiors are against superiors and superiors against inferiors, when ministers shall be divided against people and people against ministers, and magistrates against subjects and subjects against magistrates'.[22]

The ministers had no desire to eliminate these distinctions and institutions of authority as such; in fact reinforcing them was among their highest priorities, and in a time of social dissolution and individual isolation the commonplace that God sanctioned all forms of human society received renewed emphasis as an encouragement to social cohesion. 'God . . . hath ordained the society of man with man, partly in the commonwealth, partly in the church, and partly in the family,' asserted William Perkins, 'and it is not the will of God that man should live and converse alone by himself.' Each of these kinds of human association, along with the authority that governed it, was extensively discussed and vigorously supported, though perhaps the most important as an 'ordinance' of God was the first. 'Magistracy is a public power ordained of God for the preservation of order, discipline, and peace in a commonwealth by encouraging the good and by the punishment of evil and contumacious persons according to just laws.' The ordering (or reordering) of relations between magistrates and subjects was in fact among the main functions of Puritan religion. 'There is nothing (no, never so small) wherein the name, or the image, or the work, or the honor of God are involved, but hath majesty in it, and challengeth reverential seriousness from us,' declared Obadiah Sedgwick in 1648, who went on to paraphrase ironically what had once been said only of kings. 'And all these do center in magistrates, for magistrates do bear the name of God. God himself doth call them gods.' The responsibility this placed on individuals holding positions of public trust as well as on those who chose them was conveyed through the description of political office as a religious 'calling', and if there was a 'special providence' governing rational creatures, even more so political ones. 'There nothing more necessary to a magistrate than to be informed of this,' said Anthony Burges, 'that his calling is of God and that God hath a peculiar providence over such.' The description of political office as a vocation, the link between personal piety and public policy, could be (as it were) a two-edged sword: though the point was to emphasize the need for subjection to authority, the effect just as clearly was to depersonalize that authority by shifting the basis of its legitimacy from the social status of the person to the political function of the office. 'The subjection of a subject to a magistrate [is] not paid according to the grandeur of the person of the superior,' Richard Vines asserted, 'but according to the relation in which he stands.' Still, while this could and did erode traditional hierarchies of personal status, a conservative element pervaded the language of providence: in that social and political inequalities were rooted in nature, God sanctioned the existing order and worked through established authority. 'God is the God of order,' Francis Cheynell declared before the House of Lords in 1645.

He hates confusion and therefore doth approve, and make great use of, those different dignities, degrees, and orders which are established by human policy according to the light of nature in several nations throughout the world. Men are not born of noble ancestors either by chance or fortune . . . . Divine providence divides all by an unerring lot and appoints who shall be heir to the wealth and civil honor of every nobleman. If the heir forfeit his estate and honor, yet let him be . . . civilly honored till God or his deputies take the forfeiture. Private men must know their place and keep their bounds; for if malcontents may be connived at, they will quickly make as bold with the temporal estate as civil honor of the greatest men.[23]

Perhaps the real significance of such sentiments, however, even at their most conservative, was simply the need to state them and the underlying insecurity of both social status and civil order they reflected; when addressing the spiritual needs of great men themselves the emphasis was more often on the many ways in which 'civil honor' as well as 'temporal estate' could indeed be lost at the hands of God. 'My Lords, ye are men in honor, but civil honor is not long-lived,' Cheynell added. 'Honor is a tender fickle thing. It is hard to get and harder to keep . . . . We live in an age full of uncertainties and sick of jealousies.' The simple equation of order with hierarchy was tenable so long as demarcations of status were fairly clearly drawn; but in a time of rapid change and mobility, the threat to the status and honor of the great did not necessarily come in the first instance from political 'malcontents' so much as from social and economic pressures beyond anyone's control (though the distinction was not always clear). 'No man knows how soon ye may lay down your honor,' William Strong similarly warned the Lords. 'All things here below are . . . full of turnings and changes . . . . How soon that which is highest becomes lowest, a meditation which would be as fit a corrective to men in great places.' It is possible that such statements were sometimes meant to convey gentle threats; but if so they were made plausible only by wider circumstances, and providence alone carried no necessary divine authority either way as far as conferring approval or 'honor' upon even the greatest men. 'Honor is conferred upon some by providence and some by promise,' Strong explained. 'All have a commission from God, but some in approbation: some are exalted in mercy, some in wrath.' If temporal honor was bestowed by providence, after all, it could just as easily be removed in the same way, and while it was commonplace that social and civil honor ceased at death, the uncertainties of the times were such that often it was not even for that long. 'When men are thus advanced by God, he hath in this life reserved to himself a power of degradation, that no man can say he shall die in honor,' Strong warned. 'He changeth times and seasons; he removeth kings and setteth up kings . . . exalt him that is low and abase him that is high.'[24]

Such statements sound revolutionary, as indeed they were; but their appeal to some of the most powerful and exalted figures in the kingdom stemmed as much from subjective experience as from the objective principle, and the recognition that status had become fluid was as much a cause as an effect of discontent – especially if it became widely perceived that worldly 'honor' often bore little relation to integrity or ability. 'Men of servile spirits . . . are advanced, and men of princely spirits remain in low place,' Strong observed. 'This outward honor will never set a man up with God.' In a society where change and mobility had rendered the competition for honor fierce and the outcome questionable (and as economic pressures were forcing the distribution of official forms of recognition such as titles of honor less for service than for money, often upon new arrivals) the very definition of honor was seriously in doubt, and with it the value and legitimacy of the sources from which it flowed. 'God dishonors men, and this he can do upon the greatest,' Strong said. 'Kings are the fountain of honor upon earth, and by them it is dispensed; but yet he "pours contempt upon princes" . . . the highest measure of dishonor. They that convey honor unto others cannot preserve their own honor.' In these circumstances there was increasing pressure to recognize God as the sole source of honor and that honor be left for God alone to define. 'God pours the highest contempt upon persons that he hath raised to the highest honor,' Strong observed. 'All true honor is that which comes from God only.' This concern, even obsession with 'honor', which by its nature was called into question by change and mobility, came to be linked with that of God himself, so that men derived honor from God by giving it to him and the honor of men and God became mutually reinforcing. 'If ye desire to be truly honorable, let God's honor be precious in your eyes,' Strong urged. 'Herein true honor and greatness lies, when the things of God are great in our esteem and God's honor is exalted by us, and when a man falls from this he begins to be nothing though he be the greatest monarch of the earth.' People derived all their honor from God but only to the extent that they honored him, and the preachers urged their insecure listeners to project onto God that which they craved more than anything for themselves. 'We honor God when the honor of God is precious in our eyes, when . . . we do all to the glory of God,' Strong continued. 'When a man's own honor is not dear to him in comparison of God's, but he casts down his crown and falls upon his face, and he that so doth abaseth his glory that the Lord may be exalted.' This very act of abasement before God was honorable in his eyes, and God in turn would honor those who renounced their worldly honor for his, regardless of the shame and disgrace they might acquire in the eyes of others. 'We then honor God indeed when we shut our eyes against all honor and reward from men,' Strong said. 'God honors men when he doth appear for them in the dishonors cast upon them.'[25]

Such dishonors might indeed be one's lot in this world however, even as a result of God's providence, and part of honoring God was acknowledging his ability to dishonor men. 'God hath an absolute power and sovereign command over the greatest men in the world, and they owe absolute subjection to the will, pleasure, providence of the God of heaven,' Cheynell proclaimed. 'Come, acknowledge your subjection.' The point for great men or anyone else who felt insecure about their status or threatened with dishonor and degradation was to make this acknowledgment openly and voluntarily and so to acquire a sense of humility. 'God in all the changes of the world do[th] whatsoever pleaseth him both in the heavens of politic governments and in the earth of the inferior sons of men,' John Warren declared, 'that you considering who hath set you up may tremble at that power which can throw you down again.' Such humility before one's subjection to the power of a God who could abase was in itself the first step in gaining control over one's abasement and so recovering one's fragile honor. 'The greatest on the earth had need learn how to be abased,' Jeremiah Burroughs warned in his own sermon to the House of Lords. 'God knows how to abase you thousands of ways, but you must know how to be abased . . . . What are you, though nobles, earls, yea though you were the lords of the whole earth, but poor vile worms under the feet of the Almighty?'[26]

Abasement, then, was a state of mind as much as of estate, and there was a correlation between the two. 'Learn then how to be abased, notwithstanding your greatness in the world,' Burroughs urged the Lords. 'Do not stay till God forces abasement . . . . To know how to be abased – that is, humbled before God – this is of great use for men of noble families and noble spirits. It will no way hinder the nobleness of your spirits, but heighten and enlarge them.'

The point was not simply to be abased but to be self-abased, not simply humbled but humble. 'Humbling is a reflected action,' explained Richard Sibbes.

> This is that true humiliation, the humbling of ourselves; for it is no thanks for a man to be humbled by God . . . for God can humble and pull down the proudest . . . . God by this gets himself glory. But here is the glory of a [soul] . . . to humble himself; which humbling is, from our own judgment . . . to humble ourselves. Many are humbled that are not humble; many are cast down that have proud hearts still.

Such self-humbling was 'reflected' not in the crude deterministic sense that the humility necessarily followed the humiliation – all too often, as Sibbes laments, it did not – but in the sense that it should do so when correctly interpreted; indeed, in this sense the only true 'freedom' of the will, the only truly 'voluntary' action, was gained through conscious acceptance of one's unavoidable subjection and the inevitability of being humbled somehow, whether by or against one's own will. 'Holy humiliation is voluntary, for it is a reflected action, which comes from a man's self,' Sibbes explained. 'The humiliation of other men is against their will . . . . A man may be humbled and yet not humble . . . . True humiliation . . . is voluntary, being a reflected action, to work upon and to humble ourselves, but the other is a forced humiliation.' The only constructive humiliation therefore, and the way one's very humiliation itself came to be 'honorable', was insofar as it became a conscious, voluntary humiliation, a humiliation of the heart and soul as well as of the body and estate. 'I can see honor in my abasement,' Burroughs said.

> I know how to make other interpretations of God's meaning in my abasement than the world does. I know how to bear it with a quiet spirit . . . . I know how to carry myself graciously, comfortably, heavenly in my abasement, so as though the world puts dishonor upon me, I shall not by any unbeseeming carriage dishonor myself or my cause.[27]

Such eventualities, both as they objectively happened and as they were subjectively accepted, by their very nature blurred social distinctions – especially as they actually occurred, of course, but even as they only threatened to occur, since the feared abasement had become an immediate possibility for any and all. 'Consider how quickly the balance of providence may turn,' urged Thomas

Watson. 'We ourselves may be brought to poverty . . . . God knows how soon any of us may change . . . . How many have we seen . . . invested with great lordships and possessions who have on a sudden brought their manor to a morsel.' While the preachers' message for this reason could find a sympathetic hearing among persons from all ranks of society, and by its nature was not limited to any particular social class (whether 'rising' or 'falling'), it may have struck a special chord among the more deprived; and a message similar in its way to that offered to the rich and powerful was extended to those who were already, as well as to those who might become, poor and helpless. 'You who are poor, be not too much troubled with the thoughts of your poverty,' Burroughs urged his own congregation. 'Be not so impatient and impetuous in your desires after riches. Do no envy those who are above you . . . . Let thy heart be quiet and submit to God in that condition God hath set thee.' Despite the irenic and conservative tone on the surface of such injunctions, the very need to issue them stemmed from a recognition that social change, by calling into question the distinction between the rich and the poor, had indeed produced widespread and dangerous discontent throughout all levels of society. 'Condition varies: rich are made poor; whole are wounded,' observed Nicholas Lockyer. 'Men cannot bear this; therefore the land is full of discontent.' Yet the purpose of change when properly interpreted was not to produce discontent but to make people content in any condition. 'God makes changes without to make changes within,' Lockyer continued. 'He makes broken estates to make broken hearts. He brings much to nothing that he may make you content with anything, with mean things.' The preachers themselves thus not only recognized but insisted as a tenet of their theology that specific material conditions were essential for their message to receive a sympathetic hearing, though they also pointed out that the necessary consciousness would be aroused not automatically but only through a determined psychological struggle against discontent itself. 'If a man's estate is broken . . . how shall this man have contentment?' Burroughs asked. 'By the breaking of his heart. God hath broken thy estate: Seek to him for the breaking of thy heart likewise.'[28]

In this sense poverty, like abasement of any kind, like status in general, was both a relative state, being the product of change from one's previous condition and especially in relation to others, and perhaps above all for the ministers' purposes, a state of mind. 'Riches and poverty are more in the heart than in the hand,' Samuel Rogers said. 'He is wealthy that is contented with a little, and he is poor that is in want with abundance . . . . A contented mind . . . will make a supply to all thy wants . . . even in poverty.' This is not to say the ministers had a callous attitude toward material poverty; only that the poverty with which they were most concerned was an affliction less to one's estate (though they did recognize the debilitating effects of extreme poverty) than to one's soul, one's self-esteem. 'Poverty brings . . . abasement with it,' Sibbes observed. 'For the poor man is trod on at all hands . . . . Every man scorns him that is in want. They look haughty and high over [such] a man.' The relativity and the psychic effects of poverty came together in the 'esteem' or 'reproach' it conferred in the eyes of others, a consciousness of which was itself the first step toward overcoming it. 'Do not so much regard the fancies of other men, as what indeed you feel yourselves,' Burroughs urged the poor and downwardly mobile of his congregation. 'For the reason of our discontent many times is rather from the fancies of other men than from what we find we want ourselves.'

> We think poverty to be such a great evil. Why? Because it is so esteemed by others more than what people feel in it themselves, except they be in extremity of poverty . . . . Almost all the discontent in the world is rather from the fancies of others than from the evil that is upon themselves . . . . Were it not for the disgrace, disesteem, and slightings of other men, my condition would not be so bad to me as now it is.[29]

The preachers appealed to this effect of poverty by elevating to a virtue this very lack of esteem and self-esteem, to the point where God was said to have a special care for those whom they described as 'the poor' – not necessarily 'the world's poor, such as are outwardly poor', as Rogers put it, 'but God's poor, the poor in spirit, such as humble themselves before the Lord'. As with the rich, the poor were required to adopt a conscious, deliberate humility, and in this sense as well it was suddenly apparent that 'the poor' could be, or could become, anyone – both in that God could quickly alter one's fortunes and (usually as a result) one might come to realize what the preachers described as one's 'spiritual poverty'. 'Poverty of spirit should accompany us all our life long,' said Sibbes. 'There are a world of poor who yet are exceeding proud; but God sanctifies outward poverty so as it makes way for inward poverty of spirit, that as they are poor, so they have a mean esteem of themselves.' It was this weak self-esteem, rather than poverty as such, which the ministers appealed to and exploited by transforming it from a stigma into a virtue, and it was not a condition limited to the 'outwardly' poor: anyone who had come out on the disadvantaged side of change, or even one who had gained but was still conscious of a precarious position or the difficulty of finding social acceptance, might have reason to be scornful of worldly things, suspicious of success, and resentful of the honors and prosperity of others; and the rich and successful too might experience a special need to realize their spiritual poverty. 'They that abound with worldly wealth must hereby learn to become poor,' declared William Perkins. 'Poor, I say, not in goods, but in spirit. This is hard to flesh and blood, for naturally every rich man blesseth himself in his outward estate and persuades himself that God loves him because he gives him wealth, but such conceits he must strive against.' Riches or any other form of outward prosperity could thus never be any indication of God's love or approval or of one's status in another world, as the preachers repeatedly insisted. 'Riches are no signs of God's favor,' asserted Richard Greenham. 'So that the having of riches is no argument that he loveth us, nor the want of them is any argument of his displeasure toward us.' If anything quite the opposite: while both rich and poor had need of humility and consciousness of their spiritual poverty, the preachers often observed that one condition was after all more conducive to it than the other, and the 'poverty' in 'spiritual poverty' was not entirely figurative. 'Poverty and worldly lowness are the food of humility,' William Jenkyn noted. 'Riches and honors are the fuel of pride.'[30]

Especially when it came to 'poverty', therefore, a very important connection existed between providence and predestination, between material status and spiritual piety, between what happened temporally to people's estates and eternally to their souls. 'In that this outward poverty helps to inward poverty of the soul, outward afflictions help the inward disposition,' explained Sibbes. 'Hence we see likewise that providence is serviceable to predestination and election.' The connection was not a simple one in which material success or failure was reflected in one's spiritual temperament, however, but involved a complicated dialectical interaction between objective material and social conditions and subjective intellectual and spiritual responses, and one that achieved the desired effect not automatically among all who experienced the same changes in fortune but only among a select few who chose to understand them correctly. 'Poverty of estate and poverty of spirit . . . come almost in one word,' Sibbes noted, 'and indeed in God's children they are joined together.' A knowledge of providence thus did not extend to predictions regarding specific individuals, and in fact understanding this relationship required the very subjective element that constituted it; so that why some experienced adversity and others prosperity – for that matter, why some seemed to be troubled by this and others did not – was not in itself a question for the minds of men and women: the very humility required in coming to grips with one's condition brought a realization that with providence, as with predestination, there was a point beyond which human curiosity could not with humility go. 'As of election and reprobation, so of providence,' said Sibbes. 'There is no reason can be given why some of God's children are in quiet and others are vexed, why one should be poor and another rich . . . . Therefore when anything befalls us, for which we can see no reason, yet we must reverence him and adore his counsels, and think him wiser than we.'[31]

Yet the mysteries and glories of providence existed in a difficult relationship with one another, and if even the most pious could not know all things concerning the ends toward which the Almighty directed things in this world, what they could do, and what they were required to do, was to 'reverence' and 'adore' him and give him 'praise'. 'The end of all is to glorify God,' Sibbes declared. 'The work of creation, redemption, and the particular passages of God's providence . . . they are matter of praise in heaven and earth among God's people.' Perhaps it was stemming from these widely shared feelings of abasement and humiliation, the stigma that came from poverty, whether relative or absolute, and other forms of social disgrace and a consequent need for dignity and esteem, an insatiable yearning for honor and even glory, which had become so elusive and problematic, that these were precisely the attributes that were foremost to be ascribed to God himself and the various and inscrutable ways of his providence. 'The Lord doth certainly set a great esteem upon . . . the glorious actings of his providence in the world,' said John Rowe. 'We have much more reason to think

them to be worthy of ours.' Men and women were not simply to acknowledge
God's existence or recognize his control over this world and the next, therefore,
but to 'admire' and 'adore' him. 'The greater and more illustrious the appearance
of God is in any of his providences, the more ought we to admire him and adore
him,' Rowe continued. 'God is to be magnified and adored in the works of his
providence.' Why God should need this admiration and adoration, this honor
and respect, from mere men and women was not often explained, but what was
unmistakable was that they needed to give it. 'The great and eminent works of
providence which are done in the sight and face of the whole world, they should
in an especial manner be magnified and adored by us,' Rowe added, 'and we
ought to give unto them their just honor and respect.'[32]

But the state of mind necessary to see the glory of God's providence was
difficult for the best of people, and most hardly made the effort. 'While God
passeth by among us . . . by glorious and active providences his angels lay their
hands upon the eyes of most men,' Peter Sterry noted, 'not suffering them to see
the glory, the face of that divine presence, but the back part only, the change and
trouble upon the worldly part of things.' And as God confused the world, he also
confused men and women, giving them over to what John Owen called 'unstableness of mind, which makes men like the waves of the sea that cannot rest . . . . If
God give men up to a restless spirit, no condition imaginable can quiet them.'
The close relationship between the social and the mental 'confusion' was such
that as people became confused they in turn tended to panic and add further to
the general level of confusion, creating a self-perpetuating spiral of disorder.
'Alas, when poor creatures are given up to the power of an unquiet and unstable
mind, they think . . . nothing desirable but what is without their proper bounds
and what leads to that confusion which themselves in the issue are least able of
many to undergo,' Owen added. 'It is impossible but that men's hearts should be
pierced with disquietness and trouble that are given up to this frame.'[33]

Providence, though, was not confusion, however much it may have begun as
such, and at some point God would reveal his ways to the world. 'The
manifestations of God in his providences are the most precious things in the
world,' said Thomas Brooks. 'When God makes known the interpretations of
things, it will quiet your spirits.' God was said to have a purpose or, more
strongly, a 'design' in his otherwise confusing acts, and people were expected to
make an effort to understand. 'God hath a peculiar design in hand,' Owen
asserted, 'and we are to find it out.' Part of honoring God was learning to
understand this design, and people were not to balk at God's ways but to search
them diligently for meaning, to discern his purposes and to cooperate. 'I know no
better way of praising God for any work,' Owen said, 'than the finding out of his
design therein and closing with him in it.' Precisely what was this design the
preachers were reluctant to be too specific, and for good reason. 'When men have
fixed to themselves that this or that particular must be the product of God's
providential alterations, that alone fills their aims and desires and leaves no room

for any other apprehension,' Owen noted. 'When men's whole souls are possessed with a design of their own . . . they shall [not] be able to discern aright and acquiesce in the general issue of God's dispensations.' Yet whatever his design might be, one thing for certain was that God did not require great and powerful men to effect it, and the mighty of the earth were not by and large the vessels of providence. 'The Lord hath not been much beholden to the great men of the earth for the carrying on his great designs in the world . . . except some few,' Jeremiah Burroughs said. 'They have been laid aside in the great works that God hath done. "Not many rich, not many noble, but God hath chosen the poor of the world, the vile and contemptible things of the world, to carry on his most precious works by." This is a humbling consideration to the great ones of the earth.' God was in fact often especially severe against the great and mighty, since they were the most proud and powerful and therefore the strongest rivals to his own honor. 'God loves to show his prerogative and make great ones know that he is not beholden to them to do his work,' Cheynell said. 'He will let them see that he can do his work without them.' On the other hand, he could use means the world held in contempt and instruments the world despised. 'God can effect great and glorious designs by weak and improbable means,' Edward Corbet said. 'Foolish things in the judgment of the world are in great esteem with our wise God.' God in fact often used just such foolish things to pull down the power of the great. 'God is able to put as much power as he pleaseth into the least creature . . . so as though it be never so poor and weak in itself, he can make it irresistible,' Burroughs insisted. 'Hence it is that God by contemptible means hath so often brought down the power, the rage, the pride of the great ones of the earth.' Not only did God not require the assistance of great men for the fulfillment of his design therefore, but if God's design could be stated in specific terms it was precisely that of casting them down from their glory to humility and in full view of the world. 'The . . . design of providence in these dispensations is evidently to stain the glory of all flesh,' Owen proclaimed. 'What sort of men is there amongst us whose glory God hath not stained?' By the end of the decade the implications of such statements were being made explicit with increasing frequency. 'Oh 'tis high time to set light by all earthly glory,' announced Brooks in 1650, 'when God hath taken counsel to stain the pride of all glory and to bring into contempt all the honorable of the earth.'[34]

This way of turning the world upside down, even for its own sake, carried implications for the entire social order, from the spiritual condition of the individual to the political state of the nation. 'Is any civil government eternal?' asked John Warren, citing the changes experienced by mighty nations throughout history. 'What, must other countries be transformed by the all-changing providence of an unchangeable God, and may not we be changed?' Warren inquired. 'Peace and be silent before the Lord . . . who will bring all his purposes to pass and fulfill all his counsel . . . . If God will turn all things upside down, who are we that we should stand against him?' The very ability to learn this lesson, to understand the power of God against powerful men and great nations, was often said to constitute a kind of political prudence. 'It is the wisdom of a man to see . . . his aim in things when his providential voice crieth,' Owen said. 'All the works of God have their voice; those of signal providences speak aloud. . . . This carnal policy inquires not into but is wholly swallowed up in . . . applying secondary causes unto events, without once looking to the name of God.' This idea that God rather than rulers had final say over the destinies of nations for his rather than their purposes, and that a new kind of 'wisdom' was needed for their management, could express a sense of disillusionment with traditional political institutions in the face of new problems, a feeling of frustration over the unintended consequences that often resulted from acts of public policy. 'Whereas the end of all human wisdom in nations or the rulers of them is to preserve human society in peace and quietness . . . given unto them by the providence of God, it so comes to pass for the most part . . . that it hath a contrary end, and bringeth forth contrary effects throughout the world,' Owen observed. 'And what glory is there in that which almost constantly brings forth contrary effects to its own proper end and intendment?' This idea of providence as the resolution of contradictions stemmed from a conviction that human actions, and especially political actions, were by nature or design almost certain to throw up their own opposite, which in turn was destined to be resolved or defeated by the larger purpose of God. 'Those rare pieces of divine providence . . . receive their greatest beauties and embellishments from the variety of human obstructions through which they forced their way,' Warren noted in 1656. 'So in all the amazing changes and revolutions which our eyes have seen, there is a grand design of God uniformly carried on . . . through an incredible variety of men's counterworkings, all which shall serve to make it the more glorious.' The very concept of 'revolutions' as the preachers used the word was thus dialectical, and the choice for the people and rulers of England was whether they would work in opposition to God's providential alterations or in cooperation with them. 'The glorious appearances of God in these late times do with open mouth speak out God to be about to manifest himself in some more choice and remarkable way than heretofore,' Brooks proclaimed apocalyptically to the Commons in 1650.

> Surely God is a coming down to judge the earth with righteousness and the people with equity . . . and to stain the pride of all glory and to bring into contempt all the honorable of the earth. This design he is driving on for certain and will in spite of all oppositions accomplish it. The wheel of providence runs swiftly, and one glorious providence does but make way for another, which should heighten our hopes and strengthen our faith and raise up our souls to lay out all that we have received from God for the helping forward the design of God. Right Honorable, never had any men on earth such glorious advantages and opportunities to act high for God . . . . Your time is short, your task is great, your master is urgent, and your reward is sure.[35]

45

Whether they concerned the affairs of the nation or the dilemmas of the soul, God's purposes had been decreed before the beginning of time and were unalterable by any human resistance. 'Let then the great work of the Lord be rejoiced in, for it will certainly bear down all that stand in the way of it,' Owen declared; 'neither is there the least true consolation in any of these alterations but what arises from a closing with it.' To find out God's plan and to cooperate was both to serve his will and to bring contentment to the soul. 'The providence of God goes on in all things with strength and power and will not to be altered by our power,' Burroughs said. 'Let us be discontented and vexed and troubled, and fret and rage, yet we need not think to alter the course of providence by our discontent . . . . Be thou content or not content, the providence of God will go on.' The assurance that all was in the hands of God and that his purposes were inexorable never resulted in fatalism therefore, since the point was to allay the panic produced by uncertainty about the future in such a way as to allow for constructive action, not to substitute for it. '[We] should not outrun God's providence and say, what shall become of me? this trouble will overwhelm me!' Sibbes urged, 'but serve his providence in the use of means and then leave all to his disposal.' Such a frame of mind along with the humility providence encouraged led the soul to be obedient in serving God's ends. 'To yield and resign our souls unto God's disposing providence, everyone professing . . . here am I, let the Lord deal with me as seemeth good unto him,' said Edward Corbet, 'commands the soul a holy silence and in all afflictions keeps under the least rising of our hearts against the Almighty.' People were to remember that they were God's to begin with and that to deny themselves and to yield to his providence was the best way to promote stability, both social and mental. 'The less we value ourselves the better able shall we be to digest any troubles which befall us,' Edward Reynolds said. 'Who am I that I should fret against God or cavil at the ways of his providence?'[36]

The same was true of all they had or were, and people were urged to surrender their dearest attachments if necessary to the honor of the God who had provided them. 'All we are, or have, we have it on this condition,' Reynolds said, 'to use it, to leave it, to lay it out, to lay it down unto the honor of our master from whose bounty we received it.' The best preparation for the traumas of the world was 'by getting a low esteem of the things that God is thus shaking, and that upon this account, that he shakes them for this very end and purpose, that we should find neither rest nor peace in them'. A pervasive theme was learning to be 'dead to the world' (in preparation, as will be seen, for a subsequent rebirth). 'Labor to get your hearts mortified to the world,' said Burroughs, 'dead to the world.'

If our hearts were dead to the world we should not be much troubled with the changes of the world, nor the tossings about of worldly things . . . . Let afflictions and troubles find thee with a mortified heart to the world, and they will not . . . be very grievous or painful.

As with any death, the most personal objects of affection might be forsaken. 'The man that is dying is senseless, not affected with the cries of his children, wife, and friends that stand around him,' said William Bridge. 'Being a dying man he is dead to them, and if you be dead to your houses, liberties, and estates aforehand, you will be able to buckle and grapple with that condition.' Even such precious things were ephemeral anyway; the important thing was that they be sacrificed willingly and that there be no sentimental longing or looking back in regret. 'You leave your house, your habitation, your land, your riches, which shortly would leave you,' Bridge said. 'You leave it for your God, your country, your religion.' This eagerness to renounce all worldly joys and desires to join a great cause was one of the most poignant features of Puritanism and may have been especially appealing to those who had endured some losses already. 'Let offices go, let wife and children go, let estate go, be wholly for the Lord and say, What may I do? Wherein may I be employed and laid out? What is there in my head or heart, in my soul or body, in my treasury, shop, or house, which may be of any use for the Lord?' urged Stephen Marshall. 'Most gladly will I spend and be spent for such a God, in such a cause, for such an end.' Worldly ambitions, especially frustrated and disappointed ambitions, were not only among the first to go but possibly provided the greatest incentives, and becoming part of a larger cause became especially attractive for those who had come to see themselves and their lives as failures. 'Perhaps thou hast had a desire to be somebody in the world,' Owen suggested. 'Thou seest thyself come short of what thou aimedst at, say now . . . not only half but let all go, seeing that the Lord shall reign with glory.' Those who felt their lives had been wasted, that they had been irredeemably disgraced and dishonored, could look forward to an ample reward if they devoted what was left of themselves to God. 'If by an overruling providence you must part with your worldly honor (and there is no resisting providence),' Cheynell promised, 'I'll show you how you may gain a better honor, an immortal glorious honor in the highest heavens.'[37]

In the end, then, the greatest status to which one could aspire was the honor of God; and by contrast the most dreaded fate that could befall a soul, the most heinous and terrifying condition, worse than death itself, was to be cursed and shunned and to lose one's 'esteem'. 'They that dishonor and despise God shall themselves become vile and be lightly esteemed,' William Strong told the Lords in 1647.

> All sorts of contempt [shall be] cast upon [them] . . . and their reward shall be to become vile and of no esteem . . . . He that hath no esteem of God's honor shall himself (whatsoever his place and parts be, and whatever ornaments and excellencies he hath to set him off before men) be dishonored, accounted a man of no worth . . . and be separated with a curse and unto detestation before all men.

Thus the effect of change, and of the new standard of honor, was to call into question – not necessarily to deny, but radically to question – the efficacy and value of every element of the created order, both material and social, from the human will and reason to the mysteries of state and the persons who dispensed them. 'None, either persons or things, although they pretend divine authority,' asserted Joseph Caryl, 'ought to be admitted without trial.' Such statements referred to current controversies, but they had, and were intended to have, broader implications. It required no radical to carry the point to its logical conclusion: 'Will God assuredly cast contempt and shame on those that shall adventure to dishonor him?' Francis Woodcock, similarly employing the royal 'they', asked the Commons in 1645.

> Behold . . . persons of the highest rank amongst us deeply dishonoring God and God following them with greatest dishonors. Time was, their persons, names, authority were sacred among us. Now alas, how cheap are they grown, how neglected? So long indeed as it was possible means was used to hide their shame . . . by turning over the blame of all our miseries upon evil counselors, incendiaries, and the like to discharge them of it. But all in vain; it can be hid no longer . . . . God's honor hath suffered exceedingly by them, and therefore are they fallen under all this dishonor.[38]

2

SIN

A revolution is certainly the most authoritarian thing there is.

Engels

Nothing weakens a man, or nation, like to guilt.

Peter Sterry, 1645

In the political cosmology of the Puritans the distance between heaven and earth was not necessarily fixed or static; there was always room for variation, change, and adjustment. Not only did God condescend to interact with his creation, but the creatures themselves, at least rational creatures, could also vary in their proximity, their own natural tendency being to move further away. 'Behold upon us, poor wretches . . . is found that which widens this distance beyond all expression,' lamented Thomas Case. 'Sin sets as much beneath our creatureship as our creatureship sets us beneath the creator . . . . There is nothing vile and base enough under heaven to make a simile of sin.' Indeed, so alien was evil to the handiwork of God that it occupied its own dwelling place, separate from that of the creator and even his creation. 'It was the first founder of hell and laid the first cornerstone thereof,' noted Thomas Goodwin. 'Sin alone brought in and filled that bottomless gulf with all the fire and brimstone and treasures of wrath which shall never be burnt and consumed.' Almost more important however was what sin did to this world, turning the beauty of creation into something foul and corrupt, subject to the destructive powers of death and decay. 'Sin hath brought death over all,' declared Nicholas Lockyer. 'Transgression hath made mutation . . . . Sin hath subjected the whole creation to vanity.' The consequences of sin in this life and the next were not strongly distinguished, since sin itself was often so described as a kind of 'death'. 'We are all by sin dead,' Lockyer said. 'Bodily death is sad, soul death a thousand times more sad.' Sin then was the cause of all change, of all temporality, of all human weakness before the violent and inexorable forces of the Almighty. 'Sin hath its influence into the mutation of things,' Lockyer observed. 'Things are set in their course. Divine determination biaseth every state to such an end . . . . Sin provokes; justice decrees.' Sin was thus responsible not only for damnation in hell but for all worldly suffering and sorrow, and it was sin too that accounted for all social problems. 'Sin is the

49

poorest thing in the world,' lamented Richard Sibbes, 'and the cause of all beggary and poverty and misery.'[1]

The corruption of humanity, like the mutability of worldly things, was a pervasive theme in early modern literature; certainly it preoccupied the Puritan preachers, who called human nature to account for all that was wrong with their world. 'Man hath an evil root within him,' warned Thomas Brooks,

> that root of bitterness, that cursed sinful nature that is in him. 'Out of the heart proceed evil thoughts, murders, adulteries, fornications, thefts, false witness, blasphemies.' The whole frame of man is out of frame. The understanding is dark, the will cross, the memory slippery, the affections crooked, the conscience corrupted, the tongue poisoned, and the heart wholly evil, only evil, and continually evil.

Such a view of one's fellows (or oneself) was not unusual at a time when change and dislocation had weakened many traditional constraints, and while the ministers' opinion of humanity in the best of times was bleak indeed, they were also convinced that in their own age the natural evil that lurked in the hearts of men and women had been given an unusually free rein. 'Our times are times of most prodigious wickedness,' declared Stephen Marshall, 'horrible abominations in men's manners.'

> I am confident never such abominable drunkenness and general looseness in that kind, never more universal liberty of whoring, incestuous marriages, oppressions, cruelty, injustice, malice, revenge, and everything that might fill a land with ungodliness. Since we or our forefathers were born, never was there a greater deluge of wickedness than in these our times.

From such catalogues it is apparent that the most worrying forms of antisocial behavior were those unleashed by changes in the economic and social structure, as well as by an inadequate system of law enforcement and legal justice which seldom remedied and often exacerbated them: urban decay, crime, alcoholism, prostitution, fraudulent and exploitative commercial practices, family disintegration, class antagonisms, corruption of public officials. 'Go but to the places of greatest resort, market towns, populous cities, and fairs,' Marshall suggested, 'and your hearts would tremble to think how our land is overspread with these':

> oppression, cruelty, defrauding of brethren, the sensual sins of uncleanness, especially that of drunkenness . . . . Oh beloved, the generality of the people of England is extremely wicked . . . and . . . many of the nobles, magistrates, knights, and gentlemen and persons of great quality are . . . taking part with wicked men and wicked causes . . . patrons of alehouses and disorders, checking inferior officers who discover any zeal for God against an ill cause. In many of their families there is not so much as a face of civility . . . and some few others borne down in their places with the torrent of wickedness.[2]

As Marshall indicates, the role of the state was central to any effort to control such social anomie, and the impetus behind the exalted place the preachers gave to civil government in God's order was their keen awareness of man as at once a political and a very unsocial animal. 'Government is the prop and pillar of all states and kingdoms, the cement and soul of human affairs, the life of society and order, the very vital spirit whereby so many millions of men do breathe the life of comfort and peace,' Robert Bolton asserted. 'Take sovereignty from the face of the earth, and . . . men would become cutthroats and cannibals one unto another. Murders, adulteries, incests, rapes, robberies, perjuries, witchcrafts, blasphemies, all kinds of villainies, outrages, and savage cruelty would overthrow all countries. We should have a very hell upon earth and the face of it covered with blood.' This perhaps not unrealistic assessment of the human capacity for evil was the product of a society experiencing a high level of lawlessness and violence, where nothing was feared so much as disorder and anarchy, and any hatred the ministers developed of 'tyranny' was grounded in a realization that it thrived most openly when political authority was weak. 'If the magistrate were not a god to man, man would soon prove a devil to man,' said William Jenkyn. 'Violent and bloody men fear not hell so much as the halter . . . . And though their fear of the magistrate saves not their own souls, yet many times hath it saved our lives . . . . Where there be no ruler any man may be a tyrant. 'Tis just with God that they should feel the curse of anarchy who were never thankful for magistracy.'[3]

While the preachers saw the world sharply polarized between good and evil, they were reluctant to allow this more than an oblique correspondence with any polarity between persons, and both the problems of their society and the tenets of their theology dictated that the dividing line ran through each individual and that everyone without exception was depraved. 'In a sense, all men living on the face of the earth are evil men.' The description of disorders as 'evil' and the result of 'sin' and 'wickedness' was not a simplistic failure to recognize that they were also social; in fact their refusal to limit sin to those with whom they had personal or partisan differences indicates precisely the opposite, though acknowledging what would now be called the environmental causes of social deviance was not to obscure the fact that society was made up of morally responsible individuals. 'We complain of the times, but let us take heed that they be not the worse for us,' Richard Sibbes enjoined. 'The worse the times are, the better be thou; for this is thy glory, to be good in an evil generation.' Yet the ministers also recognized that social problems were not simply personal but systemic and insisted that the present disorder and dislocation of society had created conditions in which those most easily given to selfish and unscrupulous practices received more encouragement than those who made an effort to refrain from them. 'Both in church and commonwealth there is great unquietness, so that all laws both divine and human are openly violated,' Arthur Dent proclaimed in 1611. 'Good men most cruelly are dealt withal; evil men do rejoice and triumph in their wickedness without control.' In such circumstances it was the strong and ruthless who most readily

51

prospered while the weak and retiring usually ended up as their victims. 'It is ill with them that trust in the Lord, and evil men prosper,' complained John Preston, voicing the popular sentiment.

> And therefore what encouragements have I to trust in God . . . when . . .
> my life or my goods are in hazard or my name . . . . I see by experience that
> . . . politic men, and those that have the greatest means, they prosper
> whenas other men that fear God do not bring their devices to pass.[4]

This conviction that those with means and influence and without scruples were far more likely to succeed in the world than those already less advantaged was a problem the preachers have been accused of avoiding; in fact, it was the central one their religion was designed to confront. 'It is true that ill men oftentimes do prosper and that good men many times do not succeed,' Preston acknowledged. 'Evil men may prosper long and may exceedingly bring their enterprises to pass.' The danger of this perception that evil was not only rampant but all too often rewarded with success while those who tried to uphold higher ethical values often suffered as a result was its self-aggravating effect. 'How are good men despised in the world!' Sibbes lamented. 'They have little encouragements from any, but discouragements on all sides.' The problem was to prevent these discouragements from resulting in the kind of cynicism that in turn only exacerbated the problem. 'To see evil courses and evil persons flourish and countenanced in the world,' Sibbes added, 'oh, it goes to the heart of God's people and makes them stagger at God's providence.' The standard rejoinder was to remind people that this prosperity was only temporary while the final consequences were not. 'The seeming prosperity of . . . wicked men shall have an end, and their misery shall have no end,' Sibbes promised. 'Let us not be dazzled with their present happiness so as to imitate their evil ways.' As with all worldly things, the preachers assured those who failed because of their weakness or their diffidence or their honesty, the 'seeming' or 'present' prosperity of the more aggressive and successful was only transient and therefore ultimately not real. 'Let this admonish us to have nothing to do with sinful persons, nor to be troubled with their seeming prosperity,' Sibbes added. 'All their riches shall end in poverty and beggary . . . . All their honor and greatness shall end in confusion and shame.' Yet even after this was said, the conviction that injustice was not only practiced but practiced successfully, that when the unscrupulous took advantage of new opportunities for personal gain and social advancement without regard for the harm they caused to others or the public in general they often thrived and prospered – all this produced an often invisible but potentially explosive mix of moral outrage combined with bitter and abiding resentment, resentment with which the preachers' own admonitions against it themselves often seemed to seethe. 'I confess it is hard not to be troubled at the prosperity of wicked men,' Stephen Marshall acknowledged. 'But . . . enquire how able they will be to undergo the wrath of God . . . and thy envy will be at an end . . . . Never envy the prosperous. . . . Though they swim in wealth and honor and pomp in this world and have all their hearts can desire . . . never envy their lot.'[5]

Whether such resentment can be described as a form of class hatred is a matter of definition, but in a highly mobile society, where spectacular success often had its corollary in tragic failure, and fabulous accumulations of wealth came to exist (and be displayed) in conspicuous proximity to grinding poverty, the presence of 'envy' was both extensive and intense. 'There is envy in man's nature,' Sibbes observed. 'The malice of man's nature cannot abide eminency in others.' Envy was the sin of a society in transition, when traditional status was uncertain, competition keen and cutthroat, and poverty on the rise; and while the preachers condemned it unequivocally, one suspects their horror stemmed in part from what they saw of it within themselves. 'When goodness shines forth, it presently meets with envy,' Sibbes observed. 'Envy hath an ill eye.' Sins such as envy were dangerous to any society, since envious people were scheming and unpredictable. 'Envy pries into things,' Sibbes noted. 'An envious person searcheth.' Resentment of this kind brought out aggressive instincts that threatened the stability of society and even the state. 'I daresay there is no disposition or frame of soul that hath been the occasion of more bloodshed, of more injustice in the church and state from the beginning of the world, than a jealous disposition, especially in great ones.' Such rivalries fueled a tendency toward emulation, the desire to outdo others, an insatiable lust for preeminence and power, and so led to the very pursuits that aroused social discord in the first place. 'Naturally this is in men,' Sibbes observed. 'They are so vainglorious and ambitious, that when they see the lives of other men outshow theirs . . . they go to base courses . . . . Especially when it comes in a kind of competition and comparison, they love not to be outshined.' This kind of invidious comparison could be found in both individuals and groups, and the preachers' warnings of the dangers in 'envy', 'jealousy', 'discontent', and 'ambition' seem to have been directed against the aspirations of powerful individuals as much as the lower classes. 'Hence springs ambition and the vein of being great in the world . . . an unmeasurable desire of abounding in those things which the world esteems highly of,' Sibbes continued. 'There is in us naturally a competition and desire of being equal or above others in that which is generally thought to make us happy and esteemed amongst men. If we be not the only men, yet we will be somebody in the world.' This 'corrupt desire of being great in the opinion of others', especially when aggravated by quite realistic fears of failure, had obvious destructive potential for society and could expose self-destructive tendencies within the individual, to the point where 'men will sacrifice their very lives for vainglory'. Such proclivities were found among both older elites and the poorer classes and any social stratum where people felt threatened with ruin or came to be filled with resentment over the (new) prosperity of others. 'Of this mind are not only the dregs of people, but many of the more refined sort, who desire to be eminent in the world and . . . herein give up the liberty of their own judgments and consciences to the desires and lusts of others,' Sibbes observed. 'To be above others, they will be beneath themselves.' The destabilizing dangers of unbridled ambition to both the soul and society were powerfully enunciated by Robert Bolton: 'Ambition . . . is an insatiable thirst after glory and a gluttonous, excessive desire after greatness,' he explained.

> Of all the vicious passions which do possess the heart of man it is the most powerful and unconquerable . . . . Seated in the highest and haughtiest spirits . . . it is resolute and desperate in its undertakings, furious and headstrong in its pursuits and persecutions. It is venturous to remove any let and hardened for all means, many times without remorse or tears . . . . It is victorious over all other affections and masters even the sensuality of lustful pleasures . . . . It prefers a high room in the world before a temporal life – yea, and eternal life too.[6]

Such ruthless ambition was especially worrying in the realm of high politics and specifically appointments to office. 'Through the covetousness and ambition of some and partiality of others, things are so carried in a church or state that worth is neglected and worthless men advanced.' Unethical methods of acquiring and exercising office were among the abuses the preachers attacked frequently and vociferously. 'Woe therefore to those empoisoned stirrups by which so many . . . rise aloft and climb so high,' Bolton warned. 'I mean bribery, simony, flattery, temporizing, base insinuations, and such vile means . . . of going into office, benefices and high rooms by corruption.' At its worst such a system degenerated to the point where offices were not awarded according to qualifications but purchased by the highest bidder. 'Oh gall of bitterness, oh root of all evil to church and commonwealth, when authorities and offices of justice shall be bought and sold!' remarked Samuel Ward. 'Offices are not livings and salaries but charges and duties, not preferments for favorites but rewards of deserts.' This perception that power and status were being conferred in state and society more for money than merit also led to the preachers' denunciations of 'the worst of all vices incident to magistracy . . . covetousness . . . an inordinate love of money'. 'If the world once take notice that money doth the deed, men to make way for preferment will seek more to get money than merit,' Bolton argued. 'Those who should rise . . . in the commonwealth will labor rather to furnish themselves with heavy purses than noble parts.' Covetousness comprehended numerous societal ills, from enclosures and usury, which drove the poor from the land or into debt, to the exploitative and parasitic practices of the legal profession. 'What's now the reason that almost half the world is turned enclosers, usurers, or bankrupts, that the common jails have more poor debtors than desperate felons? What's the fountain of so many lawsuits and law cases . . . so many perjuries and false accusations?' asked Thomas Pestell. 'Men are sick [with] covetousness.' Though covetousness was particularly endemic among the rich and successful, it infected all ranks of society where dissatisfaction over the success of others bred a desire for similar and greater gains for oneself. 'This sickness seizes all,' Pestell declared. 'From the greatest to the least . . . everyone is given to covetousness.' Like ambition, covetousness was both insatiable and politically pernicious as it influenced official promotions. 'Many may say of their places . . . their money, not their merit, hath made them great men (but corrupt men) in church and state,' according to Samuel Garey, and the preachers often called for 'strict and severe laws against those two great impoisoners of the strongest and most flourishing states: first, bribery, secondly, baseness in coming to high rooms . . . . No kingdom under heaven harboring these two cutthroats can stand long without baseness or ruin.' The complaint kindled powerful emotions, inextricably blending genuine concern for the public good with the injured pride of those who had lost out in the scramble. 'Wicked magistrates do a great deal of mischief to a state,' Bolton protested in righteous indignation, threatening the corrupt with condign retribution at the hands of a judge who accepted no gratuities:

Many nowadays run madding after promotions and serve themselves by means and measures into offices, benefices, preferments, and being most unworthily advanced, they hold it a special happiness to have a hand over men far worthier than themselves. Let them alone; this is their day, a day of domineering . . . . Though they swell never so big with pride and disdain, look they never so high . . . they shall certainly down with a vengeance. God shall suddenly . . . throw them down into the dust. Their pride and their power shall be overthrown . . . and their poor sinful souls must presently be presented at the last and strictest tribunal, where never bribe or big look, gold or greatness bears any sway. O then they will gnash their teeth and roar and wish that they had lain in the dust all the days of their life and never known what preferment had meant, when they find by woeful experience, but too late, that to mighty men there are mighty torments prepared and that they shall be horribly plagued proportionably to the pestilent abuse of their high places and those public employments into which they have corruptly thrust themselves.[7]

Even short of outright corruption, the preachers lambasted what they saw as unabashed ambition and warned against the kind of men that would (and did) hold sway in the commonwealth. 'Not only the viler and baser and more gross ways of getting into places of preferment and rising, as by gifts, brokerage, affection, favor, etc. are forbidden and condemned, but even ambitious seeking also,' Bolton complained. 'Men of most prostituted consciences are for the most part the most pragmatical prowlers after undeserved preferments, honors, and places of advancement.' Often the preachers suggested that ambition itself disqualified and that those who sought office were by that very fact unsuitable to hold it. 'He which ambitiously seeks a place, even in so doing, makes himself most unworthy of it,' Bolton argued. 'For as those of truest worth are ever timorous and most retiring . . . so the worst men ordinarily are most ambitious and aspiring.' Those who came to power through untoward methods were usually servile and therefore cruel, likely to use their new position to satisfy a lust for domination. 'A wicked man advanced and hoisted into some high place may look big, domineer, and . . . stand to it stoutly a good while,' Bolton warned; 'but . . . he that is a slave to his lust and slavishly serves the time will be sure to . . . turn true coward when his temporary happiness is hazarded. And cowards . . . are slaves to their superiors, fellow fools to their equals, tyrants to their inferiors, and windmills to popular breath.' Sometimes the preachers went so far as to suggest that such as were most fit for office, the 'timorous and most retiring' (those, one suspects, similar to how they saw themselves), should be pressed and even compelled to serve the public. 'They that are fit and able must and will be sought to, yea haled out of their ease and privacy into the light of employment,' said Samuel Ward. 'For the prevention of all which evils unavoidably attending ambition, lighting most heavily upon the commonwealth . . . such [shall] be provided not as would have places, but as should have.'[8]

On the other hand, the resentments stemming from these very complaints were themselves a dangerous source of discontent, particularly among those who felt their own talents were not receiving their due recognition. 'Man thinks himself worthy of all honor, never considering his weakness and infirmities,' Sibbes observed. 'We willingly puff up ourselves in our own conceits of self-sufficiency, and hence arises discontentedness, when we think God is not so good to us as our merits do deserve.' This sensitivity to one's sense of 'honor', or what might now be termed status or self-esteem, as both a powerful motivating force for individuals and a potentially destabilizing one for society, the preachers often noted in their observations that injuries were most wounding, and therefore most likely to provoke a reaction that could lead to social conflict, as they afflicted one's need for respect and fear of public disgrace. 'Thought of disgrace is in every man naturally,' remarked William Perkins, 'bringing forth . . . envy, strife, emulations, dissensions, and debates.' Far more than material injuries, the wounded pride and humiliation that resulted from social disgrace and the affronts of 'wicked men' produced a resentment that was deep and abiding. 'We are more moved with reproaches than injuries,' Sibbes suggested. 'No man but thinks himself worthy of respect from some or other. Now, slanders come from abundance of malice or else abundance of contempt, and therefore nothing sticks so much as reproaches.' This awareness of the impact of social competition on the individual ego (perhaps especially the masculine ego) was the starting point of Puritan social psychology. 'Reproach . . . is that that the nature of man can least endure of all,' Sibbes observed.

> The nature of man can endure . . . a loss . . . but a reproach, especially if it be a scornful reproach, the nature of man is most impatient of . . . . Now a reproachful scorn shows disrespect, and when the nature of man sees itself disrespected, it grows to terms of impatience. There is not the meanest man living but he thinks himself worthy of some regard.[9]

This sensitivity to being 'disrespected' aroused in the socially insecure by a myriad of otherwise invisible petty slights often found its outlet in violence, sometimes semi-organized in vendettas and clan feuds. 'It is a perverse disposition of mind whereby men remember injuries, discourtesies, and unkindnesses and carry about them a purpose and desire to do like for like,' said Perkins. 'This enmity [is] everywhere among us. For we daily see person divided against person, family against family.' The preachers often complained that men (it was usually men) were excessively quarrelsome and contentious, sensitive to insult, overly jealous of their honor and status and ever ready to defend them by whatever means were available. 'Contention is carnal and sinful . . . when men contend for things for which they should not contend . . . or when contention is without forgiving, forbearing, or suffering, and that in trifling matters,' Perkins said, '. . . when men willfully defend their own private causes, no regard had whether they be right or wrong, true or false.' Private violence was still seen as a serious problem – whether it took the form of domestic quarrels in the humblest households, duels between gentlemen, or the feudal and dynastic warfare of overmighty subjects – and one which no civilized society could tolerate. 'All of us [are] set on being desperately prone both to give and execute sentence upon our own wrongs (if happily wrongs) by dint of sword and bloody death . . . for every slight affront and idle word,' another observed. 'In so quarreling a generation, and so prone to blood and violence . . . let every man have the freedom of his own sword, suffer them to abuse their own bodies and lives unto the satisfying of the bloody purpose of their . . . desperate and malicious disposition, there will soon be an end of all civil society.' The unquenchable thirst for revenge was one against which the preachers found themselves constantly having to admonish by insisting that all vengeance belonged to God. 'It is a point of injustice to revenge ourselves, for then we take to ourselves the honor of God,' Perkins said. 'Learn . . . not to requite and repay evil for evil . . . but leave all revenge unto the Lord.' Puritan preachers were hardly unique in condemning these tendencies, though they were the most active in exhorting popular audiences and seeing the prohibitions observed in practice. 'When injuries are done unto us we ought to abstain from all affections of revenge,' Perkins cautioned. 'It is indeed a hard lesson to learn and practice but is our parts to endeavor to do it . . . yea, even at that instant when other men are doing us wrong.' The ethic of loving one's enemies was by no means foreign to Puritan sensibilities; when it came to one's private enemies it was a foremost imperative. 'When a man can love his very enemies and those that have done him most wrong, it is an argument that such a man hath something above nature in him,' Sibbes suggested. 'For a man to overcome himself in this sweet appetite of revenge . . . argues the power of grace and godliness in such a one.' The ministers' objection to indulging one's lust for revenge, it might be said, was not so much the harm it did to the victim as the satisfaction it gave to the perpetrator, as well as the social devastation wrought by an uncontrolled and unending cycle of private vengeance. 'Revenge . . . begets a base, a cruel and wolvish disposition and an unnatural thirst of blood,' Bolton observed. 'We commonly see that the basest and most worthless men are most malicious and revengeful.'[10]

While in some the passion for revenge could take the form of open violence, those not in a position to indulge their hostility by force often sought more fantastic remedies for their sufferings and affronts. 'When men through crosses, wrongs, vexations, wants, etc. are in deep discontent, so that they say in their hearts, what would not they do that they might be avenged on such and such, at such times as these, the devil, by voice only or by some shape also, approacheth near to them offering them aid . . . upon his conditions,' observed Nathaniel Holmes. 'It is a common practice of many among us in these days, when God's hand is upon them to go for help to the devil; they seek for counsel to witches and wisemen.' The yearning for respect and self-respect amid fears of disgrace and destitution could send people, especially poor people, grasping at anything that might help them overcome their feelings of frustration and powerlessness and give them some degree of dignity and some semblance of control, however illusory, over their lives. 'The main causes of the practices of witchcraft [are] in man's outward estate [and] in the mind and inward man,' Perkins argued, demonstrating how Puritan sociology often combined economic with psychological explanations for the bizarre forms this search could take:

> When he lives in base and low estate, whether in regard of poverty or want of honor and reputation, which he thinks by right is due unto him, he then grows to some measure of grief and sorrow within himself. Hereupon he is moved to yield himself to the devil, to be his vassal and scholar in this wicked art, supposing that by the working of some wonders he may be able in time to relieve his poverty and to purchase to himself credit and countenance among men . . . and hence he is moved to attempt the cursed art of magic and witchcraft as a way to get further knowledge in matters secret and not revealed, that by working of wonders he may purchase fame in the world.[11]

OPPRESSION

The preachers' strictures on how to deal with one's adversities, both external adversaries and internal anxieties, may have been significant less for what they said than for the need to say it, and the recognition that both the injuries perpetrated by bad people and the bitterness they engendered in otherwise good ones constituted either side of a single problem of social discord. 'There are two great troublers of our peace and hinderers of our keeping the precepts of God,' Joseph Caryl said. 'The first is sin within; the second is oppression of man without . . . . Oppression is any wrong done to man by man.' The absence of a strong distinction was not only because oppression was itself one form of sin but also because of the moral degradation it produced in the oppressed as well as the oppressor. 'Oppression makes a wise man mad,' Caryl noted. 'Oppression doth not only spoil a man of his outward estate, but it even bereaveth him of his wits; he is as it were distracted, discomposed.' In their concern with the psychological effects of oppression, the preachers were acknowledging that moral behavior was shaped in part by social circumstances, and as an extension of the social nature of sin people were also thought to be possessed of a natural instinct to oppress. 'As there is a spirit in man which lusteth to envy,' Caryl observed, 'so there is a spirit which lusteth to oppress.' And as England was a society unusually rife with envy, so with oppression as well. 'Oppression . . . is . . . insinuated by a diabolical spirit, whereby one creature's being is too blessed in the eye of another,' Nicholas Lockyer explained, not without some moral ambivalence.

> One person better beloved, better endowed, better succeeded. If he were dead, dead in esteem or dead in being . . . then I should be all and have all. . . . Oppression is a bloody spirit . . . . 'Tis strong parts setting their feet upon weak and wringing blood out of a brother's nose. 'Tis grinding the face of the poor.[12]

Oppression could be perpetrated by and against anyone, though it was thought to be especially endemic to powerful men, who seemed to enjoy using and abusing their power over others. 'It is an ordinary thing for mighty men and men of power in their dealing to oppress those that are under them,' Charles Richardson observed. 'There is no spectacle more pleasant to their eyes than the ruins of the poor . . . . The more they increase the more they oppress and make the ruins of the oppressed as it were the steps to the oppression of others . . . till there be nothing left for the poor but lamentable desolation.' Though many forms of oppression were decried, including the political and religious, even these had their roots in what was by far the overwhelming source of oppression: that of the rich over the poor. 'Those that rob and spoil, oppress, defraud, and beggar young and old, the mother and the child upon her' earned the invective of Robert Harris in one of many catalogues detailing the effects of enclosure and other forms of social oppression, as well as the psychic scars it left on its embittered victims:

> Oh 'tis a fearful sin to ruin houses and towns, to lay whole families on . . . weeping. The cry of so many will surely to heaven, the smart of so many will deeply embitter, when children shall cry to parents for bread and they have it not . . . for coats and they have none, food and money and they have none, when they shall look one way on the miseries of their children, another way on the injustice, unmercifulness, oppression of landlords, of creditors, and see themselves forever betrayed to misery through the default of others. Oh this fills their heart with many a bitter thought, the mouth with many a bitter curse . . . . They lie at God and give him no rest till he revenge them . . . . This will work bitterness in others to us, to ours.[13]

The poor were given to their own sins, not the least of which was this very bitterness and cursing, though even that was said to redound most heavily on those who brought them to it. 'They that care not for the poor procure to themselves, yea and upon their estates (either unconscionably gotten or uncharitably kept), many a curse,' John Moore warned. 'The poor will curse them.' Though such cursing was not to be condoned, neither was it necessarily far removed from that of the Almighty himself. 'When the poor curse these hard-hearted wretches,' Moore added, 'though it be sin in them, yet there is somewhat of God in it.' Still, the bitterness of the poor did leave them susceptible to desperate temptations, not only cursing but crime and other destructive outlets for their rage and frustration. 'Poverty becomes not only a cross but a snare,' Thomas Watson pointed out. 'It exposeth to much evil . . . . The poor will venture their souls for money.' Even so, no permanent stigma was attached to the poor because of their poverty or their sins, both of which were said to be caused by the oppressions of the rich, though there was a recognition of the dangers both to the victims and to society in swelling indigence. 'Do not curse and swear and fret,' Thomas Jacomb advised the poor.

> Though you be very low . . . 'put not forth your hands to steal' . . . (which is the devil's temptation to the poor). Do not fret and murmur at the providence of God . . . . Are you now poor in estate? Be also poor in spirit . . . . Do the rich deny you mercy? Do not curse and swear and fret at them (as many profanely do) but quietly wait till God incline their hearts to show favor to you.[14]

The ministers' attitude toward the poor was not that they were to be treated any more severely than anyone else but that they were to be treated as people – not as victims or as charity cases but as people with the same selfish and aggressive inclinations as anyone else and fewer incentives to restrain them; in fact their moral responsibilities, far more demanding than those of the rich, required that not only were they not to exacerbate their condition with illegal and self-destructive ways but also they should preserve what little dignity and self-respect they had left. 'Idleness and laziness is the sin of many that are in want,' argued Jacomb (in a sermon otherwise dedicated entirely to the maltreatment of the poor by the rich).

> Whence is it that we have so many vagrants and beggars amongst us? . . .
> They go from house to house and are supplied by the mercy of others . . . .
> When they have got a little money, presently they go to an alehouse and there drink it away, and so their wives and children may starve if they be not relieved.

The sins of the poor that were most disturbing would thus seem to have been those that worsened their poverty or destroyed their social structure; compared to those of the rich, which created them, they seem to have been of minor importance. 'Oppression and theft are both of them to be accounted sins,' Richardson noted. 'Oppression is a more grievous sin than theft . . . . In oppression, beside the damage . . . there is always some indignity and reproach . . . which is far worse than the fraud or deceit which is used in theft.' In fact for all their emphasis on judgments, and for all the self-righteousness of which they are often accused, the ministers' consciousness of the societal origins of deviant and criminal behavior led them to urge, and often to demonstrate, a remarkably detached and non-judgmental attitude toward immorality, though this was considerably easier to practice with respect to the failings of the poor than the oppressions of the rich. 'Whereby we may see what it is to be wretched . . . to be subject to all miseries,' observed William Perkins, 'hence we may learn that we must not despise parties by reason of their sins or scorn and contemn them, but contrariwise lament and pity them.' At the same time, the preachers had no romantic illusions that poverty was somehow in itself an ennobling condition; on the contrary, the squalid conditions they witnessed were simply degrading: as unemployment, homelessness, various forms of dispossession created an under-class of the most destitute, poverty disfigured people morally as well as physically; it deprived them of their humanity and turned them into beasts. 'They are (for the most part) a cursed generation,' said Perkins of the swarms of vagrants and beggars that had become such an alarming feature of London and the growing towns. 'Generally they are given up to most horrible sins of injustice and uncleanness . . . . They range not themselves into any families but live liker brute beasts than men.' No one was condemned by his misery, however, and the poor were not condemned by their oppression, though they were given the dignity of being responsible for their behavior under it. 'Poverty may be a cross, but it is no curse,' another minister said. 'But beggary is a fearful curse. . . . The daily cries in our streets cry out yet . . . that the impotent poor may be sufficiently provided for, that he need not, and the sturdy beggar compelled to work, that he may not be suffered to beg.' Begging was roundly condemned, and yet the preachers betrayed a reluctance to assign blame too readily to the beggars themselves and consistently recognized that 'the neglect of provision for the poor is the cause of begging'. In fact their denunciations of begging were almost always appended to far more extensive exhortations to generosity toward the relief of the poor and were far outweighed by the abuse they heaped upon those who failed to relieve the problem or created it in the first place. 'I do not plead for beggars,' said John Moore, whose defensive tone was typical. 'For it is the shame of a well-ordered commonwealth to suffer so many idle beggars and rogues and vagrants to wander up and down out of a calling.' Even then, however, Moore went on to explain precisely why it was such a shame and who it was that was to be ashamed. 'It is a greater shame for any . . . society, city, or town to take no more care for the poor than that they be forced to beg,' he continued. 'But how great a shame is it . . . not to suppress make-beggars which make such swarms of beggars in counties, cities, and towns.' While the political authorities that failed to alleviate poverty were guilty enough, the economic exploitations by the rich (and perhaps especially the newly rich) that actually produced the problem earned the most stinging rebukes of the prophet's indignation:

Here I cannot but cry aloud . . . and tell these make-beggars their sins and these greedy gripes their transgressions, that care not how many beggars they make so themselves may be gentlemen, nor how many poor they make so themselves may be rich. I mean the unsociable, covetous, cruel brood of those wretches . . . who fall under the prophet's woe, 'that join house to house and field to field till there be no place, that they may be placed alone in the midst of the earth' and be rid of all the poor.[15]

Poverty, then, as a material condition, was in itself morally neutral (though not insignificant) in Puritan religion; only one's behavior under it made a difference. 'There is a great deal of wisdom in distinguishing between them that have sinned themselves into poverty and who by the hand of God are brought into poverty,' Thomas Watson suggested. 'All whom God, not their idleness, makes poor are to be relieved.' Riches, on the other hand, were almost intrinsically evil (and this despite the ministers' own dependence on the patronage of the gentry). 'Riches and sin have some affinity,' Richard Greenham observed. 'They are evil commonly either in getting, or in keeping, or in using, or in loving them . . . . Poverty hath been the decay of many a man, but riches of a far greater number.' There were a number of related reasons for this: in a time of social insecurity and an apparently widening gulf between the rich and the poor, social disparities as well as the exploitation and prodigal use of resources were evident and a constant source of denunciation, as well as a good illustration of how any sin was aggravated by oppression. 'Hence it is that the superfluity of men's goods, which is the portion of the poor, is lavished out and wasted in profuse and vain expenses, yea in the maintenance of base and sinful lusts,' Samuel Rogers observed, 'for by that time pride, gluttony, drunkenness, voluptuousness, and all manner of excess and riot have had their share, there is scarce a farthing left for the poor.' Rogers's catalogue provided one testimony to how the conspicuous consumption of the rich and upwardly mobile existed alongside, and in more than one way contributed to, widespread squalor:

so many pounds laid out (cost needless) in bravery of apparel, rich attire, and fantastical fashions . . . whereas so many poor creatures at the same time had not a good rag to cover them . . . such vast sums of money lavished out without any measure in feasts and banquetings, whenas the poor that were ready to perish for hunger would have been glad of the scraps and fragments that were given to their hounds and hawks, yea fain would they have been refreshed with the very crumbs that fell from their tables . . . such a treasure wasted in needless and unnecessary buildings, so many walks and galleries, turrets and pyramids, such setting up, pulling down, transposing, transplacing to make gay houses (which were very mock-beggars) and so much yearly cast away in costly furniture, with which their houses were well-stuffed and filled, whenas multitudes of poor people were driven to wander about, and had no certain dwelling place, had no other house than the wide world, no other bed than the hard ground, and no other canopy than the open heaven . . . so many hundreds spent in lawsuits for the satisfying of a self-will and as much more in sports and pastimes for the pleasing of a carnal mind, whenas never a poor creature was one penny the better for all this.[16]

This contempt for a society devoted to material acquisition, vulgar display, and frivolous pastimes formed the basis of the famous Puritan asceticism and disdain of pleasure. 'There are some that . . . in their fullness are in straits, not enjoying what they have, grudging to themselves everything . . . hidebound miserable men, who are not only unmerciful to others but even to themselves,' Jacomb observed. 'These do not so much possess their wealth as their wealth possesses them.' It is possible that the ministers' apparent inability to enjoy themselves may have been stimulated largely as a form of protest against what much of their society seemed to find enjoyable. 'Ye can throw away a great deal prodigally upon a feast, a suit, a house, a hawk, maybe upon a whore,' Jacomb accused his more well-heeled listeners, 'but when it comes to a business of charity then you can pretend inability.' While the preachers often singled out the rich for special denunciation, poverty was also a problem for all of society and one which the failure to solve could bring trouble on the entire nation, making the oppressors not simply enemies to the poor but public enemies and enemies to God as well. 'This evil of covetousness and of not caring for the poor will bring the fury and wrath of God upon . . . the most flourishing nations,' John Moore warned, 'and those that care not for the poor are the worst enemies to a commonwealth.' Oppression then was not merely a burden to the oppressed but a threat to society and the state as well, since there was thought to be an inherent connection between poverty and violence. 'It is a degree of murder,' thundered Charles Richardson. 'For a man to deprive the poor of that wherein his life consisteth is all one with God as to take away his life itself . . . . Oppression is a most filthy bottomless sink of grievous enormities.' While forms of oppression besides the social and economic were also worrisome, these too were closely connected, and the dangers of oppression to all of society were brought home by developments in the 1640s. 'Oppression maturates itself in high places,' declared Nicholas Lockyer in 1645.

> Oppression . . . is the cryingest provocation in a land and brings down the cryingest judgment, civil war, a body tearing out its own bowels . . . . We may guess our sin by our punishment . . . oppression corporal, oppression spiritual. Our possessors – to wit, prince, peers, prelates – did slay us . . . body and soul.[17]

JUDGMENT

Sin was thus as much a social as a moral problem, and by the 1640s it had become a problem of political dimensions as well. In his first appearance before the House of Commons in 1641, Edmund Calamy set the theme of many sermons throughout the decade: 'It is about the ruin and repair of kingdoms and nations, a matter suitable for you that are the representative body of the kingdom,' he said.

'Sin ruins kingdoms.' Sin was not so much a political problem in the partisan sense, as what accounted for problems generally, and conflicts themselves, aside from the issues involved or specific perpetrators, were directly attributed to sin. 'Sin is like so many great pieces of ordnance, planted and charged upon high mountains, ready to shoot down cities and kingdoms,' said Calamy. 'Sin dissolveth Parliament unhappily. Sin puts variance between a king and his subjects.'[18]

How sin possessed this destructive power varied, but the preachers insisted that all worldly misfortunes and afflictions be seen as 'judgments' from the Almighty. 'The Lord is a God of judgment,' they quoted from the Psalms, and 'the Lord is known by the judgments which he executeth'. By 'judgments' they did not necessarily mean that God interrupted the course of nature in ways that were inexplicable by the human faculties of sense and reason; this may have been the case with some of the judgments recorded in scripture, but it was generally agreed that such methods had (for the most part) come to an end. 'The Lord doth not now ordinarily discover future judgments by divine revelation as of old,' said Thomas Carter; 'neither only by their foregoing natural causes.' The preachers' prophecies of impending doom merely extended the social strife people could see all too plainly around them, and their sociology allowed that antisocial behavior might well undermine social and political order by ordinary cause and effect. 'The ruin of a nation,' said Carter, may come about 'by such evils as in their intrinsical nature are destructive to a state and bring its ruin by way of natural causation'. Carter went on to identify with scientific precision some abuses by which a nation could be so devastated:

> Divisions in a church or state, like the opposition of the planets, are of dangerous consequence and make way for civil wars . . . covetousness and ambition . . . partiality . . . worth is neglected and worthless men advanced . . . when all creatures are out of their proper place and in a motion contrary to their natural principles . . . . Licentiousness, sensuality, and luxury take away the heart, effeminate men's spirits, infatuate a people, and make them neglective of their own private and of the public good.*[19]

---

*Carter's mention of the 'opposition of the planets' illustrates how the responsiveness of God to human behavior seems to have called into question all such mechanisms of 'natural causation' in the universe, especially those governing human affairs. Citing the theories of Brahe and Kepler on the influence of the stars and conjunctions of planets, Edward Corbet conceded that 'few can be ignorant that the heavenly bodies have great power over inferior creatures and are partial causes of many alterations here below'. Nevertheless, God was free to dispense with such apparently immutable natural laws when human behavior required correction:

> But . . . the body and actions of men . . . are swayed by reason and education and religion. And God doth so control and check them at his pleasure that our sins are more to be feared than the stars, and nothing certain can be concluded from their aspects. . . . They make somewhat to foretell man's inclination and are signs of spiritual events, but they bring no fatal necessity with them, and things contingent are as far above their power as they are below the Almighty's.

There was still an element of caprice and uncertainty in God's judgments, and it was not always possible to know precisely how or when or where they would be visited; nor, by the same measure, did they necessarily appear equitable from the human perspective. 'God's administrations of judgments are various,' observed Nathaniel Hardy. 'His justice walks not always in the same path, nor with equal pace.' Some judgments were certain, such as that each soul would eventually face, as well as the 'final' judgment the world at large would someday undergo; but 'lesser days of judgment' could be expected before 'that last and great day', and while these could not be predicted with precision they were already making their impact felt at various levels of society, from the daily personal misfortunes of individuals to the shared catastrophes of entire societies. 'Whenever the sins of any church, nation, city, family, or person (you may take it as large or as narrow as you will) are come to a full measure,' promised Stephen Marshall, 'then God infallibly brings ruin upon them.'[20]

During the 1640s especially, and particularly before the Houses of Parliament, nations were those most frequently portrayed as helpless in the hands of an angry God. 'As God deals with the souls of persons,' declared Jeremiah Whitaker, 'so with states and nations.' Especially now, God seemed to be dealing with nations largely for ill. 'The days are the days of shaking,' Whitaker announced. 'And this shaking is universal: the Palatinate, Bohemia, Germany, Catalonia, Portugal, Ireland, England – there are shaking sins, judgments, sorrows, fears all Christendom over.' Recently, for some reason, God seemed to have begun a period of unusually intense shaking. 'This shaking began in the Palatinate, Bohemia, but it hath spread itself over France, Spain, and all the Christian world,' he said. 'The Lord seems to have a controversy with all nations.' All were equally vulnerable to the wrath of God; no nation was special, none favored above others in the eyes of the Lord. 'God will shake all nations collectively,' Whitaker warned. 'No nation is so stable but it shall have a time of shaking.' Most frighteningly too, no nation was guaranteed that its shakings would not end in destruction. 'There be no worldly states and monarchies of whom this can be said, their kingdom is such as cannot be destroyed,' another preacher said. 'Where is there a worldly kingdom that cannot be shaken?' God shook nations in a variety of ways, both within and without, and if the preachers emphasized the more dramatic traumas produced by wars, and especially the current succession of wars, they also used these to highlight the more subtle but also more fundamental tensions and turbulences existing throughout society and perhaps more immediately felt in the daily lives of their listeners. 'If God shake the nations, see the hand of God in all the shakings that are in your persons, families, in all the concussions that are in the world,' Whitaker continued. 'There are no persons, families, cities, states, churches, so well settled but one time or another shall meet with shakings.' The problem for any nation (or person) was to so order itself as to transcend the

In politics as elsewhere, divine determinism could liberate people from resignation to the inevitabilities of 'fatal necessity', however scientific the justification, and provide them with a measure of freedom and control.

mortality to which nations, like persons, were so conspicuously susceptible, and temporal shakings made the soul yearn for eternal tranquility. 'Bodies which are unsound, whether natural or politic, cannot endure shaking,' Whitaker noted. 'When you see all kingdoms shaken – your laws, liberty, property, life – labor to get a property and to clear your interest to that kingdom which cannot be shaken.'[21]

But while nations were often disturbed in subtle ways on the personal and social level, the most severe of temporal judgments, which more than any other brought together the mortality of natural and political bodies, was war. 'War is a judgment of God's own bringing,' said John Arrowsmith. 'War in general . . . is called evil.' But while war was lamentable, it currently seemed to be a particularly rampant expression of God's will, and the preachers felt compelled to list and illustrate the instances when God used war and to urge their audience to discern its significance. 'We all be exhorted from hence,' Arrowsmith urged, 'to contemplate the sad condition of those commonwealths that have the sword raking in their bowels.' Even before the outbreak of war in England, the Thirty Years War and more immediately the Irish rebellion offered vivid and menacing examples of how God treated nations. 'Who can think upon the desolation of Germany without lamentation?' asked Nicholas Proffet in 1644. 'Or . . . cast an eye upon Ireland nearer hand, and see it wallowing in its own blood and bleeding itself to death.' The preachers frequently went into long descriptions of the atrocities endemic to any war, sometimes indicting Roman papists, Irish rebels, or English 'malignants', but more often simply drawing attention to its horrors generally and urging that their own audience accept some measure of responsibility for what was to be seen as the fruit of sin. 'What should I speak of the lusts and uncleanness, gluttony and drunkenness, chambering and wantoning, prodigality and lavishness, excess of riot, masking and balling and sporting, when Germany and the Palatinate and other places were wallowing in blood?' asked George Gillespie. 'Who eats one dainty morsel the less, riots the less, drinks and quaffs the less, abates any one lust, while poor Ireland is slain with the sword and killed all the day long as sheep appointed for the slaughter?' Further, while any war was destructive, the most devastating by far was civil war. 'Of all wars that which is called civil hath in the experience of all times proved the most pernicious,' observed John Ley, 'when a kingdom is not united against a foreign foe but divided against itself and by that division in great danger of a desperate downfall.' Clearly this was the most severe of all God's judgments, though it was not without betraying a measure of fascination that this was explained at some length by the great Stephen Marshall (or Martial, as his name was sometimes spelled by admirers as well as detractors): 'If ever God give up a people to this . . . it is a token that the wrath of God burns hottest that it can burn against a land,' he declared.

'I will dash them one against another . . . I will not pity nor spare, nor have mercy, but destroy them,' a strange expression from a God of mercy, whose delight is in mercy. I will not pity, show no mercy! Kill, kill, kill . . . . The father shall destroy the children and children their fathers, and a man's murderers shall be his neighbors or men of his own household. You may by these plainly discern that God accounts it the terriblest of all judgments.[22]

INDIVIDUAL RESPONSIBILITY

The relationship between sin and judgment, whether as manifested in the upheavals of this world or as anticipated in the torments of the next, was such that there was not always a clear distinction between the harm people committed and that which they suffered. Indeed, in a time of moral confusion the problem of explaining why there was evil at all in a world ruled by a benevolent God was perhaps the most important consideration in the preachers' reminders that the ways of heaven could never be fully known. 'In all these afflictions and sins,' Nathaniel Holmes lamented, 'God's thoughts towards us poor sinners are incomparable and transcendent, above and beyond what we can think.' Still, if ultimate purposes were beyond human understanding immediate ones were not, and there were practical considerations to be minded even as speculative ones were to be discarded. 'Let our endeavor be, though we cannot comprehend God, to apprehend God.' In explaining evil there had always been a theoretical sense in which there was nothing to explain, since being by definition negative, evil was not fully real: 'Evil properly taken (saith the school) and by itself is not anything created or existing but signifies a mere absence of that good which should be present.' Especially as evil seemed to be unloosed with unusual force in times of change, it could be seen (to a point) in negative terms as the breakdown of order, the loss of stability, the failure of things to work properly, so that God did not so much create evil as simply withdraw good. 'The sinfulness of sin is to be ascribed not to any efficiency of God but to the deficiency of man's will,' argued Robert Baillie, 'which now is sinful and . . . weak . . . so able to change itself from good to evil.' But while God did not place any 'positive' sinfulness in people, but merely left them to their own inadequacies and imperfections, he did manipulate it for his own, ultimately beneficent purposes. 'Although we do not say that God doth infuse any positive, objective malice or wickedness into the hearts of men,' explained John Cardell, 'yet we say that he hath the ordering of all that wickedness . . . and that he doth either restrain or let it loose . . . according as he hath a purpose either to save or to destroy.' However theoretically evil might be simply the absence of good therefore, in practice it was a real and powerful force with God as directly behind it. 'Shall there be evil in a city and the Lord hath not done it?' asked Peter Smith, quoting the prophet Joel. 'Not . . . the evil of sin (there's no such evil from the Lord) but . . . the evil of punishment. And this is properly from God, what or whoever be the instrument.' This distinction between 'an evil which is sin' and 'an evil which is punishment for sin' was not meant to deny that they were closely related; in fact quite the contrary. 'Sin and the punishment of it are frequently in the scripture of the same name,' observed John Owen, 'so near is the relation.' God had numerous ways of using sin itself as a punishment without himself actually causing it. 'God can so without sin make use of sin as to punish sin with sin,' said another. 'God as a righteous judge is [said] to give over sinners to the devil, to other wicked men, to themselves, to be led in more and greater sins as punishments of the former.' The point was not limited to temporal judgments, but it did seem especially suited to explaining those troubles that afflicted society as a whole. 'Civil discord is a sin and a great judgment,' said Baillie, 'a sin to the authors and fomenters, a judgment to all, as well the innocent as nocent party.' No doubt social and political ills often did have identifiable 'fomenters', but the point was not to limit guilt to them alone but to spread it as widely as possible among all members of society, so that nobody was ever entirely 'innocent'. 'Whatever injuries are brought upon us by man, let us acknowledge them as deserved punishment of our sin in regard to God,' Nathaniel Hardy said. 'Though we have given no cause to the one, and so are innocent, yet we have given just cause to the other, and so are nocent.' Such were the ways of providence that sinners could disobey God's commands and yet unwittingly obey his will and serve his purposes. 'Our very afflictions as ruled by God have this injunction upon them to further our salvation,' said Edward Corbet. 'Our wounds are remedies, and those who contradict the precepts of the Almighty obey his providence.' Implicit in this distinction between precepts and providence was a corresponding duality between godly and wicked persons; but for the moment that could be laid aside, since being manipulated by God never excused the oppressions of wicked men. 'Let us remember this in all oppressions we meet with, that they fall not upon us without divine providence,' Hardy urged. 'As for oppressing adversaries (whether domestic or foreign), let them not account themselves safe because they execute God's judgment, since though they act his secret will, they contradict his revealed will, the only rule of our actions.'[23]

The explanation of evil and suffering, then, was not simply an academic problem but a matter of addressing real and pressing anxieties, and the fear of God served as an alternative to the fear of things and persons. 'If you be full of fear,' Jeremiah Whitaker suggested, 'turn your fear into a right channel and fear him that after he hath killed the body can cast the soul into eternal death.' The description of worldly troubles as judgments from the Almighty literally encouraged frightened souls by directing their fear toward him rather than the problems themselves or their perpetrators. 'A spirit of true courage hath all its fears swallowed up in the fear of God,' said Jeremiah Burroughs. 'The fear of God . . . drives out all base fears; by this [a soul] comes to fear nothing else but to be feared by his enemies.' This was especially appealing for those who felt themselves to be victimized by the world and oppressed by 'enemies'. 'Though they are men who bring this cross on you, yet they are God's instruments,' Burroughs consoled his congregation. 'God hath a hand in it, and they can go no further than God would have them go.' While this assurance was useful in confronting impersonal sources of misfortune, it was especially helpful in enduring the wrongs inflicted by other people, which was the kind of suffering that most concerned the ministers. 'When we suffer anything in this world, it is from ill men for the most part, except it be in those afflictions wherein we more immediately deal with God, as in sickness,' Sibbes pointed out. 'But in persecution in the world, our trouble lies with men.' Occasionally the preachers betrayed the enmity in their own hearts, even as they sought to placate it in others, when they recognized those afflictions and affronts brought on by 'wicked men', 'enemies', and 'devils'. 'All wicked men and devils are in God's hands,' said Cornelius Burges. 'All the devils in hell are not able to inflict one plague without God.' To see the hand of God behind one's afflictions and humiliations, though admittedly requiring tremendous strength of mind before the almost irresistible temptation to either panic or rage, was even said to be 'comforting'. 'This doctrine may serve for comfort and support unto God's people, to remove and mitigate sorrow, especially in the . . . saddest times of smiting,' said Nicholas Proffet. 'This doctrine being remembered, that it is God that smiteth . . . when Turk or traitor, some Irish rebel, English papist or atheist, is the sword, yet the hand of God doth order and guide it, and whatsoever their malice or bloody cruelty may be, yet it shall do no more . . . than he shall carry it . . . this will quiet their spirits and stay their fears.' The natural tendency when afflicted with misery or injustice after all, especially when wrongdoers seemed to be readily identifiable, was either fear or enmity or both; but to believe that adversity resulted from one's own failings and that there was no one else to blame was both to place difficulties within one's own control and also to alleviate the kind of bitterness and hate that could poison the soul from within. 'This may direct us to look over and beyond all the instruments of our . . . miseries, which are but subservient unto a higher hand that is correcting us,' John Strickland said. 'While we look upon second causes and . . . instruments only, we profit not by God's judgments and afflictions that are upon us, but rather are provoked to passion and revenge . . . . But this quiets the spirit from all impatience and passion and is the way to beget a dutiful submission in whatsoever we suffer.' This concern with 'impatience' under suffering, especially unmerited suffering, made it imperative that social injustice be seen as part of a larger divine justice. 'We should patiently bear all afflictions and troubles whatsoever,' Thomas Mocket insisted, 'because we suffer justly and most deservedly; the Lord is righteous in afflicting us.' Applied successfully, such an attitude would even make the stricken soul 'cheerful' in adversity. 'Consider that afflictions and troubles . . . what or whosoever be the instruments, yet God, a good, wise, and gracious father, is the author of them,' Mocket said. 'This should make us not only patient but cheerful also under affliction.' This effort to inculcate not only the theory but the practice of quiet suffering, with its apparently conservative attention to the moral responsibilities of the victim rather than the wrongdoer, was intended less to apportion blame than to assuage (though also to divert) the resentment and lust for revenge; and yet if the message was to suppress one's feelings of victimization, perhaps the significant point is that it thrived on the existence of people who felt victimized. 'Enemies may traduce thee, and oppress thee, and calamities like a storm may fall upon thy head,' said Thomas Valentine. 'And these may be borne; but if thy spirit be impatient and unquiet that's an earthquake in thy soul and will do thee more hurt than the malice of thy worst adversary.' It was not that there was necessarily anything theologically original about this (or any other) point that distinguished the Puritan ministers, and the idea itself was not difficult to grasp; what is significant was their determination to see the injunction upheld in practice, especially under the hard strain of adversity. 'This point, I know, is a very difficult task for flesh and blood to perform, especially when the hand of the Lord lieth heavy upon us,' confessed Nicholas Estwick.

'Tis one thing to contemplate this truth and another thing when we are put to the trial to practice it . . . . To submit willingly to God when we are very ill and do live in great distress is a high point of learning, but this we ought to do.[24]

This theodicy, which might seem like simply a convenient formula for blaming the victims of oppression for their own misery, was in fact a method of helping people cope constructively with their problems and frustrations, and the enormous strength of character and self-control required to repress one's malice in the face of misery and injustice demanded repeated exhortation. 'Let us feel sin more,' Anthony Burges urged, 'and we shall feel outward troubles less.' The ministers' aim was to internalize all external problems, to shift social conflict from that between individuals to that between man and God, where it was then subject to constructive remedies. 'We may then see that the great quarrel and controversy originally is not betwixt man and us, but between God and us,' Henry Scudder said. 'We must therefore first submit to him, and make our peace with him, else we shall make no peace, or no good peace, with man. It is not any policy, or power, nor any other means (though never so good, and so necessary that we shall sin if we use them not) can remove our evil from us, but as we shall obtain it of God, who hath appointed it.' Such injunctions were never a substitute for positive action, but whatever the problem, it first had to be solved within oneself. 'Would you overcome difficulties without?' asked William Sedgwick. 'Labor first to overcome yourselves.' Often the various outward difficulties served as metaphors for the conflict within, and the metaphors could be suggestive. 'Your worst enemies lie in your own breasts,' said Obadiah Sedgwick. 'None ought to be more carefully watched than the traitors within our own bosoms.' While the principle no doubt had its origins in dealing with one's private enemies, once developed it could then be turned to other uses, becoming politically important during the 1640s in organizing a collective response to what were increasingly described as the public enemies of the kingdom, and even after the outbreak of hostilities the preachers would constantly remind their listeners of the war within. 'We speak much of a malignant party,' Robert Harris told the House of Commons in 1642, 'but . . . our sins be the malignant party, yours and mine and those whom we represent this day.'[25]

What emerged as paramount here was less the amount of sin as such than one's attitude towards dealing with it. 'It is not the greatness of thy sins but thy willingness to be still in thy sins,' Sibbes advised. 'It mattereth not so much what ill is in us, as what good; not what corruptions, but how we stand affected to them.' Here sin was becoming defined in not simply moral but ideological terms, and the failure or refusal to see God and one's own shortcomings behind misfortunes, and instead to blame other things and persons, was itself a sin, one the preachers called 'murmuring'. 'A murmuring heart is a very sinful heart,' Burroughs said. 'When thou art troubled for such an affliction thou hadst need to turn thy thoughts rather to be troubled for the murmuring of thy heart, for that is the greatest trouble.' That murmuring was itself a sin and one both occasioned and aggravated by adversities demonstrates how afflictions caused sins as much as the other way around. 'We must remember the author of our afflictions . . . and the providence which directs them,' said Edward Corbet. 'Murmuring may enrage our crosses but cannot remove them. It may increase our guilt and bring upon us new judgments; it cannot take them off.' Murmuring was familiar from the Old Testament, where the children of Israel, newly-liberated from their captivity, complained about their hardships in the wilderness rather than working to overcome them. 'In all their murmurings they never blame themselves for their sins,' Anthony Burges noted. 'Sometimes they complain of God, of the instruments, of the evils themselves, but never one word of their own sins.' Such was also the tendency of many in England, who grew impatient when things did not go their way quickly or easily enough. 'At this day there has been, at least lately, as much murmuring in England as there ever was,' said Burroughs in 1645. 'The Lord brings the plague upon men for this sin of murmuring. He does it in kingdoms and families and on particular persons.' Though even the best of men and women were occasionally guilty of murmuring, and though murmuring was usually occasioned by the exactions and oppressions of 'wicked men', taken far enough a murmuring heart would itself become a wicked heart and lead to dangerous and destructive ways. 'It causes shiftings of spirit,' Burroughs warned. 'Those who murmur and are discontented are liable to temptations to shift for themselves in sinful and ungodly ways.'[26]

Sin was thus a matter of attitude as much as behavior, and the aim was to channel the fear of adversity into guilt for one's own part in it. 'Guilt is the breeder of fear,' observed Thomas Watson, though the point might just as well have been put the other way around. 'It is not affliction without but sin within creates fear.' The effort to internalize conflict, though 'comforting' insofar as it placated the soul from its frustration and rage against the outside world, nevertheless in the very process produced violent internal conflict in the form of 'conscience'. 'God's end is merciful when his hand is heavy,' said Edward Reynolds. 'So troubles may be bitter to the palate but profitable to the conscience.' The principle encouraged the tendency, when faced with adversity, to assume one had done something to deserve it, and to shift fear from things and persons to God was to arouse and awaken the conscience. 'Commune with your own hearts,' Thomas Manton urged. 'Guilt works best when it results from your own consciences.' In no sense did the ministers ever exalt the autonomous private conscience or advocate what came to be known as 'liberty of conscience'; nevertheless, they did believe the conscience was a powerful force if it could be co-opted for their cause. 'If you have any conscience,' Henry Scudder said, '[it will] work mightily upon you to the pulling down of the strongholds of sin.' This appeal to the conscience was based on the conviction that the soul retained enough (and only enough) natural goodness to begin to realize its natural corruption. 'If a man be guilty, and his conscience come once to be opened and convinced of injustice,' Samuel Torshel said, 'that man's soul will tremble.' An appeal to the conscience did begin with an appeal to fear therefore, though the fear and the guilt were mutually reinforcing, and a troubled conscience was the cause of a faint heart or worse. 'The guilty conscience always makes a coward,' noted William Carter. 'A guilty man hath two mischiefs at once to grapple with, oppositions from without and within the wrath of God upon his soul, both which put together is a burden that will wound and sink the spirit.'[27]

To a large extent, therefore, the fear of God was in reality a fear of oneself. 'Passionate men are . . . afraid of their own consciences,' said Richard Sibbes. 'Such men are . . . afraid of nothing more than themselves.' Certainly at least the terror of one's conscience made the fear of God more vivid and likely. 'If we cannot stand before our own consciences, how shall we be able to stand before that judge who . . . knoweth all things?' Thomas Case asked. 'Conscience is but God's deputy in every man's breast. And as conscience judgeth now (if not erroneous), so will God judge hereafter and condemn them upon the evidence of their own consciences.' The 'hereafter' was more plausible to a guilty conscience, and while the preachers advocated a literal belief in hell, they also stressed that it was made possible by the condition of the conscience. 'Sure the worst hell is in the conscience,' Francis Cheynell said. 'Hell is not only the center of torment but the sink of sin.' This in no way derogated from God's power to afflict, since the 'affliction' of the conscience was itself an act of God. 'You need not dispute where hell is,' Thomas Hill said, 'for they that know what terrors of conscience mean, they will tell you. God can make a hell in a man's bosom.' And yet this 'hell' was also a necessary stage through which every sinner had to pass in order to come to a full realization of the seriousness of his or her ways:

O saith conscience! What hast thou done . . . to provoke the holy and righteous and great God? I know the several acts of thy sinnings, and times, and places, and persons, and circumstances, and . . . that great God . . . hath commanded and deputed me . . . to speak his wrath and displeasure unto thee, and in his name I charge upon thee all thy sins and all his just wrath revealed against them.

Obadiah Sedgwick's account of the anguish and horror aroused within the awakening soul can only speak for itself:

And now the proud and stout heart of a sinner begins to throb and fear and tremble. He thinks that every threatening which he reads is a cloud of tempests against him. He thinks that every judgment he hears of another is a sword drawn to cut him off also. He thinks that all the hell and torments thereof mentioned in the scriptures will ere long be his portion, whereupon his distracted soul cries out, O that I had never been! O that I had never sinned! O that I might never be! If I should now die, good Lord! what will become of me? If I should yet live, will the Lord ever be merciful to me? The sins which I see are many, the wrath which I feel is great, and that which I fear is infinite. If I live, I see I am an accursed creature, and if I die (O let me not yet die!) I fear I shall be forever (O my soul breaks at that endless word of misery!) a damned sinner. But yet cries out this sinner, Lord! Lord! Is there no mercy, nor hope of any mercy for me, a most vile sinner? With these mind racking breaking thoughts away hastens this burdened, broken sinner . . . and with much confusion of thoughts and fears he spreads all his sinnings before God, confessing one, and then another, and then with fervent agonies begs of the Lord (more than for his life), Mercy Lord! Mercy, mercy for a lost, for an heinous, for an undone sinner! Canst thou pardon me? Wilt thou pardon me? O Lord pardon me! O Lord be reconciled unto me! O that I might hope, any hopes, the least hopes, that thou wouldest be merciful unto me![28]

The most horrifying torture then was that aroused within the soul itself. 'God, when he will humble a man, need not fetch forces from without,' Sibbes observed. 'God . . . can not only raise the humors of our bodies, but the passions of our minds also to torment us!' Such 'spiritual judgments' were no less severe than those provoked by social 'forces'; if anything they were much worse. 'Spiritual judgments are more fearful than any outward judgments,' said Jeremiah Burroughs. 'Spiritual judgments are the greatest judgments of all.' Sin was once again its own punishment, even within the individual. 'Sin carrieth vengeance in its own bowels,' said John Maynard. 'Sin itself is a misery; holiness itself is a reward.' In this sense too God punished sin with sin, and sin was itself the worst of all afflictions, torturing the conscience and tormenting the soul and producing, if not quite a desire for punishment, at least a fear of affliction threatening from within that far exceeded any from without. 'Punish me, O Lord, with all thy scourges, with poverty, with dishonor, with loss of parents and children,' exclaimed Samson Bond, 'but . . . to punish sin with sin, Lord, scourge me not.'[29]

For some, these terrors and torments of conscience proved too much, and for them the hell was permanent: they were the ones whose hearts were 'hardened'. 'The sin of hardening the heart against God is a certain forerunner of utter destruction,' Stephen Marshall said. 'When men do thus harden their hearts against God, be it a family, be it a kingdom, be it one or be they many, this . . . is a certain forerunner of utter destruction.' Hardness of heart, like murmuring, was a refusal to submit to the chastisements of God for other sins and so itself a judgment from on high. 'The most tremendous judgment of God in this world is the hardening of the hearts of men,' John Owen said. 'This seals them up for the most part to destruction.' Here again it can be seen not only how the sins of some were judgments against others but also how the sins that provoked them were caused by, were, in effect, the same as the judgments themselves, and hardness of heart was the foremost among psychological sanctions. 'It is one of the greatest of spiritual judgments,' said Obadiah Sedgwick. 'A hardened and unbroken heart is (in some respect) a judgment worse than hell.' Hardness was especially dangerous because it placed the soul on a kind of self-perpetuating and self-destructive spiral, and once chastisements were shown to be of no value to a hard heart, God would give up on such sinners. 'This is such an evil as draweth on eternal perdition after temporal ruin,' Robert Baillie said. 'So that this hardening is very oft the sign of a reprobate to whom God shows no mercy.' The same was true of entire nations, as illustrated by the obvious parallel, the stiff-necked people of Israel. 'As it is said to Israel . . . it may truly be said of England,' warned Nicholas Proffet. 'Notwithstanding all warnings, menaces, corrections and severe punishment, they are not bettered, they yield neither to words nor blows but hold on their sinful course, continue obstinate, although grievously afflicted and oppressed.' While the notion of hardness was intended to arouse anxiety within each sinner that he was a desperate, unabashed, impenitent sinner, the preachers also gave their listeners an out through the assurance that, like any sin, hardness could be overcome, the first step being an awareness it existed. 'To feel hardness of heart,' said Marshall, 'is softness of heart.'[30]

The appeal to the conscience, then, was intended to create an intense self-consciousness – or at least to gain control over what self-consciousness was already aroused by instilling an awareness that God was within, watching and manipulating in ways the soul itself might not be fully aware of. 'He himself is more in the midst of you, and within you, every one of you, than your own selves,' said John Ward. 'He knows not only our works and ways, but the inward frame and temper of our hearts.' Even thoughts themselves were not free, since God knew and punished them as well. 'The most secret cabinet designs of man's heart are all unlocked . . . before the Lord,' Thomas Watson said. 'God doth as strictly observe and severely censure all inward sinful thoughts, although never so secret, as he doth outward acts of sin.' It was impossible that any sin could escape the attention of God. 'How would it fill every heart with trembling and every face with shame to consider that God . . . knows all our sins, our secret sins, our darkness sins, our midnight sins, our closet sins, our curtain sins, our bosom sins,' Matthew Newcomen said. 'Would we seriously consider . . . that we cannot hide it from the righteous God, how would it make us stand in awe and not sin?' The theme was a favorite with Newcomen, who explained how terrifying, and how effective, it could be. 'Whoever thou beest that art guilty in this kind, know it (and know it to thy terror) there is no sinner upon earth whom God hates more than he hates thee,' Newcomen said, 'for there is no sin that is more directly contrary to the nature of God . . . than this sin of dissembling.' The fear and guilt reinforced one another in such a way that the preachers could expect an audience that themselves expected to be punished, in one way or another. 'Thou has had some secret evil it may be which thou hast not yet repented of, and though the

Lord has forborne thee in one particular yet he will meet with thee in another way,' Thomas Horton warned. 'Be sure your sin will find you out . . . . It's impossible that any willful sinner should absolutely and totally lie hid.'[31]

Yet while the eye of God could be terrifying, the point of instilling this terror within was to minimize the need for that from without, and the emphasis on the conscience suggested the importance of non-coercive measures for controlling the nation's sins. 'The people may be taken by the conscience and not only conformed by law,' Richard Vines told the House of Commons, 'for the strength and continuance of a reformation lies not all in the magistrate but in this, that the people receive the truth into them and among them.' This idea that 'reform' or 'reformation' began within 'the people' had long been fundamental to Puritanism and was often distinguished from the kind of coercive control that was exercised from without. 'We see the necessity of the minister's industry as well as the magistrate's in reforming times,' said Thomas Ford. 'For though it be the power of the sword which must conform the outside, yet it is the power of the word which must reform the inside of the people.' Religion or the fear of God existed to do what the state was unable, and the ministers argued that the sword alone was unable to exact the kind of obedience that was reliable and permanent. 'The sword may work an unwilling subjection,' Joseph Caryl insisted. 'Only God can work a subjection of the will.' Alexander Henderson captured the ministers' position succinctly, not denying some role for coercion but expressing a clear preference for persuasion. 'The laws of men may do some hurt for repressing outrages,' he acknowledged, 'but . . . there is a great difference betwixt outward restraint from man and inward mortification from God. Where religion taketh place men neither dare nor will commit sin.' It followed that religious reform had indeed to be inculcated thoroughly, not resting content with immediate contingencies or temporary circumstances as did other, more 'political' remedies. 'Circumstantial reformations, I grant, are more easy and quick, but those which are deep are ever most safe,' Sedgwick cautioned. 'It is better to cut it down to the root than to hire men many days to cut off the limbs.' Sedgwick indicated how 'radical' was the preachers' position when he distinguished reforms rooted in love from acts growing out of fear. 'Those of fear may be more strong and stirring for the present . . . but those of love are most acceptable and constant,' he said. 'Voluntary acts, though sometimes more slow, yet are at all times more successful . . . . No private or public work of reformation will come to good which is derived only from a fear of evil and not from a love of good.' Whether Sedgwick is referring to personal hypocrisy or state-imposed coercion is not clear, but the point was the same. 'Whether you limit it to a repentance that is personal or extend it to a reformation that is national holds true in both,' he continued. 'The one and the other must be so dispersed that it may not prove vain and lost but effectual and successful.' The result of this kind of grassroots reform, perhaps paradoxically, was a kind of political revival in which 'the soul of the public state will answer that of the person.'[32]

COLLECTIVE GUILT

Personal repentance and public reform were thus not mutually exclusive but mutually reinforcing approaches to the nation's problems, which, insofar as they had social roots, demanded solutions that were 'radical' in the root sense of the word. 'We should not only as surgeons look at the outward wound of a kingdom and seek the cure of that by outward applications, but like a physician look into the causes of these evils and labor to procure a remedy for those inward distempers whence the outward do spring,' said Thomas Carter. 'If we have not the evils removed that provoke the wrath of God by a thorough reformation, as well as the outward judgment, if by true repentance peace be not made with God as well as an outward peace in the kingdom, surely though . . . we cut off only the branches, the root will sprout again.' The words 'reform' and 'reformation', which had already come to have strong political associations, thus began as largely synonymous with 'repentance', and in practice the terms were often used together. 'The sins of England are the enemies of England,' said Edmund Calamy, invoking one of his favorite metaphors. 'But . . . repentance and reformation repairs and upholds kingdoms and nations. This is their fortress and tower of defense, their munition, armor, and wall of brass.' Though God had his own time, repentance was said to work on terms of virtual certainty, and again for both persons and nations. 'Personal repentance, if right, will always save thy soul from hell,' Calamy promised. 'Repentance, if it be sincere and national, is an infallible way to save a nation from ruin.' Further, just as repentance could be extended to the entire nation, so reform began with the individual, where it was almost always a prelude to reforming elsewhere. 'Begin with a personal reformation,' urged Cornelius Burges, 'then shall you be better able to carry on and advance the great work of reformation of others.' Like repentance, only more so, however, reformation was by its nature a 'national' undertaking. 'As this reformation must be personal, so also it must be national,' Calamy insisted. 'A particular man by turning unto God may turn away a particular judgment. But when the sins of a nation are general, and the judgments upon a nation general, the turning must be general.'[33]

How the nation could be generally guilty varied, but the social consequences of sin were reflected in the principle that all shared in the failings of their society. 'There is none of us all but we have had a hand in the sins of the times,' said Richard Sibbes. 'The best of all conditions are guilty of them . . . . We are all guilty in this respect, we receive some taint and soil from the times we live in.' One effect of this, at least initially, was to minimize the distinction between good and evil people or the even more difficult division of the godly and the ungodly, much less visible political parties. 'Yea among them, God's own people, who profess his name, even they will be too much tainted with the common sins of the times and places wherein they live,' said Henry Scudder. 'God's people are so far from being always clear of procuring national judgments that sometimes judgments have come upon nations for the sins of some of God's people among them.' It was even possible that extraordinary guilt could correlate with special status and that

God's people were especially responsible for the nation's difficulties. 'The word of God makes it evident,' noted Herbert Palmer, 'that . . . the sins of those that are God's people by more special profession (and sometimes even of his most faithful servants . . .) have a special influence to bring national judgments.'[34]

The political implications of sin, then, were more complex than simply assigning it exclusively to one's private or even the nation's public enemies, since social troubles constituted a shared experience about which all were expected to feel concerned. 'A broken spirit grieves and mourns for the sins of others,' Francis Roberts said, 'especially for the public abounding sins of the times wherein it lives.' Moreover, one was obligated not only to be sorry for others' sins but also to do something about them. 'Let us mourn for our own sins and the sins of the times wherein we live,' urged Sibbes. 'And let us not only mourn for the sins of the times but labor also to repress them all we can.' So important was this directive that people were to be held accountable not only for what they did but also for what they did not do. 'There's a great deal of guilt and iniquity even in sins of omission,' argued Thomas Horton. 'The neglect of what we should do is a business which we are accountable for as well as the venturing upon that which we should forbear.' And the first thing people were to do, beyond attending to their own sins, was to restrain the sins of those around them. 'We sin in others while we suffer them to sin,' Joseph Caryl said. 'We become guilty of other men's sins not only by commanding, counseling, and approving them, but (if we may) by not stopping and restraining them.' The injunction had egalitarian and potentially radical implications, since the lowest could be held liable for the sins of even the highest, and the guilt carried a similar message that all people were obligated (to a point) to restrain even their social and political superiors. 'They do not seldom become guilty of the sins of others by too much complying with kings and princes that seek to mold them to their own designs, although never so wicked or injurious,' Burges said. 'Kings should not be permitted to commit such public sins, but counsel, Parliament, people, and everyone according to his place and power should hinder them.'[35]

The preachers believed in working through established authority as far as possible, and those who already stood as political and public figures had the most weighty obligations. 'An ill executor of the laws is worse in a state than a great breaker of them,' Robert Bolton told the assizes. 'Not to punish an offense, being under your charge and in your power, is to commit it.' The responsibility was both passive and active, and even both at the same time. 'Whatever sin is in your power to restrain, if you do not restrain it, you commit it,' Elidad Blackwell instructed the councilmen of London. 'Whatever good is in your power to advance, if you do not advance it, you hinder it.' A strong political dimension characterized the concept of national sin in that a special importance attached to the role of public authority. 'Take an evil, and though it were never so private before, yet if it pass here it will take a higher degree and commence national wickedness,' William Bridge told the House of Commons in 1641. 'This is a fearful evil, and very dreadful, that a personal sin should become national.' One criterion for such national wickedness was the role of the law, making national sin somewhat more impersonal than personal sin. 'A sin is . . . (among diverse other ways) properly said to be the sin of a nation when it is established or at least tolerated by law,' Thomas Case informed the Commons, 'by the government of a nation, not only some governors in a nation.' It was not a precise distinction however, since men made and enforced laws and so were personally accountable to God for those under their jurisdiction. 'You must look upon yourselves as trusted with the making of all necessary laws and the strengthening of those already made . . . for the purging the land from whatever filthiness is in it,' Cornelius Burges told the members of the House, 'which till you be careful to effect, the sins of particular persons will become national and the guilt thereof will lie at your door.' There was, thus, no incompatibility between the principles of individual responsibility and collective guilt, since they existed alongside and even reinforced one another. 'Personal sins are made national when they are not punished by authority,' Case asserted, 'and national sins are made personal when they are not laid to heart by the subject.' No strong distinction separated personal and national sins, the private and the public, officials and ordinary persons, and the duties of public officials and those of private individuals were by no means mutually exclusive. 'How vainly do many private persons bless themselves in casting off the blame and danger of the sins of the times upon great men in places because they think it not their duties to reform these things but those that have power and authority in their hands to suppress them,' Samuel Fairclough remarked. 'And how vainly do many of our magistrates . . . wash their hands from the sins of towns and families by saying, we have nothing to do in these sins of the times, we join not in the practice of drunkards, swearers, and incest, etc. when yet they accessarily and occasionally are guilty of all those which by their counsel, power, and authority they might have restrained.'[36]

Sin and guilt were not private matters, then; they were social and political in their impact, and one succinct method of conveying this was through organic imagery: 'What breeds distempers in the body natural carries some resemblance to that which causeth distempers in a body politic.' This imagery, in itself a commonplace of the time, was given new and almost literal meaning by the Puritan preachers, who more than others used the metaphor to emphasize these 'distempers' and 'diseases' and the need for remedies, perhaps drastic ones, by those in positions to administer them. 'The commonwealth is a body politic,' Blackwell declared. 'Offenders and offenses in a commonwealth, they are (as it were) the peccant and noxious humors and diseases in that body. Judges and magistrates, they are (as it were) physicians for the healing and curing of those diseases.' The idea that the nation as a whole constituted a 'body', within which Parliament stood as the 'representative body', and which in turn was composed of individual bodies, linked private and public morality and with it the transmission of guilt among the limbs or members. 'You may keep the disease from proving epidemical, for as for the general body of this people it hath well nigh overspread all,' Anthony Tuckney told the 'state physicians' in Parliament, 'and therefore the

78

representative body's integrity must stand for all, one body for another, you representing us all, as well to God as to man, and so being for the present the only means that is left of keeping off national guilt and so the wrath of God from this whole nation.' Great men and public figures, especially (but not only) as they sat in Parliament, were so important to the spiritual status of the nation that they were said to embody it, both as individual persons and as a collective 'body'. 'Let me consider you . . . as you are united into one body,' Calamy told the House of Commons.

> All the sins of the kingdom which are committed by your connivance, or allowance, are the Parliament's sins, and they call for a Parliament repentance. Search and try your hearts, and consider how far you are accessary to the sins of the kingdom, that so you may be wrought up not only to a personal but to a Parliament humiliation. And if it doth appear that you have taken more care in settling your own liberties than in settling of religion . . . this is a crying sin, and this makes you accessary to a thousand sins that are committed in the kingdom. Again, if you do not labor according to your duty, and according to your power, to suppress the errors and heresies that are spread in the kingdom, all these errors are your errors, and these heresies are your heresies, and they are your sins, and God calls for a parliamentary repentance from you for them this day.[37]

Parliament was thus the 'representative body' of the kingdom, and members of Parliament and other public figures 'represented' the nation, as one put it, 'synecdochically' – not so much its rights before the King as its responsibilities before God: their repentance was the repentance of the nation, and if they were personally reformed the nation would be publicly reformed. 'If you that are the representative body of this nation, as you stand under this relation, be reformed, the nation itself may be said to be reformed,' Calamy said. 'For you are the nation representatively, virtually, and eminently. You stand in the place of the whole nation, and if you stand for God's cause, the whole nation doth it in you.' Yet again, however, even the personal morality of magistrates was in turn defined by their public duties, and if the nation could be said to be reformed in them, they in turn were only reformed insofar as the nation was. 'If a nation sin, the repentance must be national,' Cornelius Burges demanded. 'But yet when all cannot, or will not . . . the representative body of it . . . must fall down before the Lord . . . . In all national provocations, they who represent the nation must be careful to . . . repent . . . not only in respect of their own personal transgressions, but in reference also to the sins of the whole kingdom.' Only by assuming responsibility for the sins of others was the individual, especially the magistrate, himself truly reformed. 'Look upon yourselves as public persons that must both bear the sins of others whom you represent, and purge out the sins of others, or be guilty of them yourselves,' Burges continued. 'Do not think any humiliations for your own personal faults and failings will find acceptance with the Lord until you take care to punish the offenses of others and to prevent the like for time to come.'[38]

No sharp distinction separated personal and public morality; especially in regard to 'public persons' there was nothing that could legitimately be considered 'private'. 'Private self-respects prove great hindrances to most necessary duties,' said Herbert Palmer, and it was what Burges called 'private respects in public debates' that effectively defined sin. 'Have you no personal sins left among you to pull down what others of you build?' he asked. 'No private respects in public debates? . . . Have you no sins as you are a body? Is it not possible to find some want of zeal and courage? . . . No neglect of God's cause and work?' God was concerned only with the 'public good'; private ends amounted to selfishness and sin. 'If there be any among you that drive your own designs, and seek your own ends more than the public good, and seek your own ends to the detriment of the public good,' Calamy warned, 'these are crying abominations, and the Lord calls for a Parliament repentance this day.' Those who neglected public affairs to devote themselves to private matters were simply atrophied or diseased members of the body politic, fit only to be cut off. 'Surely it is a great pity that any man's pivate respect should hinder the common good,' John Greene said. 'Nor will it be well with the body politic, where it is not with this as in the natural, which will willingly lose a great deal of blood . . . will endure the cutting off a limb or two, to preserve the health and life of the whole.' Organic imagery tied the individual to the collective body in such a way as to make everything public and even political, and the near-literal understanding with which the preachers used the metaphor to describe political affairs was perhaps most powerfully set forth when it was reversed, so that the individual in turn was described as a kind of political unit: just as the body politic might be forced to discharge noxious humors or amputate useless limbs, so each person was required to institute a reign of terror against the public enemies incorporated within his own carnality. 'Every man hath a little commonwealth within him,' said Thomas Case. 'Call a parliament . . . in thine own heart. Thither call every offender before thee. Sit as a ruler, a judge, and arraign and execute every rebellious, traitorous lust.'[39]

This tendency to describe sin and all aspects of life in political terms indicates how the preachers saw people, for all their antisocial tendencies, as at least potentially political animals and in need of political instruction and practice. 'God hath made every man a governor over himself,' said Richard Sibbes. 'The poor man, that hath none to govern, yet may he be a king in himself. It is the natural ambition of man's heart to desire government . . . . When we have learned to rule over our own spirits well, then we may be fit to rule over others.' One of the most frequently mentioned institutions of such 'government' was the family, the most basic unit of authority any man (or woman) could have to rule over others, and for that each head of household was responsible before God. 'Every master of a family stands accountable to God for his family as well as for himself.' The family linked the private and the public and so effectively combined the various understandings and practices of authority. 'Family authority, domestical, paternal, may and ought to be more exact and strict than public and that which is more extensive,' argued Thomas Coleman. 'Successful reformation is by gradual ascension: family, congregation, kingdom – the less constitutes the greater.' The family was the basic unit of 'society', as well as the most personal object of affection, and therefore the training ground for political – including 'radical' political – activity. 'Families are the first root of human consort and communion,' Francis Cheynell said, 'for government was first settled in those little nurseries. Now if the root be rotten, what will the branches be? A kingdom consists of so many families united . . . for the common good, and if families be poisoned and corrupted, what will become of the towns and cities, and how will the kingdom flourish?' The foundation of all politics was thus 'economic' in the seventeenth-century understanding of the word. 'It is well and generally known that all civil unions begin in a family, in a house, in those three combinations of husband and wife, parents and children, governors and servants,' Humphrey Chambers noted. 'By the union of houses, cities and townships are constituted; by the union of cities, kingdoms are composed; and so upwards, out of the union of kingdoms arise large and comprehensive empires or states of the earth.' Great men and members of Parliament had special responsibilities within their own, politically influential families as well as the nation, which itself could be described as a kind of family. 'You that are Parliament men are members of an honorable house,' Cheynell added. 'The kingdom is your household; the commonwealth is your family; and by doing justice and judgment you may not only command but persuade the kingdom to walk in the way of Jehovah.'[40]

In theory such comparisons might work both ways, but the effect here was arguably less a patriarchal view of the state, since responsibility was being devolved from a single head to all householders, than the politicization of the family, and indeed of all social relationships; in fact it was with special weight attached to the family that what one preacher described as 'the links and bonds of politic and civil society' provided that 'many may be guilty of the sin that one commits'. 'The scripture tells us of . . . political guilt,' observed the notorious Samuel Fairclough,

> merely passive and no ways active, not of the sin at all, not punishment eternal, but temporal and external, which arises from the links and bonds of politic and civil society, whereby as members of the same body they are made partakers of the good and evil belonging to either of them in politic things . . . . In political guilt . . . we see in the death of infants for their parents', subjects for kings' sin and transgressions.

Fairclough acknowledged that biblical standards of justice might seem cruel, though he contended that the concept in fact vindicated God's justice by explaining why seemingly innocent people suffer: 'political' or collective guilt 'serves to vindicate the justice of God in bringing public calamities and troubles by and through wicked men's actions upon people that may seem to be actually innocent of these crimes'. Punishment in times of crisis was justified by benefits in times of stability. 'It is by political guilt, wherein yet the equity of God's justice and dispensation may be cleared,' Fairclough added, 'that as innocent persons, by virtue of political ties and bonds, partake of many temporal rods by occasion of wicked men's sins, so do they also receive many temporal commodities from their services.'[41]

Moreover, God's eternal perspective over temporal things allowed him to know how human actions had ramifications beyond what human perceptions tended to realize, and as God saw all events simultaneously he knew how sin had consequences not only throughout society but over time as well and apportioned his punishments accordingly. 'That a whole nation in general may be guilty of the sins and punishment committed by one in particular . . . is of most undoubted truth,' Fairclough insisted. 'God imputed the sin of one man in particular not only to a whole nation present, when the sin was committed, but to a future generation living long after the offender was departed.' It followed that people could similarly be held responsible for sins committed not only by others but by others before they themselves were born. 'This humiliation for the sins of our nation must extend to the sins of our forefathers,' declared Herbert Palmer.

Especially if in anything we find that any worldly commodity we enjoy is the fruit of their sin . . . . Human politics excuse or justify or commend those sins that redound in appearance to worldly security or advantage, as the letting evil men or practices alone which might have been redressed and suppressed.[42]

In yet another sense, therefore, the line between the temporal and the eternal was thin, since punishments were not necessarily limited in time. 'The wrath of God reacheth to the soul as well as to the body,' declared Alexander Henderson, 'to kingdoms as well as to particular persons or families, to the posterity as well as to the present generation.' By the same measure it was sometimes said that the punishment incurred through such guilt would be merely 'temporal', though precisely how temporal was often left ambiguous. 'The destruction that the family and friends of the offenders are enrapped in is only temporal,' Palmer said, 'unless they be guilty of the same sin or the vengeance of God reckon with them also for their ungodliness in other respects.' In any case, the sins and consequences that carried over time were those by which the nation derived some lasting advantage – sins that had had political and even historical importance and that had left an impact on subsequent events and especially on the current state of affairs: sins whose injustice in some way still remained, invariably described as sins of 'blood'. 'Bloodguiltiness is another provoking sin,' Edmund Calamy proclaimed. 'How much hath been shed heretofore and the murderers either not brought unto judgment or not prosecuted in judgment? This polluteth a kingdom with blood, and this blood crieth loud for vengeance upon those into whose hands God did put the sword of justice to revenge for him and to execute wrath upon such as are murderers and do it not.' While private violence was still feared, blood guilt usually involved forms of specifically political repression. 'The land is guilty of blood,' Cornelius Burges told the House of Commons in 1642, 'and blood, you know, defiles the land.' Citing Old Testament examples, Burges interwove different strands in the theme of blood as it affected political authority in the sense of both family and violence – each of which, or both together, transmitted guilt to posterity – when he called on Parliament to repent its complicity in the atrocities committed by earlier regimes. 'I speak not now of ordinary murders committed by private persons for which the law hath provided,' he said, 'but of blood, shed by the whole kingdom, even in Parliament itself':

> Witness the blood of many hundred saints and martyrs, shed in England in times of popish persecution, to which the bloody paramours of the scarlet whore hath been enabled by diverse laws made in Parliament in the reigns of Henry IV, Henry V, Henry VIII, and Queen Mary and for which the land was never sufficiently humbled unto this day . . . . I leave it to your wise and pious consideration whether England and the Parliament of England be not deeply concerned in the butcheries and burnings of so many holy and precious men and women as (perhaps by the hands or procurement of some of their ancestors who now sit in Parliament) have been destroyed by those bloody laws of this kingdom at the instigation of the man of sin.

Blood guilt on the royal houses of England was an emotive theme in both popular literature and official propaganda, though with the religious twist the blood feud became not a private quarrel between actual families but a public affair between the nation and God. Though Burges does exploit the ambiguity to suggest that guilt for blood is transmitted though the blood lines of great men such as kings, noblemen, and members of Parliament, he also seems to indicate that that very fact confuses and calls into question the legitimacy of those same family lines as the basis of political authority:

> Trace the streams of blood that issued from that first law made in 2 Henry IV out of the veins of the two houses of York and Lancaster. Above fourscore of the blood royal lost their lives, together with many thousands more of the nobility, gentry, and common people, before the quarrel ended in the joining of the two roses into one. And yet perhaps Henry IV might plead a kind of necessity for giving way to that bloody law of burning all whom the popish Antichrist pronounced heretics, because by the help and strength of the popish faction, rather than by a just title, he grasped and wore the crown. And for the same reason Henry V might tread in the steps of his father which after cost his son and the kingdom so dear before God could be appeased.[43]

More recent persecutions, including the exile of many godly men and women, established that blood guilt still remained on the house of England. 'The guilt of the misery our brethren have suffered,' warned Jeremiah Burroughs (himself an exile before the war), 'the guilt of their blood is upon the whole kingdom in as much as the whole kingdom hath not risen even as one man to prevent it.'

Moreover, so collective was the guilt of the nation, and of such 'temporal' significance in any sense of the word were the sins that carried over time, that the nation could be held liable not only for the persecution of the godly but even for the damnation of the wicked; thus the frequent warnings regarding what the preachers called the 'blood of souls'. 'Blood guilt is a sad sin,' Oliver Bowles remarked, 'but guilt of soul blood is more dreadful and inexpiable.' That no guilt was ever purely individual was illustrated by Herbert Palmer's graphic account of how, by this 'most prodigiously frightful guilt of the blood of souls', England was literally going to hell:

> Thousands and millions gone to hell, out of this kingdom . . . for want of good laws and through wicked magistrates, civil and ecclesiastical, and wicked ministers and neighbors . . . millions, I say, now howling in hell . . . damned through the undeniable defect of sufficient means of salvation . . . and through the damnable persecution . . . a wickedness for which alone it is next a miracle that God hath not sunk the whole kingdom into the bottom of the sea long ere this.[44]

Other institutions were also cause for concern insofar as they threatened society. 'We have yet the consideration of our armies to be affected with,' Herbert Palmer reminded the House. 'The sins of our armies do in a special manner call us to humiliation . . . for their sins as well as our own.' Like the sins of any other sector, those of the armies could prejudice the welfare of the nation as a whole, and given developments during the 1640s, they seriously threatened to do so. 'Let us lay . . . to heart the disorders of all ranks, commanders, officers, and soldiers in our camp,' urged William Reyner. 'For as the sins of the country may prejudice the success of the army, so the sins of the army may hinder the peace of the country.' Armies were not only a means of achieving religious ends, but through godly discipline something of the end was achieved in itself. 'Your armies are reforming armies,' Thomas Case said. 'Let it be your care to make them reformed armies, and you may humbly expect that God will go out with them to enable you to do exploits.' Purity or 'holiness' seems to have been particularly important for armies. 'Holiness is as proper and comely for soldiers and armies as for any other of God's servants or societies,' said Reyner. 'They that fight the Lord's battles ought to be holy . . . . They should be not only a holy family or a holy church or commonwealth, but a holy army also.' While this emphasis on holiness was applicable to other societies and institutions, somehow it seemed to come out more readily in the injunctions to armies and soldiers, perhaps because of the dangers involved. 'Soldiers carry their lives in their hands and look death in the face daily,' Reyner noted. 'They cannot be . . . in preparation for death until they be in a posture of holiness.' If actual soldiering intensified religious devotion, social breakdown did the same to some extent for everyone else, and the uncertainties in the life of a soldier were often paralleled with those of any frightened soul. 'We cannot be all soldiers to fight the Lord's battles in the field,' said Henry Hall, 'but there is a holy war which we all may and must wage.'[45]

JUSTICE

The preachers often emphasized that the measures they demanded of magistrates and others were necessary because of the injustice God was permitting in society; it was not that God was not merciful, nor that human authorities were not to be merciful as well, only that God's own acts of justice could not be ignored. 'I am a minister of God's mercy,' said Stephen Marshall, 'and take no pleasure in pressing to such a work as judgment and severity were it not that I am assured that if we should not do justice where God requireth it to be done he will do it without us, and he will do it upon us.' Human justice was thus intended to reflect that of God, which it could to some extent forestall. 'When men execute their just judgments, then God removes his,' said Anthony Burges. 'We shall hereby prevent the public judgments that may come upon a land.'[46]

Human justice was in fact closely connected to God's, whose own role as 'judge' in the great matter of redemption was said to be manifested politically in the authority he delegated to subordinate 'gods' for making not dissimilar decisions in the administration of public affairs. 'I do not look upon God [only] as sitting upon his own immediate throne of divine judicature as the supreme judge of the quick and the dead, judging to, or saving from, eternal death and damnation,' Thomas Case explained. 'But I look upon God [also] sitting upon these inferior thrones of judicature among his delegates and deputy gods . . . there directing and commanding them what sentence they shall give, whether of life or death, when they shall spare and when they shall strike.' The problem was to preempt God's judgments (of whichever kind) by incorporating his justice into the legal and political system as a standard for public officials, and the ministers' task was to train these lesser deities in the habits of officious and conscientious behavior, to teach them to dispense justice effectively and impartially, to make them continually ask themselves, 'What would God do if he were on the bench?' as Case put it, 'How shall I be able to answer it to God?' Human tribunals became part of the circuit of the great court of heaven, and those who occupied positions of public trust were accounted assistant gods. 'You are not only vice-kings but deputy gods,' Case told a gathering of London municipal officials in 1644. 'For judges to deflect and turn aside in judgment to the right hand or left is to abuse their deputation as much as in them lies, to un-god themselves and God too.' This technique of devolving the divine image, and the responsibilities that attended it, onto lesser public figures was forcefully articulated by Elidad Blackwell in a passage typical of the numerous exhortations delivered to assemblies of local magistrates in the decades before the war. 'You judge not for man but for the Lord,' he instructed the Lord Mayor and Aldermen of London in 1645.

The ordinance of magistracy, it is the ordinance of God. The person who judgeth is a person sent of God . . . . He is God's vicegerent, God's delegate, God's deputy. The persons and causes to be judged are God's. The man is God's, his life is God's, his estate God's. The judgment too, if righteous and just and good, it's God's. God will own it, approve it, defend it, reward it. Consider that. You have your commission from God, receive your office from God, derive your power and authority from God, sustain God's person, do God's work, execute God's judgment.

And along with the godly commission came an equally weighty burden of responsibility. 'Take heed therefore what you do,' Blackwell continued.

Do nothing but what God would do, if he were in your room. Now would God punish the poor and pardon the rich? Would God justify the wicked and condemn the righteous? Would God pervert justice? Would God accept persons? Would God receive gifts? Would God be corrupted? Why, no more be you. You execute God's judgment; make God your pattern in the execution of it. Follow his rule. Imitate his example. He accepts not persons, nor takes rewards, but without respect of persons judges according to every man's work. The greatest potentates and the highest monarchs in the world, if wicked and ungodly, can no more escape the vengeance of God than the poorest wretches that live upon the face of the earth . . . . God carries himself equally and indifferently to all in the execution of judgment. Do you likewise. Set up God for your pattern, your precedent. Imitate God.[47]

Such exhortations, however unexceptionable they might seem, served a pressing need in a time of rampant official corruption, and the preachers' outraged demands for 'justice' reflected a conviction that not only was injustice in many forms epidemic throughout the land, but human judicatories, far from providing an effective remedy, were often part of the problem. 'That horrid, not neglect but perverting of judgment that hath abounded in these latter years among our judges!' Case harangued the London magistrates in 1644. 'The places of judicature were so crowded with violence, partiality, bribery, and projected perverting of judgment,' he alleged. 'Yea, robbery and violence, murder and treason which were wont to stand at the bar have for many years together sat upon the bench till the land was filled with oppression and blood . . . . Blood and perverting of judgment cry aloud in the ears of God.' Such accusations may have had as much to do with the development of more rigorous and less personal standards of official conduct as with any actual increase in corruption as such, but the two were impossible to separate, and the ministers themselves were in the vanguard of the reform, popularizing and promoting the new moral strictness and seeing it put into practice. 'A difficulty lies before you of keeping to the rule,' Case admonished, 'this interest and that relation, this bosom friend and that powerful advocate, whispering and pleading and beleaguering you with armies of temptations to bias your judgments to their interest and affections, and yet all under the fairest and candidest pretences of equity and justifiable mercy.' However they might be deputy gods in office therefore, the most exalted political figures were still fallible humans in person, vulnerable to seduction by the temptations of a corrupt and corrupting world. 'You are but men,' Blackwell reminded his distinguished audience, 'gods indeed, but yet but earthen gods: men, weak men, frail men, flesh and blood.'

> You have the same carnal principles in your hearts that are in the hearts of others . . . pride . . . self-love . . . base, slavish fear . . . ambition . . . covetousness . . . temptations from Satan . . . solicitations from men . . . evasions in offenders to avoid justice. Friends' entreaty; enemies' obloquy. Such a world of snares, so many respects to work upon your affections, so many occasions to turn you out of the way, so many impediments to justice: this relation and that relation, kindred, acquaintance, fear, favor, hope of reward, frowns, smiles.

A large part of Puritan preaching consisted simply in exhortations to impartiality and to be on guard against temptation and corruption, to understand that political office was a duty demanding dedication, sobriety, and a high standard of professional integrity. 'You must be impartial,' Case demanded. 'God accepts no man's person. God accepts not the rich because he is rich, nor the poor because of his poverty; not the cause for the man, but the man for the cause.' As God did in the great court above, the same pattern was be expected of administrative gods in lesser courts below. 'You must be incorrupt,' Case added. 'With God there is no taking of bribes. In God's court no man can buy off a hell.'[48]

The preachers' concept of 'justice' was not precisely social justice in the sense of leveling social distinctions, though officials were told 'you must be patrons and protectors of the poor', and the egalitarianism in the demand that human courts and political assemblies institutionalize the great tribunal of heaven did conflict with traditional notions of privilege and hierarchy. 'In impartiality judgments must be little types of God's great assizes, where sin shall be judged in all persons alike, saving that the greatness of the person shall add to the punishment,' said Thomas Scot. 'The greater the man, the greater the sin . . . . Greatness and eminency of person is of itself neither virtue nor vice, but yet it gives a great addition to either.' Perhaps more important was how the demand for strict, impartial justice was motivated by indignation over the manipulative leverage of powerful men and diffidence on the part of lesser ones. 'Judge . . . warily yet . . . boldly,' urged William Est. 'Not to stay judgment though it be against mighty men . . . . A fearful judge that standeth in fear of the mighty will be swayed by the authority of the mighty and is made such a slave to his affections that the least thing will corrupt him.' The preachers recognized that conquering this 'fear of men's greatness who will be offended at justice' was not easy, but it was essential for any equitable and efficient system of justice that it be controlled. 'If judges and ministers of justice be fearful to offend [great men] they shall hardly deal well for good causes of mean men for fear of the persons of great men,' William

Pemberton warned. 'This servile fear troubles the mind, distracts the thoughts, and corrupts judgment.'

This psychological leverage, exerted by those in positions of privilege over those in positions of justice (no longer necessarily the same), called for considerable 'strength of mind', as another described it, 'to govern and manage passion and unruly affections, which he that rules at will is stronger than he that subdues a city and conquers a kingdom'. 'He needs to be of some spirit and resolution that must neglect the displeasure and frowns, reject the letters and suits of great men and superiors,' Samuel Ward remarked. 'It is incredible to those that know it know it not what strength great men will put to for the upholding of a rotten alehouse, countenancing of a disordered retainer, etc., the resistance whereof requires . . . some spirit.' A certain amount of such 'spirit' could be generated simply from the resentment such practices aroused, perhaps especially among the lower orders and other victims. 'With what bitterness of spirit do men groan under delayed and perverted justice when it . . . turns them out of their wits,' Ward observed, 'some of them ready to destroy themselves, their adversaries, yea and sometimes their judges!' While the ministers were reluctant to condone extra-legal measures, they recognized the dangerous level of public dissatisfaction and warned that blocked, perverted, or simply delayed avenues of legitimate redress for social injustices would exacerbate the crisis. 'It grieves the heart and excruciates the soul of the party oppressed,' Pemberton explained. 'Grief constraineth the just, who finds no relief by just order of law, to take unjust and unlawful courses, as calumnies, quarrels, contentions, and brawls, to relieve and remedy their unrighted wrongs, and sometimes . . . poisonings and murders of their oppressing adversaries.' The problem was compounded all the more when the law became an instrument for, rather than against, oppressive practices. 'There is oppression in judgment,' Charles Richardson observed, 'making that a means of oppression which was ordained to be a protection of the poor.'[49]

Yet, while the preachers were acutely aware of the social dangers of injustice, they emphasized that the first place to execute judgment was within. 'Let them beware of all corruptions in judgment to respect persons, take bribes, directly or indirectly, neglect the widows and fatherless,' said Lazarus Seaman, 'to be partial, to prefer private interest before the public, are all abominations in the sight of God.' Self-examination was the continual requirement for those who held political office. 'Examine whether you keep and detain in your hands that which is due unto others,' Vavasor Powell urged the members of the Rump Parliament, 'for as you have many opportunities to enrich yourselves in these days, so you will not want temptations to improve them for your own advantage.' The preachers seemed especially concerned about those newly arrived in positions of power and prestige (in whatever way); they were the most likely to be insecure and ambitious, perhaps servile and obsequious, possibly ruthless and cruel as well, and therefore most susceptible to the temptations of power and most in need of instruction in the principles of moral and official rectitude. 'When many come into places of dignity and power,' Jeremiah Burroughs observed, 'they think of gratifying their friends . . . of respect and honor that they shall have abroad in the world and be accounted somebody . . . of revenging all their wrongs, of making up of all their broken titles.' In a society where the competition for power and status often left bitter feelings in its wake, those who had arrived at the highest positions, such as city magistrates or members of Parliament, were in need of constant admonition. 'Do not seek to drive on your private designs by that power of judgment God hath put into you hands,' Burroughs warned. 'I am now a Parliament man; I have power in my hands; I will improve my advantage . . . . These thoughts are very vile . . . . Know that you have less opportunity to revenge your own wrongs now than ever you had before you were chosen Parliament men.' Not only private interests and relations, then, but most troubling was this thirst for private revenge. 'Private revenge is not within your commission,' Robert Harris felt it necessary to warn the House of Commons in 1642. 'Ye visible gods . . . remember that God avenges by you!' While vengeance might indeed come to be exacted for public offenses it was never to be appropriated to settle private scores, and to divert public authority to private quarrels was a serious infraction. 'It is not a private but a public power, a power authorized by a lawful commission to execute as the Lord's avengement for sin, justice and judgment upon arraigned and convicted malefactors,' William Sclater enjoined. 'All they who take the sword . . . to satisfy their own private revenge . . . shall for that sin be smitten by the public sword.'[50]

Further, the requirements of righteousness were such that public officials (and possibly others as well) might have to make a special effort not only to forgo the most egregious breaches of public trust but even to deny many otherwise legitimate personal urges and private relationships. 'A judge when he puts on his robes ceaseth to be like other men,' said Thomas Scott, 'but puts off all personal respects, knows no friend, no kindred, no acquaintance, no favorite.' The only guarantee that the highest ethical standards would be reliably kept was to insist that all private attachments be sacrificed at the altar of justice. 'You are to be . . . without father or mother or any private relations,' Anthony Burges enjoined, '. . . that you may not be charmed with the oratory of delinquents, nor bewitched with their tears, that you may see nothing that may cause affection to mist your judgment.' What seemed like reasonable standards for those acting on behalf of the public were taken to extreme and even fanatical lengths during the revolution as the preachers called on their followers to put aside much of what might otherwise be regarded as natural human compassion. 'The righteousness of God . . . "makes us hate father and mother and wife and children and brothers and sisters",' said Joseph Caryl; 'that is, it breaks all ties, whether natural or civil, when they stand in the way.' It was even with a kind of chilling fervor that the public spirited were required to remove themselves from all human feeling. 'Oh right honorable, take glorious resolutions to yourselves,' urged Thomas Brooks. 'Though your fathers may stand before you, and your brethren and friends press about you, though your mothers should hang on you . . . throw down the one, and break the other, and trample on the third, that your souls may cleave to the ways of God, to the ways of justice and righteousness.' And though these injunctions were urged with special solicitude on those with the highest positions of public trust, while they were acting in that capacity, by the very nature of the ethic it was not always possible to distinguish sharply public from private persons. 'All this hath been spoken not to judges and justices of peace only,' explained Samuel Ward, ' . . . but to all from the highest and greatest to the lowest and least instrument of justice.'[51]

Though the problem of sin and judgment could (and did) become intertwined with partisan division, the first task was less to appropriate the terms of justice to any particular 'cause', as such, than to make the administration of impartial justice itself a cause, to encourage the magistrates of England to deal conscientiously with pressing social problems. 'My Lords, two or three things I desire to mind you of,' Elidad Blackwell included in his exhortations to the London Mayor and magistrates.

> What swarms of poor, lame, maimed, wounded soldiers lie up and down the streets, crying to everyone that goes by! . . . And oh the many poor, sad, desolate widows, and the many fatherless children! . . . And oh the throngs of beggars that wander up and down the streets!. . . Look into the prisons too, my Lord. Oh the world of wickedness that is there! . . . Look into taverns and inns and alehouses and gaming houses too my Lord. Oh the abuses and disorders that are there, what drunkenness, what swearing, what whoring, what neglect of callings, of families! . . . Now the Lord help you! You have more work to do than I can speak.

Such problems would not be easy to judge, let alone solve, and the preachers' attitude could be at once compassionate and brutal, often with no more than a general indication of which was appropriate in any given instance. 'Those that are able to work, let them work – or let them starve,' Blackwell demanded for the beggars, the problem of which had reached chronic proportions. 'Those that are not (through age, or lameness, or blindness, or the like), let them be provided for.' What precisely was the difference would have to be determined in specific cases, though the preachers did sometimes put forth schemes for dealing with them; Blackwell's suggestion that the enforcement of fines for immorality would at once repress vice and provide funds to relieve poverty was typical of the kind of social engineering with which Puritan magistrates were experimenting. 'Were all the penal statutes executed upon drunkards, swearers, sabbath-breakers, common gamesters . . . (besides the restraining of these God-provoking, land-devouring, soul-damning abominations) what plentiful provision would there be for the poor?'[52]

In most instances, however, the point was less to advocate specific policies or rules of administration than to urge officials and emerging citizens to address problems in the first place, not so much how problems were solved than that they were solved at all. 'It would pose the greatest critic either in law or divinity to lay down exact and distinct rules for you to steer your judgment by in every particular case that shall come before you,' Case confessed in a sermon to the London magistrates in 1644. 'You will meet with many knots hard to untie, to know whom to smite and whom to spare, when to clothe yourselves with severity and when with mercy. You will find it a very hard thing to balance the scales of justice so even that the guilt shall not weigh down your censure nor your censure the guilt.' Such decisions would be agonizing, though some guidance was provided by the great judge of heaven himself. 'If you condemn whom God would absolve, or if you absolve whom God would condemn, you contract the guilt of blood upon yourselves and families,' Case enjoined. 'Guilty blood cries because it hath not been spilt; innocent blood cries because it hath been spilt; and God hath drawn his sword to avenge both.'[53]

The preachers remained convinced that coercion would not change people's hearts, though as with God himself, magistrates were required to use stronger measures when words alone failed. 'Men of a servile disposition will not be amended by so easy means as bare instructions,' Nicholas Proffet insisted.

> Compassion is to be used towards some and severity towards others . . . .
> Men must be dealt with for the saving of their souls . . . . God himself doth
> take the rod into his hand when the word is contemned, and if lighter
> strokes will not serve, he hath heavier blows for those that be impenitent
> . . . . The word and the sword must be joined.

Proffet was perhaps stretching a point to suggest the sword was capable of saving souls, but if God could smite sinners while still loving them, so could magistrates. 'Charity is not contrary to justice,' according to Joseph Caryl. 'We may love the person while we reprove, oppose, or punish the offender. God himself punisheth where he loves . . . . And man may forgive where he taketh vengeance.' Sinners could thus be punished, even brutally, for their own good. 'Not to bear evil is a mercy, not only to the good, but to the evil,' Caryl added. 'You cannot be more cruel to them than in sparing them. . . . Is it not then a kindness to smite them?' From the point of view of the redeemable sinner there would presumably be little difference between the 'judgments' visited by God generally and those coming through the hand of the righteous magistrate. 'These acts of justice, being the appointment of God, they may be blessed by him to the awakening and rousing of men's consciences,' Anthony Burges suggested. 'God hath suffered all this to fall upon them in mercy to their souls.' Yet while the preachers held out hope that coercion might awaken the conscience, often they settled for restraint of the body. 'Howsoever, if justice do not work the salvation of their souls, yet it works to the restraining of their sin,' Burges added. 'The measure of their wickedness is the less.' In most instances the preachers did not bother with euphemisms but were straightforward that physical restraint was not without its value. 'Let it ever be thought an evil consequence among reasonable men,' William Strong urged, 'that because magistrates cannot constrain men's consciences, therefore they may not restrain their actions.' Still, the conscience was swayed to religion in the first instance by fear and even terror. 'Bear not the sword in vain,' exhorted Elidad Blackwell. 'Draw it and cut off those that will not otherwise be reclaimed. Make wicked and ungodly men afraid of you . . . . Let not sin dare any longer to affront word and sword.'[54]

The preachers' notion of justice seemed brutal at times to the point of cruelty and was justified by the thin line separating justice and mercy. 'Right Honorable,' Thomas Brooks told the House of Commons, 'it is cruelty to the good to spare the bad.' The principle elevated the welfare of the 'whole' or the 'public' above that of the private individual, which could be sacrificed with apparent ruthlessness. 'When you pity the bad, you are hard-hearted to the good,' Anthony Burges reiterated. 'Besides, pity the whole rather than the part . . . so that there is no just public act, though it seem never so severe in respect of a person, yet it is a merciful act to the commonwealth.' In this respect there was a difference between offenses purely against God and those against the public as well, since magistrates had the survival of the state on their consciences and so could not afford to be as liberal with the well-being of others. 'Herein spiritual punishments differ from civil,' according to Burges. 'In spiritual if the party repent they ought not to inflict them; but in civil the magistrate he doth it howsoever, because he looks at the good of the commonwealth.' So while temporal tribunals were intended to reflect the eternal one, there was a similar distinction in the nature of their punishments. 'Even where sometimes he useth his prerogative royal for the pardon of sin against himself and remitting the everlasting punishment,' Case argued, 'he yet commandeth his deputies and vicegerents not to forgive the trespass, whether it be against a private person or a public state, but to execute the proportionable penalties, a substance for substance, life for life, and blood for blood, without showing any mercy at all.'[55]

A danger was presented by excessive mercy on the part of magistrates when God was demanding justice. 'He that spares any sin doth what lieth in him to ruin Parliament, army, city, kingdom, king, and all,' William Greenhill said. 'Peace is a desirable thing, yet . . . such peace we desire as will keep the God of peace with us.' Public officials were told that guilty blood, like innocent, would indeed be avenged and was even to some extent contagious. 'All that guilty blood that God requires you in justice to shed, and you spare, God will require the blood at your hands,' said Edmund Calamy. 'All the bribery, all the cosenage, and all the robberies which are committed in the kingdom which you can punish and do not, these are all your sins.' When in doubt it was best to execute justice. 'God is angry, and he seems to ask . . . Will you execute judgment or will you not?' according to Thomas Case. 'I will have the enemies' blood, and yours too if you will not execute vengeance upon delinquents.' The incentive was such that it would indeed be a thorough justice. 'Be not wanting in the execution of justice,' urged John Strickland. 'You know there is a curse pronounced against them that do that work of the Lord (though it be a bloody work) negligently.' God had many ways of fulfilling this curse, though in his usual method of using causes to make the punishment fit the crime he used those who deserved justice against them who failed to execute it. 'God oftentimes makes them who are unduly spared to be the destruction of those who did not execute justice upon them,' Cornelius Burges pointed out. 'When God doth not punish them with the wicked, he usually punishes them by the wicked.'[56]

Who precisely were 'the wicked' was not always clear, especially since those who failed to punish them were among them; while they began with the 'swearers and drunkards and filthy persons', also included were those who came to be in opposition to the Parliament and God. 'The magistrate hath the power of the sword,' said John Ley, invoking a famous passage from Romans, 'not only against one single offender but against many, if many deserve it, and to do justice upon many may require many swords (so many as make up a whole army); and if there be military force raised to hinder justice, there may military force be used to pursue it to effect.' The distinction was becoming increasingly blurred, as calls for 'the speedy execution of justice on offenders' and 'the vigorous prosecution of the war' were frequently made in the same breath; still, the distinction itself does indicate that the need for the state to execute justice at least began as its political or policing, rather than military, authority and the one was sometimes said to be an alternative to the other. 'When the sword of justice glistens, the sword of war shall rust,' Joseph Caryl said. 'Draw out the sword of righteousness, and God will sheath his sword of wrath.' Yet if the two swords were not strictly identical the existence of the one at least made the use of the other more urgent. 'If we follow righteousness we shall be sure that either our war will quickly conclude in peace, or that our peace shall be concurrent with our war,' Caryl suggested. 'It is true that war and peace in propriety of speech are inconsistent . . . but . . . a prosperous war is accounted peace.' War was peace in the sense that internal justice could substitute to some extent for external war. 'A little execution of justice is of more victoriousness than a great deal of military preparation,' John Lightfoot argued. 'This way must you either quell and conquer this devil of injuriousness and oppression or he will spoil your cause; he will overthrow your armies.' If the difference might appear negligible to those on the receiving end of justice, it nevertheless had its purpose in promoting a 'cause' that was connected to the means used to further it, and any setbacks in the cause were to be attributed to a lack of justice – never to the cause itself, since the cause itself was justice, but to an absence of justice within it. 'What may we think the cause of this disaster to be?' Matthew Newcomen asked in a September 1645 sermon 'to set forth the right use of the disasters that befall our armies'.

> I will tell you what we may not think it to be. We may not, we must not think
> that . . . the ground and cause of the war is unjust and sinful because of this

disaster . . . . No, though God should frown yet further upon us . . . never repent that we have embarked ourselves in the quarrel, for the sin lies not in the cause itself.[57]

The problem of sin and justice, therefore, was always internal, and though the enemy without was also deserving of justice, the first problem was those within. 'Why should any think that God will give into our hands those delinquents that are in arms against the great judicatory of the kingdom,' Herbert Palmer asked, 'if justice be not done upon those that are in our hands already?' Yet even as justice remained an internal problem it was constantly related to the external one, since these were the terms on which God would allow the war, and England, to prosper. 'The rebels are our enemies; our sins are God's enemies,' declared Case. 'If thou wouldst have God do execution upon thy enemies, do thou execution upon his.' Precisely which delinquents and rebels were to be executed was often ambiguous, though John Cardell could hardly have been more explicit in 1649. 'Our enemy and the destroyer of our country is now apprehended and brought before you, worthy magistrates of this renowned city,' he told the London magistrates shortly before the trial of the King. 'Arise therefore, honored patriots, unto a speedy and faithful execution of justice and judgment upon this grand incendiary, and let all the world see that your actings of late have been high and extraordinary and far beyond the proportion of former times and ages, so that ye have had nothing in your eye therein, and nothing of your own so much as the glory of God . . . and the good of the public.' War, after all, was simply the extension of justice by other 'means'. 'The magistrate bears not the sword in vain,' Robert Ram quoted from the standard text, 'but the civil sword many times would be vain and useless without the help of the military sword.' The distinction between a soldier and a magistrate, therefore, was not always a sharp one. 'Soldiers are instruments of justice, a kind of magistrates,' Ram told the army. 'The sword is put into their hands to bring those to justice and condign punishment which the civil magistrate could not reach . . . . Every soldier is a justice of peace . . . . Your business is to do what justice would not or could not do.' War was, thus, a common element between the two types of 'judge', God and magistrates (or soldiers), and as such it too constituted a 'court of appeal' – much as did the political institutions whose authority was now dependent on its outcome. 'The high court of Parliament is the great, ancient, venerable, high throne of the kingdom,' Case proclaimed.

War is another formidable throne which God hath newly erected in this land, the great court of appeal, whither both sides provoke for judgment, crying out (as it were) with a loud voice when they draw near to the battle, O thou Lord of Hosts, give out a righteous judgment this day between us. Every council of war is a subordinate throne, and God hath seated you noble and worthy commissioners upon one of the most eminent . . . . Your work is . . . to make inquisition for blood . . . to inquire after the innocent blood that hath or should have been spilt in England and this city. There have been . . . courts formerly set up to shed blood. And I hope you will not be less active in avenging it than the enemies have been in spilling it.[58]

3

COVENANT

Sir, I will presume that you are so well read in scripture as to know what God himself hath said concerning the shedding of man's blood. Genesis 9 [and] Numbers 35 will tell you what the punishment is and which this Court in behalf of the whole kingdom are sensible of, of that innocent blood that has been shed, whereby indeed the land stands still defiled with that blood, and as the text hath it, it can no way be cleansed but with the shedding of the blood of him that shed this blood. Sir, we know no dispensation from this blood in that commandment, 'Thou shalt do no murder.' We do not know but that it extends to kings as well as the meanest peasants, the meanest of the people, the command is universal . . . . That God that we know is a King of kings and Lord of lords, that God with whom there is no respect of persons, that God that is the avenger of innocent blood – we have that God before us, that God that does bestow a curse upon them that withhold their hands from shedding of blood which is in the case of guilty malefactors, and that do deserve death. That God we have before our eyes, and were it not that the conscience of our duty hath called us unto this place and this employment, sir, you should have had no appearance of a court here.

John Bradshaw at the trial of Charles I

As indicated at the start, the preachers demanded a recognition not simply that a god created and governed the universe but that one particular God had revealed and recorded the terms by which he did so. That in most instances God adhered to predictable laws or 'causes' meant that in normal circumstances there was no necessary need for further information and no obvious sense in which written revelation was any more special or sacred than any other. But when the logic by which God acted was not altogether clear, when events seemed to interrupt the routine workings of 'ordinary' providence, and when some special authority seemed to be required to restore a sense of order – at this point it became necessary to have recourse to something more transcendent than what existed in nature alone. This was what Puritanism exalted above all else: 'the word'. 'There is very much of God in his word,' said Jeremiah Burroughs, 'more of God there than in all his works of creation and providence.' Events alone were often uncertain and inscrutable, and essential as they were for preparing people to receive the word, the very inclusiveness of providence, comprehending the behavior of human creatures for evil as well as good, meant that worldly occurrences in themselves provided no infallible moral guide. 'If the providence of God extendeth unto all our actions, good and evil . . . then there is no certain rule or judgment to be made from thence,' William Bridge argued. 'If the providence of God do thus extend to our very sins, then we cannot make up our judgment and our rule from a bare providence, but you must make up your judgment and rule from the scripture and the word of God written.' The principle prevented the kind of cynical casuistry into which justification by providence alone could degenerate, whereby people simply made up the 'rule' as they went along. 'Though the Lord doth sometimes guide us with the eye of his providence, yet if I make the providence of God the rule of lawfulness or unlawfulness, then am I in a great error,' Bridge warned. 'The scripture and the word of God – it is the only rule whereby I may and must make up my judgment of lawfulness and unlawfulness.'[1]

This need for a 'rule', a standard by which to 'judge' what was just and 'lawful' when all existing moral values were in doubt, stemmed from a conviction of not only flagrant and widespread injustice, but also of the power of human corruption to distort understanding even of itself. 'Self hinders the knowledge of itself all it can,' Richard Sibbes remarked. 'Sin naturally hinders the knowledge of its own foulness.' And yet a certain level of human 'dignity' did at least allow the soul to be made aware of its own failings and inadequacies. 'Man hath judgment to know what he hath done . . . to judge of his own actions,' Sibbes insisted. 'This shows the dignity of man.' This capacity for self-awareness and self-judgment was the conscience, whose role as the arbiter of 'lawfulness' was graphically conveyed in the preachers' fondness for describing the human soul as a court of judicature. 'God hath erected a tribunal in every man,' Sibbes said. 'He hath set up conscience for a register, and witness, and judge. There are all the parts of judicial proceeding in the soul of man.' The description of the individual conscience as a fully developed system of criminal justice suggests its role as one means of redress against the many forms of injustice throughout English society, as well as an alternative to the limited effectiveness of institutional civil courts, and in this it was but the first stage in a more extensive system of appeals culminating in that great court above of which God himself was Chief Justice. 'God hath set up a court in man's heart, wherein the conscience hath the office both of informer, accuser, witness, and judge,' Sibbes explained. 'And if matters were well carried within ourselves, this prejudging would be a prevention of future judging . . . and so prevent public disgrace. But if there be not a fair dispatch and transaction in this inferior court within us, there will be a review in a higher court.'[2]

Yet, as Sibbes indicates, the conscience on its own could not always be depended on to dispense justice equitably; like existing civil courts it was often corrupt, partial, liable to error, and so had to be guided by a rule or law. 'Judge of the goodness of the way by the rules of holy scripture and not only by the seeming light of your own conscience,' Thomas Hill urged. 'Conscience may conclude that to be a lawful way which is unlawful, and it doth not oblige thee to practice, neither can it warrant thee therein.' Conscience was itself compromised by sin and likewise no infallible guide to right and wrong. 'Thy conscience by the fall of Adam was defiled . . . and even in the regenerate is sanctified but in part, not freed wholly from darkness and error and so cannot be a pure and perfect rule,' Hill warned. 'If you make your conscience your only guide, you will soon be misled into gross offenses.' The ministers had great respect for the power of the conscience, but they did not allow it any absolute autonomy for right other than negatively, as the mechanism for identifying wrong. 'To command religion without information of the minds is rather tyranny over the conscience than true zeal,' Samuel Rutherford could say, but such statements stemmed not from any confidence in the ability of the unaided conscience to make correct determinations regarding religious truth or 'information' as from a recognition of its reliability to defend that truth once so informed. 'If conscience goes against the word get conscience better informed,' Thomas Watson enjoined. 'Conscience being defiled may err.' However solicitous the ministers became about how to instruct the conscience, justification by conscience alone was never their creed (let alone was 'liberty of conscience' ever their politics). 'An erring conscience . . . will not . . . justify thy sinful practice,' Hill added. 'Conscience is . . . a rule to thee only so far as it receives information from the word of God.'[3]

Neither worldly providence nor the private conscience, then, but the 'word of God' alone was as eternal and immutable as God himself, applicable in all circumstances and binding on all rational creatures. 'It is universal in regard of time, place, and persons,' proclaimed Anthony Burges. 'No person or persons are exempted from the obligation of the word.' In the face of instability and dislocation, as an alternative to all fallible human faculties, authorities, values, and institutions, the ministers called for the return to a society in which people's lives would be ruled throughout by the word of God. 'The word of God is extended to all causes, all persons, all conditions of life,' declared Alexander Henderson, 'all which are to be ruled by the word.' While this plea often involved highly technical exegesis and bitter disputation in a variety of academic forums and polemical fronts, it was most thoughtfully expressed in the popular medium of the sermon (itself often described as simply 'the word'). 'Not by tradition, not by custom, not by councils, not by . . . antiquity,' Joseph Caryl argued. 'Whatsoever truth came from heaven . . . shall never feel decay. . . . The trial cannot be made by . . . antiquity but by that which transcends all human antiquity, customs, councils, and traditions . . . the word of God.'[4]

The principle that 'what cometh directly from God is not subject to change or decay' was not a simplistic appeal to whatever might happen to be written. That the word had been set down in 'scripture', and was 'old', did in itself give it a certain stability in contrast to human traditions, though even then the word was said to be more transcendent than simply the writings. 'The word of God is ancienter than the scripture,' said Sibbes. 'The scripture is but that mode, that manner of conveying the word of God.' The word did have to be conveyed through the scripture, though the point was that it interpreted what was occurring here and now; and while the word of God was more important than his works, the ministers recognized that a willingness to acknowledge any authority had to begin with what was accessible to human perception. 'We read him more easily in the patent of his works than charter of his scriptures,' Nathaniel Hardy said. 'We soonest assent [when] we see with our eyes, feel with our hands, and put our fingers in the print of God's works.' The metaphor emphasized the close interaction between the two in the mind of believers as a kind of living exegesis. 'The word expounds the works, and the works of God do interpret the word,' Thomas Case said. 'The works and word face one another and answer over one to another . . . the book of the word and the book of the works.' The relationship began with adversity, which is how the description of God's acts as a 'book' was usually made, and the word alone meant little to those who had not suffered affliction to make it plausible. 'We ought to conform our wills in case of all crosses . . . to the holy revealed will of God,' said Nicholas Estwick. 'When God reveals his will to us by any cross . . . the outward work is a book written in great text letters what is God's good pleasure towards ourselves and others.'[5]

THE LAW

Troubles and afflictions then led people to the word, which infused them with order and purpose by placing all God's acts within the terms of a 'covenant'. 'It was always God's way to deal with man in a way of covenant,' said William Bridge. 'No sooner was man made but God entered into covenant with him.' Covenant began simply as the idea that God limited himself to working according to certain rules (or 'laws'); that he ordered his creation, including sins and judgments, according to natural 'causes' was often described as the 'covenant of nature'. 'The covenant of nature is that whereby God, by right of creation, doth require a perfect obedience of all mankind and promises a most blessed life to as many as do give it him,' said Samuel Bolton; 'but against those that deny him this perfect obedience he doth denounce eternal death.' Covenant was especially associated with written revelation, however, and while sin and judgment were grounded in the law of nature, they were also defined by that of God. 'Sin is the transgression of the law,' declared one minister. 'The foundation of every judgment is in the law.' The 'law', as the preferred term for the covenant of nature as codified in scripture, consisted in simply those rules of natural equity that when violated resulted in suffering and worldly trouble and so could be equated with natural law. 'This word "law" in its natural signification both in the Old and New Testament, doth signify any doctrine, instruction, law, ordinance, or statute, divine or human, which doth teach, direct, command, or bind men to any duty which they owe to God or man.' The law consisted simply in natural human morality along with obedience to human authority, and though both were subject to some strain during the 1640s, the preachers continued to insist throughout that it provided a standard as stable and unchanging as God himself. 'The moral law is perpetual and immutable,' Bolton said; 'that law of nature engraven in the heart of man in innocency . . . which cannot be changed or abolished any more than the nature of good and evil'.[6]

The codification of natural law in scripture might seem almost humanist in its reference to the divine image in each individual; in fact, it proceeded from the ministers' dim assessment of human civility and their determination to civilize human conduct, to repress the aggressive and antisocial instincts – 'our natural fierceness and cruelty' – of which they had all too acute an awareness. 'If God had not given a severe and terrible law against sin, such is the vileness of men's spirits they would have acted all villainy,' Bolton charged. 'The law chains up the wickedness of the hearts of men, that they dare not fulfill those lustful inclinations which are in their hearts to do . . . . What one man does, all men would do were it not for . . . the law.' In addition to its usefulness on people's spirits, the law could be used, much like the civil version it paralleled, to impose restraint upon their bodies. 'There are two main ends for which the law was promulgated,' Bolton said; 'one was political; the other theological or divine.' The two were not always so easily distinguishable in practice, but the 'political' seemed especially necessary for those to whom the other did not apply. 'The political use is . . . "for the lawless and disobedient, for the ungodly and for sinners, for unholy and profane, for murderers of fathers and murderers of mothers",' Bolton claimed. 'It was made for them if not their rule, that it should be their punishment. This is the political use of the law.' Historically, this had indeed been the original one. 'The Jewish commonwealth had the laws of God's own making to punish all manner of transgressions,' observed Herbert Palmer, who suggested that this was an example that might profitably be adopted in England and other modern states. 'Since other commonwealths have taken to themselves (I am afraid further than God allows) a liberty to count themselves free from his penal laws, it is manifestly possible that they may be wanting in necessary laws to suppress ungodliness and then they make the nation guilty of such sins as for want of good laws are practiced.'[7]

There were limitations to the effectiveness of the law, whether politically or theologically: like the coercive power of the state, the law could restrain outward actions but it could not alter inward character, and while it was an end in itself for some, for others it was but a means to a higher end. 'The law was given to . . . restrain wicked men in sin, though it have no power to renew and change them,' Bolton said. 'The law doth remain . . . to discover sin to us.' Since sinners were incapable of obeying the law, its practical value was limited to the negative one of revealing to them this very weakness and serving to prepare them for another covenant that alone could provide them with the strength to overcome it. 'It acts . . . that we might be kept humble . . . and sensible of [our] own guilt,' Bolton said, ' . . . that so we may be kept humble and vile in our own eyes and that we might live more out of ourselves.' The law convinced the soul of its moral depravity and brought it to a harsh realization of how helpless and powerless it in fact was. 'The terms of the law were intended to awaken men and convince them of their own impotency, to humble them for their impotency,' Bolton continued. 'In the law, God's sole purpose is . . . that man might become convinced of his weakness and helplessness . . . to convince him of his impotency, to humble him for it, and to drive him away from all hope in himself.' The law on its own therefore did not itself create this weakness and helplessness but articulated a consciousness of emotions that were already present, that they might be first identified and then addressed. 'The Lord gave not the law purposely to damn men, but to drive them to an holy despair in themselves,' Sibbes said. 'They that despair in themselves, they come to see their whole hope of comfort to be in the face of God in Christ.'[8]

Because humanity had failed to keep the covenant of nature, its own nature was defiled, corrupted, and 'dead'. 'Every man naturally is dead,' said Sibbes. 'Sin itself, it is not only a cause of death . . . but . . . an intrinsical death.' This death was as much one of the spirit as the body, and the law not only defined the guilt before God but also provided for the awareness of this guilt within the conscience of the sinner. 'We are dead in law as well as in disposition,' Sibbes added. 'This death in law is called guilt . . . . It breeds horror and terrors in the soul.' This death was 'eternal' in more ways than one, being inherited from the first sinner and continuing to live on (as it were) through repeated violations. 'Hereupon comes a death sentence upon us, being damned both in Adam's loins, and likewise adding actual sins of our own,' Sibbes said. 'If we had no actual sin it were enough for the sentence of death to pass upon us, but this aggravates the sentence.' Adam had bequeathed a kind of eternal, even immortal, or at least hereditary death, by which human flesh existed in a state of constant 'corruption', successively revitalized with each new generation, only to have the process resumed in a self-aggravating spiral of perpetual decay. 'Adam's person first corrupted our nature, and nature being corrupted, corrupts our persons, and our persons being corrupted, increase the corruption of our nature,' as Sibbes described it. 'Corruption . . . swelleth bigger and bigger . . . propagated from parents to their children . . . till our natures are altered.'

Whether this legacy of original sin reflected an awareness of social and psychic disorders as rooted in childhood development and dysfunctional family life – and the popularity of familial metaphors throughout Puritan literature, as well as the ministers' obsession with the regulation of domestic relationships and household discipline, would seem to bear this out – the doctrine of original sin did constitute a kind of sociology, expressing a sense of moral frustration over the social origins of deviant behavior. 'It is not these actual sins that defile me only,' Sibbes said, 'but if I look back to my first conception, I was tainted in the spring of my nature.' This suggestion that blood was 'tainted' combined the metaphor of family generation with that of criminal law, so that hereditary sin constituted a form of 'treason' against the sovereign authority of the King of heaven. 'Man is in soul misery judicially,' said Nicholas Lockyer. 'Corruption is got into the blood; generation is marred . . . . Treason stains the blood; the first man proves a traitor

. . . and then begat as he made himself . . . and so doth all the posterity to this hour . . . a piece of mere putrefaction.' Insofar as both original and actual sin continued to carry both temporal and eternal consequences, the mythical and contemporary elements merged into an atavism by which current social and political troubles were seen as the symptoms of a persistent hereditary and even phylogenic pathology. 'Old diseases are long in curing, so especially those that are hereditary and so become natural to our temper and constitution,' Anthony Tuckney noted. 'Oh that in washing this day with our tears our still-bleeding wounds we could . . . weep over our first old sore, acknowledging it to be bad flesh that is so ill to heal, and that sure our blood is tainted, that continues the quartan so long and turns it into a continued fever.' This idea of societal ills as 'diseases' (or increasingly, 'wounds') in the body politic gave new social signifi-cance to 'birth' and perhaps especially 'blood', even as it called their political value into question. 'Lay to heart the vileness of sin which hath stained your births,' Jeremiah Burroughs urged the House of Lords. 'Your births otherwise are honorable, but every one of you have your blood stained with high treason against the God of heaven.' Given the epidemic proportions of such congenital diseases throughout all ranks of English society, ties and lines of blood had become meaningless if not positively dangerous as indications of health or legitimacy within the social organism. 'Nobles used to be proud of their birth,' Francis Cheynell observed before the Lords; 'they are too often puffed up with the glory of their progenitors.'

> Nobles are by nature the children of wrath, even as other common men, and can you be proud of your foul conception and foul birth? My father Adam, was he not your father? Oh my father Adam, your father Adam, was once a man in honor . . . but his blood was tainted by sin, nay your blood was tainted by sin . . . . And are you still proud of your birth and blood when you are thus polluted in your own blood with your birth sin? Can you still be proud of your original when your original, your blood, your very nature is stained and tainted with original corruption? . . . Oh base ignoble birth, we are born slaves of sin, born like heirs apparent of hell, with the seeds of damnation in us. Can you still be proud of your progenitors, when they derived a sin upon your high-born soul which will sink it as low as hell?[9]

The 'corruption' that originated in Adam had thus grown to the proportions of a plague over English society, infecting the great as well as the mean. 'Guilt and corruption hath been derived by the fall into . . . all conditions,' Sibbes observed, 'from the king that sitteth on the throne to him that grindeth on the mill.' Corruption was thus a leveler, and all descendants of Adam were created, and corrupted, equal. 'All men are equal in their original, in their creation, Adam, and in their fall, Enosh,' said William Strong. 'Only God makes the difference and appoints one vessel to honor and another to dishonor, here as well as hereafter.' This attainder and corruption of human blood corrupted all collectively and equally, and any apparent differences in the moral quality of people were the result not of any natural or inherent goodness with which some might seem to be endowed but only of how successfully their tendency toward corruption had been repressed by religion and other constraints. 'The differences that be in some men . . . arise not of this that they have not more or less original corruption but of the restraint and limitation of man's corruption,' argued William Perkins. 'For in some God bridleth sin more than in others, and in them is found civility.'[10]

'Corruption' still carried more biological than political associations, though the organic and religious metaphors were coming to connect the two, and the ever-increasing tendency toward death and decay propagated across the generations could also spread through the body politic as well, so that the explicit socialization and politicization of sin and judgment – the idea that guilt pervaded all society, the family and the nation, even over time – was something that had long been implicit on the level of myth. 'By one man sin entered into the world, and death by sin,' Samuel Fairclough pointed out, showing how consistent it was that God should visit his wrath collectively on the entire nation for the sin of one individual, 'especially if he be in place of power and authority in church or commonwealth or both'. Adam was just such a figure of power and authority, and one of the central symbols of Christian theology was politicized as a kind of prototype of the corrupt public official. 'Adam must be considered not as a private man but as . . . a public person representing all his posterity, and therefore when he sinned all his posterity sinned with him,' Perkins explained, 'as in a Parliament whatsoever is done by the burgess of the shire is done by every person in the shire.' The precariousness of Adam's position and his fall were given added plausibility by similar instances of social and political mobility in the contemporary world, and Adam was made something of a negative 'role model' for the way many public figures were in fact behaving. 'When magistrates are in Adam's condition, too busy with forbidden fruit in the garden, God, it may be, turns them out,' George Cokayn warned members of the Long Parliament in November 1648. '"I have said ye are gods, but ye shall die like men." God may bring you to Adam's condition . . . even to be thrust out from your pleasure and power.'[11]

A variation on the theme of original sin – as well as the corruption of 'blood' – was what might be called original crime, mythically represented in the murder of Abel by Cain, whereby biblical myth was politicized even more explicitly from simply 'sin' to 'oppression' and 'violence'. 'The same spirit that actuated Cain to kill his brother Abel . . . ha[s] actuated these men to kill the saints,' declared Richard Heyricke in 1646. 'The devil was a murderer from the beginning; the whole world lies in the wicked one.' The crime of Cain symbolized the violent origins of human civilization and identified persecution with 'a vein of malignant and active contrariety which hath run down from the days of Cain to this very hour'; as represented by Cain and Abel, contemporary political conflict in England was set in the context of an atavistic instinct to kill. 'The cry of violence and oppression, but above all the cry of blood is gone up to heaven and cries in the ears of the Lord of Hosts,' proclaimed Thomas Case in 1644. 'For if of one righteous Abel's blood had a tongue to cry to God for vengeance, then how much louder doth the blood of more innocent persons than Abel had drops of blood in his body, poured out in England and Ireland like water upon the ground cry in the ears of a righteous God against the fratricidious, yea and parricidious Cains of our times, "Vengeance, vengeance"?' While vengeance belonged to God, measures not permitted to those acting in a private capacity were permissible by, and in fact incumbent upon, office holders acting in the name of God and public order, and the crime of Cain provided a clear case of the kind of transgression that public officials, like God, could not afford to forgive. 'These men are guilty of all the blood that hath been shed in this kingdom in the cause of liberty, of privilege, of religion,' Heyricke alleged.

> God will lay all the blood to their charge. He will not lose one drop of the blood of his saints. Abel's blood yet cries for vengeance. God when he comes to make inquisition for blood, he will account for every drop of blood. He that pardons all other sins will not pardon innocent blood. Tears shall not wipe away the guilt of blood.[12]

THE GOSPEL

Yet the harsh and unforgiving justice of the law was not the only justice at God's disposal. 'Justice in actions is either legal, rigid, strict justice,' said Thomas Valentine, 'or else evangelical, tempered, allayed justice.' Both were indeed forms of 'justice', and whether in 'temporal' or 'eternal' affairs the two had to be (and in some sense already had been) reconciled. 'Not that there is any kind of inequality,' John Cardell explained. 'When a person or a people are saved, either temporally or eternally . . . the mercy of God . . . is [not] greater than his justice . . . for . . . mercy cannot anywhere take place until justice be fully satisfied.'[13]

Justice would be satisfied and mercy 'justified' because God did not simply eliminate evil and replace it with good, without reference to the causes and means of the world, but manipulated evil in such a way that good would come out of it. 'It is the way of God to bring all good out of evil,' observed Jeremiah Burroughs, 'not only to overcome the evil, but to make the evil to work toward the good . . . not so much by removing the evil, as by . . . changing the evil into good.' The opposition between justice and mercy, evil and good, was not mutually exclusive, then, but dialectical: God would bring forth good, not simply despite evil but out of the very evil itself. 'The manner of God working in things . . . is by contraries,' said Richard Sibbes. 'He bringeth light out of darkness, glory out of shame, and life out of death . . . . God worketh all by contraries . . . . Out of misery he bringeth happiness, and by hell bringeth men to heaven.' The very essence of God as creator and governor was after all dialectical. 'God, as a God properly, makes something out of nothing,' Sibbes explained. 'That is to be a God, for nothing but God can make something of nothing.' And what God performed in the creation he could also bring to pass in the hearts and souls of people. 'As he raised all out of nothing, order out of confusion, so . . . he can raise comfort out of discomfort, life out of death,' Sibbes continued. 'He can create out of that which is contrary.'[14]

Just as providence had both its dark and light side, then, so these, along with the often confusing passages of scripture, were systematized into two dialectically interacting covenants. 'As there are two Adams, and the one was the type of the other,' said Thomas Goodwin, 'so there are two covenants, the law and the gospel.' A favorite technique was to intermingle the promise of 'mercies' (to be discussed later) with the threat of judgments, each cast in terms of the covenant by which they were dispensed. 'There are but two ways to cure a stony heart,' said Edmund Calamy, 'either by the heart-cutting threatenings of the law or by the heart-melting mercies of the gospel.' Both were in continual operation at any given time, the law through judgments and fear, the gospel through mercy and love. 'The mercies of the gospel do kindly work upon the heart . . . melting it into tears,' Calamy said. 'The hammer of the law will batter and bruise the soul, but the cross still remains in it. But the fire of the gospel, the furnace of God's love, will . . . purge out the filth that is inwardly got into the soul.' As some of the imagery indicates, the distinction could be a fine one: each covenant had its sanctions, and even 'dreadfuller woes are pronounced under the gospel than under the law'. 'Legal sins will bring legal curses,' Calamy said, 'but gospel sins (unless there be gospel sorrow) will bring a gospel curse, which is above all legal curses.' Moreover, while judgments were sometimes said to work 'outwardly' on the body and mercies 'inwardly' on the soul, the correspondence was not precise: even judgments, it seems, could be 'spiritualized' by the gospel. 'In the times of the gospel . . . we find generally the judgments of God to be more spiritual upon the hearts and consciences of men,' Burroughs noted. 'Spiritual judgments upon men's souls . . . are the most terrible judgments.' It was because afflictions on the conscience were so terrifying that gospel preaching was full of fire and brimstone. 'The gospel hath fire in it,' announced Richard Byfield, with revivalist ardor:

It is true, life and immortality are brought to light by the gospel; and it is no less true that hell fire and damnation is language peculiar to the gospel . . . . To preach hell is gospel preaching . . . . For the greater and more glorious are the manifestations of God's grace, the greater is the sin and heavier the wrath and condemnation due to the refusers.[15]

Even so, the gospel brought a compliance not of fear but of love, which in the long run was more effective. 'The breaking up of sinful hearts is a singular means to prevent the breaking down of a sinful nation,' declared Obadiah Sedgwick, who contrasted the alternatives: 'Legal attrition is only the pinching of servile fear and despair . . . but evangelical contrition is the melting and lamenting of filial love and hope,' he said. 'An attrite heart may . . . become negatively penitent . . . but the contrite heart . . . becomes positively holy.' Each covenant had a role in working this 'holiness' though only one actually achieved it: the first provided for a modicum of moral sense and outward civility, but as that came to be 'dead', holiness required that a new law, one of 'life', be inscribed within. 'I do not . . . mean by holiness the mere performance of outward duties of religion, coldly acted over as a task,' Ralph Cudworth maintained, 'but I mean an inward soul and principle of divine life that spiriteth all these, that enliveneth and quickeneth the dead carcass of all our outward performances whatsoever.'[16]

This 'spirit of life', as opposed to the mere 'letter' which was 'dead', animated and inspired both the word and the soul. 'All scripture is given by inspiration, the 'breathing' of God,' Thomas Case said. 'Holy men of God spake as they were inspired by the Holy Ghost.' Scripture then came to be resurrected as it was inscribed in the hearts and lives of similarly inspired persons, and the preachers were anxious to emphasize that a crude biblical literalism would be of little lasting value. 'The scriptures in the letter are but a shadow,' said Peter Sterry. 'The scriptures in the letter are dead.' Like the law in particular, the scriptures in general were dead so long as they were taken only literally by a 'dead' person, one devoid of any 'spirit' or 'life'. 'The law and the letter . . . as they are alone are old and dead.' Sterry said. 'The scriptures thus taken signify nothing except you bring some living power or principle to them. Lay them before a dead man, and they are as dead as he.' Further, the letter of the scriptures, though itself dead, had an active role in 'killing'. 'The scriptures in the letter are killing,' Sterry added. '"The letter killeth, but the spirit quickeneth."' Whether a given soul was killed or quickened depended on the amount of spirit, as it were, in that soul. 'That which to the faithful is a quickening spirit,' Robert Baillie said, 'to the misbeliever is a killing letter.'[17]

And yet the alternatives were not necessarily so simple, as Sterry indicates, since not only being dead but being thoroughly, almost positively, even consciously, 'dead' through the active process of 'dying', or at least the passive one of being 'killed', was the necessary preparative to being reborn. 'The law then findeth us dead and killeth us,' said Sibbes. 'It findeth us dead before, and not only leaves us dead still, but makes us more dead.' Only once the law had killed the soul, rendered it utterly lifeless by stripping away all vestiges or illusions of value and worth – only then would the soul be in a condition to be revived, 'regenerated', by a life outside it. 'Till the law as a covenant . . . be dead to you and you to it . . . you will never look for righteousness and life in another,' Samuel Bolton said. 'But when once the law hath killed you . . . then will you look for life alone by Christ.' This dialectical interaction of 'life' and 'death' was (literally) crucial to the operation of the covenant within the soul of the regenerate. 'I through the law am dead to the law, that I might live to God,' Bolton quoted from the scriptures. 'The law having now slain me, I am forever dead to it . . . . All my life is in Christ.' And this 'life' provided by another to the dead soul was described as a new birth or 'regeneration'. 'This is called regeneration, or being born again, because it hath a former birth . . . presupposed,' Robert Gell explained. 'The regeneration is . . . of those who are conformed unto the death of Christ by dying unto sin and to his life by conformity unto his resurrection. Such regenerated ones are they who are born from the dead with Christ and so become children of the resurrection.'[18]

In this process of spiritual death and resurrection, the human spirit itself was not entirely passive, though its active role was limited essentially to one of self-renunciation and self-destruction, since God's spirit could only breathe new life into a soul whose own spirit had been thoroughly expired. 'Labor to be emptied of yourselves,' urged Sibbes. 'In what measure we are emptied of ourselves, we be filled with the spirit of God.' For the holy spirit to enter the soul the human spirit first had to be thoroughly 'broken', since only a broken spirit could be reduced to the required level of abasement and humility. 'A broken spirit is a humble spirit,' said Francis Roberts, 'low in its own eyes . . . broken and spiritualized with godly sorrow.' Such a spirit was not only aware of its unworthiness, it seems, but anxious to make it complete. 'A broken spirit is a self-debasing spirit, can lay itself low before God, is vile in its own eyes . . . vilifies himself, dejects, debases, and abhors himself . . . debases himself exceedingly,' Roberts said. 'Oh a heart thoroughly broken for sin . . . can be as anything, can be as nothing, that God in Christ may be all.' Only a spirit that was not merely willing but eager to undergo this process of self-abasement and self-vilification could attain the degree of sincerity the ministers demanded. 'A broken spirit is a true and sincere spirit,' Roberts continued. 'It . . . ingenuously spreads open all its own vilenesses before the Lord, takes the shame of all upon its own face . . . spares not even his foulest and shamefullest miscarriages, could be thoroughly purged from all.' With the sincerity produced within this purged and broken spirit came not simply obedience but unquestioning obedience, a passion for obedience, an obedience that could be relied on. 'A broken spirit is a dutiful, tractable, obedient spirit,' Roberts added. 'A melted softened heart will bend and bow as God will have it. . . . Such a heart is fixed and resolved upon all dutiful compliance with God's commands.' And the reward for the total obedience that only a broken spirit could be made to exhibit was the promise that a thorough abasement would lead to an eventual exaltation, this time on God's terms. 'He casts down that he may lift us up. He crusheth that he may console us. Yea, he kills us that he may more gratefully revive us,' Roberts promised. 'Behold how God, how Christ loves a broken heart.'[19]

This determination to break the spirit, to render the soul malleable in the hand of its maker so as to be readily shaped to his will, a prelude to steeling it for his service, was one those not already acquainted with some sense of disaffection and dejection and in need of strength and direction might look upon as perverse and unnatural. 'There is a vast odds and disparity betwixt that account which God and that which the world hath of a broken spirit,' Roberts explained. 'With God a broken and a contrite spirit is most acceptable . . . . But on the contrary this brokenness of heart is with the world . . . looked upon as a sad, mopish, melancholy disconsolate distemper.' A tendency toward depression, often severe, did accompany certain stages of conversion and greatly concerned the ministers themselves, who nevertheless argued that their religion, though it brought such distempers into the open, was not the cause but the cure. 'The best Christians are subject to be troubled, to be pensive and dejected more than should be,' Sibbes acknowledged, adding that this was not the responsibility of religion itself, which only applied itself to an already existing frame of mind in an effort to furnish a remedy. 'You will say, religion breeds a great deal of trouble and pensiveness,' he conceded. 'It is indeed the speech of the shallow people of the world, "religion makes men sad." Aye, but the same religion will cheer them up again,' he rejoined. 'Yea, it casts them down that it may raise them up.' This systematic process of first beating down and then raising up the spirit was a response to the oppositions and contradictions of worldly change, and its purpose was first to make people aware of these alterations and then to impose upon them a measure of order and control. 'Our life is woven of matter of sorrow and joy, and . . . affections should be sensible of both,' said Sibbes. 'Our life is nothing but as it were a web woven with intermingling of wants and favors, crosses and blessings, standings and fallings, combat and victory.' The dialectic taught people that to understand and overcome these unsettling vicissitudes it was necessary to confront them methodically – first to accept the disappointments and the sorrows and only from there to appreciate the wonders and the joys. 'If a man will be joyful, let him labor to weep first, that the matter that interrupteth his joy may be taken away,' Sibbes urged. 'Those that will be joyful . . . must needs with shame be brought back to sorrow.'[20]

The dialectic of spiritual death and resurrection then was not a static assortment of unrelated tenets but a systematic operation that took place within the innermost depths of the soul, beating it down into nothing that it could be lifted up again as something. 'You must let Christ kill anything,' insisted Nicholas Lockyer, 'so he will but make alive your souls.' Nowhere in fact were these contradictions and oppositions more poignantly brought together than in the complex metaphors of life and death. 'Life took death that death might take life,' Sibbes observed. 'Christ's life itself took death that we . . . might take life. . . . The death of Christ . . . is the death of death.' The frantic obsession with 'life' in Puritan rhetoric found its nexus in the figure of Christ, who embodied not just life but the life brought forth from death. 'Christ is the universal principle of life,' Sibbes declared. 'As Adam was a principle of death . . . so . . . we are begotten again to this inheritance by the resurrection of Christ, who is risen again to quicken himself and all his.' The preachers insisted that the spiritual life was, if anything, more 'real' than the natural one, being eternal life and never to be terminated by death. 'There is a life besides the natural life, and the root of it is Christ,' said Sibbes. 'There is a better life than a natural life . . . for this life which we live in the flesh is . . . but to make a beginning for a better life.' 'Life' by definition required both body and soul, and however it might be assumed that religion pertained to some postulated 'afterlife', the ministers did not draw a categorical distinction between 'this' life, meaning that lived before 'death', and the 'next' one, which followed it: Christ put vitality into what had to be lived now as much as any hereafter. 'The glory of Christian religion is in the resurrection of

Christ,' Sibbes proclaimed, 'and to consider that . . . cannot but infuse life and vigor into all our actions, estates, and conditions, be they never so mean.' The very distinction between life and death seemed to melt away in Christ, himself the 'death of death'. 'It is not properly death, for misery dieth, death itself dieth; we do not die,' Sibbes said. 'Therefore it is no great matter what kind of death a Christian dieth, because he dieth in the Lord.'[21]

This shared vigor gave Christ the quality of not simply a savior but the archetype of the charismatic leader: 'the prototype of holiness'. 'Christ is our pattern, whom we must strive to imitate,' said Sibbes. 'Christ . . . is the prototype, the first type and idea of all perfection.' Christ personified a complex set of ideas that embodied the concept of covenant in its fullest sense of defining and limiting God in his relations with man. 'He is not a God simply, but a God in covenant,' Robert Harris said, 'and that covenant is made with Christ, and by virtue of that same covenant Christ and we are both heard.' Through Christ salvation became a covenanted act, one which took place not despite that but because God had bound himself to abide by his own justice. 'By virtue of this covenant God cannot but accept of a poor penitent sinner laying hold upon Christ for pardon,' Edmund Calamy said. 'God is not only merciful but just to forgive us.' But though the preachers addressed the fears of each individual sinner, Christ embodied the worldly and collective nature of Puritan religion: God did not simply remove isolated souls into some abstract or distant 'other' world without reference to the sufferings and sorrows of this one; rather, an atonement, a sacrifice in expiation for the sins of men and women from all time, had vicariously satisfied his justice. 'The way of man's salvation it was by a mediator,' Jeremiah Burroughs pointed out. 'It is not only by God's mercy, God's saying that he is offended by sin but he will be content to pass it by; no, but it is through a mediator . . . . There is required a great work of God to make an atonement.' This great work not only had required, but might continue to require, the greatest of human sacrifices. 'He hath subjected himself to the breaking of his body and to the pouring forth of his blood for the reconciling of us,' Burroughs continued. 'It is not merely . . . that God saith, I'll pardon them, but Christ undertaking to make peace between his father and us, it cost him the breaking of his body and the pouring forth of his blood.' But while the preachers stressed his role as 'mediator', the Puritan Christ was less an intercessor to be propitiated than an example to be imitated and a leader to be followed. 'Oh what should we be willing to suffer for Jesus Christ in our bodies, even to resist unto blood,' Burroughs added, 'seeing Christ hath been content to have his precious body broken and his blood shed for us!'[22]

The salvation of humanity was thus by the blood of Christ: the blood of God. 'We are by the blood of God saved,' Burroughs proclaimed. 'The same person that was God had a body and blood; that body and blood was united into the divine nature . . . to reconcile God and us together.' Through the united sacrificial death of God and man, 'God performed the law,' as one said, 'God died for us.' Only by sacrificing himself could the wrath of God be justly appeased. 'God must be satisfied . . . and there could be no satisfaction but by blood,' Sibbes said; 'and there could be no equal satisfaction but by the blood of such a person as was God.' In Christ, God had willingly degraded himself to the status of a victim, a condition expressed both in his incarnation and more violently in his 'humiliation, to frailty, guilt, shame, horror, death'; and as the purpose of the law was to humiliate and 'kill' the human spirit, God's willful humiliation and death of himself under the law alone could fulfill it. 'Christ's humiliation did consist in his subjection to man's miserable condition, as to "become sin" and "a curse" for mankind, to come under his own law and to be judged by his own justice,' said Vavasor Powell. 'Oh what a low degree of humility was this for Christ to yield to a death . . . which was so shameful, miserable, and cursed.' While the symbolism of Christ doubtless appealed to something universal in the human condition, it touched an especially sensitive nerve among those who saw themselves as the victims and outcasts of society. 'He became not only a man but a curse, a man of sorrows,' said Sibbes. 'He was broken, that we should not be broken; he became a curse that we should not be accursed.' In Christ as the prototypical victim the preachers described their own anxieties and insecurities, and with them their hopes and aspirations. 'They looked upon him as a poor, despised, mere man and that had nothing of worth in him,' said Fulk Bellers, 'when he seemingly suffered himself to be overpowered on earth, to be apprehended, buffeted, scourged, and crucified, to see him that was the creator of nature to suffer death by his sinful creatures.' The same could apply to the petty scourgings and crucifixions that those sinful creatures themselves had to contend with, and if the preachers were indulging the considerable capacity of their audience for self-pity, the aim was to channel it into sympathy for Christ, with whom they then identified as a surrogate victim. 'Art thou censured and scorned by men?' Sibbes asked. 'Make use of it, but not to discouragement. Remember Christ was despised, counted a worm, judged wicked, and then say . . . "though I fall I shall rise again".' The sufferings and degradation of Christ thus gave dignity to those of ordinary men and women and made them less wounding, holding out the promise that all was but the necessary prelude to a final triumph. 'Our evils are nothing to Christ's sorrow,' Nicholas Estwick said, 'and the lowest and meanest member of Christ in any condition is more excellent than the highest monarch in the world.' Here the conventional and unexceptionable symbols of Christianity took on new and potentially explosive meaning as the cruelty and indignity endured by Christ were offered to help people cope with their own feelings of inadequacy, failure, and shame. 'Am I disgraced or dishonored?' asked Jeremiah Burroughs.

Why, Jesus Christ he had dishonor put upon him . . . . All the foul aspersions that could be were cast upon Jesus Christ, and this was for me, that I might have the disgrace that is cast upon me sanctified unto me. Whereas another man his heart is overwhelmed with dishonor and disgrace, and he goes this way to work to get contentment: Perhaps if you be spoken ill of you have no other way to ease and right yourselves but if they do rail upon you you will rail upon them again, and thus you think to ease yourselves. Oh, but a Christian hath another manner of way to ease himself: Others rail and speak ill of me, but did they not rail upon Jesus Christ and speak ill of him? And what am I in comparison of Christ? And the subjection of Christ to such an evil was for me, that though such a thing should come upon me, I might know that the curse of it is taken from me through Christ's subjection to that evil. Thus, a Christian can be content when anybody speaks ill of him . . . . So if men jeer and scoff at you, did they not do so to Jesus Christ? They jeered and scoffed at him, and that when he was in his greatest extremity upon the cross . . . . Now I get contentment in the midst of scorns and jeers by considering that Christ was scorned.[23]

In Christ the very abasement exalted, the very humiliation glorified, the dishonor honored, and disgrace opened the soul for grace: Christ synthesized the divine and the human by literally incorporating the central dialectic at the nexus of an intricate matrix of other dialectical relationships – the resolution of contradictions, the reconciliation of opposites. 'A Christian's estate is carried under contraries,' observed Sibbes, 'as Christ was.'

'He was rich, and became poor.' He carried his riches under poverty. He was glorious, but his glory was covered under shame and disgrace. So it is with a Christian: He goes for a poor man in the world, but he is rich; he dies, but yet he lives; he is disgraced in the world, but yet he is glorious. As Christ came from heaven in a way of contraries, so we must be content to go to heaven in a seeming contrary way. Take no scandal therefore at the seeming poverty and disgrace and want of a Christian. Christ himself seemed to be otherwise to the world than he was. When he was poor, he was rich . . . . When he died, there was nothing stronger than Christ's seeming weakness. In his lowest abasement he discovered the greatest power of his Godhead.

What was true for Christ could also be true for the Christian, then, and what made the dialectic operative for each soul was a consciousness both of its own inadequacies and of Christ's limitless capacity to supply them. 'We [are] to be restored by a way contrary to that we fell,' said Sibbes. 'We fell by pride; we must be restored by humility.' A conscious and complete humiliation in imitation of Christ was the only way to confront the humiliations of a hostile world, and whatever the human frailty or suffering – humiliation, abasement, weakness, poverty, shame, and death – it had to become a state of mind before it could be overcome. 'Christ humbled himself, being God, to become man for us, and by his death restored us to life,' Sibbes said. 'When we are weak, then are we strong in the Lord: when we are abased, then are we readiest to be exalted; when we are poor, then are we most rich; and when we are dead, then do we live.'[24]

Moreover, the dialectic was constantly moving onward and upward to heights ever more grand and glorious, so that if pride was responsible for the initial fall, and humility necessary for the return, the reward for undergoing degradation was not simply restoration to one's previous, neutral condition but nothing less than the greatest imaginable 'glory'. 'The more affliction the more glory . . . and passing all the glory of this world,' Sibbes promised. 'In glory there is such a degree of excellency as is victorious and convincing . . . conquering the contrary that opposeth it.' Once one had endured humiliation one's former existence would never again be adequate; nothing would satisfy but glory. 'Glory is the end of all,' said Sibbes. 'The reward of humility . . . is riches, glory, and life . . . . The glory then we speak of is an eternal glory.' There was no going back; the only course in the face of trials and tribulations was forward, and only the stirring promise of unsurpassed glory could inspire the meek and dispirited with the bold confidence to surmount the difficulties and discouragements they would encounter. 'A man that hath this calling unto glory,' Sibbes remarked, 'oh how marvelously may such an one be joyful in all tribulations, sorrows, and crosses.'

> Oh but, says one, I am in poverty, what shall I do? Stay a while, and glory will come, and thou shalt be rich as the best. Oh, may some other say, but I am tormented with sorrow and sickness, yea, am so loathsome as doth make me stink in my own sight, and be a burden to myself and others . . . . Oh but think then even this loathsome vile body is appointed unto glory, and glory will come ere it be long.[25]

This appeal to the combined emotions of self-hatred and self-pity gave confidence to those with little self-esteem, whom it encouraged even further in their humility with the assurance that they would be raised up again in glory. 'Those that God loves, he will have them vile in their own esteem,' Sibbes said, 'for it is his method first to beat down, then to raise up.' People came to love Christ the more they hated themselves, the more they could see their own wretched and wasted lives in his, and the more they could see their own disappointments and failures acquire significance in his death. 'He should be the dearer to us the more vile and base he was made for us,' said Sibbes, 'and he should be most lovely in our eyes when he was least lovely in his own, and when he was deformed, when our sins were upon him.' The more a soul loved Christ then the more conscious it became of its hatred of itself. 'In what measure any man . . . hath any opinion of himself that he is something, just so far he detracts from Christ,' said John Preston. 'Every Christian may truly say, God loves me better than I do myself.' Through the love of Christ, and an awareness of the relationship he established between humiliation and exaltation, disgrace and grace, the soul was encouraged to yet further feelings of self-hatred, to pursue an active course of 'self-judging, self-loathing, self-abhoring, and self-searching', and to despise itself as thoroughly as possible. 'His wisdom, holiness, power, and strength . . . will make us abhor ourselves,' Sibbes exulted. '"I abhor myself." . . . "I am not worthy".'[26]

Christ thus appealed to the estranged and the disaffected, those with little self-confidence and sense of self-worth, assuring them that, not merely despite, but because of their conviction of the worthlessness which the world seemed to fasten upon them, they would be precious to him; and when successfully applied the dialectic transformed the very self-hatred itself into a source of spiritual comfort. 'God's own dear children . . . because they find no deserving in themselves, are therefore discouraged at the sight of their own unworthiness,' Sibbes observed; 'whereas, quite contrary, the sight of our own unworthiness should make us the more fit subjects for Christ's free love, which hath nothing to do with them that stand upon deserving.' In fact the only thing Christ would value was a conviction of one's inadequacy, and the only thing he would reject was a claim to some personal worth. 'None ever received Christ, embraced Christ, and obtained mercy and pardon from Christ but unworthy souls,' said Thomas Brooks. 'Christ hath bestowed the choicest mercies, the greatest favors, the highest dignities, the sweetest privileges, upon unworthy sinners.' All value was in Christ alone, and far from requiring any worthiness or sense of worth, Christ would only come to the soul from which such conceits had been thoroughly purged. 'If the soul will keep off from Christ till it be worthy, it will never be one with Christ,' Brooks continued. 'God hath laid up all worthiness in Christ . . . . God will account none worthy . . . but believers who are made worthy by the worthiness of Christ.' The only impediment to the union of the soul with Christ was any lingering self-valuation, the remnants of some illusion of personal merit which the preachers regarded as the sin of pride. 'If you make a diligent search into your own hearts, you shall find that it is the pride and folly of your own hearts that puts you upon bringing of a worthiness to Christ,' Brooks added.

> The Lord calls upon moneyless, upon penniless souls, upon unworthy souls . . . but sinners are proud and foolish, and because they have no money, no worthiness to bring, they will not come, though he sweetly invites them . . . . Well sinners! Remember this, it is not so much the sense of your unworthiness, as your pride, that keeps you off from a blessed closing with the Lord Jesus.[27]

What was rejected by the world was accepted by Christ, and for that very reason, so those who felt despised by the world, and as a result had come to despise themselves, were taught that their insecurities were not only acceptable but admirable and decidedly to be encouraged – indeed, to be made as complete as possible. 'A man must be emptied of all opinion of worthiness in himself,' Preston insisted. 'He must think himself of no worth at all. He must be empty of all opinion and conceit . . . [and] see that he hath no ability to help himself, that all his redemption must come from Christ.' To some extent such requirements described what already existed, and a soul that already harbored a certain measure of alienation was most likely to undertake the effort in the first place; beyond this, however, the preachers demanded that such feelings be not only conscious but deliberate and thorough, and to be loved by Christ and to follow Christ required a total surrender of all personal qualities and attachments, all feelings of self-worth, all pride, all affections, all loyalties, all desires, all opinions, all identity. 'None can come to Christ but he must first strip himself of himself,' Sibbes demanded. 'He must not own his own wit, will, or affection. He must be emptied of himself wholly. He must deny himself in all his aims after the world, in the pleasure, profit, or preferment of it. He must not respect anything if he will follow Christ.' Christ demanded a complete voluntary surrender of the will, as if the only thing the human will was able to do was to admit its inability to do anything and to deny itself entirely in submission to the will of Christ. 'A Christian . . . must think what Christ thinks and submit his judgment to him,' Sibbes continued. 'He must have no will of his own; he must give it up to . . . Christ and be content to be ruled by him in all things.' Everything was to be surrendered unconditionally and unquestioningly to Christ, so the Christian became simply a conduit to convey the will of Christ, an instrument to be manipulated by Christ. 'A Christian gives himself and all his to Christ,' Sibbes insisted.

> I have given up myself to him, therefore I renounce all others . . . . If he will have me die, I will die. If he will have me live here, I will. I have not myself to dispose of any longer. I have altogether alienated myself from myself. I am his to serve him, his to be disposed of by him. I have renounced all other.

All worldly possessions, dignities, positions, enjoyments, affections, attachments, livelihoods, cares, existence itself – all were to be forsaken if necessary for Christ. 'Thou must be contented . . . if need be to leave all as he did,' Nicholas Lockyer enjoined, '. . . riches, honors, pleasures, blood, life, to follow after Christ . . . . Though Christ will take nothing for anything he hath, yet you must come to him with all that ever you have in your hand and lay it at his feet. Think nothing too good for him: Here is now estate, wife, children, yea here is body, soul, self – do with all what thou wilt; drown all, burn all if thou wilt.' To love and follow Christ was to renounce all other affections than Christ, to love and follow nothing else. 'You must have a transcendent, a heroical love to the Lord Jesus,' Francis Cheynell demanded. 'You must love him better than your friends, better than your estates, better than your honor . . . . Nay, you must love Christ better than your lives.'[28]

This need to strip the self of all individual identity, along with the new identity it would be given by Christ, was again succinctly conveyed in the concept of 'honor' – in some ways more important than 'life' and to the soul, as they said, 'eternal' life itself. 'Lay down all your honor at the feet of Jesus Christ . . . and God will in due time exalt you to such a degree of honor as will make most for his glory and yours,' Cheynell promised. 'Leave all to him . . . that disposes of honor and power, victory and glory . . . . This is the way to recover all your honor.' Whatever might befall Christians in the world, and however they might be called upon to lose their personal identity in allegiance to Christ, they could have the consolation of knowing they would be accounted 'noble by their intimate relation to Christ', and to be esteemed a Christian was to be granted a 'glorious title of honor'. 'This one title of honor doth outshine and eclipse all the admired titles of honor in the most flourishing commonwealths,' Cheynell announced. 'It is not the birth but the new birth that makes men truly noble.' If those who claimed nobility by virtue of their birth found the title increasingly vapid compared to the meager acceptance they received from the world, and if those without noble birth found themselves envious and searching for some other measure of their own dignity, either could find compensation by claiming a new kind of nobility through a new birth – one which seemed to offer the promise of a renewal in life, a fresh start for those who may have felt disappointed that their own lives had not turned out to be everything they had hoped or expected. 'You may be more ennobled by a new birth, by a second birth, than you were by your first birth,' Cheynell told the House of Lords, 'for in your second birth ye are born to a heavenly kingdom, and ye are born not of blood (mark that) nor of the will of the flesh, nor of the will of man, but of the will of God.' Here the preachers enhanced the appeal of their message with concepts and metaphors designed both to control and to exploit the discontents arising from emerging status if not class consciousness, and in such a way that their ideas simultaneously thrived upon and transcended social divisions. 'The greatest honor that we can attain to is to be of the offspring of God,' Cheynell declared, promising his audience a pedigree from the Lord of lords himself:

> The highest honor is to be his offspring by regeneration, to be his sons by adoption, for then we are truly noble, highly descended indeed, more noble than the proudest of them . . . for every regenerate man is born of God and bred of God, and therefore it must be granted that he is well bred and born.[29]

Those who felt rejected by the world and inferior within society could now direct their feelings of victimization into a religion that would at once mitigate and make use of those feelings by telling them that their rejection was not personal but for their allegiance to God. 'For reproaches and disgraces that [a soul] meets withal in the world,' Sibbes said, 'he wears them as his crown, if they be for religion.' This enhanced sense of honor or self-esteem was not an easy one, however, and arose not simply because the ministers said so but because it would impel the soul to a superior moral standard in an effort to live up to its new prestige. 'We should have a holy esteem of ourselves, as when we are tempted to sin,' Sibbes urged. 'What! I that am an heir of heaven, a king, a conqueror, the son of God, a freeman, shall I stain myself? God hath put a crown upon my soul, and shall I cast my crown into the dirt? No, I will be more honorable. These are no proud thoughts but befitting our estate.' If one aim of Puritan religion was to teach the most dejected and self-deprecating souls, as the phrase now goes, to feel good about themselves, it was not a vacuous exercise in good feeling but in order that the dignity derived along with the divine image would encourage them in a bold new effort to be worthy of it. 'Shall God be one with us in our nature in heaven and shall we defile our natures that God hath so dignified?' Sibbes asked.

A Christian should have high thoughts of himself. What! shall I defile the nature that God hath taken into unity of his person? . . . Our nature is dignified by . . . his blood. It is God that died . . . . Hereupon comes the dignity of whatsoever Christ did and suffered . . . . Whatsoever was done by Christ . . . had its worth and dignity to prevail with God.

And this 'dignity' in turn provided the most disheartened and withdrawn with a new confidence and even boldness, a sense of resolution and purpose and holy mission that assured them that they and what they did would be 'justified' by their religion. 'This should encourage us . . . to proceed on a resolute course of Christianity,' Sibbes exhorted. 'Though the wicked world laugh at us, and scorn us, God the judge justifies us, his children justify us.'[30]

THE POOR

There were various reasons why people might be brought to a condition where they would seek refuge from the laughter and scorn of the world; another metaphor indicates perhaps the most common apprehension by which the human spirit came to be bruised and broken and vulnerable to the appeal. 'Blessed are the poor in spirit,' William Perkins quoted his Savior. 'Christ ascribing this happy title of his heavenly kingdom to them that be poor, and of a contrite heart, doth herein minister a sovereign remedy against all temptations from outward poverty and distress.' As with 'brokenness', it was the 'spirit' of it that alone could make 'poverty' holy, as Jesus himself had promised. 'What is meant by "poor in spirit" is . . . that those poor are blessed who by means of their distress, through want of outward comforts, are brought to see their sins and their miseries thereby,' Perkins explained, 'so as finding no goodness in their hearts they despair in themselves and fly wholly to the mercy of God in Christ for grace and comfort.' More than anything it was poverty that created the self-loathing that left the soul in need of the self-affirmation Christ could provide, and though the term was used figuratively to describe a state of mind and spirit, there was thought to be at least an oblique correspondence with that of the body and estate. 'Christ's poor here pronounced blessed are such as by reason of their poverty are miserable and wretched, wanting outward comforts,' Perkins explained. 'Christ opposeth them to the rich, who abound with all worldly delights.' In one sense, everyone existed in a state of spiritual poverty; to be truly poor in spirit was to be conscious of it. 'Every person and all people are but poor and beggarly if they want Christ,' said Perkins. 'To feel . . . spiritual poverty and so become poor in spirit . . . [is] to feel our own poverty, how by nature there is no goodness in us, but we are utterly destitute of the grace and favor of God, that so we may go out of ourselves and in regard of ourselves even despair of our salvation. For till this poverty of spirit be wrought in us . . . till we be beggars in ourselves we never begin to be rich in Christ.' While poverty (and especially 'beggary') was a dangerous and potentially damning condition in that the shame and despair it created exposed the poor to desperate and destructive temptations, it also, by virtue of that very despair, left them more susceptible to the means of their salvation. 'Doubtless poverty is a grievous cross, not only in regard of the want of bodily comforts, but especially because of that contempt and reproach which in this world doth hang upon it,' Perkins acknowledged, 'whereupon many do esteem their poverty as a sign of God's wrath against them and thereby take occasion to despair, thinking the kingdom of darkness belongeth unto them.' Yet insofar as this contempt and reproach produced the correct consciousness, that of self-contempt and self-reproach, the effect would be precisely the opposite:

> If a man in outward distress can be brought to feel his spiritual poverty and the wretchedness of his soul by reason of his sins, then he is so far from having just cause to despair of God's favor by reason of his poverty, that on the contrary he may gather to his soul a most comfortable assurance . . . that the kingdom of heaven belongs to him.[31]

Puritan religion, then, was not itself responsible for somehow creating that 'contempt and reproach' the preachers so often observed as attaching to poverty and other forms of failure; what it did was articulate and exploit that vulnerability so as to teach people that however impoverished and degraded they might feel in themselves, by virtue of that very demeanor, and because Christ had voluntarily made himself 'poor', they could become rich and honorable in him. 'Notwithstanding thy outward poverty, yet thou art rich in God,' Perkins consoled the materially and spiritually indigent. 'Men are rich in God . . . when they are reconciled to God in the merits of Christ. Christ became poor for our sakes that we through his poverty might be made rich.' While the lives of the poor were wretched to the point that they were sometimes deemed the 'damned' of society (which might be taken simply as a way of characterizing their temporal condition), they also tended to make up a greater share of the saved of God. 'Though the promises of God's grace be not denied unto the rich, yet sure it is, riches do choke the seed of grace in the heart and hinder the care men ought to have for spiritual riches,' Perkins added. 'Hence it cometh that more of the poorer sort receive and obey the gospel than of the rich.' Nor, for all the spiritual 'riches' of Christ, was following him any way to generate outward wealth (whatever the tendencies of later generations who may have found it advantageous to adopt this language). 'True religion and piety will not free any from outward poverty,' Perkins admonished, 'and therefore let no man think because he is godly he shall be rich or not fall into poverty.' On the contrary, the preachers warned that the pious could only expect to suffer all the more because of their piety. 'Being destitute of temporal blessings . . . [they are] afflicted both in body and mind . . . tormented . . . banished and driven to extreme poverty . . . deprived of all goods and of all society of men . . . and evil entreated of all men.' If anything was distinctive about the Puritans' social conscience it was not that they failed to address the problems of poverty in their society, as is sometimes alleged, but the determination with which they made political capital out of the readiness of their audience to believe they were the most egregiously victimized by it. 'God's servants may be overwhelmed with manifold calamities at the same instant,' Perkins continued, 'pressed down with crosses in goods, in body, mind, friends, and every way.' To follow Christ, they insisted, was almost to guarantee trouble in this world. 'Even those who are so dear to Christ that their case he accounts as his own may nevertheless in this world be in a needy condition,' Samuel Rogers warned; 'hungry, thirsty, strangers, naked, sick, and in prison.' While spiritual poverty did have some correspondence with material indigence therefore, the 'spiritual riches' inherited from Christ were intended as an alternative to material acquisition and to direct the sense of deprivation into the pursuit of things more valuable and enduring. 'Jesus Christ was so rich that he was 'heir of all things',' noted John Cardell. 'And yet . . . he became so poor that there was hardly anyone poorer in regard of outward things.'

> This poverty he did voluntarily subject himself unto that we through his poverty might be made rich. Let the same mind be in you . . . that was also in Jesus Christ; and as he humbled himself and emptied himself for the good of you all, even so be ye willing . . . to humble yourselves and to empty yourselves for the good of one another.[32]

THE MAGISTRATE

More important then (and more radical too) than the obligation of the rich to relieve the poor was this empowerment of 'the poor' with the psychological means to relieve themselves, encouraging their transformation from passive economic recipients into active political participants; and in fact the contribution of Puritan religion to the political thought and practical politics of the revolution was this use of Christ as what might now be called a role model to make a sense of deprivation and disaffection an incentive to an ethic of self-sacrifice and public service – turning the 'poor in spirit' into the public-spirited. 'Never was the world acquainted with such another example of self-denial, with such another precedent for publicness of spirit as that which Christ held forth,' Cardell declared. 'He came from the highest degree of sublimity, and he stooped to the lowest degree of ignominy; for he did not only . . . bleed for us and die for us, but he was made vile and of no reputation.' This way of phrasing the message appealed as much to those who had some 'reputation' to lose (or to gain) as to those with a more literal experience of spiritual poverty; and if those who felt rejected and marginalized by society were most ready to identify with Christ, those who already held positions of respect and responsibility in the common-wealth – and with them the divine image in some measure – might have their own need for a religious title commensurate with the honor. 'Magistrates are called gods,' Obadiah Sedgwick reminded a local political gathering. 'It is not a naked title which conveyeth nothing of substance and reality with it. He who hath given this name of excellency unto them hath derived an answerable power and authority in regard of which they may be justly called gods.'[33]

Yet the divinity of magistrates resided not in the private persons but in the public positions. 'The divinity is not stamped upon their persons but upon their office,' William Spurstowe told the London officials. 'Their divine constitution doth not change their native condition.' For those conscious of the discrepancy – perhaps especially those recently elevated who harbored doubts about their worthiness to fulfill the responsibility or disappointment over the degree of social acceptance they received – Christ offered a way of reconciling the difference, and magistrates were often observed to be similar in their way to Christ, at once human and divine and standing representatively for others. 'By our Savior's own exposition they are called gods . . . which doth prompt us to believe that magistrates were types of Christ,' George Cokayn noted. 'In a subordinate way, they are resemblances of the Lord Jesus Christ.' Like Christ, they would receive little gratitude for their pains and very likely be scorned and despised for them, but that was why magistrates were necessary: they were 'those who will be saviors to a people if that be the work God would have done', and often whether or not the people themselves would have it done. 'Our Savior Christ is . . . in you . . . whom God hath called to be saviors of this kingdom,' William Carter assured the House of Commons.

> You must do it for many that will ill requite you, ungrateful and unworthy persons, such as consider not your faithfulness, nor travel, nay, even for such as will revile you and reproach your actions, for base-minded men that will do nothing for themselves. Thus doth Christ, and thus must you.[34]

Christ, after all, was the archetypal godly magistrate: as God incarnate he embodied the collective virtues demanded of members of Parliament and other 'public persons'; he had taken upon himself responsibility for the sins of others, while himself guilty of none, and made expiation for them with the sacrifice of his blood. 'He hath brought you into a relation of his own, which is of public and common persons,' John Ellis told the Commons in 1643. 'He is the chief representative person that ever was . . . . In like manner each of you stands for multitudes: some for hundreds, some for thousands, some for ten thousands.' Christ, in other words, was a metaphor for the integrity and self-sacrifice expected of the concientious public official, and like the fall of Adam his act of atonement was frequently characterized by political analogies describing the ethic of selfless public service and devotion to duty now being required of political figures and citizens. 'Christ upon the cross stood not as a private person but as a public person in the room, place, and stead of all the elect,' explained William Perkins. 'Therefore when he was crucified all believers were crucified in him, as in the Parliament when the burgess gives his voice the whole corporation is said to consent by him and in him.' The political vocabulary of 'representative' or 'public' or 'common' persons describing not only Adam but especially Christ in a religious sense much as magistrates stood in a political capacity in fact significantly predated the 1640s. 'Only Christ was he that died in whom all died; he was crucified in whom all were crucified; and he rose again, in whom all rise, he being a public person,' said Sibbes. 'Other particular men died, and themselves died only. Let us look upon God incarnate and see ourselves in him, see God in Christ, see Christ a public person.'[35]

Christ thus atoned for guilt in the same collective terms as people incurred it through Adam (and one another), and the collective guilt and atonement now being explicitly applied to practical politics had long been latent symbolically at the heart of Christian theology. 'Adam . . . stood as a common person for us all . . . and if Adam had performed the condition, we all had performed the condition,' William Bridge noted. 'Jesus Christ is a second Adam, and he stands as a common person . . . . Although the first Adam did not perform the condition for his seed, yet the second Adam hath performed the condition of the promise and of the covenant for his seed to the full.' While the act of the 'common person' comprehended those of his posterity or 'seed' in the sense that his descendants incurred the guilt or benefited from the pardon, it did not substitute for, nor did it necessarily 'determine', those of ordinary men and women in such a way as to preclude individual responsibility, any more than did the duties of magistrates for the general citizenry; particularly in the covenant of the 'second Adam', it still remained to be seen whether specific individuals were to be included. 'Christ was a common person,' Bridge explained. 'Christ did not die for himself nor obey for himself; but he did die for us and obey for us, and all his seed were in him as in a common person.' And yet it was more than simply a matter of example, since both status and behavior were collectively identified with the prototype, whose act was somehow the act of each member of his 'seed'.

> Therefore . . . you are not barely to say thus and thus Christ resisted for my example, but in his resisting, I did resist, in his overcoming, I did overcome. For as I did eat in the first Adam's eating, and yield in the first Adam's yielding, so I did refuse, and resist, and overcome in the second Adam's refusing, resisting, and overcoming. Thus with all the saints and people of God who are the seed of the second Adam.[36]

The role of the identifying soul was thus simultaneously passive and active, since just as the seed of Adam was phylogenically tainted with the corruption that led individuals to commit sins of their own, so part of the legacy Christ bequeathed to his spiritual offspring was a measure of his own divine strength that would enable them to rise above their corruption. 'Jesus Christ as a second Adam doth beget children after his own image,' William Ames said. 'The first Adam brought forth children in his own likeness . . . . So doth the second Adam propagate his posterity and give unto them his own spirit.' Much as each soul transformed original into actual sin with its own violations of the covenant of nature, so this spirit in turn was realized in each soul as it 'accepted' or 'gave' itself to the covenant of grace. 'There is in the work of thy turning to God the giving up of thyself to God in an everlasting covenant,' Jeremiah Burroughs said. 'As thou takest Christ, the head of the covenant, to be thine, so thou givest up thyself to Christ . . . . There is the resignation of the soul wholly to God in an everlasting covenant to be his.' While the entire seed acted in Christ therefore, the element of personal responsibility was preserved in the requirement of mutuality at the heart of the covenant. 'It is the nature of covenants to be mutual,' John Brinsley observed, 'and such is the covenant betwixt God and his people.' While in the aggregate Christ acted on behalf of his seed as a whole, a reciprocal act of self-resignation was still required from each individual soul to be included. 'There is a mutual commerce between God and man, and there is nothing that God doth for man . . . but there is somewhat in man wrought by the spirit to answer it again,' said Sibbes. 'It is not sufficient that God is reconciled in Christ, because God will always have a reflex act from man.' To be chosen, in short, one was required to choose. 'As he chooseth man, so man by grace chooseth him,' Sibbes said. 'Our choosing . . . is an evidence God hath chosen us.'

Technical quibbles about whether God or man actually chose first were largely academic, since the whole point was that Christ synthesized the two. 'Christ was chosen before all worlds to be the head of the elect,' Sibbes said. 'He was predestinate and ordained by God . . . . He was chosen eternally . . . and all others that are chosen are chosen in him.' The principle of mutuality was not simply that God initiated the covenant and man responded in such a way that each had his own respective role while otherwise remaining distinct persons; through the synthesis of Christ the two were joined dialectically so that the role of each was also that of the other, and people were said to reciprocate the covenant only in the sense that Christ was the 'common person' who not only performed God's part but also enabled them to perform theirs. 'Christ was chosen first as a head and we in him,' said Thomas Goodwin. 'He as a common person and a head was first elected and we in him.' The question of the respective roles of God and man or precisely how much 'freedom' the human will had in choosing was also academic and in this context almost meaningless: the whole point of Christ was that he gave the power of God to impotent man; he provided weak souls with the divine strength to do what otherwise they were powerless to accomplish. 'The spirit of Christ is a spirit of power and strength,' said Sibbes. 'It will enable us . . . to overcome ourselves and injuries . . . it will make us able to live and to die, as it enabled Christ to do things that another man could not do. So a Christian can do that and suffer that that another man cannot do and suffer, because he hath the spirit of Christ.'[37]

It was not that nothing was required of the human will in its own salvation, therefore; on the contrary, it was precisely because so much was required that weak and helpless souls were incapable on their own of doing it, which was why they needed a savior and why what was demanded of man had to be performed by God through Christ. 'Not that we answer by our own strength, for it is the covenant of *grace*,' Sibbes emphasized. 'It is a covenant of grace not only because the things promised are promised of grace, but because our part is of grace likewise.' In the covenant, human helplessness was supplied by divine power, so while people would inevitably fail to fulfill the covenant, the consequences were not necessarily so dire since the covenant of grace by its nature was equipped to deal with failure. 'When we have done all we can do, yet we shall fall short of that exactness of obedience which the law requireth,' John Brinsley conceded.

> But let not these discourage . . . . The covenant that God's saints are under is not a covenant of works but a covenant of grace . . . the Lord requiring from us not exactness but truth, sincerity, uprightness. So as every failing . . . is not a breach of covenant so long as the heart is upright.[38]

Imperfect obedience in itself was not necessarily a problem under the covenant of grace so long as the effort was 'sincere'. 'For thy own part, there is no more required of thee but sincerity,' John Preston said. 'Under this gracious covenant sincerity is perfection.' The catch was that even sincerity was never perfect, since the soul itself would always have doubts; ultimately therefore the only determination of sincerity was relentless effort, a life of perpetual struggle. 'In the covenant of grace . . . sincerity is our perfection,' Sibbes said, 'which is known by a strife against the contrary.' The covenant dialectic operated between the poles of anxiety and confidence, in which the conflicting soul could have the assurance of knowing its failings and inadequacies would be overlooked but only so long as it never ceased to demonstrate unswerving dedication to the cause. 'Though there may be many slips and failings in the walking of God's people . . . yet walking before God with all their hearts in uprightness and sincerity, the Lord will keep covenant with them and show mercy to them . . . performing unto them all the conditions of the covenant on his part,' Brinsley explained. 'And therefore let all our care and solicitude be how to perform the conditions on our part.' Provided this was kept firmly in mind and one constantly persevered in the struggle against all oppositions, the covenant worked on terms of virtual certainty. 'If you keep covenant with God, the great God will keep covenant with you,' Edmund Calamy promised, 'and all the blessings of the covenant . . . shall be your portion for ever and ever.'[39]

The purpose of the covenant, then, was purpose itself, and it perhaps says something of the sense of powerlessness in those who eagerly absorbed the message that what they found 'comforting' was not a doctrine that offered the possibility of doing something to improve their chances of being chosen, a view they rejected as implausible, but precisely the contrary, one that assured them there was nothing they could do to diminish them. 'See here the good will of God in the rise of predestination,' noted Nathaniel Holmes; 'predestination is . . . of choosing, of purpose.'

> These purposes of favor are unmovable and unchangeable . . . . So that against all fears of change, this becomes an assurance, that whom he loves, he loves to the end . . . . For God is not unresolved . . . as a man is unresolved oftimes . . . . God is unmovable from his purposes of mercy by anything that is in us or from us.

Predestination, then, was an answer to the anxieties and uncertainties of worldly change, assuring the bewildered that they would not be made the victims of their own inabilities and inadequacies, and God could be counted on to be constant in assisting sinners to persevere in the second covenant despite the discouraging sense of failure produced by their own violations of the first. 'The covenant with Adam was broken and all forfeit and lost because mutable,' Thomas Mocket explained. 'But the covenant of grace hath for ground the immutable promise of God that it shall never cease and Christ who ever liveth.' And Christ communicated this 'unchangeableness and stability' to individual men and women. 'If thou wouldst be unchangeable in thy covenant get interest in Christ who is the covenant,' Thomas Case said, 'the unchangeable covenant . . . the faithful and true witness, yesterday and today, the same forever.' The virtue of the covenant was its certainty; it provided a set of stable and enduring values when all else had been called into doubt. 'Alas, there's no sureness here in these things,' Jeremiah Burroughs lamented. 'I can be sure of nothing here, especially in these times . . . . There is no sureness in the things of this world; but . . . the covenant is sure.' And it followed that Christ's covenant was by its nature more powerful than Adam's, since, by being unchangeable, constancy and good were by definition stronger than corruption and evil. 'The image of God in the second Adam is more durable,' said Sibbes. 'For all excellencies and grace [are] more firmly set on Christ than ever they were upon Adam.' The very certainty for which people were searching was itself the mechanism that assured them they would obtain it:

When God set his image on the first Adam it was . . . decayed and lost . . . because he was a man changeable. But Christ is . . . eternally united to the godhead, that shall never be altered. Therefore we are renewed . . . and that is why the state of God's children is unalterable, why being once gracious they are so forever.[40]

How far this contrast between the two covenants involved a chronological sequence was deliberately ambiguous, but as Christ brought a more stable covenant, he rendered the covenant of Adam – indeed, the entire world of Adam – 'old'. 'Care not for this world,' Thomas Goodwin urged. 'It is old Adam's world; it brings oftimes much loss to saints; it's well if thou canst get handsomely rid of it.' Through Christ, by contrast, God was offering a 'new' world, a 'world to come'. 'As this world was ordained for the first Adam,' Goodwin said, 'so there is a world to come for the second Adam.' But this world to come was not so much an 'other' world in the sense that it was somewhere else as the same world newly created, new modeled from the old. 'As God made this world for Adam,' Goodwin explained, so 'God appointed a world for the second Adam, Jesus Christ.'

God doth take the same world that was Adam's and makes it new and glorious . . . . Even as God takes the same substance of man's nature and engrafts grace upon it, so he takes the same world and makes it a new world, a 'world to come'.

And a new creation required new creatures, new men and women whose natures had been 'renewed', restored to life by the atonement of Christ. 'Christ's mighty power . . . brings them to become new creatures,' John Lightfoot promised. 'This is the next work of wonder and power to the work of the incarnation, for as in that God became man, so in this man becomes like God.' This renewal of the world through the renewal of human nature, one soul at a time, meant that personal regeneration and social reform were not mutually exclusive but mutually reinforcing, and its potential for making all things new, as much as chronologically, made the gospel itself the 'new' covenant. 'In such a respect as gospel blessings are called "better",' William Gouge explained, 'they are also called "new"':

> as a 'new covenant', a 'New Testament', a 'new Jerusalem', a 'new heaven and a new earth', a 'new name', a 'new commandment', a 'new way', a 'new heart', a 'new spirit', and a 'new song'. These and other like things are called 'new' in opposition to old things, which decayed and vanished away. . . . These new things shall never wax old; they are new, not only in their beginning but also in their perpetual continuance. They shall ever be fresh and flourishing.[41]

Christians could have a share in these new things, provided they were also renewed with the creation. 'There is a necessity that we be changed, and that we be new,' said Sibbes, 'or else we can never be inhabitants of the new heavens and the new earth.' The old was corrupted and decayed, while the new would always be fresh and alive. 'The nature of man . . . is corrupted,' Sibbes said. 'We must have new judgments of things, and new desires, and new esteem, new affections, new joys, new delights, new conversation, new company. All the frame of the soul must be new.' With the exciting promise of a new world the preachers tried to make their listeners comfortable with change, which was no longer to be feared and resisted but now could be controlled and therefore welcomed. 'It is an alteration, a change, a new man, a new creature, new birth,' Sibbes added. 'We see the necessity of a change.' Christians were newly created not only as they experienced a new birth, but also as they acquired a new honor, lived new lives, and as their old status was buried. 'If you desire this new honor, you must lead new lives, and you'll never do that till you have new natures, new hearts by a new creation,' Francis Cheynell proclaimed. 'Therefore you must all, high and low . . . be made new creatures in Christ.'[42]

The vision was given a political twist as the inhabiting of a new 'kingdom', even being made 'kings' – not by birth or generation into the hereditary succession that legitimated the decayed and corrupted kingdoms of the earth, but by a rebirth, a spiritual regeneration as heirs to a new and ever-flourishing domain. 'All real Christians are spiritual kings,' Cheynell said. 'We are kings by birth, born to a kingdom by a new and miraculous birth.' Other political analogies also endowed Christians with monarchical status. 'We are kings by conquest,' Cheynell added. 'Our Lord and master hath conquered principalities and powers . . . the world and the devil . . . even our own selves for us . . . and therefore we are more than conquerors through him that . . . overcame our spiritual enemies for us.' Unlike earthly monarchs, Christ shared the magisterial image along with the divine one, and his kingship was not monopolized by him alone but devolved upon all his 'subjects'. 'He is such a king who maketh all his subjects to be kings,' said Stephen Marshall. 'He takes possession of their hearts by his power . . . making them kings in his kingdom, and bringing them infallibly into glory.' The first conquest in this alliance of the soul with Christ then was over itself, obtaining a kingdom within. 'The soul is subdued to God,' Burroughs said. 'Then it comes to receive Jesus Christ as a king, to rule, to order, and dispose of him how he pleases.' Such subdual and occupation could fortify the soul against whatever threatened it externally amid the old and crumbling kingdoms of the world. 'A Christian then whatever he wants he can make it up, for he hath a kingdom in himself,' said Burroughs, so that whatever earthly kingdom one was a subject of, 'it is much better to be a subject . . . of the kingdom of grace, for grace knoweth no old age, nor hath grace an internal principle of corruption . . . and though the powers of the earth may subvert the foundation and fundamental laws of earthly kingdoms, yet cannot Christ's kingdom or the constitution of it be broken'. This kingdom that would know no 'corruption', in whatever sense, could transcend the power of earthly kingdoms. 'The administration of the covenant of grace in the gospel of Christ is no other thing than the very kingdom of heaven,' Marshall proclaimed. 'Let the men of the world esteem it a bondage, a drudgery, yet it's no less than a kingdom, yea a kingdom of heaven, which doth transcend all the kingdoms of this world.' It transcended them in the sense of providing for the kind of inward subjection and obedience of which no civil or coercive 'administration' was capable. 'The glory of Christ's government to his people stands in . . . being a king over them,' Marshall said, 'which no other government reacheth to, no not in any degree further than it is in subordination to Christ.'[43]

Like the law, then, civil governments demanded only 'political' compliance, but the preachers argued for something more secure. 'There is a twofold righteousness,' Obadiah Sedgwick said; 'one is political or civil, which consists in the due administration of justice or judgment; another is spiritual or heavenly, which consists in a renewed conformity of man's heart and life to the revealed will of God.' While only the one was 'political' in the traditional (and somewhat pejorative) sense, the other could also come to serve as an ethic for the pious public offical, and magistrates were expected to be merciful as well as just. 'Rulers must be men of mercy as well as of justice,' Sedgwick said, 'and it is the excellency of Christ's government that it is full of purity, and of equity, and of mercy.' Christ also served as the role model for the merciful judge, official, and citizen. 'What would Christ do nor not do in such a case?' Sibbes urged the conscientious soul to ask when faced with any moral uncertainty. 'Would Christ be cruel if he were on earth? Would he swear, and look scornfully upon others? Would he undermine others and cover all with a pretense of justice? Oh no! It is the devil's work to do so.' Mercy may not have been urged upon officials as frequently as was justice, but the point was that the two had to be reconciled in the office of a magistrate no less than they had been in that of Christ. 'The highest manifestation of God's justice . . . in which it and mercy did seem to be at an irreconcilable distance . . . [was] by making his son a surety to suffer punishment for man's sin,' said William Spurstowe. 'It should therefore be the greatest care of those who are called gods on earth to preserve the unity and concord of justice and mercy in the exercise of their office.'[44]

BLOOD

Yet this mercy and conciliation of Christ's government came at a price: not unlike earthly states, Christ's kingdom had been conceived in violent death, and the same might well be required of those who sought to enter it. 'If men will go to heaven they must be violent . . . sometimes to venture life itself and whatsoever is dear and precious in the world,' Sibbes warned. 'A man must be so violent that he must go through all, even death itself, though it be a bloody death, to Christ.' Christ was an agent of peace and conciliation, but even that was effected through a sacrifice: 'Without blood there is no remission of sin.' While the blood spilt founding and preserving earthly kingdoms continued to hang over the land as national crimes demanding vengeance or expiation, however, the blood of Christ did not necessarily call for revenge. 'The blood of all the prophets and righteous men, from Abel even unto Christ, fell so heavy upon the Jews that it is not yet fully expiated unto this day,' Cornelius Burges could declare, but such remarks had little practical relevance, given immediate circumstances; more typical was the emphasis on Christ's blood as that of forgiveness, which superseded any need to avenge it. 'His blood speaks better things than the blood of Abel,' William Price said. 'The one calls for vindictive justice, the other for pardoning mercy.' Arguably, the entire point of Christ's blood was that, unlike the human violence symbolized by Cain and Abel, it could not be revenged on earth; it provided a mechanism to end the vicious cycle of vengeance killing by directing the retribution against each and every soul. 'The blood of Abel cried against the wicked Cain,' said William Carter; 'much more the blood of Christ against our sins.' The blood shed by the secular state defiled the land; but blood, or at least a certain kind of blood, was also capable of washing (or purging) it clean again. 'Blood is of a defiling nature, but the blood of Christ cleanseth because it is a satisfactory blood,' said Sibbes. 'He died and was a sacrifice as a public person for us all.' The preachers exhibited an intense fascination with the cathartic power of 'blood', which symbolized both death and life and the dialectical relationship between them. 'Life comes through death; God comes in Christ, and Christ comes in blood to save,' said Nicholas Lockyer. 'The choicest mercies come through the greatest miseries; prime favors come swimming in blood to us.' While this imagery was present all along, it was made increasingly graphic by the events of war and revolution. 'God makes his way most beneficial when most bloody and difficult,' Lockyer proclaimed in 1645.

The like I may say of the blood that is now shed in England. Truth by fiery trials is made famous; Christ is clothed with scarlet and crowned with glory here . . . . What a noise hath Christ's blood made all the world over! And so the blood of martyrs, is it dried up yet? What virtues and graces smell so sweet and look so glorious as those that are died rose color with blood? . . . Blood hath a very crying voice: it cries up guilt to heaven, and so it cries up grace in heaven and earth; it makes Christ terrible, holiness immortal, truth eternal. What is written in blood never goes out, and all that read wonder.[45]

Christ's blood was his most significant feature – far more important than the good deeds he performed in his life. 'Was not the holy life of Christ enough?' William Carter asked. 'No, he must die, and it must be a cursed death. Nor will his body's death suffice; his soul must die . . . . Nor had all this been sufficient had not the blood of Christ been the blood of God.' Despite the apparent morbidity, there was a certain optimism in the assurance that Christ's blood could expiate more than the world could defile. 'Nothing can satisfy or appease [God's] anger but an infinite price,' declared James Nalton, 'even the precious blood of Jesus Christ, which being the blood of a person that is God as well as man is therefore called "the blood of God".' God took a body purely in order that its blood might be shed, which blood could also signify and sanctify those acts of self-sacrifice required in dedication to Christ, beginning as an allegory for simple repentance and extending literally as far as violent death itself. 'Without blood there is no remission of sin,' Samuel Bolton declared. 'Christ was wounded, and thou must be wounded; Christ did bleed, and conscience must bleed, before ever thou art pardoned.' The sacrifice of Christ remained superior to any other, whether literal or figurative, though it was often suggested that more might be necessary in imitation of his. 'No soul affliction will procure us peace and pardon without a sacrifice, for "without shedding of blood there is no remission of sin",' Lazarus Seaman declared. 'Neither may we trust so much to the sacrifice as to neglect the humbling of ourselves. But this is our comfort under the gospel, our atonement is already wrought out.'[46]

Christ might still be the prince of peace, but by directing the guilt and retribution for his blood against each and every sinner. 'There was no little price paid for little sins,' Edmund Calamy said. 'The least sin cost the shedding of the blood of the eternal God.' Moroever, the sins of England continued to spill not only Christ's blood but others' as well, and in this sense all sinners incurred the guilt of Christ's death. 'Oh consider what it is for so many thousands in England to remain guilty of the body and blood of the Lord Jesus,' lamented Francis Cheynell. 'Can a deluge of our blood wash away a guilt of so deep a dye?' Thomas Hill took the point further, asserting that, as with that of martyrs, God would eventually revenge the blood of his son. 'Oh then take heed of abusing the precious blood of this lamb by your sins,' he warned. 'As God will make inquisition for the blood of his saints, so for the blood of his son, and if now he should search England . . . would not many of our nobility and gentry, magistrates and ministers, as well as common people, be found guilty of the blood of Christ?' As with the blood of martyrs, the blood of Christ exalted his magistracy, nobility, and kingship above any human version, and the fear of violence and death for which his sacrifice atoned elevated the 'blood' of sacrifice above that of descent, which of all ranks alike was otherwise attainted. 'Ah what is an ocean of our blood to one drop of his?' asked Thomas Case. 'The best blood that runs in our veins is tainted with bastardy and treason. If we will not lose it for Christ and his gospel, we may lose it and Christ and his gospel.' Whatever value superior blood may have had, it was still mortal blood, or worse, tainted blood, and in any case worthless beside the blood that had been shed for their sins. 'The blood which you contemn is nobler than the noblest blood that runs in your veins,' Edmund Calamy told the peers. 'It is the blood of the eternal God, of that God before whom the great as well as the small must appear at the great day of judgment.' Increasingly, one's honor and nobility came to be defined by 'blood' in a very different sense than previously: '[not] by the blood of his progenitors but the blood of his martyrdom', as Francis Cheynell said, 'not by his birth but by his death'. While Protestant theology consistently recognized that in itself 'martyrdom is no merit', to be sacrificed as a martyr for Christ became the highest form of nobility. 'He dies the noblest death who dies a martyr,' Cheynell declared. 'You cannot be preferred to a higher degree of honor than to be esteemed the friends of Christ here and made co-heirs of Christ in glory.'[47]

Further, in a world threatened by corruption, death, and decay, Christ's blood promoted healing and life, including that of the ailing body politic. 'How much . . . will the powerful and gracious presence of . . . Jesus Christ put a new life into a dying soul or people?' Anthony Tuckney asked; 'the precious blood of our Savior, sprinkled upon whole nations as well as upon particular persons'. Yet healing might still involve the purging of bad blood, as the preachers liked to say. 'Christ can heal all our differences,' Jeremiah Whitaker told the House of Commons in 1643. 'He made God and man one, Jew and gentile one; he can much more make King and Parliament one, breaking down the walls of partition. That the blood of sprinkling may come upon our nation to expiate the blood and all the other crimes of this kingdom.' Christ's blood might still bring conciliation, including political conciliation, but the terms seemed to presuppose that some would refuse to be reconciled. 'God hath begun graciously to solder our divisions with . . . the blood of his son, the blood of reconciliation,' Thomas Case noted in 1642. 'Lords and Commons, city and country, brethren and brethren begin graciously to combine for the joint opposing of the common adversary and the carrying on of the great design.' Thus were civil as much as sacred affairs increasingly to be conducted, and to succeed or fail, according to the issue of blood. 'Know honorable worthies,' Nicholas Lockyer told the House of Commons in 1646, 'that the maturity of all results and debates, whether divine or civil, are to be looked upon by us . . . as the price of much blood, much precious blood – to wit, the blood of Christ and of many gallant men.' The blood of Christ, like that of gallant men, was sacred because it had been spent to obtain a kind of freedom – a 'spiritual' rather than a 'civil' freedom perhaps, but a freedom nonetheless. 'If civil freedoms are so precious and to be maintained, how much more our spiritual freedom, the freedom . . . so dearly purchased by the blood of Christ,' remarked Samuel Bolton. 'You esteem your civil freedoms the better in that they cost so much of the blood of your ancestors . . . . How much more should we esteem our freedom which was purchased by the blood of Christ.'[48]

What came to be known as 'the cause' of Christ would be advanced by the blood of Christ, the means and ends becoming indistinguishable. 'If you desire to be victorious,' urged Thomas Hill, 'appeal from second causes unto Jesus Christ and the merit of his blood.' Worldly affairs, as much as other-worldly, were to be seen as the fruits of sacrifice. 'We are to look upon outward deliverances as the fruit of Christ's blood,' said Jeremiah Burroughs. 'By the blood of the covenant are we delivered.' Further, the blood of Christ's testament came to be of special political significance as human blood came to be both endangered and defiled. 'God hath showed us in our blood what a fearful thing it is to be guilty of the blood of his son.' Especially insofar as the entire nation had come to be implicated in guilt and defilement, even the blood of kings might be required, the preachers were saying by the end of the decade, as expiation for that of the King of kings and his royal subjects. 'Thus will the Lord have blood for blood,' William Cooper proclaimed in 1649, 'not sparing the effusion of royal blood to avenge the blood royal of his children, whom he hath made kings and priests to himself through Christ Jesus and which cost the blood of his dear son.' Though the preachers may have insisted that the blood of Christ's followers was to be the first sacrificed in allegiance to him, the blood of those whom they described as his 'enemies' would also be required. 'There is a fire of civil war kindled in England, still burning in the bowels of it,' Edmund Staunton declared before the Long Parliament in 1644, 'and for my part I think there is but two bloods will quench it: the blood of Christ and of his desperate enemies. Free grace in God hath poured out the one; full justice in your honors should help to pour out the other.' Christ's blood was both the cause itself and the terms by which his followers were required to further it. 'Go you on, noble and resolute commanders, go on and fight the battles of the Lord Jesus Christ,' Stephen Marshall exhorted Parliament the same year. 'Christ shed all his blood to save you from hell. Venture all yours to set him upon his throne.' In the end, though, the preachers' enthusiasm for the power of blood and the bond it created, as well as the complex and confused emotions which these repeated demands for cleansing were an attempt to resolve, found no more cogent expression than in the haunted cadences of the tormented Nicholas Lockyer: 'The death of Christ . . . makes a death of guilt and a death of the very being of sin,' he announced in 1645.

The sin of this age is bloody wickedness; therefore do we bleed . . . . We crucify Christ, his truth, his people; therefore doth he crucify us . . . . You that kill not the lusts of this world, you kill Christ . . . and his blood shall be upon you, not to take off guilt, but to bind on guilt, till you die, till blood go for blood. 'Tis a very bloody time in which we live . . . . Poverty is marching towards us like an armed man; all is falling. Flesh shakes at this and treads upon Christ and treads out his bowels to keep up . . . . Christ is now avenging the blood of his covenant upon all that tread upon it. Men that do not take hold of his blood and death as to bleed and die with him – in name, main estate, in person – shall bleed and die by him.[49]

4

FAITH

How many truths . . . are by some in this age called into question . . . which former ages ever looked upon as undoubted and unquestionable.

John Brinsley, 1645

For all the emphasis on sin and judgment, a loving and merciful God was as much a part of Puritanism as was an angry and just one. One politically suggestive way of describing the problematic relationship between the two was as a series of 'laws' or 'contracts', under which the arraigned malefactor was first 'convicted' and 'sentenced' to death and then pardoned through the advocacy of Christ. 'When we are one with him once by faith, we have life from Christ, the life of reconciliation in law, opposite to our death in law and in sentence,' said Richard Sibbes. 'By nature we are all dead and damned . . . in sentence. Now by Christ there is a reversion of this sentence . . . . By our union with Christ we are alive in sentence. We are absolved in God's court of justice.' The accused was not so much acquitted as pardoned, and while some degree of rehabilitation was required, the pardon or 'justification' was owing not to any redeeming quality in the criminal but entirely to the 'free grace' of the judge. 'Free grace can find arguments for redemption when deserved justice might clothe us with desolation,' said Jeremiah Whitaker. 'No other ingredient goes into justification . . . but only free grace.'[1]

Yet grace did not simply erase guilt but satisfied the demands of justice by reforming the transgressor. 'God's forgiving and our forgoing sins are equal,' Samuel Bolton said. 'Grace in God forgives all sins, and grace in us enables us to forgo all sin.' Free grace did not abrogate moral responsibility then, and strictly speaking it did not even dissolve the freedom of the will, apparent polemical positions notwithstanding. 'Grace is that whereby God is free in giving to us,' Richard Vines said, 'and grace is that which makes our hearts free in obedience to him.' It was not that God did not use the will and that human acts were, therefore, not voluntary any more than that God suspended second causes in his punishments and deliverances; it was more that God simply controlled it as he controlled all things, and human actions were free only 'in obedience'. 'The will of man chooseth to come, and cannot do otherwise,' said Thomas Valentine, 'for it is moved and guided by a supernatural power.' The freedom of the will, then,

131

was a matter of definition, since a will in conflict with God was 'free' only for a futile struggle against overwhelming forces that he alone could control. 'There is nothing contrary to God in the whole world, nothing that fights against him but self-will,' Ralph Cudworth said. 'Happiness is that inward delight that will arise from the harmonious agreement between our wills and God's will.' The freedom or bondage of the will was to some extent determined by the attitude of the will itself, therefore, since only a will that freely accepted the supremecy of God's will and subjected itself to it could become what the preachers considered truly 'free'. 'When we have cashiered this self-will of ours, which did but shackle and confine our souls,' Cudworth continued, 'our wills shall then become truly free, being widened and enlarged to the extent of God's own will.'[2]

The relationship between divine determinism and human freedom, then, was not necessarily mutually exclusive but dialectical, since on the one hand there was a sense in which the human will on its own was indeed 'free' – free to rebel against its actual captivity. 'That which we call free will [may be] taken for a natural power [by which] the will is always free in earth and in hell,' Sibbes said, '. . . free to evil.' This was arguably not a 'true' freedom, however, but an illusion for what in reality was a kind of bondage. 'The will of man is slavish altogether without the spirit of God,' Sibbes continued. 'The spirit of God puts a new life into the soul of a man, and then . . . there is a liberty of will to that that is good.' Though divine grace was by definition not dependent upon human capabilities, it itself provided capability, since by enlightening the understanding grace freed the soul to make the only correct choice. 'The soul chooseth freely of its own will anything when it doth it upon discovery of light and reason,' Sibbes added. 'Then the soul doth things freely . . . . So that grace takes not away liberty. No, it establisheth liberty.' The soul was indeed required to 'choose', therefore, and was accountable for the choice it made, doing so 'freely'; but through grace that choice was made or 'determined' already. 'Where there is liberty and freedom there is an enlargement to understand more things than one, or else there were no freedom,' Sibbes said, 'and though the soul be determined to choose one thing and not many, yet of itself it hath power to choose many things.' By so freeing the will that it was at liberty to make a predetermined and correct 'choice', the spirit of grace saw to it that the human will was, in effect, forced to be free. 'When the spirit sets a man at liberty to holy things he is confined to good,' Sibbes said. 'He is . . . determined eternally to that that is good.'[3]

Yet one did not have to be utterly depraved to be without grace (or less than completely free), and the truly gracious continually strove for more. 'How is it possible that we should have too much of that whereof we can never have enough?' asked Henry Hall. 'A man that is in a violent strain . . . never thinks he hath virtue and grace enough; still he is aspiring and reaching after more.' Grace came to the soul during conversion, a process that demanded intense resolution and commitment. 'Conversion . . . must be . . . not merely philosophical to some low and general dictates of reason . . . not merely political, to credit or profit or secular ends,' said Edward Reynolds, but 'a full, thorough, constant, continued conversion, with a whole, a fixed, a rooted, a united and established heart, yielding up the whole conscience and conversation to be ruled by God's will in all things.' Such a conversion was not instantaneous but required a continual and even lifelong effort to bring the will into harmony with the will of God. 'A Christian is often converted,' Joseph Caryl asserted. 'His whole life upon earth is a continued conversion. A great deal of a Christian's progress is to go backward and much of his work the undoing of what he hath done.' The same could be said of entire nations: they were not converted quickly or once-and-for-all, but sometimes over many generations, often being interrupted by lapses and backslidings, and having to be converted all over again. 'It is a noble and a glorious undertaking . . . to take care that nations and kingdoms may be brought near to God,' Caryl told the House of Commons in 1646. 'Oh that it may be the honor of this present Parliament yet to advance a . . . conversion of England, that England may be converted beyond all former conversions.'[4]

This idea that conversion, whether of individuals singly or entire nations together, involved 'progress' (along with occasional digress and regress) was graphically represented in the familiar allegory describing conversion – and life – as a kind of 'journey' or 'pilgrimage', with the time on earth as a period of 'wayfaring'. 'A Christian's life is a mere pilgrimage,' John Whincop said. 'We are all strangers and pilgrims here, and the path we walk in must be humility.' In an age when travel was hazardous, the metaphor highlighted the difficulty and problems along the way, but also the transitory nature of the undertaking and the assurance that it was all leading somewhere, that there was to be a destination, a goal, an end. 'You have a great journey to take, from hell to heaven, from Egypt to Canaan, through the wilderness of this world,' Thomas Hill told Parliament. 'It is God's indulgence to offer himself to poor travelers . . . that going on they shall find rest for their souls . . . . Black clouds shall be blown over, the storm shall cease, travelers towards Zion shall enjoy a haven of tranquility.' Journeying involved continuous motion in which 'not to go forward is to go backward'. 'Walking is a moving forward . . . so that you make some progress,' Hill added. 'Though you be in the right way, yet if you stand still, you do not walk.' One also had to be sure one was indeed in 'the right way'. 'The Lord would have you carefully inquisitive after the good way because there are so many wrong and by-ways wherein you may miscarry,' Hill cautioned. 'The gate is strait, the way is narrow which leads to heaven, the passage is so difficult, the passengers are but few.' But the important thing was to keep moving, eyeing the final destination while disdaining the obstacles and hardships along the way. 'You must be industrious, inquisitive, persevering travelers,' Hill enjoined. 'Keep your eye upon your journey's end: look homeward; look heavenward. Though the journey itself be long from hell to heaven, the way narrow, full of difficulties . . . yet it leads to life.' In this pilgrimage through a cruel and hostile world God would be a constant companion, and diligent observation of his ways would impel the traveller onward by providing assurance of safe passage. 'This is indeed walking with God in the good way,' Hill said, 'observing of his daily providences, obediently delivering up yourselves to his commands, moving according to them.' In this way would the soul be moved 'voluntarily', from an inward motive that heavenly grace alone could provide. 'This walking must be a voluntary, a willing motion,' Hill said. 'Every godly man . . . moveth not like a terrified hypocrite from outward motives . . . but . . . there is an internal principle and a motive within . . . . He is not drawn nor driven, but he spontaneously moveth. . . . God's people are volunteers.'[5]

The metaphor of journeying was often coupled with another that might also apply to either persons or nations, or both together, and one that similarly suggested movement. 'As Christians . . . you are both wayfaring and warfaring men.' Matthew Barker said. 'Oh let nothing be able to divert you in the race you are running or to dismay you in the battles you are fighting.' This metaphor was elaborated with similar detail and could also be used in a personal as well as a collective sense. 'Every Christian's life is . . . a warfare,' Obadiah Sedgwick declared in 1639. 'We are no sooner born Christians but we enter ourselves soldiers.'

This world is the field. The faith of Christ is the quarrel. The army against us is large and strong, led on by that great general of all mischief, the devil. The main body of it consists of sinful flesh and many thousands of noisome lusts. The world flanks it on the right hand with many brave troops of honors, riches, and favors, on the left hand with many disgraces, contempts, troubles, losses, and death . . . . For the successful managing of this war against all these enemies we need more direction than our own.

For this management God had appointed his own commander, one who embodied the virtues of grace and charisma, along with all necessary materiel. 'You have a brave general to follow,' Sedgwick continued:

Jesus Christ; goodly weapons to handle, all the armor of God; a plain ground to fight on, his gospel; base enemies to set upon, sins and devils; a singular work to secure, your own souls; a little time for all this, your life; and after all a great reward, eternal glory.

Here too there was no standing still or going back, no halfway measures. 'March on still in the faith of Christ,' Sedgwick urged. 'Be not secure nor rash nor faint. Of necessity you must either conquer or be conquered . . . in this Christian warfare.'[6]

This, too, could be taken literally, though it involved a complex operation, the first step in which was a battle in its own right. 'Repentance is not without strife and conflict,' declared John Marston. 'It stirs up war in the soul.' As the first stage in conversion, repentance was an agonizing and often frustrating process, not simply being sorry for one's sins but coming to a full realization of the loathsomeness of one's entire self and pushing to the limits of consciousness one's sense of self-hatred. 'Repentance doth include not only a loathing of sin but also a loathing of ourselves for sin,' Thomas Brooks charged. 'True repentance will work your hearts not only to loathe your sins but to loathe yourselves.' Repentance then was not easy, particularly for those whose self-loathing made them especially conscious of their inadequacies. 'Repentance is a mighty work, a difficult work, a work that is above our power,' Brooks said. 'Repentance is a changing and converting . . . the whole man . . . both heart and life.' Repentance was assured of success however, because if sincere it involved not only a negative regret for evil acts but a positive process of 'turning' toward constructive ones. 'Repentance is not only a turning from all sin but also a turning to all good,' Brooks said. 'Repentance . . . includes an aversion from sin and conversion to God in Christ, whose blood cleanseth from all sin.' Moreover, as with the individual sinner, repentance could have a redemptive effect on entire nations as well, not only preserving but greatly improving them. 'National repentance will divert national judgments and procure national blessings,' said Edmund Calamy, 'so willing is [God] to encourage all men, especially . . . the representative body of his people, to . . . true repentance.' There seemed to be no middle ground, no purgatory between hell and heaven, and the reward for repentance was not simply survival, but welfare, even great prosperity. 'If that nation against which he hath pronounced the evil of punishment turn from their evil of sin, then will God repent of the evil he intended to do unto them,' Calamy promised. 'And not only so but he will build and plant that nation and of a barren wilderness make it a fruitful paradise.'[7]

Conversion, then, though it began with a negative repentance, was foremost a positive belief. 'A truly broken spirit is also a believing spirit,' said Francis Roberts, who saw the two as brethren in the spiritual rebirth. 'Faith and repentance are inseparable twins, bred together in one and the same sanctified womb of the converted soul.' While repentance was the pivotal act of turning from sin to God, faith alone engaged the covenant of grace and made it operative in the soul. 'We come to enter into this covenant with Jesus Christ . . . by faith alone,' Calamy said. 'Faith is that grace on our part by which we are grafted into the second Adam and so in his covenant.' Without faith the operation, the very notion of the covenant of grace, was meaningless. 'We have no more good out of the covenant of God than we have faith in it,' said Joseph Caryl. 'We live no more in the sphere of a covenant than we believe.'[8]

TRUTH

Faith of course was the essence of all religion, though in none was it integrated with such conscious determination into the content of its own doctrine as in Protestantism: faith not only constituted the central tenet of Protestant doctrine but also made the doctrine itself work by 'applying' the covenant of grace to the believing sinner. 'Not upon us but Christ he hath laid the punishment,' John Ellis said. 'He is reconciled by the blood of his son which . . . leaves . . . no blame or accusation, so that it being applied by faith, God himself hath nothing to lay to our charge.' This stipulation that religion, however 'true' in the abstract, required for its efficacy a practical 'application' through the faith of living souls transformed Protestant theology from an abstract dogma into a vital and dynamic ideology. 'True faith doth answer this particular love and gift of Christ by applying it to itself,' said Richard Sibbes. 'True faith is an applying faith. It doth appropriate Christ to itself . . . . The nature of faith is to make generals become particulars.' This tension between faith as an abstract objective 'truth', which could never be questioned, and a practical subjective 'application', about which there would always be lingering doubts, described a sharp spiritual conflict within the soul of the struggling believer. 'A man never enjoys his own assurance of Christ's particular love, but with a great deal of conflict,' Sibbes observed, explaining that 'there are two grounds that faith lays: that general truth, that whosoever casts himself upon Christ shall be saved; the particular application hereof, but I cast myself upon Christ, therefore I shall be saved'. To believe the first was relatively easy; it was with the second that the trouble arose:

> This particular application, which is the work of faith, is mightily assaulted, more than the general . . . . There is a mighty conflict before it comes . . . . There is no Christian but he finds his particular faith strongly assaulted, more than his general . . . . All who have experience know what this spiritual conflict with an unbelieving heart means, when it comes to application.

'Faith' thus involved a complicated dialectical interaction between the objective and the subjective, the theoretical and the practical – 'either the principles of Christian religion', as Sibbes said, 'or the inward disposition of the soul towards them'. The inseparable interplay between the two was conveyed with a deceptive simplicity in the use of the common term. 'The same word implies the truths themselves, and the affection and disposition of the soul toward them,' Sibbes observed.

> Why is religion itself called faith, and the grace of the soul also called faith? To show that faith, that is, the truth revealed, it breeds faith, and must be apprehended by faith. Therefore one word includes both the object, the thing believed, and likewise the disposition of the soul to that object.[9]

For the gospel to come true – effectively for it to *be* true – it had to be believed, and above all it had to be believed for oneself. 'The gospel, though it be a sovereign and medicinal thing in itself, yet the mere knowing and believing of the history of it will do us no good,' Ralph Cudworth warned. 'We can receive no virtue from it till it be made ours and become a thing living in our hearts.' The 'truth' involved was understood to be objectively and absolutely true, and the preachers (at times) denied that it was the belief itself that actually made the doctrine true. 'We are bound to believe that the thing is true before we can believe our share in it,' said John Preston. 'We do not therefore make it true because we believe, but our believing presupposeth the object of our faith . . . . The very believing doth not cause Christ to be given, but he is given, and therefore we believe.' And yet there was an inescapable sense in which believers did make it true because they believed and their very believing did cause Christ to be given, and even the doctrine itself insisted as much. 'This very belief, that faith shall be victorious, is a means to make it so indeed,' Sibbes pointed out. 'Believe it, therefore, that . . . it shall prevail.' Faith was self-fulfilling, since the very 'truth' of the doctrine itself was 'twofold': '*objective*, as it lies in the scriptures', and '*subjective*, as seated in us, which we seek from the word'. Not only were the two inseparable, but neither could conceivably be effective or true without the other, and the result was described as a 'double faith': 'the true doctrine of faith' and 'the saving grace of faith'; 'one which is believed is called doctrinal faith', 'another by which we believe is called habitual faith'. The two acceptations of the word 'faith' interacted dialectically to reinforce the 'truth' which together they contained, and in fact they were often then synthesized into a third which may indicate the purpose behind the connection between them: 'It is a useful distinction of "faith" into a faith *which we believe* – thus our creed is objectively called our faith – a faith *by which we believe* – the habit, the grace of faith . . . – and a faith *by which we are believed*, trusted by others . . . . We are used to call it fidelity or faithfulness.' This last applied not only to man but to God as well, and in such a way that each guaranteed that of the other. 'Now this fidelity is expressible towards God and towards man,' William Price said. 'And indeed the one seconds and attends the other.'[10]

In their doctrinaire moods the preachers insisted that faith had to be inculcated simply as objective and absolute truth. 'The judgment is to be enlightened by doctrine before the affections are set on fire,' said Thomas Watson. 'Doctrine . . . is of use to strengthen the faith of weak Christians, and to put courage into them that are fearful and cowardly in our land, now in these perilous times.' But if Protestant doctrine, even more than others, seemed by its nature to demand the indoctrination of believers, the preachers demanded more than simply a blind assent to a series of abstract tenets and in fact encouraged a strong measure of incredulity in the acceptance of any dogma. 'Try all things,' urged Thomas Hill. 'Take nothing upon trust . . . . Swallow not things credulously, but consider, examine them . . . . It is not safe for any to receive matters of religion without serious examination.' The preachers saw a place for dogma, but they did not want a faith that was that alone and urged scrutiny if not skepticism even in examining what they regarded as the truth. 'No man should be moved by an implicit faith,' Simeon Ash warned, 'but everyone should be fully persuaded in his own mind.' True faith was more than simply being persuaded in an abstract, purely intellectual sense, since by its nature faith would have to be tested and relied upon in times of hardship and trial. 'Faith is more than a naked, hungry, and poor assent to the truth,' said Samuel Rutherford. 'There is in it a fiducial acquiescence and a leaning upon the Lord.' One had not only to agree in theory but to believe in practice, and for all their moral absolutism, almost inseparable from this was a kind of relativism that defined truth in terms of the subjective attitudes and social circumstances within which it proved itself. 'There must be a *consent* as well as an *assent*,' Preston demanded. 'It is the act of the understanding to assent to the truth . . . but . . . there is also an act of the will requisite to consent unto them . . . to apply them to a man's self.' Faith activated the 'truth' of the doctrine and actually made it 'real' to the believer, working its way not merely into the mind but into the soul. 'Let us labor to make those truths which we understand our own by mixing them with faith,' urged John Maynard. 'We cannot make the truth our own . . . unless we so mix and temper it with faith as that . . . our souls become one with it.'[11]

The preachers, in fact, never assumed belief and sought adherents who would believe not simply because custom and tradition led them to believe, or because they were taught to believe or because their parents believed. 'It is a base thing to say, I believe as my parents believe,' Sibbes remarked. 'A Christian doth not say, I was brought up to this, or I cannot do otherwise, but I do it from a principle . . . . That is the nature of faith.' In the restless search for certitude amid the bewildering perplexities and disappointments of the time, the true Christian believed in faith because there was nothing else left to believe in. 'It is no easy thing to be a Christian,' Sibbes lamented. 'His life is uncertain, his estate in the world is changeable here, his life is as a vapor, and the comforts of life are less than life . . . . Yet a Christian hath comfort here, the promises are . . . made his own by faith.' What may appear as an eagerness to surrender one's critical faculties in blind devotion to a simplistic ideological escape began at least as precisely the opposite, a searching skepticism that defiantly refused to place unquestioning faith in anything other than faith itself, and far from being the easy answer of the ignorant, the doctrine of faith alone constituted the final culmination of a process of relentless inquiry that was only credible once every other potential object of faith had been called into question and found wanting. 'When all things else leave him . . . when riches leave him, when friends leave him, when honor and great places leave him, when his life and senses leave him, when all leave him, yet faith will never leave him.'[12]

Yet, if the logic of this unsparing sense of disbelief was to reject every tangible, material object in favor of an abstract doctrine that was not subject to verification except insofar as people believed it, the burden this placed on the believer was almost unbearable. 'If thou wilt search into the bottom of thine heart, and not superficially,' said Matthew Barker, 'thou shalt find it a hard matter to believe and rest steadfastly on God.' While in theory the ministers unequivocally 'believed' in a creed of justification by faith therefore, in practice, as they were the first to insist, the most difficult feat for the human will was to believe. 'When once you come to know what it is to believe, you will say, Oh it is a harder thing to believe than to do anything,' William Bridge warned. 'I do not know anything in all the world that is so hard as to believe.' A faith that was merely routine or habitual was certainly a faith that was false, and all sin could even be traced to unbelief. 'All . . . transgressions . . . may . . . be . . . reduced to . . . unbelief,' argued John Lightfoot. 'Unbelief is as level to our sinful nature, and as daily acted, as any sin whatsoever.' By equating all sin with unbelief the preachers turned all sins into ideological sins, sins not simply of the body and flesh but of the mind and soul. 'A man can never believe as he should who is not humbled for his unbelief,' said Bridge. 'And he is not far from faith . . . that is humbled for unbelief.' The only way to truly believe was first to realize how far every failure and inadequacy stemmed from insufficient belief. 'If you would be truly humbled and not be discouraged . . . then [trace] all your sins to your unbelief,' Bridge urged. 'Say, this hath my unbelief done. . . . Oh, what an unbelieving heart have I! The Lord heal my unbelieving heart.' And as Bridge said, the dialectic so worked that, if sin was attributable to unbelief, the fear of this very unbelief was the first realization of faith. 'So far as a good man is sunk in unbelief, so far he will rise in faith,' Bridge added. 'So much as a man is shaken by unbelief . . . so much he will rise . . . and be confirmed and steeled in it.'[13]

The first thing the preachers assumed about their prospective followers, then, was not that they were believers but that they were by nature unbelievers. 'We are all by nature enemies to God,' Francis Cheynell said. 'We do naturally conceive an atheistical hatred against him.' Such an attitude would seem to indicate a certain ambivalence however, in which not only did people naturally not believe but they did not want to believe, and possibly the first emotion they felt toward God as they did begin to believe was, in fact, hate. 'The carnal heart of man is a poisonful thing and hates God naturally,' Sibbes argued. 'It wishes that there were no God . . . . He wisheth with all his heart, Oh that there were no God!' Faith may well have originated as a method of controlling hate, which it first directed at God; certainly the preachers were aware of its ferocious power. 'Hatred [is] the strongest, deepest, and steadiest affection of the soul,' said Sibbes. 'Hatred is an implacable and irreconcilable affection.' After hate God was to be feared, and fear, whether of one's own unbelief or of the external adversity that exacerbated it, was arguably the beginning of faith. 'Fear is (in some respect) God himself,' said Obadiah Sedgwick. 'Fear doth . . . deify God.' Fear decidedly was to be encouraged, since fear was also one of the strongest of human motivations and faith was a means of harnessing its power. 'Faith will teach you to fear, and fear will prevent feeling,' said William Jenkyn. 'There is nothing more suspicious and more inquisitive than fear.' A recognition of God's presence began with fear, and true faith required a large measure. 'This fear must be serious,' Sibbes demanded. 'This fear must be total.' If love was the vanguard of faith, fear followed up the rear. 'Fear doth guard all our guards,' Sedgwick said. 'All our graces are preserved by fear . . . . Oh that we did repent and fear, believe and fear, pray and fear, do every fit work and still fear.' Fear alone was not faith, however, and the two could be sharply contrasted. 'Fear may restrain, though it cannot renew men,' said Samuel Bolton. 'Fear may suppress sin, though faith alone doth conquer and overcome sin.' Further, faith could even act as an antidote to fear. 'They who have little faith have much fear,' said Joseph Caryl, 'and they who have no faith are in a readiness to be all fear, to be slain by fear.' But the two also worked in close cooperation with one another. 'As faith hath promises and experiences as its ground,' said John Bond, 'fear hath threatenings.'[14]

The reason for the apparent ambivalence was that faith did refer to 'threatenings' as well, even temporal ones, though in this it merely extended the natural faculties of sense and reason into the future. 'The Lord foreshoweth the ruin of a nation to his own people in . . . his word,' Thomas Carter explained, 'and by an eye of faith it is discernible.' In contrast to a simple understanding of 'natural causation', faith alone made even threatened judgments certain and the believer a prophet. 'Not only when it is so near that obvious to sense or discernible to reason in the natural cause of it but while it is afar off . . . before it comes forth and only discernible by an eye of faith,' Carter added. 'And indeed though the judgment be future and at present invisible, as being not yet existent, yet by faith it is made as evident and certain to the faithful as if [it] was now acting before their eyes.' This orientation of faith toward the future, with respect to judgments initially, became far more important as it foresaw mercies, and if it merely augmented sense and reason in perceiving the threatenings of the law, it stood alone in comprehending the promises of the gospel. 'There is nothing in nature that can help us to the attaining of faith,' explained John White.

> Sense cannot help us, for the objects of faith . . . have no present being but are in hope and expectation only. Much less can reason help faith, seeing that takes all her grounds from sense . . . . No, sense and reason are so far from helping faith that they are the most dangerous . . . to hinder it or overthrow it where it is.

In that judgments and adversity took place through nature, they might be perceived and understood through sense and reason; but while faith too had reference to judgments, sense and reason had no role in perceiving or understanding mercies. 'It is the proper work of faith to look on both sides of God's dispensation and of our own condition,' said William Bridge. 'There is a dark side of a dispensation, and there is a light side thereof. Sense and reason look on the dark side alone; faith seeth both sides.' As a result, sense and reason produced discouragements in the face of adversity, since they could perceive and calculate weakness but not strength. 'The principles of sense and reason can behold and view all the power that is against them,' Stephen Marshall explained.

> The temptations and allurements of the devil, the world, and the flesh are all agreeable to our corrupt nature, and . . . the opposition which the wisdom, authority, and power which all the kingdoms and men of the world make against the saints appear in its full strength . . . . Sense and reason sees their weakness but sees nothing of their strength.[15]

In times of adversity, sense and reason produced 'pretexts', which in the preachers' view were little more than excuses, and believers were urged to shut their eyes and ears to whatever apparent facts the devil might place in their path. 'These pretexts are used against a God that gets over all excuses,' William Jenkyn asserted. 'Satan undoeth most this way; if he can make them stop and stagger and hesitate by an excuse, he will soon make them fall.' These pretexts and excuses, though some might be tempted to regard them as unpleasant realities, were for the faithful nothing but 'appearances' (or what the preachers called, in another context, 'images'). 'The shadow of a pretext may more affect us than the substance of a precept,' Jenkyn said. 'And why should it be followed, suggesting only appearances, when as it will not let us follow God, though he propounds realities?'[16]

Things comprehended by faith were thus as 'real' as those known by the natural faculties. 'Divine objects seen by faith carr[y] with them as much evidence, certainty, and assurance as any natural thing that we apprehend by any or all our natural senses.' What these divine objects were was not important, since unlike the knowledge of tangible things, faith was its own 'substance' and supplied its own 'evidence'. 'The object of hope is things invisible,' Jeremiah Whitaker said, 'and faith must be the ground of such things hoped for, and the only evidence we can have for those things that are not seen.' That faith did not fasten on material objects was precisely its strength: it provided its own 'substance'. 'Faith is the substance of things hoped for,' William Reyner quoted Paul. 'It . . . gives comfort and confidence concerning them.' Similarly, unlike faculties of perception, faith did not merely not use evidence but was itself evidence. 'Faith is the evidence of things not seen,' Walter Cradock pointed out. 'He doth not say that faith is an opinion, a probability, a conjecture or a wild guess, but faith is the *evidence* of things not seen.' Faith broke down the limitations of time and provided believers with the perspective of the eternal and omniscient one himself. 'Faith doth give a man the true prospect of things, past, present, and to come, and of things as they are,' said Willliam Bridge. 'If you would see things past, present, and to come, then grow in faith and . . . shall you be able to see things afar off.' That an object of faith seemed to have no present existence told nothing against veracity of faith or the reality of what it foresaw across the barriers of time and temporality. 'So our faith might prevent time and make those things present to our minds for the comfort of our hearts, which in themselves are future and have no being at all,' Francis Cheynell urged, 'let us fix our faith in Jehovah our God.'[17]

Faith, then, which often seemed to take the form of a stubborn refusal to recognize obvious facts, was, in reality, a defiant refusal to accept the world as it was or as the empirical and rational faculties of the mind insisted it must always be, and this rejection of the claims to primacy made by the methods of observation and logic, along with the usual understanding of 'substance' and rules of 'evidence', was not necessarily a resort to the imaginary or the irrational by ignorant minds, but a desperate groping by destitute souls after what the preachers called 'hope'. 'Hope is the main supporting grace of the soul,' said Richard Sibbes, 'springing from faith in the promises of God.' Religion may not have given people much else in this world, but it could not be denied that it did at least give them hope. 'This is God's constant dispensation, while we live in this world we are always under hope,' Sibbes said. 'We are children of hope. We are saved by hope.' Because faith did not promise anything concrete, did not depend upon any of the untrustworthy things perceived or understood by human faculties, it was able to provide this hope. 'If thou hast faith, thou hast hope,' said John Preston. 'Hope is the property of faith; where there is faith there is hope.' Hope was among the most basic of human needs, especially in times of trouble and among those who saw themselves as the uprooted and rejected of the earth. 'A hopeless condition is a very sad condition,' lamented Thomas Brooks.

> It is the worst condition in the world; it makes a man's life a very hell . . . .
> The loss of hope will make the soul languish; it will make it choose strangling rather than life; it will make a man's life a continual death . . . . A man had better part with anything than his hope.

Hope promised the soul that things would someday be better and so gave it something to look forward to amid present hardships and the strength of mind to stand against otherwise overwhelming difficulties and to overcome endless obstacles and discouragements. 'A saint's hope will outlive all fears and cares, all trials and troubles, all afflictions and temptations,' Brooks promised.

> Saints have much in hope, though little in hand . . . . A saint can truly say, 'I hope for better things.' . . . Hope can see light through darkness, life through death, smiles through frowns, and glory through misery. Hope . . . makes a Christian to stand and triumph over all afflictions, oppositions, and temptations.[18]

Hope was the combined product of fear and love, as well as the avoidance of either presumption or – most dreadful of all – despair. 'Presumption and despair are both of them contrary to hope,' Thomas Valentine said. 'Both are bad, but the very name of despair seems more horrid . . . . Presumption lifts men up as high as heaven and then lets them fall as low as may be. Despair throws them directly down to hell.' There were many possible sources of this most feared of conditions; any kind of human misfortune or sorrow, disappointment or failure, could bring a soul to the brink of despondency. 'The miseries before man are the dangerous snare which the devil lays for the destruction of the soul,' said William Perkins, '. . . that the soul of man may be swallowed up of the gulf of final despair.' Hopelessness and despair were evidently widespread in English society at the time, judging from the attention the preachers devoted to them, and possibly the greatest problems they confronted among their most devoted followers. 'Despairing sinner . . . thou art in hell upon earth,' declared Nicholas Lockyer. 'Despair is the black seal of the bottomless pit.' Despair was the fear of being overwhelmed by the forces of adversity, feelings of helplessness and inadequacy out of control. 'Many despair of help because of their own unworthiness, as though there were no hope of God's mercy,' said Richard Greenham. 'He which despairs makes all the promises of God to be false.'[19]

And yet, while despair was naturally more horrifying than presumption for the soul experiencing it, despair was also by its nature a condition to which God-fearing people were especially prone. 'When a godly man is tempted to any sin, if he fall into it, then he is tempted again with unbelief to . . . aggravate his sin and to despair,' said William Bridge. 'When a wicked man is tempted to what is evil, if he fall into it, then he is tempted to presume, tempted to excuse his sin.' This very understanding of the dialectic not only brought hope amid despair but could make the despair itself the source of hope. 'A holy despair in ourselves is the ground of true hope,' said Sibbes; 'not the despair of the damned, but a good despair, when we are utterly out of all hope of salvation in respect of our own strength, virtues, works, or anything that we can possibly do.' It was not always easy to discern the difference in practice, but that was part of how it worked, since despair, however terrifying in itself, was necessary for hope to follow. 'In true humiliation is a holy desperation,' Perkins said, 'which is when a man is wholly out of all hope ever to attain salvation by any strength or goodness of his own, speaking and thinking more vilely of himself than any other can do.' Faith by its nature even thrived on despair, and whether one's despair was 'holy' or not depended on understanding the seemingly contradictory ways of God. 'Despair is oft the ground of hope,' said Sibbes. 'That which to a man unacquainted with God's dealings is a ground of utter despair, the same to a man acquainted with the ways of God is a rise of exceeding comfort.' A soul that made use of the dialectic to take renewed resolution from the very frightenings and frustrations that tormented it was a soul that could also learn to thrive on sorrow and adversity. 'The soul must be raised to right grief,' said Sibbes. 'Despair to such is the beginning of comfort, and trouble the beginning of peace. A storm is the way to a calm, and hell the way to heaven.' Like God's ways in the world, like the covenants of scripture, faith itself, especially when it came to providing hope in the midst of despair, was by its nature dialectical. 'Faith . . . will believe in contraries,' said Sibbes. 'Faith knows that God works by contraries.'

When a man is in despair . . . faith knows that it is God that comforts the abject, raises the dead . . . making our extremity his opportunity. So faith reasons . . . Doth he thus and thus work by contraries? Then I will answer his working the same way; I will believe one contrary in another, I will expect . . . wonderful changes in our greatest miseries.[20]

In that it was conceived in the first place to derive hope from the throes of despair, glory from the depths of shame, strength from the face of weakness, faith, and with it the true believer, was strengthened by opposition. 'Considering all things conduce unto our good, though in appearance never so opposite . . . then I must believe against belief; I must stand firm against contraries; my faith must answer his manner of working and believe that God can bring me to honor by shame and to heaven by hell,' said Sibbes. 'For if it be his course first to cast down and then to lift up, by disgrace to bring his servants to glory, then in all my extremities I must rest upon God, who is never nearer unto his to succor them than when he seems to be furthest off.' Faith was born of struggle and opposition, and the presence of strife and conflict, whether in the outer forces of the world or in the inner torments of the soul, or both together, was itself an indication that the dialectic was at work. 'Contraries, the nearer they are one to another, the sharper is the conflict betwixt them,' Sibbes said. 'The more grace . . . the more antipathy to the contrary; whence none are so sensible of corruption as those that have the most living souls.'[21]

Faith thus turned the power of evil and adversity back against itself, augmenting its own strength in the process, and so was able to survive and increase when all else faltered. 'Faith liveth and breatheth in the grave, in the throat of hell,' said Samuel Rutherford. 'Faith can make a passage between hell and heaven.' The entire purpose of faith was to help the soul overcome adversity, discouragements, obstacles, temptations, guilt, and spiritual 'disquiet', and far from requiring any human ability or strength, sense or reason, love or assistance, faith could operate freely only in their absence. 'We should learn to come to Christ with an empty hand and not to be discouraged for any want that we find in ourselves,' said John Preston. 'Faith . . . doth its work best alone, and faith is so far from requiring anything . . . that necessarily he must let go all things else, otherwise he cannot believe.' This very demand for renunciation of all possible helps and hopes that might compromise faith was what the preachers meant when they insisted on justification by faith 'alone'. 'Faith is so far from requiring anything to be added to it to help it in the act of justifying that of necessity it excludes all things else,' Preston insisted. 'For faith hath this double quality, not only to lay hold of Christ offered, but to empty a man of all things else.' Faith by definition worked only when nothing else did and had efficacy only when there seemed to be efficacy in nothing else, and the anguished soul only came to truly believe in Christ once it had reached the point where it could no longer believe in anything else, and above all when it could no longer believe in itself. 'Every man is apt to think that it is impossible that God should accept him unless there be something in him why God should regard him,' Preston observed. 'He thinks that Christ will never look after him. But you see that faith requires nothing . . . for all that faith hath to do is only to take from Christ that righteousness that we want ourselves.' Faith enabled weak and fearful souls with a new strength to surmount whatever difficulties and afflictions they might encounter by uniting them with the power of Christ. 'Can I have the strength of Christ?' Jeremiah Burroughs asked. 'Yea, it is made over to thee by faith . . . . Faith draws strength from Christ.' The faith of Christ supported and strengthened those who had lost faith in themselves, and believers were to live entirely in Christ and to believe that though they themselves might be worthless and poor, they would be powerful and honorable in him. 'A believer is strong in Christ, rich in faith because rich in Christ,' said Francis Cheynell. 'He is nothing in himself and all things in Christ.'[22]

Faith thus took people who, owing to the fact or fear of poverty, frustrated ambitions, disappointed expectations, or from whatever form of social disgrace or personal failure, lacked a sense of self-respect and self-esteem and taught them a different standard by which to measure their worth. 'Faith teacheth a man, when he is an heir of heaven, not to value himself by earthly things,' Sibbes explained. 'He values not himself by his honors, nor dignity, nor by the things that he hath here; nor he doth not disvalue himself by poverty or disgrace . . . . Christians are kings and heirs; they esteem not or disesteem of themselves by what they have here below.' This yearning for 'esteem' lay at the heart of Puritan faith, as indicated by the vehemence with which the preachers endlessly lavished it upon the Almighty himself. 'There must be an estimation, an esteem of God and Christ,' Sibbes asserted. 'There must be a high esteeming, and valuing, and prizing of God above all things in the world.' However bleak one's prospects might appear, faith restored self-confidence amid the despondency of failure, and while Puritanism has come to be synonymous with a dour and ascetic disposition, the preachers themselves insisted it was all merely a necessary stage through which the soul had to pass in preparation for a final joy. 'Humble, broken-hearted Christians . . . so mopish and cast down, as though Christianity were a life of perpetual sorrow and not rather of perpetual rejoicing' was a character trait Sibbes both recognized and lamented. 'Our blessed Savior indeed shows that mourners are blessed, but it is chiefly because it ends in joy.' This joy was not an unbridled, temporary enthusiasm but on the contrary a sober, constant, enduring quality that itself came from the protection it provided from erratic and violent swings of mood. 'Joy is the constant temper which the soul should be in,' said another minister. 'Our joy is not a riotous, loose joy, but a religious, regulated, sober joy.' A consistent cheerfulness under all circumstances, however elusive to attain and painful to maintain, indicated a sound and successful faith. 'Where there is faith there is joy,' Preston proclaimed. 'If thy joy be right . . . a joy that is so great as that it exceeds all other joy, if this joy do but hold out in tribulation, it is a certain sign thy faith is good.'[23]

Though faith was important for its own sake, it had to be defined in specific terms, and it had to be the same for all. 'Remember that your faith must be the faith of Christians, not the faith of devils,' Francis Cheynell said. 'It must be such a precious faith as . . . assents and consents to Christ.' And the original source of all Christian faith was 'the word'. 'We must be sure to build our faith upon a firm foundation,' John White asserted, 'which can be none other than the faithful word of God.' The Bible itself commanded faith, and the most effective foundation for any faith was a written one. 'Faith and the word of God must run parallel,' Anthony Burges said. 'All that is written must be believed, and all that is believed must be written.' When people changed, when the world changed, the writings alone were constant. 'Let us build our faith upon that which shall stand forever, upon the word of God only,' Cheynell said. 'Our faith builds for eternity, and therefore we had need build upon that which will stand forever.' A faith so constructed upon the word would make the believer as constant and enduring, as immutable and eternal, as scripture itself. 'Such a man will be sure and constant in his way,' Burges promised, 'for as the truth is yesterday, and today, the same forever, so also will the frame and temper of the man be the same forever.' By absorbing the scriptures as faith, the soul too could remain constant amid the upheavals of the world. 'Thou mayest safely build thy faith upon the holy scriptures,' Cheynell urged. 'Though the kingdoms of the earth be shaken, yet the words of God will stand and stand forever.' Indeed, scripture provided the solution to, as well as simply an escape from, the shaking kingdoms of the earth. 'There is as much ground in scripture for faith to build on for the present temporal salvation of this distressed kingdom,' Joseph Caryl said, with some understatement, 'as any man at first hath or had in scripture to believe his eternal salvation.'[24]

Scripture sustained faith because, while it did describe 'threatenings', scripture was most important as literally the 'word' of God: it contained 'promises'. 'Faith acts in the strength, upon the truth and goodness of a promise,' Caryl said. 'Faith . . . must have a promise in the word or promise in the works of God to rest upon.' The promise in the 'works' of God will be discussed later; foremost was that of his 'word'. 'He not only gives us his word, but a binding word, his promise,' said Sibbes, 'and . . . hath entered into a covenant with us . . . sealed by the blood of the Lord Jesus.' The power of promises was that they were, in one sense or another, certain. 'God's promises concerning things most difficult and impossible things in man's eye are notwithstanding certain and infallible,' said John White. 'The promises of God are as certain as if they were already accomplished.' In what sense they were certain and were to be accomplished was variable, but it was this that impelled the ministers in their devotion to 'truth'. 'He is a God of truth,' John Owen asserted. 'The truth of God in his promises and engagements requires an accomplishment of them whatever it cost.' Whatever else happened in the world, the God of truth would remain trustworthy and keep his promise. 'God cannot be worse than his word,' said Thomas Palmer.

> God will not deceive those that trust to him, that depend upon him. Deliverance may be deferred, but it shall not fail. . . . [He] will have a great care to keep his word, his promise. . . . The very fabric of the world may be dashed and broken, yet God will not break his word.[25]

This need for 'truth', for something trustworthy and dependable when all else was either in doubt or proved to be false, was not simply a rhetorical abstraction but an essential element of any stable social order, and if faith was the essence of religion, faithfulness was central to the maintenance of secular society as well. 'No one thing does more strongly unite or hold together a commonwealth,' asserted John Cardell, 'than fidelity.' For any society to operate there had to be a modicum of mutual trust and credibility among the members, since no business of state or society could be effectively conducted amid an atmosphere of suspicion and distrust. 'Because man is a sociable creature, one man naturally oweth that to another without which human society cannot be preserved,' Charles Richardson explained in more secularized terms. 'Men cannot live and converse together unless they believe and trust one another, as manifesting the truth one to another.' And yet for all the commonplace assertion that man was such a sociable creature, in actual fact the uncertain condition of society had made it all too apparent that most people were not always dependably 'faithful', worthy of 'trust', and manifesting the 'truth' to one another. 'Every man is a liar,' Sibbes declared; 'that is, he is false.'

> But God is essentially true . . . . Therefore ever, when thou art disappointed with men, retire to God and to his promises . . . . With men there is breach of covenant, nation with nation, and man with man. There is little trust to be had in any. But in all confusions here is comfort. A religious person may cast himself boldly into the arms of the Almighty, and go to him in any distress, as to a faithful creator that will not forsake him.

The promises of God were thus a substitute for those who felt they had been let down by the promises of society, and when people seemed most unfaithful, most deceitful and scheming and devoid of scruples, ever ready to defraud or betray one another for the sake of their own private gain or advancement, whether in the world of commerce or law or government or any other public or private relationship where the absence of good faith could create rivalry and discord – then was the time to go to him who was always trustworthy and could never lie. 'Considering therefore that God is so faithful every way in his promises and in his deeds,' Sibbes urged, 'let us . . . in all the unfaithfulness of men whom thou trustest depend upon this, that God is still the same and will not deceive thee.' This sharp polarity between the trustworthiness of God and the falseness of men may well have expressed the disillusionment fostered by the ruthless practices of an increasingly competitive and commercial society. 'This should comfort us when men deal loosely with us and fail in their promises . . . when men deal falsely with us,' Sibbes said.

> There is nothing that makes an honest heart wearier of this wicked world, than the consideration of the falsehood of men in whom they trust. Oh! it is a cruel thing to deceive . . . . It is a treacherous thing, but this world is full of such treacherous dealing that a man can scarce trust assurances . . . . But there are things thou mayest trust . . . there are promises . . . there is a God that keeps covenant.[26]

At a time when no one could be safely 'trusted' these were the qualities to be found in God and imparted to believers by religion: those of 'truth' and 'faithfulness'. 'Another attribute is God's faithfulness,' Jeremiah Burroughs said. 'Thou hast to deal with a God of infinite truth and faithfulness. And likewise thou must bring a faithful heart suitable some way to this faithfulness of God.' God was not only himself faithful, but also the font of all fidelity elsewhere, even the imperfect trustworthiness of man. 'Whence is it that men are faithful in their relations one towards another?' asked Sibbes. 'Is it not from God? . . . Shall not he be most faithful that makes other things faithful?' Moreover, just as knowledge of faithfulness created trust, so conversely the very act of trusting itself encouraged fidelity, and when 'honored' with trust, God too would prove himself worthy of it. 'We must trust God if ever we expect any good at his hands, and our dependence on him binds him to be the more faithful to us,' Sibbes said. 'Trust begets fidelity . . . . When God is honored with our trusting of him, it makes him faithful.' This honor which God derived from being trusted was also the reason that unbelief was so fearful, since it constituted perhaps the supreme 'dishonor' to God. 'God stands upon his truth and faithfulness . . . and we cannot dishonor him more than to distrust him, especially in his promises,' Sibbes said. 'We make him a liar and rob him of that which he most glories in, his mercy and faithfulness, if we rest not securely upon him.' To place unswerving trust in God then was not only to give God supreme honor but reflectively to receive it oneself. 'Can you honor God more than in believing the gospel?' Sibbes asked. 'Can you dishonor him more than to call his truth into question?'

What an honor is this, that God will be honored by you! . . . In not believing, what a dishonor do you do to God! . . . God vouchsafest to be honored by weak sinful men believing of him, and that faith that honors him he will be sure to honor.[27]

What precisely it was that God promised was not often stated explicitly, and the preachers tried to avoid overexpectation, inevitably followed by disappointment, by saying that Christ himself was the central promise from which all others emanated. 'The promise of Christ himself is the first grand promise,' said Sibbes. 'All promises, they were all accomplished in him.' And yet from the way the preachers spoke of the other promises they clearly were assumed to include a 'salvation', and at some point a salvation in time. 'Promises . . . are all we have to build our faith upon for eternal salvation,' said Joseph Caryl, 'and these we, or any other nation that is under the same condition, hath to build assurance upon for temporal salvation. There are promises of free grace to nations, that God will deliver and save them . . . . Such a promise we have, though the name of England be not expressed in it.'[28]

Promises for either salvation were perhaps equally certain, though the latter kind, especially in the short run, tended to be conditional. 'Promises of deliverance . . . are to be understood in a double sense, literal and spiritual,' John Ellis argued. 'In the former, they are not always fulfilled; in the latter they never fail. All things are not ours literally . . . . We have a deliverance spiritual . . . but temporally we may even for one sin be kept from entering into Canaan.' And yet the reason such distinctions were seldom invoked was that ultimately there was no distinction at all: in that faith eliminated all distinctions of temporality, or even temporality and eternity, it made the promises 'as certain as if they were already accomplished' – an understanding that not only brought assurance that the promises would be accomplished, but in one sense itself accomplished them. 'Learn to live by faith upon a promise,' John Strickland urged, 'to live upon a promise yet unfulfilled.'

There is . . . an excellent substance in a promise made by God to support the heart though it be not yet fulfilled. And faith hath an excellent virtue to extract and bring to present enjoyment that which is virtually in the promise to comfort and strengthen the spirit. Faith hath (if I may so speak) a kind of creating power and can make a man to enjoy that this day that shall not be actually accomplished, it may be, many years hence by giving a substance to things future and an evidence to things invisible . . . . This is an excellency of faith, that it brings all things to the present enjoyment of the believer, even things that are past many years ago and . . . far off to come. Faith can foresee and as by a perspective present them to the soul as if in being.[29]

Promises, then, were accomplished when they were 'applied' by faith. 'It is the proper work of faith to fall in with a suitable promise and to apply the same,' said William Bridge. 'A promise, once given unto a soul, shall never be reversed or repealed.' Faith had the power to activate promises, to demand of God his own 'faithfulness', and make them true. 'Faith hath a strange faculty to . . . require an account of his promise, power, and faithfulness,' William Sedgwick said. 'Faith works upon his promise and so prevails with him.' The interaction between faith and promises made each effectively self-fulfilling, as the preachers not only admitted but insisted. 'Faith in the promises and the accomplishment of the promises are inseparable,' said John Owen.

The promises of God do signify . . . that the believer of them shall be the enjoyer of them . . . . Upon believing . . . the deliverance of his promise is mine . . . . The promises of grace are general and carry a truth to all that there is an inviolable connection between believing and the enjoyment of the things in them contained. And in this truth is the sincerity of the promiser . . . . Here lies the sincerity of God towards thee.

God was thus infinitely 'sincere' or 'faithful' when he made the promises; what was required from each soul was the similar sincerity for the promises (for that soul at least) to become 'real'. 'The promises of God, and God in all his promises, are full of sincerity,' Owen said, 'so that none need fear to cast himself on them; they shall be real unto him.' The self-fulfilling quality of promises completely eliminated any distinction between object and subject. 'Though it do not make the thing believed to be (the act cannot create its own object),' Owen argued, 'yet applying it, it makes it the believer's. It is the bond of union between the soul and the thing promised. He that believes in Christ, by that believing, receives Christ. . . . It is a grace uniting its subject and object, the person believing and the thing believed.'[30]

And yet, as Owen indicates, this very quality of the promises raised the possibility that through unbelief the promises could be rendered false. 'It is true, if a man stand disputing and staggering, whether he have any share in a promise and close not with it by faith, he may come short of it,' Owen explained, 'and yet without the least impeachment of the truth of the promise or sincerity of the promiser, for God hath not signified by them that men shall enjoy the good things of them, whether they believe or not.' This might not be an insurmountable problem (though neither was it an insignificant one) so long as a fairly clear distinction was maintained between the objective truth of the promises as they applied to the elect in the aggregate and the subjective faith of each individual, God's secret will alone accounting for the fact that some did not believe and so the promises did not apply to them. 'God's promises are not declarative of his secret purposes and intentions,' Owen warned. 'When God holds out to any a promise in the pardon of sin, this doth not signify to any singular man that it is the purpose of God that his sin shall be pardoned. So that though everyone to whom the promise is held out hath not the fruit of the promise; yet this derogates not at all from the sincerity of God in his promises, for he doth not hold them forth to any such end and purpose as to declare his intentions concerning particular persons.' Yet such a distinction was tenable only to a point, even for the individual soul, who was after all relying on the truth of the promise to help it believe; but further, the more widespread was unbelief throughout society as a whole – and the preachers always insisted it was very widespread indeed – the more it threatened to turn the promises themselves, as opposed to simply the particular application of them, into lies. 'The stability of a people is founded on promises,' Joseph Caryl explained, with carefully worded ambiguity:

but unbelief attempts to shake the promises, and more, to make them of none effect . . . . Yea, unbelief (as to us) destroyeth the promises . . . so that they cannot . . . help us. Yet further, unbelief (as much as in it lies) turns all the promises into fallacies and the truth of God into a lie. Faith feeds upon the goodness of the promises, and unbelief devours the truth of them. Surely they shall never receive the good of a promise who deny and destroy the truth of a promise.

The parenthetical qualifications indicate the obvious danger: that the subjective faith, or lack of it, should come to abrogate the objective doctrine and unbelief should make God a 'liar' – a problem that was terrifying enough as it arose within the individual but one which became critical politically insofar as it was rampant throughout society and therefore visible to the world. 'What if some d[o] not believe?' Caryl asked. 'Shall their unbelief make the faith of God without effect?'

This [i]s the attempt of unbelief even to make the faith of God – that is, the faithfulness of God – of none effect . . . . This is it which these by their unbelief would do, or to do which there is a tendency in unbelief. God doth and will right himself in honor, show himself faithful, though all the world should prove liars and unbelievers. But no thanks to unbelief; that would put the highest dishonor upon God, even that of falsehood to his own word and unfaithfulness to his own people.

But if literally 'all the world' should prove unfaithful or infidel it would be difficult to see in what sense God remained true, and in the end the truth of God's promises could be vindicated before the world only by virtue of at least some believing. 'Though all ought to increase and strengthen faith in darkest times, both in themselves and others, yet let no man despair because some, or many, do not believe,' Caryl assured the faithful. 'For as their unbelief shall not make the faith (that is, the faithfulness . . .) of God without effect, so neither shall it make the faith of other men without effect.' While sincerity ultimately had to be determined between each individual and God if the promise were to be made good for that soul, the personal terror of the promise proving untrue for each individual through his or her unbelief also came to be involved with, and even inseparable from, the collective cause of proving God's promises true at all; and from this came the passion among those who did truly believe to proselytize, not only to spread the truth but to agitate and even fight for the truth, so that anxiety over the fulfillment of promises came to be externalized as an ideological commitment to seeing that they be accomplished in and before the world as vindication or 'justification' of God, his 'truth', and his 'faith'. 'Thousands of standers-by be ready to call in question either the faithfulness of God or the infallibility of those truths which God's people have so many years together professed and suffered for,' noted Thomas Case, who countered that this very contention established the truth being contended for: 'Those truths for which the saints have contended . . . the truth . . . of God's promise . . . the truth of doctrine . . . which w[as] preserved . . . did preserve them. They fought for the truth, and the truth fought for them.'[31]

In this way, each soul's anxiety over the sincerity of its own faith became intertwined with the need to vindicate the sincerity and fidelity of God and yet in such a way that all doubts had to issue from the soul over its own faith and never from the truth of God's promise. 'Not the least occasion imaginable is thence administered to staggering or doubting,' Owen argued. 'He that disputes the promise and knows not how to close with them must find out another cause of his doing so; as to the truth of the promise, there is no doubt at all.' All doubt was placed in the subjective experience of the individual, never in the objective truth of the promises. 'Is it for want of fullness and truth therein?' Owen asked. 'Not at all, but merely for want of faith in thee that keeps it off.' Even more than other sins, unbelief in the promises came to be self-perpetuating in that it was fostered by itself: as the soul came to look upon its own worthlessness arising from sin, especially the sin of unbelief itself, it became even more discouraged and unbelieving. 'To stagger then at the promise is to take into consideration . . . all the difficulties that lie in the way for the accomplishment of it as to a man's own particular, and there so to dispute it in his thoughts as not fully to cast it off nor fully to close with it,' Owen explained.

> The soul considers the promise of free grace in the blood of Jesus . . . but withal takes into his thoughts his own unworthiness, sinfulness, unbelief, hypocrisy, and the like, which as he supposes, powerfully stave off the efficacy of the promise from him. Hence he knows not what to conclude . . . and what to do he knows not. Let go of the promise he cannot; but here he staggers and wavers to and fro.

A nightmare was thus created in the soul, that 'unstableness of mind' the preachers saw as a reflection of worldly confusion and change, but now made articulate and brought between the poles of the covenant dialectic. 'A poor creature looking upon the promise sees, as he supposes, in a steadfast closing with the promise that there lies presumption; on the other hand, certain destruction if he believes not,' Owen went on. 'And now he staggers; he is in a great strait. Arguments arise on both sides; he knows not how to determine them, and so hanging in suspense, he staggereth.' At this point the only choice before the soul was to sink down into despair, either to remain there perpetually or to emerge from there with renewed determination and strength by using that very despair as a dialectical mechanism to recognize the hopeless depths of its unbelief and with it its own faith in the promise – and doubtless for many a troubled soul it was the very recognition of unbelief, the very horror of doubting, that established its ultimate belief. 'I believe; help thou my unbelief, says the poor man,' according to Owen. 'It is of sincere faith to unlade our unbelief in the bosom of our God.'[32]

As the tortured soul struggled with these contradictions it could come to realize that the contrary forces tearing it apart could be used propel it forward through focusing on the dialectical figure of Christ, to whom believers were encouraged to look rather than to the promises of more temporal things, whose fulfillment was more problematic. 'A gracious heart looks upon every promise as coming from the root of the great covenant of grace in Christ,' Jeremiah Burroughs said. 'Other men look upon some particular promises that God will help them in straits . . . but they look not upon the connection of such particular promises to the root, the covenant of grace.' Through Christ what God promised was not so much particular deliverances at particular times or even final 'salvation', though these were included. 'He that performed the grand promise in giving Christ in the fullness of time, will for Christ's sake perform all other promises,' Sibbes promised. 'The death and resurrection of Christ . . . is a pawn and pledge to us of the performance of all things to come.' The essential promise was of faith itself, and more specifically fidelity: 'his fidelity or faithfulness in the discharge of his promises'. 'He is a most faithful, covenant-keeping God,' said Simeon Ash. 'He is God, the faithful God, which keepeth covenant and mercy.' This fidelity of God was established in and vindicated by the sending of Christ, who in turn provided for the faith and fidelity of the believer. 'Christ is called the word of God,' noted Burroughs, 'and is said to be faithful and true because he will discover the truth and faithfulness of the promises.'[33]

The mutuality of the covenant was such that 'if we keep covenant with God then God will keep covenant with us', and believers were equally expected to be faithful to the covenant to acquire the divine image. 'We must keep covenant with God that we may be like unto God,' said Thomas Mocket. 'Since God is faithful in keeping covenant with us, we must be faithful in keeping covenant with God.' But this was only possible because Christ himself vindicated God's fidelity by making the believer faithful, and Christ was himself the word or promise because he was the subject as well as the object of faith: he was not only that in which the soul believed; it was also he who enabled the struggling soul to accomplish its own belief. 'Thy faithfulness in keeping covenant with Christ must issue from the faithfulness of Christ's covenanting with thee.' The idea that the promises established God as infinitely sincere or 'faithful' to his word by transmitting that faithfulness to man, while all failure to realize the promises stemmed from the inability of man to exhibit similar fidelity on his own, was the central paradox in the perhaps oxymoronic concept of a 'covenant of grace'. 'The covenant of grace is so called because God is so gracious as to enable us to perform our own part,' Sibbes said. 'It is a covenant of *grace* . . . not only because the things promised are promised of grace, but because our part is of grace likewise.'

> We believe of grace . . . . All is of grace in the new covenant. God requires not any answering by our strength . . . . When he commands us to believe and obey, he gives us grace to believe and obey. It is ourselves that answer, but not from ourselves, but from grace. Yet notwithstanding let us . . . answer God's promise by faith and his command by obedience.[34]

This deliberate tension contained in the oxymoron, not wholly expressed by the idea of a mutual 'covenant' alone, was better conveyed as that word was combined with the notion of a more one-sided 'testament'. 'The covenant of grace is not only a covenant which requires duties of our parts,' Sibbes said, 'but also it is a testament wherein these graces are given us in a way of legacies.' Where a 'covenant' implied that mutuality which the preachers demanded even as they insisted the will could never meet its requirements alone, a 'testament' carried the connotation of a 'gift' or 'legacy' given freely without respect to the ability or response of the recipient. 'The new testament . . . is all one with the new covenant,' Burroughs explained. 'It contains the substance of the new covenant but called 'testament' in this regard':

> To show that the Lord doth do all in the new covenant . . . and therefore the same thing that is sometimes called a covenant is called a testament – that is, the will of God wherein the Lord doth bequeath his rich legacies to his children . . . so that all the good things in the covenant of grace they are bequeathed by way of testament as well as covenant . . . . For indeed when they look upon the way of the gospel as in a way of covenant, why then they think this, this requires somewhat of our parts to be done, and indeed God will keep covenant on his part, but it may be we shall not keep the covenant on ours, and so we may fail at last. But now when thou lookest upon all the good things in the gospel dispensed in the way of a testament . . . this is a mighty comfort to the soul.

Like a covenant, a testament centered on the prototypical figure of Christ, though in a slightly different role than that of 'mediator': now he became a 'testator', one who had left a free gift not simply to others but to future generations – though crucially, only by virtue of his death. 'A testament . . . is a covenant sealed by death,' Sibbes noted.

The testator must die before it can be of force. So all the good that is conveyed to us by the testament it is by the death of the testator, Christ. God's covenant with us now is such a covenant as is a testament, sealed with the death of the testator, Christ; for 'without blood there is no redemption.'[35]

The two roles of mediator and testator, conveying the tension between the bilateral and the unilateral, were often combined into yet another that placed Christ in the role of a kind of collateral – ensuring the faithfulness of God for the keeping of his word in covenant and one that could be forfeited in the event of his unfaithfulness (and one which, owing to that of man, already had been). 'Men use to give hostages for the securing each other of the faith and truth of all their engagements that they may be mutual pledges of their truth and fidelity,' John Owen observed. 'Jesus Christ is the great hostage of his father's truth, the pledge of his fidelity in his promises.' As Christ was simultaneously a 'mediator' between God and man and a 'testator' from God the active giver to man the passive receiver, so he was himself also a 'hostage' or 'surety' – a kind of mediator, as it were, turned testator. 'Christ was a surety as he was a public person,' said Owen. 'A surety is one that undertakes and is bound to do a thing for another.' Christ was a surety foremost on God's part, but also to some extent for the believer as well. 'Christ is called the covenant of God, the surety or undertaker of the covenant,' said Thomas Case. 'A surety on both sides, the surety of God's covenant to them, for all the promises of God are in him . . . and Christ again is the surety of their covenant unto God.' As the surety of God, Christ fulfilled both sides of the covenant, vindicating God's fidelity by providing it to man. 'It is Christ who makes the covenant good on both sides,' Case continued, 'as God's to his people, so his people's to God.'

> Christ [is] the undertaker, the surety of the covenant. As he paid the debt for time past, so he must see the articles of the covenant kept for the time to come. For want of such an undertaker or surety the first covenant miscarried . . . . But the second God meant should not miscarry and therefore puts it into sure hands . . . . God hath furnished Christ where-with all to be a surety, to make good his covenant to his people.[36]

MERCY

Logical as all this might be in the abstract, believing in theory was often very different from believing in practice. 'It is so with us in our view of the promises,' Owen observed. 'While we consider them at large as they lie in the word, alas! they are all true, shall be all accomplished, but when we go to venture our souls upon a promise, in an ocean of wrath and temptations, then every blast we think will overturn it.' Just when the soul may seem to have convinced itself that it did believe, some fresh adversity or obstacle would come along and renew the turmoil, since 'inward discouragements [are] caused very much by outward afflictions'. Further, the certainty that promises would be accomplished did nothing to lessen God's inscrutability and capriciousness in determining how or when (or to whom). 'His ways are past finding out,' said John Strickland, 'that is to say, in what manner or when he will perform his promise, though the promise itself may perhaps be known.' Precisely how and when he would do it was up to him, and while providence was an object of faith it was not in itself the primary one, being difficult to interpret at times and often seemingly opposed to the ends of the promise. 'Believe the promise and rest on the promise, notwithstanding that providence seems to cross the promise,' Thomas Brooks urged. 'It is nothing . . . to believe . . . when the promise is made good . . . but to do gloriously is to believe the promise, to stay upon the promise, when providence in our apprehension crosseth the promise.' God never promised that deliverances would necessarily come how and when they were desired, and one was never to place faith in uncertain worldly things or in the fulfillent of one's own immediate expectations. 'For the most part we live upon successes, not promises,' Owen noted. 'Unless we see and feel the print of victories, we will not believe.' God had his own purposes, 'eternal' ones and 'temporal' ones, and while the two were intricately connected they were not precisely the same. 'Take heed that ye do not measure God's eternal affection by some present dispensation,' William Bridge cautioned. 'Eternal displeasure . . . cannot stand with eternal love; but eternal love and present displeasure may stand together.' Those who confused the two would allow themselves to be depressed and discouraged by every setback:

> Some there are that do walk by particular providences . . . and when they have them, then they are much refreshed; if they want them, then they are much discouraged and say, Ah, Christ loves me not . . . . But if God's present dispensation seem to run cross to his eternal purpose, why then should they be discouraged?[37]

Only when people properly understood the promises of the word and applied their faith to them could they begin to look on the God's works in the world as encouragements to faith. 'When we are rightly principled by the word, we shall learn by it to see God in his works,' said Henry Scudder. 'You must first believe, and then you shall know.' Once this was firmly understood, then faith applied alongside sense and reason could begin to show the believer that God's outward works of providence similarly promised hope. 'The works of God have a promise in them as well as the word of God and are therefore the objects of faith,' said Joseph Caryl, 'not only as faith notes the believing of what is done, but also as it notes the believing of what is to be done.' To a point experiences could even substitute for lack of faith in promises, though this was dangerous. 'If we will not believe the promises . . . yet let us believe our own experience this way to trust in him,' Robert Harris urged. 'Hath not God been gracious to us in particular, hath not he been gracious to us in common for the public? . . . Let this encourage us . . . in all our afflictions and distresses, whether they are personal or whether they are public.'[38]

155

Even as the preachers dwelt upon the terrible anger of the Almighty then, they also recognized that 'pure wrath and displeasure in God would utterly destroy faith and not exercise it'. It was here that God began to bestow temporal 'mercies', and their descriptions of how God dispensed mercies often simply paralleled those of judgments: some took place in the ordinary course of things, while others were 'special', revealing more starkly his concentrated attention. 'Such mercies as come in an ordinary way are commonly interpreted to come from an ordinary love,' Stephen Marshall explained, 'but mercies and deliverances coming in an unexpected time, in an extraordinary way and manner, in them God's love and goodness is most apparently seen and acknowledged.' The idea that there were temporal 'mercies', like judgments, in the plural was in itself nothing new, and they could similarly be described according to the communities affected: 'the city mercies, the country mercies, the family mercies, the soul mercies'. Judgments would continue, even as mercies began to issue forth, and the two together were directed to an end that God alone had determined. 'God is the author of all good . . . the permitter of all evil . . . the orderer and disposer of both,' another minister said, 'by his mercy rewarding the one, by his justice revenging the other, and by his wisdom directing both to the ends of his eternal glory.' Both were in continual dialectical operation and could be expected to continue as such. 'There is no figure in all the prophets more usual than this, to interweave judgments and mercies,' Owen observed. 'Is it not so in our days? Precious mercies and dreadful judgments jointly poured out upon the land!' And the juxtaposition of judgments and mercies, when properly understood, was intended not to have people similarly ebbing and flowing but, precisely the opposite, to keep them on a steady and constant course. He keeps the heart of his in an even balance, in a continual dependence upon himself, that they may neither be wanton through mercy nor discouraged by too much oppression,' Owen said. 'Our heavenly father is therefore neither always feeding nor always correcting.'[39]

Nevertheless, while adversity was still to be expected, it was being manipulated for some higher end in which mercy would triumph, because good by definition was more effective, enduring, and so 'eternal' than evil. 'Acts of mercy are God's proper work towards his people, which he will certainly awake and keep alive in the saddest times,' Owen promised. 'My thoughts of anger are but for a time, but my thoughts of mercy are everlasting.' The whole point of mercy was that eventually, in one sense or another, it removed or neutralized judgments, or at least softened their impact. 'It is the glory of God's mercy that it preventeth judgment,' said Nathaniel Holmes. 'The spirit of God extenuates evils and crosses and doth magnify and amplify all mercies and makes mercies seem to be great and all afflictions seem to be little.'[40]

In this way mercies, like judgments, quieted the soul from its discontent, and this was especially important with those mercies shared by the community, who were all expected to share and rejoice in the common blessing. 'Public mercies . . . should quiet our hearts and keep us from discontent,' Jeremiah Burroughs

156

enjoined. 'The sin of discontent for private afflictions is exceedingly aggravated by the consideration of public mercies of the land.' Thus again the sin of murmuring, made even more grievous under mercies than judgments. 'To murmur when we enjoy an abundance of mercy,' Burroughs added, 'the greater and the more abundant the mercy that we enjoy, the greater and viler is the sin of murmuring.' Even mercy included an implicit threat in case of insufficient gratitude, and the dialectic carried the warning that 'sins against mercy' could still produce destruction in the end. 'If mercies do not work upon love, let judgments work upon fear,' Edward Reynolds suggested. 'When neither judgments nor mercies bring a heart to fear, the Lord usually pours out the full vials of his heaviest wrath.' In the same way that the gospel brought 'eternal' judgments, so they tended to come after temporal mercies. 'The abuse of eminent mercies and deliverances provokes God to inflict eminent judgments,' warned William Spurstowe, 'and many times a total and final ruin.'[41]

Mercies were said to be abused when recipients were not sufficiently grateful – 'when eminent blessings are received without any notice being taken of them' – and especially over time it was often lamented that 'great mercies, and such as before they come are most highly esteemed, are commonly little set by when we once enjoy them'. For this reason mercies were 'to be diligently observed and exactly numbered'; above all, they were to be remembered. 'Great deliverances call for frequent remembrances,' said Owen. 'Former mercies with their times and places are to be had in thankful remembrance unto them who wait for future blessings. Faith is to this end separated by them.' Mercies contained a promise in that 'deliverances past are pledges of future deliverances', and like faith, the remembrance of past mercies could break down the barriers of time and make future ones present to the believer. 'Faith looketh backward and forward, to what God hath done and to what he hath promised to do,' said Owen. 'Faith gives a present subsistence to sore past works as recorded and future mercies as promised to support the soul in an evil day.' Ultimately, the distinction between promises and experiences was thin, since while scripture did contain explicit promises or 'prophecies' for the future, it was itself largely a record of mercies (as well as judgments) of the past; and while biblical examples were the most frequently cited, those of recent times were increasingly worthy of notice. 'Thus should we make use of former deliverances and experiences to increase our trust and dependency upon the Lord,' urged John Strickland, who, while he went on to list many biblical examples, added: 'But I know not whether God hath not equally showed his power and love and faithfulness towards us in signs and wonderful works, even at this day, not to speak of those never to be forgotten wonders, the armada in eighty-eight and the powder treason. What heaven-born discoveries have we lately seen and had experience of in this kingdom.' Such major deliverances came to be treated with a reverence otherwise reserved solely for scripture. 'If then at any time you think yourselves scanted in promises,' Joseph Caryl suggested to Parliament in 1645, send back your thoughts to those many experiences, both of elder and later days: the invincible navy in eighty-eight overcome, the secret powder plot discovered and blown up, your yesterday protections, deliverances, successes, victories should all be served up to the table of your hearts for faith to feed upon and nourish itself up into a holy confidence, that he who hath delivered you from so great a death . . . will yet deliver you.[42]

Often the preachers requested that mercies be 'recorded' so as to be more readily remembered and referred to. 'It's good to have a register of God's favors,' Robert Baillie suggested, 'both to the public and thy person.' The assiduous recording of temporal mercies marking the spiritual progress of the individual soul and presaging its final salvation had long been the impetus behind a familiar Puritan practice: 'For this end the diaries which many use to have, wherein they register special mercies and blessings on the day wherein they were wrought, are commendable.' The model for this practice was scripture itself, and one's own personal record was intended to supplement the Bible in furnishing material for daily contemplation and for recollection in times of spiritual stress and doubt. 'The Bible is God's Book of Record,' noted Thomas Palmer. 'Be persuaded to keep a soul book, that you may know how your spiritual estate stands.'

This recording of revealed truths and soul experiences [is] of great importance in times of trouble and trial. The calling to memory of former experiences of God's love, power, and providences helps a soul exceedingly to trust God for the future; it strengthens faith mightily in extremities.[43]

As an extension of this the preachers often took the lead in publicly listing mercies bestowed upon their local community or the wider society, and during the war the parliamentary preachers especially would also frequently catalogue from the pulpit (and often in expanded form from the press) temporal mercies granted to England in general and the parliamentary cause in particular. An outstanding example was the sermon preached by Edmund Calamy at the first regular fast in February 1642, shortly before the war began, which extended back to the earliest years of Christian Britain but concentrated on those of and since the Reformation: 'God hath made us not only Protestants but reformed Protestants,' Calamy pointed out. 'We have enjoyed the gospel . . . for almost a hundred years.' As with others, the two major deliverances given to England in particular initiated his list. 'In this century God hath multiplied deliverance upon deliverance,' he noted. 'We have had our eighty-eight and our gunpowder deliverance.' But above all Calamy concentrated on the extraordinary deliverances since 1640. 'The mercies of these two last years do far exceed all the mercies that ever this nation did receive since the first reformation,' he declared, 'mercies that deserve to be engraven in every one of our hearts':

the happy pacification between England and Scotland . . . the Protestation against all popery and popish innovations . . . the great hope we have of a reformation of the church and state . . . the many grievous yokes that God hath freed us from . . . from the late Canons . . . from the Star Chamber and from the terrible High Commission . . . from those two terrible oaths . . . the discovery of the secret underminers that have these many years labored to blow upon religion and under the name of Puritans to scare all men from being Protestants.[44]

Throughout the civil war the preachers continued to describe and catalogue in painstaking detail great mercies – most often military victories – as God awarded them to England and Parliament. 'Let former mercies be an anchor of hope in time of present distresses,' John Owen urged at a thanksgiving for the surrender of Colchester in 1648. 'Where is the God of Marston Moor and the God of Naseby? . . . Oh what a catalogue of mercies hath this nation to plead by in a time of trouble? God came from Naseby and the Holy One from the west.' Owen went on to narrate the precise circumstances and events of the battle, emphasizing the tremendous odds against which the parliamentary forces fought and ascribing the overcoming of each obstacle and every turn of events to the hand of God: 'in leavening the counsels of the enemy with their own folly . . . in ordering all events to his own praise . . . by controlling with his mighty power the issue of all undertakings', and so forth. 'It cannot be denied but that providence was eminently exalted in the work of your protection and delivery,' Owen proclaimed to the Commons. 'Doubtless the hand of God was lifted up.'[45]

Sometimes the preachers went further to suggest that such control of nature resulted in not merely 'mercies' and 'deliverances', but occurrences considered somehow beyond the abilities or understandings of mere mortals. 'God sometimes bringeth plentiful deliverances and mercies for his people from beyond the ken of sense and reason,' Owen explained. 'Consider whether the mercy celebrated this day ought not to be placed in this series of deliverances brought from beyond the ken of sense and reason.' It was not that there were not 'means' and 'causes' involved which others might choose to comprehend through 'sense' and 'reason', but those were not what the faithful would look at. 'Let us [consider] whether or no the present great work of salvation and reformation that is in your hands (for 'tis a work of salvation) be . . . a plain work of common providence in which ordinary causes do bring forth their wonted effects and issues without any remarkable variation,' John Bond urged the House of Commons. 'Or rather is it not an extraordinary, elaborate, shadowed masterpiece, altogether made up of strategems, paradoxes, and wonders? If thus, then comfort yourselves, you may conclude it will be a great salvation.' It was for this reason that, if not ordinary, at least entirely explicable events were seen as 'providences', 'wonders', even 'miracles'. 'Have not our deliverances been wonderful and many of our victories little less than miraculous?' asked Simeon Ash after a series of parliamentary victories. 'There is not only mercy but miracle in our deliverance.'[46]

Often, too, the preachers described mercies, much like their denunciations of judgments, as having an affinity with the ultimate reward usually thought to be reserved for the next life. 'As our life is subject to many miseries, in soul, body, and estate, public and private,' said Richard Sibbes, 'so God hath many salvations.' Yet the various 'salvations', like the similarity between 'lesser' and 'final' judgments, were perhaps even more frequently and strongly emphasized during the 1640s. 'Of salvations, there are two sorts,' said John Bond. 'First, spiritual, reaching to the soul; of this the Lord is the sole author. And there are temporal, outward, civil salvations to the body and estate.' This latter type of 'salvation' was more complex; God controlled them as much as he did the other, though the extent to which his providence employed 'causes' varied. 'These are wrought either by an ordinary and common providence or by special and extraordinary,' Bond explained. 'By ordinary providence . . . as when the greater number doth beat the lesser. But they are extraordinary salvations when . . . the Lord doth elevate and heighten them above themselves.' And faith not only brought both kinds of 'salvation' to realization but brought them together as well. 'Faith in our redemption and faith in God's providence go together,' said Richard Greenham. 'Believe God's providence . . . towards thee.'[47]

Whether or not temporal mercies were truly miraculous, then, their occurrence was seen as a vindication not simply of God's determination to 'save' but of the terms by which he did so in either world. 'National mercies come from free grace, not from free will,' Calamy asserted in 1642.

> If free grace hath preserved England, let England bless God for free grace. . . . Let us ascribe all our deliverances and all our mercies, the mercy of the pacification, the mercy of reformation, the mercy of the union of both Houses of Parliament, the discovery of all plots and treasons against this church and state, our freedom from all our yokes, and all the good things that God hath done of us unto free grace . . . . If free gace hath preserved England, not free will, let England maintain free grace above free will.

And their experience of how salvation was delivered in this world helped shape people's understanding of how it would be bestowed in the world to come. 'And certain it is,' Calamy added, 'if temporal deliverances be the fruits of God's free grace, much more are spiritual and eternal.' The conflict between free grace and free will was not merely abstract or academic, therefore, but represented a fundamental difference of social and political outlook, so much so that the collective 'salvation' of England, as much as of the individuals distributed within in, came to be at once dependent upon, and itself evidence for, the vindication of the doctrine of grace. 'Let us maintain the doctrine of free justification,' Francis Cheynell urged, adding with ambiguity, 'our salvation depends on it.' The political and military conflicts of England, in other words, were fought out less over the issue of religious doctrine than according to the terms of it. 'Free grace hath been spoken against, preached against, and printed against, though it have been the best friend that ever England had and is not yet weary of doing England good, which is the highest confutation of the lies and blasphemies of the adversaries that can be,' declared Thomas Case in 1642. 'For surely free will hath had no share in these blessed revivings of our hopes and comforts. This salvation of God . . . is . . . a wonder of free grace.' And by believing this doctrine, and acting out of that belief, the doctrine itself would come to be true and be 'proven' so before the world. 'And truly if the Lord please to carry on the work in ways proportionable to the beginning,' Case promised, 'England's deliverance will be the most irrefragable confutation of popery and Arminianism and the highest monument of free grace that ever was set up in the view of the world.'[48]

Moreover, in that each deliverance promised more and strengthened faith to expect more, the 'stream of mercies', as one called it, was not simply an assortment of isolated or discrete phenomena but a single continuous process of redemption which augmented itself over time, each mercy building upon the last. 'It is the way of the Lord to make his last mercies better than the former,' Peter Sterry said in 1655. 'The present salvations of our Lord in the midst of us have exceeded all that ever were to this day.' The present deliverances of England even seemed to take on historic significance comparable to the greatest of antiquity as chronicled in scripture. 'Our times are times of deliverance, the greatest deliverances that I think the Lord hath wrought since he brought Israel out of Egypt,' announced Stephen Marshall in 1646, ' . . . the fruit of free grace wherein the Lord hath exceeded . . . our faith.' The preachers also urged their listeners to be conscious of the mercies, like the sins, of past generations and of the sacrifices that had been made to obtain them. 'You should account deliverances granted to your ancestors to be yours, for you enter into their labors who now sit in their places,' William Strong told the House of Commons, 'and you reap the fruit of all their hazards and dangers.' Similarly, faith could prognosticate mercies for the generations to come, giving the believer prophetic powers as well as renewed resolve to do his or her part to see them fulfilled. 'I look upon the mercies of many years to come,' Joseph Caryl announced. 'My faith begins to prophesy, and my spiritual prospective draws before me the blessings of many generations, even blessings for the children yet unborn.' Faith thus created a solidarity across the ages in which believers came to their rest knowing that future generations would reap the rewards of their devotion. 'Thou shalt establish the foundations of a generation and a generation,' Thomas Coleman said, 'not thy own age only, but the next and the next shall fare the better, God remembering his mercy to a thousand generations of those that love him.' While individuals might have to settle for rewards beyond the grave, faith brought not only assurance of this, but also the knowledge that salvation would come to the community of the faithful in time. 'They shall be blessed everlastingly,' promised John Strickland. 'Though they should never live to see the promises of temporal salvation, which they wait for, yet they shall have a day wherein they shall receive the waiting servant's blessing.' Such had been the fate of many of God's children in the past: the patriarchs 'died in hope not having obtained the promises', Coleman noted; 'they only by the eye of faith saw them afar off'. Such too might be the fate of many in the present generation: Coleman himself may have had premonitions of his own early demise in 1647 when he assured his people that he had been to the mountain, and though he might not make it there with them, through faith he knew that England, in some way, in some form, would reach the promised land. 'Such a one, a godly minister, an old disciple . . . having given a good testimony of their faith . . . died, not having obtained the promise,' he said.

It is possible then, nay more than probable, that I shall also come short of ever seeing this glory dwelling in our land . . . . These thoughts may be true, and though true, yet let no man's heart fail him . . . . If you shouldst, it is no prejudice to thy everlasting being; thou shalt not have one seat lower in heaven for it.'[49]

In yet another sense, then, did faith transcend the limitations of time, since by foreseeing the inevitable faith broke down the distinction between temporal and eternal. 'The prosperity of our worldly affairs, as well as of our heavenly, depends upon and flows from the actings of our faith,' Caryl insisted. 'Faith is the pledge and security of eternal salvation, and therefore may well be the pawn and forerunner of temporal redemption.' God's works of 'temporal' as of 'eternal' salvation could thus be said to be appointed from everlasting, predestined in his eternal decree. 'Exercise faith upon . . . these thoughts of mercy,' Nathaniel Holmes urged. 'They are conceived from God's . . . predestination, appoint-ment, purpose, or choosing.' What precisely was the difference was increasingly unclear, as faith seemed to bring together the beginning with the end of time. 'Faith is . . . sown in the beginning,' said Sidrach Simpson, 'it's known at the end of the world.'[50]

PRAYER

Redemption, then, came on essentially the same terms here as hereafter, and the preachers issued similar warnings against reliance on human power for salvation in either world. 'As in our spiritual salvation we are prone to dote much on the power of our wills,' Obadiah Sedgwick warned the House of Commons in 1644, 'so in our temporal salvation we are as apt to rely too much upon the power of creatures.' To be sure, an awareness of the limitations of worldly instruments was no excuse for failing to seize the opportunities God had provided. 'Outward means indeed are not to be neglected,' Thomas Carter admonished the House. 'As we must not idolize the means in trusting in them, so neither tempt God in neglecting of them.' Still, the first means they usually suggested were those within. 'The great means of all, that which . . . can let out all the floodgates of God's mercy to quench the heat of his wrath,' Stephen Marshall asserted, 'is unfeigned repentance.' Yet repentance was itself highly involved and led on to the next means, one to which the preachers devoted extended passages and sometimes entire sermons: 'The establishing of an unsettled kingdom calls for the holiest and most spiritual motions of faith in praying.'[51]

Prayer was the means of bringing temporal as well as eternal mercy. 'Eminent mercies are the fruits of eminent prayers,' said William Spurstowe in 1644. 'The wonders of these years . . . have been wrought by prayer.' Yet precisely how prayer worked was problematic, and everyday experience would seem to suggest that prayers were not always effective on earth, at least not immediately. 'It is usual with God's own people and dearest children to say and think sometimes that the Lord doth not answer their prayer when the Lord doth,' explained William Bridge. 'There is a twofold answer of prayer . . . a visible return of prayer and . . . an invisible return of prayer.' While people prayed 'for' things, prayer was directed at least as much to the feeling of helplessness as to anything tangible, and the very act of praying was itself a mercy, especially when outward ones were not directly forthcoming. 'Sometimes a waiting frame of heart is a greater mercy than the thing waited for,' Bridge suggested. 'It is a mercy to pray, though I never receive the mercy prayed for . . . and a great ease to a burdened, troubled spirit.' As with any other human action, the calming effect on the soul was at least as important as the 'salvation' – or in some sense was the salvation. 'This means is better than the end,' Joseph Caryl said, 'and God to whom we pray is better than any spiritual thing we pray for.'[52]

Still, prayer was said to be efficacious for national as well as individual deliverances. 'Act faith for the kingdom as you would for your own souls,' Joseph Caryl urged. 'Hath not God given his people sometimes as clear evidences, as strong assurances, that their prayers have been heard about temporals as about eternals?' The factors ensuring this were what constituted sincerity and in what sense it would prevail; the ministers had no illusions that prayers for particular temporal deliverances would necessarily be answered in the short run. 'Spiritual things may be prayed for absolutely,' Jeremiah Burroughs cautioned, 'but outward things must be prayed for conditionally.' God had his own reasons for not always seeming to answer prayers immediately, and they could even be merciful ones. 'Though the Lord be a God ever hearing the prayers of his servants, yet this hearing of request is not always by granting the things requested,' Jeremiah Whitaker explained. 'God may deny in mercy and grant in fury.' The logic and justice of how God answered prayers were even closer in terms of the fates of individuals in relation to the community. 'It may be thou shalt not see the answer a great while, possibly not till thy death come,' said Stephen Marshall ambiguously. 'Nay peradventure, the greatest of thy prayers shall be when thou art dead and rotten in thy grave.' Further, it could simply be asserted that for prayers to work they had to be 'sincere', indeed zealous. 'Prayer is said to prevail if it be fervent,' another preacher said. 'Indeed, we seldom read of any of the saints of God in prayer but some way or other we may observe this kind of zeal and vehemency.' And sincerity after all was something of which there could never be too much. 'They must not be dead prayers, lifeless, formal, slight, perfunctory, customary prayers, not the saying over of prayer . . . without spirit, understanding, devotion,' said Stephen Marshall. 'Prayer must be . . . the pouring out of the soul; it must be fervent prayer; it must be humble prayer; it must be from a pure heart and faith unfeigned . . . . These things must at least be aimed at and endeavored in prevailing prayers.'[53]

Further, not only was such sincerity difficult to determine within the individual, but the level of sincerity might vary among the members of the community, and while the preachers exhorted all to intensify their faith, they also claimed that only the prayers of the truly faithful would be heard. 'The persons praying must be holy men,' Thomas Carter asserted. 'Their prayers only are prevalent.' The prayers of such holy men for the welfare of the nation could even give them a kind of 'representative' function, similar to that of the public officials who had usually been taken as the representatives of the nation before God. 'The prayers that are useful for the saving of a nation from ruin . . . are of two sorts,' said Carter; 'first, the prayers of the nation itself; secondly, of God's own people for the nation.' The first is familiar and parallels the way in which God regards sin – with particular weight given to those of magistrates or the 'representative body' without neglecting those of the 'body' or nation at large: 'First, the prayers of the nation itself, which also are twofold,' Carter explained:

> First of the representative body of a nation: for . . . the acts of the representative body of a nation, not only acts civil but sacred, even in their heartbreaking and repenting prayers offered up for a nation in the name of the whole . . . surely these acts interpretatively are the acts of the nation, and therefore in and by them the nation prayeth. Secondly, the prayers of the essential body of a nation: when a kingdom in all its parts, if not all or the most men in it universally, yet generally . . . shall be up in prayer . . . the nation prayeth.

As against both of these, Carter set another sort of prayer, equally representative of 'the nation': 'The second sort of prayers available for the procurement of a nation's safety are the prayers of God's own faithful people for the nation,' he said, 'for though they are very few, yet their prayers are exceeding prevalent for that purpose.' Yet from whomever they proceeded, there was no guarantee that prayers would necessarily result in immediate temporal blessings, or that even the prayers of the faithful would save a nation the majority of which remained recalcitrant – only that, as always, they would bring final rewards to those whose endeavors were true. 'Yet howsoever the prayers of God's people are effectual means, yet have we no certain assurance that they shall actually save such a stiff-necked people from ruin,' Carter concluded.

> The safety of a nation is but a temporal blessing, though a great one, and we have no absolute promise to obtain them by our prayers . . . . Outward blessings are only . . . good in reference to certain ends. Though holy men should entreat for them, yet shall they save but their own souls.[54]

Yet even as they repeated such warnings, the preachers issued urgent appeals to all who would listen to continue to pray for just such temporal blessings. 'Prayer hath done mighty things in battles,' Jeremiah Burroughs declared. 'This name of God shows us our duty to seek him much by prayer in times of war and to depend upon him wholly for success in it, for he is the Lord of Hosts.' Of all the endeavors for which the preachers urged prayer, war was the most frequently mentioned. 'A praying army must be a victorious army,' Samuel Rutherford asserted. 'Prayers draw forth the armies of the living God.' Again, it was difficult to tell what was figurative and what was literal, but that was what gave the imagery (and prayer) its power. 'The saints of the most high God can pray down empires and kingdoms and the towers and castles and walls of the proudest enemies,' declared Thomas Case. 'It is safer standing before the mouth of a cannon than before the prayers of the saints.' Whatever the fortunes of worldly armies, those of the Lord would prevail. 'An army of prayers is as strong as any army of men whatsoever,' Burroughs proclaimed. 'Yea, one man praying may do more than many men fighting.' Perhaps most significantly, prayer involved even the most humble in a sort of participation in national and political affairs – if not directly at first, at least vicariously – while at the same time mobilizing mass support for the cause. 'Let us strive with God in prayer while our brethren are striving with the enemy in battle,' Burroughs urged. 'Great things depend upon the success of these wars. He is an unworthy member of church or commonwealth who hath not a heart to pray now.'[55]

WORK

Yet prayer was a preparation, not a substitute, for action, and no prayer was truly sincere without all possible effort to see the 'salvation' realized. 'You must not think your work done when your prayers are ended,' said Christopher Tesdale. 'You must then act over your prayers and live over your prayers.' Especially for the redemption of the community, prayer was the first rather than the only 'means'. 'We may pray for the accomplishing of all . . . promises,' Lazarus Seaman said, 'but we may not pray for the end but with reference to all known means ordained thereunto.' What precisely were the 'ends' toward which the 'means' were directed – or at what point the ends came, like faith itself, to 'justify' the means – was not always spelled out, though the question was at least raised. 'Faith doth not take away the use of means,' said Richard Sibbes. 'Nay, he that is most certain of the end should strive to be most careful of all means used to that end.' Joseph Caryl was perhaps more specific in reference to the political nature of the ends: 'To despise the instruments of our civil as well as of our spiritual salvation is to . . . mock God when we use not all possible means to accomplish what we pray for,' he said. 'If we be desirous to have a kingdom of heaven upon earth, we must spare for no cost, but . . . venture all we have.'[56]

Prayer, then, was the beginning of the other logical extension of faith: work on the part of those who themselves sought to be among his means or 'instruments'. 'As we must pray, so we must do,' said William Sedgwick. 'Work in prayer, and work with prayer.' Work became a kind of active prayer or simply an extension of prayer by other means. 'God loves to see our prayers live in our deeds,' Sedgwick continued. 'It is unbelief, base fear, or worse, hypocrisy to say to God in private what we will not act in public.' Prayer connected abstract inward faith with practical outward work, and all actions, all the affairs of life, were to be undertaken as an act of prayer. 'Live by faith in Christ,' Thomas Hill urged. 'Not only pray in faith, but work, fight by faith, expecting all from Christ.'[57]

Activism was in some ways what distinguished Puritan religion. 'Reformation ends not in contemplation,' said George Gillespie, 'but in action.' If Protestantism made Christianity into something to be believed, the Puritan application of those beliefs made Protestantism and Christianity above all something to be done. 'Christianity is a busy trade,' said Sibbes. 'What a world of things are required to be a Christian.' To be a Christian was to be an activist, not believing only, but constantly doing. 'The estate of a Christian is a working estate, not idle,' Sibbes added. 'Christianity is not a verbal profession, nor speculative.' Simply believing in the abstract meant nothing; to be a true believer one's faith had to be applied, one's knowledge put to 'practice'. 'What makes a true Christian?' asked Sibbes. 'When he nakedly believes . . . the articles of the faith – doth that make a true Christian?'

> No . . . . For religion is a truth . . . not according to speculation only . . . . Religion . . . is a knowledge of things directing to practice. The gospel is divine wisdom teaching practice as well as knowledge . . . . He that is godly, he believes aright and practiseth aright.[58]

Faith, after all, was itself a matter of practice, the 'application' of abstract religious precepts to the concrete dilemmas of one's soul. 'Indeed, faith is nothing but knowledge with application,' Sibbes added. 'Knowledge with application is faith.' Faith, therefore, and the ministers' own faith in particular, far from excluding work, initiated it. 'If a man have faith, he will show it by his works,' John Preston said. 'If thy faith be a true faith, it must be a working faith, or else it is nothing.' Faith preceded work in Protestant theology, because correct theory had to direct practice, but so intimately was faith defined by activity that it was itself said to be a kind of labor. 'Faith is all,' said Preston, 'but it must be such a faith as works . . . . Though it be by faith, yet it is not an idle faith.' There was no opposition therefore between faith and work: faith took precedence, but work in turn applied theory to practice. 'Faith doth justify works,' Thomas Watson said. 'Works do testify faith.'

> Faith alone justifies, but justifying faith is not alone . . . . Good works, though they are not the causes of salvation, yet they are evidences. Though they are not the foundation, yet they are the superstructure. Faith must not be built upon works, but works must be built upon faith.[59]

Works testified faith insofar as they involved struggle against a hostile world, and 'work' could be defined as both 'active and passive', 'doing and suffering'. 'Working is in doing or suffering,' said Preston, 'for in suffering there is a work as well as in doing, only it is a work with more difficulty, a work with more impediments.' A godly act undertaken with resolution and continued with steadfastness when met with opposition from a threatening world was evidence of true faith. 'As you will be ready to do much, so you will be ready to suffer much also,' Preston added. 'Suffering is a kind of doing, only it is a doing of things when there is difficulty and hardness.' When the outside world was actively hostile, 'suffering' was the usual way of testifying faith, and as long as oppression and persecution threatened, suffering would continue to be necessary. 'To suffer imprisonment and disgraces for good causes, this is a good work,' said Preston, 'for it is a great work to suffer.' Increasingly however, passive suffering was to be seconded by the more active work of 'doing'. 'Be doers,' Preston exhorted. 'This is the great business which we have to do and the thing which for the most part we all fail in, that there is no doing, no acting, no working of our faith . . . . Show it by doing something . . . . It is not for you now to stand idle; the time of your standing still is past; it is for you now to work . . . to be much in actions.'[60]

While work applied faith, however, it could not outpace faith or it would become 'hypocrisy': 'Hypocrisy is to do the outward action without the inward sincerity.' The relationship was difficult to pin down, since on the one hand action without sincere faith directing it was hypocritical. 'God looketh more at the will than the work,' Joseph Symonds said, 'and by how much our actions exceed our wills by so much the more are we hypocrites in the things which we do.' On the other hand faith itself could not be considered sincere unless it was executed as action. 'It's not enough to resolve, but we must do it,' Symonds added. 'Not purposes but actions are recompensed.' The two had to reinforce one another, since God required both the soul and body, and the preachers were concerned that outward actions could be substituted for inward convictions. 'When God calls for the whole man, outward and inward, deny it not,' John Whincop urged, 'still remembering . . . to take heed . . . they be . . . from an inward principle of grace within, not an outward conformity only and compliance without.'[61]

What distinguished the Puritan ethic of work from the traditional theology of 'works' was that, rather than isolated acts of charity, work was to become a systematic effort, a relentless struggle directed to a single-minded purpose, to an all-encompassing 'cause'. 'Laborious working in a good cause is very pleasing unto God,' according to Joseph Caryl. 'God is himself a pure act, and he loves to see man active.' Work became a cause as it was faithful effort directed toward the accomplishment of those things foreseen by faith. 'Be faithful in doing all the work of God whereunto you are engaged,' John Owen urged, 'as he is faithful in working all your works whereunto you are engaged.' Work engaged not only God in it but effectively his own 'works'. 'If you would give God no rest, you must take none,' William Sedgwick said. 'The best way to make God restless is to be restless in seeking; our activity works upon God . . . . Let action be your rest . . . . God cannot rest until you give over working. He will work with you so long as you work with him.'[62]

It was through this interaction that believers were selected as 'instruments' of God. 'If we have the honor to be God's instruments we must do the office of instruments and be active,' said Edward Corbet. 'It concerns us to answer providence with industry.' Work was even encouraged for its own sake, as an alternative to the destructive and self-destructive temptations of boredom, and to do work was almost in itself to do the Lord's work. 'The idle man is Satan's agent,' Caryl said, 'and the laborious man is God's . . . . The more active we are, the more like we are to God.' Work was important both as it was directed toward the elimination of evil things and as itself an alternative to the kind of dissipated courses that became tempting when people lacked a sense of direction in their lives. 'An unemployed life is a burden to itself,' said Sibbes. 'God is a pure act, always working, always doing, and the nearer our soul comes to God, the more it is in action and the freer from disquiet.' The meaningless and purposeless existence to which unemployment gave rise was considered a potentially dangerous condition for both the individual and society, since there was no limit to the wayward pursuits to which people might resort when searching for some sense of purpose and fulfillment. 'Idleness breeds temptation,' William Bridge noted. 'When we are least at work for God, then is Satan most at work about us. By doing nothing we learn to do evil.' There was a sense then in which one had no choice but to work; it all depended on whom it was one worked for. 'Christians, fall to work, do it early, earnestly, uncessantly,' urged Thomas Watson. 'Either you must do the work that Christians are doing, or you must do the work that devils are doing.' God's work was public work and not the kind of private pursuit that was likely to be selfish or mischievous. 'The subject of this activity . . . is not the works of the world or our own private works, much less the works of sin, but the works of the Lord.' It was after all the first 'work of sin', the violation of the covenant of 'works', that created the imperative for continued work. 'No sooner was man fallen but he was put upon sore consuming labor,' Caryl noted. 'Sin brought in sweat, and now not to sweat increases sin.' Conversely, the inability of human works to fulfill that covenant made the 'work' of Christ himself necessary as the object toward which faith was directed. 'They who work for Christ should imitate Christ in his work for us,' Caryl suggested to the Commons.

> Christ . . . will yet work a work for us. Shall we think any labor too great for him? Christ by his own labor in your cause hath outbid all the labor you have or can bestow in his cause . . . . I know you have labored in the midst of many crosses, but Christ labored for us upon the cross. I know you have wrestled with many difficulties, but Christ was in an agony; he sweat blood, and he spilt his blood . . . . Whenever Christ looks upon a believing, repenting soul, he sees in that the travel of his soul.

Christ's work on the cross epitomized the virtue and honor of self-sacrifice, and to work for his cause and glory was to work in the service and the image of Christ. 'Thus Christ glorifies his father upon earth,' said William Strong. 'He lays out himself to the utmost in service.'[63]

The close connection between religious commitment and civil employment, between faith and work, was concretized in the concept of the calling, or callings. 'Vocations . . . are of two sorts: general or particular,' explained William Perkins.

'The general calling is the calling of Christianity . . . . The particular is that special calling that belongs to some particular men: as the calling of a magistrate, the calling of a minister, the calling of a master, of a father, of a child, of a servant, of a subject, or any other calling that is common to all.' This idea of a twofold calling, religious and secular, though the relationship between them was not direct, was essential to understanding either. 'We show religion, that is our general calling, in our particular calling,' said Sibbes, 'and what we do in either of these callings is the way to heaven.' Certainly no worldly calling, however exalted, was simply to be equated with the heavenly one. 'We must not think that the particular calling of men, either to magistracy or ministry, is this calling to glory and virtue.' But the two were intended to reinforce one another as devotion to the Christian calling enhanced the performance in the secular calling, which in turn served as an outlet for one's Christian piety and could itself help keep the soul on a straight moral path. 'The calling of Christianity is showed in particular callings, which are sanctified by God to subdue the excess of corruptions,' said Sibbes, who remarked that 'men without callings are exceedingly vicious, as some gentlemen and beggars.'[64]

As Sibbes indicates, among worldly callings two were exalted above all others, reflecting the duality between sacred and secular. 'There are two callings which are the highest in the world, and also the heaviest in the world,' asserted Obadiah Sedgwick, 'the minister's calling [and] the magistrate's calling.' Yet to whomever it pertained the calling was usually described as an employment within specifically 'civil' society. 'We do ordinarily take the word "calling" for our civil employment and outward occupation [or] for our outward state and condition,' said William Bridge, '. . . for there is no state or condition that we are called unto but some occupation, employment, or calling is to be used therein.' But while the idea of an 'occupation' or 'employment' in the sense of a livelihood was included, the calling connoted much more public than private duties, and the division of labor it described and encouraged within the various sectors of 'civil' society was one less of production than of authority. 'Neither family, church, nor commonwealth can stand without distinction of particular callings and labor in the same.' The insistence on callings as 'civil' did not mean they were divorced from the calling to Christianity, but that they were for public benefit rather than private gain. 'A vocation or calling is a certain kind of life, ordained and imposed on man by God for the common good,' said Perkins. 'Every person of every degree, state, sex, or condition without exception must have some personal and particular calling to walk in.' The emphasis on the 'common good' dictated that all persons of whatever status had something to contribute and were required to contribute it, and to work solely for personal profit or advancement was to violate the most basic rule of the calling. 'He abuseth his calling, whosoever he be, that against the end thereof employs it for himself, seeking wholly his own and not the common good,' Perkins enjoined. 'Everyone, rich and poor, man or woman, is bound to have a personal calling in which they must perform some duties for the common good.' The calling could indeed be described as an 'economic' concept (especially in that the family was an institution within which the calling was most stressed), but more important was its role in the promotion of moral rectitude and political authority, not only to impel people to do good but in the very process to prevent them from doing evil. 'Sloth and negligence in the duties of our callings are a disorder against that comely order which God hath set in the societies of mankind,' Perkins maintained. 'Idleness and sloth are the causes of many damnable sins.'[65]

Moreover, not only was lack of diligence in a lawful calling dangerous, but not all enterprises and endeavors were necessarily recognized to be legitimate callings, and those who exploited the poor and helpless of society for their own gain or contributed nothing to the common good were condemned in no uncertain terms. 'There is no calling but it is for public good,' Sibbes reiterated. 'As an usurer, for whose good is he? . . . And such are they that live in a course of oppression, that live by the ruin and spoil of others.' Here the interplay between the two vocations was instructive, since only those worldly callings proceeding from a religious one were likely to be acknowledged as legitimate. 'Wheresoever these two callings are severed, whatsoever is in show, there is nothing in substance,' observed Perkins. 'Some be usurers and oppressors, some engrossers, some use false weights and measures, some lying and swearing, some are loose and lascivious.' The calling in fact originated as one answer to the deterioration of society caused by fraudulent and oppressive economic practices, and it was in this context that the preachers denied as socially acceptable callings those ways of life the poor were forced to adopt as a result of what such exploitation had done to their ability to maintain productive livelihoods. 'It is a foul disorder in any commonwealth that there should be suffered rogues, beggars, vagabonds, for such kind of persons commonly are of no civil society,' Perkins insisted. 'To wander up and down from year to year . . . to seek and procure bodily maintenance is no calling but the life of a beast.' For the poor therefore, as for the rich, work meant dignity and, indeed, redemption. 'You must be painful and diligent in a calling,' Thomas Jacomb urged them. '"He that will not work let him not eat." . . . If [the idle] would but work they might eat of their own bread and not be chargeable to any.'[66]

The economic importance of the calling, then, which was indeed real, was not to encourage the unfettered pursuit of private gain but, precisely the contrary, to impose control upon chaotic social relations and unaccountable commercial practices and make people morally answerable for the disruptions they created, as well as to rein in the high rate of mobility in English society. 'Every man must judge that particular calling in which God hath placed him to be the best of all callings for him,' Perkins enjoined. 'This duty is the stay and foundation . . . of church and commonwealth, for it maketh every man to keep his own standing and to employ himself pain[stakingly] within his calling; but when we begin to mislike the wise disposition of God and to think other men's callings better for us than our own, then follows confusion and disorder in every society.' Conservative as this may sound, the significance again may have been simply the need to state it and the recognition that new forms of social mobility and new economic opportunities had resulted in dangerous ambitions and discontents; as an expression of class hostility it almost certainly stemmed less from a fear of social subversion from below than of political sedition from above. 'Hence come treacheries, treasons, and seditions, when men, not content with their own estate and honors, seek higher places and being disappointed, grow to discontentments, and so forward to all mischief,' Perkins continued. 'Therefore . . . the good estate of the church and commonwealth is when every person keeps himself to his own calling.'[67]

Moreover, the particular calling was not the only one, and if social order was best preserved by each minding his own calling without envy and discontent, it was even more effectively strengthened through the dedication to the only calling that all could share equally in common without rivalry or ambition. 'Every man must join the practice of his personal calling with the practice of the general calling of Christianity,' Perkins continued. 'Every particular calling must be practiced in and with the general calling of a Christian.' The relationship was essentially that between faith and works, but in less abstract, more concrete form. 'The general calling of Christianty without the practice of some particular calling is nothing else but the form of godliness without the power thereof,' Perkins said. 'Therefore both callings must be joined, as body and soul are joined in a living man.' Precisely how they were joined varied, however, and one of the most powerful messages the higher calling sent to those who had lost out in the competition for worldly callings in a time of aggressive ambition was that they might have compensation for their inferior status in the egalitarianism, or even the moral superiority, of a religious vocation more prestigious than any to be found in human society. 'Though thou hast but a mean calling in this world, and so art not regarded as a man of use in the world, yet if thou beest a Christian God hath called thee to a higher calling,' Jeremiah Burroughs told his London congregation. 'The angels in heaven have not a higher calling than thou hast.' In the end, this most basic concept of the calling infused, and by the same measure eclipsed, all others:

> Thou that perhaps spendest thy time in a poor business, in the meanest calling, if thou beest a dung raker, to rake channels, or to cleanse places of filth, or any other thing in the world that is the meanest that can be conceived of, thy general calling as a Christian doth advance thee higher than any particular calling can advance any man in the world. Others, indeed, that are called to manage the affairs of the state, they are in a high calling, or ministers, they are in a high calling; but thine in some respects is higher.[68]

If a humble calling in society was conducive to a more honorable one in religion, it was because it encouraged diligence with humility, and the sole criterion determining the value of work was not the achievement of one's performance or the status of one's calling but the meekness of one's attitude. 'In doing our works . . . we [should] look upon God as all and ourselves as nothing in them.' Works were indeed required for whatever kind of salvation, but no one was to derive any pride of accomplishment or sense of having earned whatever it was they might achieve or procure. 'We plead not for the merit of them, but we are for the use of them,' said Thomas Watson. 'Though we shall not be saved without working, yet not for our working. We do not work out salvation by way of merit.' Far from endorsing the recent notion of a 'Protestant ethic' of justification by success, the cornerstone of Protestant theology was an uncompromising refusal to acknowledge 'any merit or degree or shadow of merit' in any human action and a denial that anyone could ever earn or deserve what one obtained in this world or the next. 'Merit? Away with it,' declared Thomas Jacomb. 'There is nothing merited at the hand of God.' The same rejection was central to Puritan social ethics, and not only the disavowal but the outright disdain the preachers consistently expressed for new middle-class values such as merit stemmed from a conviction that in practice what people called merit was usually little other than servility. 'Away with the conceit of merit!' Sibbes demanded. 'We merit nothing but destruction . . . . God indeed uses [us], but hereby do we not deserve anything.' The conviction that merit would or could receive its just reward was after all the creed of the successful, but the ministers' remedy for a society where merit more often than not went unrecognized and unrewarded was not so much to try to reinforce the ideal so that deserts and emoluments more nearly corresponded (at least not directly) but to reject the notion of merit altogether as the self-serving illusion of the powerful and privileged, to point out that the weak and deprived knew all too well that the merit of this world was an empty conceit and that the only true merit flowed in blood. 'Work low; be humble; think not to merit by your working,' Watson urged. 'Look up to Christ's merit. It is not your sweat but his blood saves. That your working cannot merit is clear.' A radical egalitarianism proceeded from the denial of justification by merit in favor of faith, since while one's achievements or position were declared worthless in the sight of God, one could console oneself with the knowledge that those who appeared more successful or prosperous were equally devoid of value, and the conviction that what people might have accomplished in this world in the way of possessions or status or office bore no relation whatever to what they deserved played no small part in their similar understanding about how rewards were distributed in the world to come. 'If we merit not outward deliverance . . . what can we do for eternal life?' Sibbes asked of the 'spiritual beggars' he addressed. 'It is . . . a mere foolish conceit then to think that the beggar merits his alms by begging . . . . What doth the beggar merit by begging? Begging, it is a disavowing of merit.' The refusal to recognize merit might not appear fair to those who were puffed up with a sense of their own accomplishments and all the 'work' they had done to attain them, but the service of Christ was not for the high but for the humble, those who knew it was God's work and not their own and so would not allow themselves to derive pride or complacency from whatever they might seem to have achieved. 'They that be humble . . . are willing to take him on his own terms,' said John Preston:

> to keep his commandments and not think them grievous, to bear his burden and think it light, to take his yoke and count it easy, to give all they have for him and think all too little, to suffer persecution for his sake and rejoice in it, to be content to be scoffed at and hated of men, to do, to suffer anything for his sake and, when all this is done, to regard it as nothing, to reckon themselves unprofitable servants, to account of all as not worthy of him.[69]

None of this was to say that God did not reward works; on the contrary, the preachers insisted that he did reward them – just not the same way the world did, and this was what Preston meant when he said that 'God rewards men according to their works, not according to their wealth.' God did indeed reward works, not because of their merit, but despite their lack of it. 'Though we merit not any good, yet God he overlooks the illness of our works and accepts and reward the good that is in them,' Sibbes said, 'giving us comfort and assurance of our justification.' The critical factor in this justification was not the quality of the works, and certainly not the status of the person, but the 'faithfulness' of the heart. 'Thy faithfulness may be rewarded by God with as great glory as a king that hath swayed his scepter for God,' promised Jeremiah Burroughs, 'because the Lord doth not so much look at the work that is done as at the faithfulness of our hearts in doing it.' The demands of faith, far from the 'meritocracy' with which they are sometimes credited, were in some ways precisely the opposite, an ethic that sought to level even those distinctions based on ability. 'May not I be faithful as well as another? I cannot come to be as rich a man and as honorable as others, but I may be as faithful as any other man,' Burroughs suggested. 'You that are the poorest and the meanest may be as faithful as the greatest.' This may even have had the potential to become more of a 'mediocracy', or rule of the failures, though the aim was to spur the most inadequate and diffident souls on to constructive activity by assuring them that their duties were rendered acceptable for the same reason as were their souls: because they were faithful. 'Faith is . . . that that makes all acceptable to God,' said Preston. 'It is faith by which both our persons and services are accepted.' The Protestant creed of justification by faith and the Puritan 'work ethic', then, were not somehow imposed upon people by an insidious conspiracy of dour killjoys but a burden they imposed on themselves in an effort to satisfy perhaps the greatest need they could feel, this need to be 'accepted'. 'Our good works shall be rewarded . . . but the reward is grounded upon a free pardon and a gracious acceptation,' Francis Cheynell explained. 'If we were not first justified, our works would not be accepted nor rewarded. Because our persons are accepted in Christ, therefore our works are rewarded for Christ.'[70]

Faithful work was certain of reward, then, but it did not follow automatically according to natural causes but was often postponed considerably, sometimes even into the next life, to ensure that people continued working throughout this one. 'God doth as other masters that keep their wages till the work be done,' Edmund Calamy explained in social terms.

> This life is the time of working; hereafter we shall have wages enough . . . . If they had a great part of their wages aforehand, they would do but little work . . . . And indeed we see it too true in many great rich personages that have so much of their pay beforehand . . . whereas indeed it ought to be an obligation to greater service.

The point of warning that returns might be withheld for a time was to help people understand that in this world instant gratification of one's desires was not always possible and to instill the habit of accepting the promise of gratification that was often significantly delayed. 'Take heed that you do not lay the stress and weight of all your comfort upon duty . . . or the immediate answer of it,' William Bridge warned. 'So much will you be discouraged in case you either want duty or an answer to it.' The message was to not expect immediate success in one's endeavors, however worthy, or be discouraged when they seemed to fail at first, but to continue on, looking beyond present obstacles toward the future, if necessary the distant future, even eternity, for the satisfaction of one's deepest needs and the fulfillment of one's dearest hopes and expectations. 'Those whose minds are so fixed on, and swelled up with, some end (though good) which they have proposed to themselves do seldom see good days and serene in their own souls,' John Owen observed. 'They have bitterness, wrath, and trouble all their days . . . . There is a sweetness, there is a wages to be found in the work of God itself.' By giving them something to look forward to, faith assured people that the work they were put to would in some sense succeed and at some point be rewarded, a knowledge that was itself a kind of reward. 'Our reward is certain, not of worth but through grace,' Lazarus Seaman promised. 'Thereby beloved, be ye steadfast, unmovable, always abounding in the work of the Lord, forasmuch as you know that your labor is not in vain in the Lord.' The assurance of eventual success allowed believers to devote themselves to the work itself rather than chafing in anxious expectation of what the work was meant to achieve, and so made work its own reward. 'Your labor *is* not in vain,' Matthew Barker emphasized. 'The very work is wages. A man is reaping while he is sowing.'[71]

Rewards, then, did have a place in moving people to action, at least when contrasted with punishments. 'Heaven hath more force by an attractive power to draw our desires than hell hath operation by way of terror,' said Thomas Valentine. 'The fear of hell troubles not so much as the want of heaven.' And yet the very terms used to make this point indicate that their ends were best achieved through this emphasis on 'love', as distinct from fear, in motivating action. 'Love . . . is one of the greatest and most radical virtues,' said John Preston. 'Faith and love . . . are the radical virtues which indeed make up the new creature.' Faith and love were 'radical' in that they changed human nature from the root, moving it to action. 'Wheresoever there is faith and love, there is a change of nature,'

Preston said. 'Nature is changed; it must needs be active.' Love enabled work to be undertaken voluntarily, not from the outward compulsion provided by fear but from a motivation within. 'To do a thing in love is to do it in sincerity,' Preston said. 'The love of Christ . . . draws one to serve the Lord . . . from an inward inclination of the mind, from an inward principle.' Through love the distinction between works and rewards, means and ends, freedom and servitude, disappeared altogether, since one no longer worked for the reward but for the satisfaction derived from serving God. 'The nature of love . . . is this, to be free in doing that it doth, and not to stand to examine how much they should do and how much they shall receive for doing of it, but to do it with liberty and freedom,' Preston added.

> If your love be right to the Lord . . . you will not stand considering what you are bound to do of necessity . . . . But love will rather say, what shall I do to recompense the Lord? It will be devising what to do; it will be glad of any occasion of doing anything that may be acceptable to God . . . . Beloved, if there be love in you, you will strive to do the utmost of your power; it is the nature of love so to do.

Faithful service undertaken out of love was thus its own satisfaction. 'He that loves God only for heaven loves God for that which is inferior to God,' Edmund Calamy said. 'This is my heaven to be obedient.' The service of God was itself, in effect, a kind of heaven on earth. 'God's service is a type of heaven,' Calamy proclaimed, 'wherein is fullness of joy.'[72]

Just as sin created its own misery, therefore, so good work provided its own compensation. 'As sin is punishment enough unto itself,' said Daniel Evance, 'so to do good is reward enough unto itself.' Yet the main impediment to this joy was sin itself, its own punishment in part because of its antipathy to work. 'He that is employed for God shall have the sin of his own heart against him,' William Carter warned. 'Sin hath reason for it, because the works of God are its destruction. Where his work prospers, woe to sin; it fades and dies.' It followed that God's work was most effectively conducted by those whose sins had been forgiven through their faith. 'The work of God doth prosper best in such men's hands whose sins are pardoned and whose peace is made with him.' It was never denied that God also used wicked people as his instruments; nevertheless, there was said to be a difference. ''Tis true, God serves himself sometimes upon his enemies, and they shall do his work,' Carter continued; 'but still his business prospers best with such who are his friends.' Many of the efforts demanded by God of his people could, in fact, be paralleled with the followers of Satan. 'Let us but look on the antichristian party in this kingdom and see how industrious they are,' Henry Wilkinson admonished in 1644, 'how vigilant . . . to make use of all advantages to promote their designs.'

> They do not offer to the devil that which costs them nought. He is a hard master, and his service is very troublesome, dangerous, desperate service, and yet how zealous are they in it? How many lives have been sacrificed in

it? Let it never be said that Satan should have more cost bestowed on him, more pains and care and time laid out in his drudgery than the noble and honorable and glorious work of God now in your hands should have bestowed on it.[73]

Such also were the instruments of God and in their fashion served his purposes as well, but not in the same way. 'Those that serve God upon such terms, they are not servants but slaves,' said Evance, 'and truly those that prove servile, they can never prove serviceable.' If the human will existed naturally in a state of bondage, by willingly binding themselves to the service of God the wills of men and women – and the men and women themselves – could become truly 'free'. 'Let us then go to our work as bound, yet free,' urged Joseph Caryl, 'free to our work, not from it, working from a principle of holy ingenuity, not of servility or constraint. The Lord threatens them with bondage and captivity who will not be servants in their covenant with readiness and activity.' Freedom was defined not as freedom from subjection to God but as a voluntary subjection to his power and 'service'. 'God's people are a free people,' said Sibbes. 'God's people are all volunteers, doing holy duties freely; for they are freed from exaction and coaction. The spirit . . . setteth them at liberty . . . . It cost Christ's blood, who redeemed to serve him without fear.' This was the meaning of Christian liberty, the only real liberty in the ministers' view, when the soul was free to work and serve voluntarily. 'Christ's service is the only true liberty,' said Sibbes. 'Those that take the most liberty to sin are the most perfect slaves, because most voluntary slaves.' To serve God with dedication was nothing less than emancipation, even liberation. 'Be assiduous, indefatigable in service,' Gaspar Hickes urged, 'that you may be freemen of heaven.' And thus the dialectic paradox at the heart of Puritanism between bondage and freedom. 'There is a service which is freedom,' said John Geree, 'the service of Christ; and there is a freedom which is servitude, freedom to sin. There is a liberty which is bondage and . . . a bondage which is liberty.'[74]

This was more than simply a platitude, since the service of Christ was indeed rigorous. 'It is a kind of bondage, and abridgement of liberty,' Henry Wilkinson said, 'to devote oneself to the service of Christ.' Christ himself was sometimes described as the humblest of servants, one whose calling was to bear the burden of others. 'Christ took upon him the form of a servant,' Sibbes noted. 'He was lowest of all servants . . . for none was ever so abased as our glorious Savior . . . . He was a servant to us, because he did our work and suffered our punishment. . . . He is a servant that bears another man's burden.' Though Christ had offices higher up the status scale, his servitude was what many of his followers in England seemed initially most ready to identify with. 'Was not this wonderful, for . . . the glorious God to abase himself, to be a servant?' Sibbes asked. 'For the living God to die . . . for glory itself to be abased, for riches to become poor, what a manner of wonderment is here!' All liberty for Christian 'freemen' then was purchased by Christ's bondage and servitude. 'Our liberty comes from his service and slavery,' Sibbes said, 'our life from his death.' And outside that liberty, for even the highest, was nothing but continued 'slavery'. 'Out of Christ we are slaves, the best of us are slaves,' Sibbes added. 'In Christ the meanest of all is a freeman and a king. Out of Christ there is nothing but thralldom.' The doctrine of the 'bondage of the will' was thus intimately associated with the bondage of humanity, and like the will humanity was in bondage to the extent that it was the captive of sin. 'The more [one] is enthralled to sin the more he is in bondage to the devil,' said Sibbes, 'and he becomes the enemy of God.'[75]

Slavery and freedom, then, were to some extent conditions of mind, and such was the thralldom of many that they seemed to prefer their enslavement to the liberty that came from serving Christ. As Oliver Bowles remarked contemptuously, 'Men will endure much so be it you let their sin alone.' For this reason liberty was especially difficult for leaders, who had to contend with not only their own sins but also those of the people, who often became ungrateful and discontented as difficulties arose. 'It is very hard for governors themselves to lead a people out of bondage into freedom and not to provoke God much by their own sins,' Anthony Burges noted. 'The ingratitude and discontents of people are such under reformers that they make their condition very hard and uncomfortable.' Such again was familiar from scripture, where God's people, disoriented and frightened by their new freedom, sought security by returning to bondage. 'We are like unto the children of Israel,' Calamy observed, 'who when they came first out of Egypt did almost deify Moses and Aaron, but afterward, as soon as ever they began to meet with straits and difficulties, they began presently to murmur against them and to call their fidelity into question and to accuse them, as if they had a design to bring them into the wilderness to destroy them. Just so do we.' This Old Testament episode illustrated the consequences to those whose servility had inured them to bondage and who sought to evade freedom. 'We see those of the Israelites who had a mind to go back again into Egypt did all perish in the wilderness,' Sibbes noted. 'It is a pity they should ever be delivered that are in love with bondage. Those that will serve and be slaves still, it is a pity but their ears should be bored to perpetual servitude.'[76]

To be enlisted in the service of true religion, by contrast, far from demeaning the servant, entailed honor and even nobility. 'To be the Servant of Christ is [a] title of honor,' declared William Strong, 'and to be the servants of God is the honor of the saints.' The honor derived from such service guaranteed that it was conscientious and sincere. 'Honor God by service,' Strong urged. 'We . . . honor God when we think ourselves honored by the service of God.' To be so honored was to derive no honor from the service itself but to give all the honor first to God and then to gain it only reflectively from him, and to be an 'instrument' at once humbled and exalted the soul. 'A man honors God by ascribing all unto him when he hath labored in his service with all his might,' Strong said. 'Men employed in the highest works upon earth are but instruments and weapons in the Lord's hand, and as to be used in service is a man's highest honor, so to take to himself the glory will be a man's shame and dishonor forever.' While the preachers encouraged work as its own reward, this appropriation of honor may have provided the most powerful motive. 'The highest honor . . . is to be used,' Strong said, 'and the greatest reproach to a man that can be is to be laid aside.' The opportunity to be employed and needed for a great work may have been especially appealing to those of whatever status who felt their services and talents had not received sufficient recognition from society. 'God doth honor men by giving them honorable employments,' Strong promised.

> They that are most serviceable are most honorable. Those honorable titles carry in them great services . . . and whatsoever may set forth a man useful in church or commonwealth. That any of you should be so far used and honored as . . . to deliver an enslaved people . . . to fight the Lord's battles . . . these are the greatest and most honorable services that any men in the world can be employed in.[77]

Yet, while it was all very well to inform people that such toil was to be undertaken cheerfully and for its own sake, discouragements would indeed be encountered. 'Though God do raise up men on purpose to do some great work for him,' Burges said, 'yet there will be many difficulties and stops in the way.' This was the basis of the preachers' concern about hypocritical performances – that they were unreliable and in the face of obstacles would lead to apostasy. 'Apostasy and hypocrisy are like the symbolical elements whereof one quickly slips into the other,' noted Obadiah Sedgwick. 'A hypocrite is a kind of secret apostate, and an apostate is a hypocrite uncased.' While hypocrisy, which tended to exist in times of relative ease, might seem innocuous, and in any case could only be known for certain by God and the sinner (if even the sinner), apostasy would quickly manifest itself to the world at the first sign of difficulty or danger. 'The same grounds which persuade men to hypocrisy when times go well,' Jeremiah Whitaker warned, 'will carry them to apostasy when times go ill.' Apostasy thus had the same roots as hypocrisy, those of unbelief and infidelity. 'Unbelief will carry a man to apostasy,' said Thomas Brooks. 'It hath been the great reason of many men's apostasy and backsliding from God and his ways, that they could not . . . trust in God by faith.' Without the constancy provided by faith, one simply worked, and failed to work, along with the uncertainties of the world. 'We live in an apostatizing age,' Brooks complained. 'Men wheel and turn about as second causes work and are not steadfast with their God.' Lack of faith guaranteed 'unfaithfulness' or inconstancy, possibly even betrayal, not only of God but others as well. 'Want of faith is the cause of all the unfaithfulness that ever was in the world, the very root of apostasy both from God and man,' Joseph Caryl said. 'Faith keeps the heart steady and will see us die rather than offer a thought of withdrawing from a known duty.' In the course of the revolution such abstract principles came to have increasingly critical practical consequences as the faithful developed a mounting stake in the success of what they had perpetrated and with it a suspicious apprehension regarding treachery within their own ranks. 'Have you been steadfast in your hearts and affections?' Matthew Barker asked the members of the House of Commons in 1648. 'Have they been firm and borne up stoutly against all opposition and discouragements that you have met with in that great work which hath been under your hands? Or have you not been closing, at least some of you, with indirect means for your own security in case the cause should miscarry?'[78]

While the sincerity of an individual's faith was ultimately known only to God, it was continually being tested and testified visibly by unrelenting struggle against a hostile world and could be indicated only by 'constancy' in the face of difficulties and 'perseverance' through dangers. 'Sincerity is accompanied with constancy and perseverance,' said Sibbes. 'Always constancy and perseverance are companions with simplicity and sincerity . . . . Where there is truth . . . there is perseverance to the end.' Perseverance was an indication of fidelity and therefore of faith, though it was God's faithfulness as much as that of the soul. 'The case in perseverance is not how faithful we are but how faithful God is,' Sibbes said. 'A Christian may be assured of his salvation, of his perseverance, because Christ is Lord of all.' As Sibbes indicates, the doctrine of perseverance, the knowledge that one would persevere because God would allow one to persevere, was closely related to another, one of the most central tenets in Calvinist theology, that of 'assurance'. 'These truths follow one the other, assurance of salvation and perserverance,' Sibbes said. 'The one follows the other, because . . . as it assures us of salvation, so it assures of perseverance.' Assurance by its very nature was especially necessary in times of change and confusion. '[Assurance] is useful to the saints at all times but especially in changing times,' said Thomas Brooks. 'In the midst of all these turmoils and revolutions . . . happy are those souls that have gained a well-grounded assurance . . . made sure to them in changing times.' What precisely it was assurance of was not tremendously important; in times of uncertainty assurance was valued for its own sake. 'When poor souls shall come to enjoy assurance who have been long tossed up and down in a sea of sorrow and trouble,' Brooks noted, 'how will they with joy cry out, Assurance, assurance, assurance!' But assurance was possible because God assured that the soul would persevere, that perseverance was itself guaranteed by God, and so, in fact, assured. 'The doctrine of perseverance . . . is this,' Sibbes said, 'that God's children, as they may be assured of their salvation, so they may be assured that they shall hold out to the end.' By elevating perseverance to the status of a doctrine, the preachers were again attempting to ensure that by that very fact it happened, fusing the dogmatic tenet with the imperative duty in such a way as to render any other outcome inconceivable. 'Be rooted and established in the doctrine of the perserverance of the saints,' Edmund Calamy urged. 'Believe that whosoever is truly united unto Jesus Christ by a lively faith shall be so preserved by Christ . . . that he shall never totally fall away.' With this doctrine in particular the actual believing of it played a very practical part in making it true. 'If God . . . hath decreed the perseverance of the saints, if he hath promised that they shall persevere, and that he will enable them by his power unto it . . . then we may safely conclude that it is our duty to be steadfast and unmovable in it.' As with the initial inclusion within the covenant

179

itself, the comfort of perseverance was that God enabled people to fulfill and continue in it. 'God in the covenant of grace doth not only promise to give us heaven if we believe and persevere,' Calamy pointed out, 'but also to give us the use of means to believe and persevere.'[79]

What the preachers sought to promote, then, and argued that only faith with its self-fulfilling doctrines such as assurance and perseverance could promote, was not simply work, but work that would be constant and reliable, enduring and conscientious, work that was undertaken willingly, cheerfully, eagerly, even fervidly. 'Men do good actions as a task; they are glad when they be over,' John Preston observed. 'But do you them with much inten[sity], much fervency, much desire; be you a people zealous of good works . . . . The Lord respects no service but as it is joined with fervency.' This fervor or 'zeal' would generate not simply motivation for work but enthusiasm. 'Zeal is the height of faith,' Francis Cheynell declared. 'For zeal can never boil high enough unless it be raised by faith.' The notion that zeal could be measured by temperature suggested the presence of energy, of 'life', as against the mass of society that seemed to exist in a state of interminable listlessness – those whom the preachers described as the 'cold', the 'lukewarm', and the dead. 'Heat is a sign of life; cold is a forerunner of death,' Thomas Valentine noted. 'Zeal is a spiritual heat kindled by the spirit of God whereby all the affections are drawn out to the utmost for God.' The preachers never doubted that such fire did burn within the hearts of the most dispirited; the problem was to get it fixated on the right objects. 'What ardent desires, what flames can they send after their sins and how dull, how sluggish in seeking him whom our soul should love!' remarked Henry Wilkinson. 'Zeal is nothing else but the inten[sity] of all holy affections and actions . . . to look only to the Lord.' Zeal was not irresponsible or nihilistic; on the contrary, it was carefully controlled and disciplined. 'It is regular, guided by rule,' according to Thomas Wilson. 'Zeal is bold, but not blind; it is not rash or indiscreet but wisely discerning.' Sometimes however it was difficult to tell precisely the difference. 'There is much discretion to be used in the managing of our zeal,' said Henry Wilkinson. 'But discretion doth not abate the heat of love, but direct it; prudence doth not remit our diligence and zeal, but guide it . . . . He which is on a right course and goes slowly is not moderate but idle.' The virtues of 'discretion' and 'moderation' were among those the preachers occasionally extolled but usually in a defensive tone and with significant qualifications. 'Moderation in a right course is not moderation but lukewarmness, and coldness,' said Preston. 'If you mean by moderation to go a slow and easy pace in the ways of God, that is coldness, idleness, carelessness. There is no excess in any good way.' Certainly moderation never carried the connotation of compromise in the struggle against any evil or adversity, and zeal demanded precisely the opposite. 'Zeal . . . yields to no encounters,' Wilkinson insisted, 'but it is increased by opposition.' The ministers' pleas for zeal, a kind of impassioned, fanatical pursuit of self-control, illustrate the moral nightmare in which they were placed and their effort to give this confusion vent in practical activity. 'Zeal is a mixed affection of love and anger,' Wilkinson said, ' . . . and produceth effects both of love and hatred.' In practice this tended to mean love towards God and anger and hatred towards everything else. 'Our love to God and zeal to the truth can never be too intense,' Wilkinson urged. 'It must be total and it must be superlative; if we love him we must love nothing else . . . . Serve him with ardent zeal, strong affections, and love inflamed, always going on with courage and resolution, continuing with patience and constancy, that so we may end with glory.'

God demanded passionate love, even exclusive love, and while zeal emanated from love, love itself existed almost inseparably in a dialectical relationship not only with fear but also, as Wilkinson says, with hate. 'Zeal . . . is an inten[sity] of the affection of hatred,' observed Preston, 'and it is required that you hate sin.' Hatred was an 'affection' that shared many of the characteristics of love and faith, and here too it was sometimes difficult to distinguish. 'Hatred . . . is a constant affection, it abides with us,' Preston noted. 'Hatred seeks the utter destruction of the thing hated.' To serve God zealously then meant to work for nothing less than the total destruction of evil from the earth. 'Zeal doth the work that God's vengeance should do,' Stephen Marshall said. 'Zealous men are endeavoring to exterminate all things that are evil.' Zealotry then was not simply a feature the ministers exhibited in moments of excess but a quality they advocated as a positive good for its own sake, and all the more so as true zealots were not numerous in the land. 'Think how few are to be found in any place or any rank or society of men who are to be numbered among them whose hearts are truly zealous for the Lord,' Marshall lamented. And yet, paradoxically perhaps, there were still others whose zeal seemed to be directed against the zealous – indeed, against zeal. 'Have we not abundance that live this day . . . who have a zeal against zeal,' Marshall asked:

> who are with all the heat that can be kindled in them set *against* zealous men, casting all the opprobrious nicknames on them that can be, branding zeal for God with madness, with turbulency, with indiscretion? . . . These are miserable and accursed men . . . and as true zealots are set on fire from heaven, so these men's fire is kindled from hell.[80]

Because of such adversaries to the faith, as well as the cold and lukewarm, there arose not only in practice a contention between true zealots and others but the imperative for deliberate, active contention and agitation, what the preachers described as contention for the faith. 'Contend for the faith,' Preston urged. 'The work must be to contend for it . . . . You must be men of contention . . . . Let not pretense of indiscretion hinder you . . . . That is your work now to contend for the faith.' This idea of active agitation, in many forms and on many fronts, illustrates the inseparable relationship between faith and work, the one being the practical application of a theoretical ideal, and applying the terms of a doctrine to the very process of vindicating it. 'It is the common faith; therefore every man . . . should contend according to his place and power,' Preston maintained. 'We should strive and contend . . . and we should do it earnestly . . . contend with

God in prayer; contend with our superiors by entreaty, with our adversaries by resistance, with cold and lukewarm men by stirring them up, by provoking one another to good works.'[81]

Moreover, as such contention became political agitation, faith could be turned outward to create an ethic of political officialdom and political activism. 'Faith will keep you to a rule,' William Sedgwick told the House of Commons, 'and so make you exact in justice.' Those who held positions of public trust were keepers of the faith of the kingdom – and of the Almighty as well – and the very knowledge that one was entrusted with the 'public faith' was intended to inspire a sense of faithful duty in defending it. 'You have not only the public faith of the kingdom but the public faith of heaven also,' Thomas Case told Parliament. 'Though others prove faint and false, yet you that have engaged the public faith, be ye faithful unto death, and God shall give you the crown of life.' The personal need to believe and have faith was thus a preparation for the public commitment required to preserve and deliver the commonwealth. 'Until you know how to believe for your own souls you will scarcely know how to believe for a nation,' said John Owen. 'He can hardly be faithful to a state that is not faithful to his own soul.' On the other hand, those beyond the faith, those without faith, and the unfaithful were by definition fallible and their devices destined to fail. 'Wicked men cannot do public service so successfully as the faithful,' William Goode said. While all public service was encouraged, that in the cause of faith itself, and against those who were out of 'the faith' or not devoted to the cause, was the noblest, and though the ministers did have a concept of 'charity', it was defined by faith. 'Much more is it an act of faith to be valiant in the defense of the faith,' Francis Cheynell said. 'And if you talk of charity, consider that . . . that is not true charity which will not consist with faith . . . . Be out of charity with the whore and the beast; they are fitter objects of thy hatred than of thy charity.' Faith at once strengthened weak souls and in the process empowered otherwise hopeless political causes. 'We have . . . kingdoms to subdue . . . justice to execute . . . violent fire to quench, a sharp-edged sword to escape, popish alien armies to fight with,' Joseph Caryl proclaimed to the House of Commons in 1643, 'and we are but weak.'

> How then shall we out of our weakness become strong, strong enough to carry us through these mighty works, strong enough to escape these visible dangers if . . . not by faith? . . . We must go to counsel by faith and to war by faith; we must pull down by faith and build by faith.[82]

Contention against opponents of the faith was therefore undertaken not only for the faith but by the faith as well, which served as the ideological mover of both political and military conflict. 'The soldiers by this triumph, and the enemies fall,' declared Thomas Wilson. 'Faith is the warrior's target, the soldier's shield.' As agitation became active conflict, the preachers urged that it be conducted according to the dictates of faith, the means as well as the end. 'Fight the good fight of faith,' urged Thomas Hill. 'Such have the best cause. It is God's. Such fight the Lord's battles. The best captain, Jesus Christ the captain of their salvation. The best fellow soldiers . . . with certainty of victory.' Of all the works a believer was to undertake the most important was war, the final forum for the glory of self-sacrifice, and in this 'fight of faith' the metaphor of warfare came to be most graphic. 'There is a fight in faith,' Francis Peck said. 'No sooner is a man a believer but he is a warrior.' In the same way as faith was the hardest thing for a soul to undertake, so war seemed the best description of the dimensions the fight could assume. 'In fighting there is much difficulty,' Peck continued; 'so in believing, the hardest thing in the world is to believe . . . . In fighting there are encounters and strong opposites; so in this fight of faith it meets with strong opposites, flesh and the devil.' Here in the 'fight of faith' the distinction between metaphor and reality seemed to dissolve altogether, and a direct continuity can be seen between the war within and that without. 'This fight of faith is twofold,' Peck explained, 'internal, when a believer fights against his lusts and corruptions and Satan's wiles, [and] external, when a man courageously stands up in the cause of Christ and suffers afflictions and persecutions for Christ and is not overcome by them.' The two came together most intensely in the readiness faith provided for the supreme sacrifice: a willingness to die for the cause. 'To make a man willing to die . . . is not done without a combat,' Peck added. 'Believers only are willing to die, and faith makes them so.' Whatever might happen to individual believers, the cause for which they suffered and died would continue, as in a sense would they with it. 'May not Christ's soldiers be foiled?' Hill suggested. 'The cause may prevail when the persons miscarry and grow great out of the ruins of such as suffered for it . . . . There will be a speedy resurrection of them and the cause.' Faith thus became as powerful for political as for spiritual purposes, and so blurred did the distinction become between 'temporal' and 'eternal' that faith, like those who had it, was predestined to triumph. 'Faith in God being so mighty,' Wilson said, ' . . . believers be most valiant victors, the chiefest conquerors.'

> Godly men relying on the word be stronger than all the world; their spirits be heroical, their arms made strong by the mighty God of Jacob. Kingdoms cannot stand before them. Through faith they subdued kingdoms . . . . It is the honor of all the saints to triumph over all contrary royalty and nobility, to bind kings in chains and nobles with fetters of iron.

And in that faith was not only that for which one contended but also that by which one fought, those who fought for the 'truth' were 'justified' by their faith in doing so, vindicating both before the world. 'Thousands of standers-by be ready to call in question either the faithfulness of God or the infallibility of those truths which God's people have so many years together professed and suffered for,' Thomas Case declared apocalyptically in 1643.

> Much of the credit of those truths for which the saints have contended into this apostate generation . . . depends upon the success of the battles between Michael and his angels and the dragon and his . . . . Thou has

given thy people occasions of joy and triumph in their victory over their enemies. Why? Because of the truth . . . of God's promise . . . the truth of doctrine . . . which w[as] preserved . . . and therefore the truth of the promises did preserve them. They fought for the truth, and the truth fought for them and crowned them with a multitude of victories.[83]

Nothing less than the 'truth' of God himself and his very 'faithfulness' to his own word came to be dependent on the success of the great work he was bringing to pass in England which, however 'temporal' a salvation it might be, came to be transformed into an event of historical and even 'eternal' importance. 'Your eternal salvation lies upon it,' Elidad Blackwell asserted. 'Your and our temporal salvation also.' Thus did the temporal redemption of England come to be intertwined with the eternal redemption of those whom God made use of in effecting it. 'Laws, liberties, lives, gospel, religion, church, state, kingdom, all lies upon it,' Blackwell continued. 'According as you manage your work, even so may it fare with England for ought I know, and the children that are yet unborn will have cause either to stand up and bless you or to stand up and curse you.' In fact, the one reliable indication within this world of the faithfulness of one's service was to hold out to the end, however it might come, especially in the face of overwhelming odds. 'For a soul to hold on and to serve his generation, against all and notwithstanding all the reproaches and dirt and scorn and contempt that is thrown on them,' said Thomas Brooks, 'this is to do gloriously.' The idea of serving one's generation meant that a willingness to endure to the death was the final determinant of faithful service and self-sacrifice, and those who served their own generation faithfully could have the consolation of knowing that another could be counted on to rise up and continue the work. 'When this life is finished, and we gathered to our fathers, there may be a generation out of our loins to stand up in this cause,' said Philip Nye, 'that his great and reverend name may be exalted from one generation to another.'

Faith created a solidarity through the ages, from the generations long gone, through those currently engaged in the struggle, to others yet unborn. 'One generation soweth and another reapeth,' said Thomas Case. 'If any of you die before you see this great salvation of the Lord, your posterity shall inherit the blessing, and for you it is honor enough that you expire in so great a cause.' No body was so important that it could not be dispensed with, and at some point God would dismiss each of his servants who had been faithful to the cause. 'There is an appointed season wherein the saints of the most eminent abilities, in the most useful employments, must receive their dismission,' John Owen said. 'Be their work of never so great importance, be their abilities never so choice and eminent, they must in their season receive their dismission.' But however expendable each individual might be as but a part of the larger cause, the faithful soul could have the consolation of the praise it would receive from the generation of the firstborn. 'Be you never so excellent, never so useful, yet the days of your service "are as the days of an hireling" that will expire at the appointed season,' Owen said. 'This is the praise of a man, the only praise whereof in this world he is a partaker, that he doth the will of God before he fall asleep, that he faithfully serves his generation until he be no more.' Thus the honor one would receive for faithful service, like the 'salvation' that one may or may not live to see here, would be, in more than one sense, eternal. 'The children of God, who in their lives have had a special care to honor God, God hath had a special care to honor their memories in future times,' promised William Goode. 'After this life God doth honor them with a sweet and a precious name . . . and their memory shall be blessed among the posterities to come.' Like God himself and the mercies he granted, those who were instrumental in procuring them would be held in honor and 'esteem', not by the world at large perhaps, but within it by those who truly mattered. 'God honors men by giving them a high esteem in the hearts of the faithful,' said William Strong. 'And to have an interest in the hearts of the faithful is more than to have the favor of all the princes of the earth.' And finally, at the conclusion of the long and arduous struggle, the weary pilgrims and soldiers who had proved themselves faithful to the last could look forward to what the preachers described as an eternal 'rest'. 'They rest from all trouble and anxiety that attend them in their pilgrimage, either in doing or suffering for God,' Owen promised. 'God wipes all tears from their eyes. There is no more watching, no more fasting, no more wrestling, no more fighting, no more blood, no more sorrow.'[84]

Increasingly, then, faith created a self-defining bond of mutual obligation among 'the faithful' from all time, centering around the example of, and allegiance to, Christ. 'Jesus Christ laid down his life for us,' John Goodwin said. 'Having such a pattern and example before us . . . it is but matter of equity and duty in us to be so far raised and carried out in our affections of love towards those that are . . . partakers of like precious faith with us as to lay down and part with our lives for them.' Such solidarity was not merely in imitation of Christ; through faithful devotion, in some sense it was Christ. 'By such excellent expressions of your love to your brethren in the faith as are required of you, you shall glorify the name of Christ on earth and convince the judgments and consciences of ignorant and wicked men.' Justification by faith acquired practical political significance as the acts of believers in fidelity to the ideal of Christ justified their own belief, and the truth of the faith came to be vindicated by the fidelity of its adherents. 'Your faithfulness justifies your faith afore men as your faith justifies your persons afore God,' William Price said. 'Fidelity sets a grace and gloss upon Christianity.' As the faith would be 'justified', even in the sight of the world, so it would in turn 'justify' those – and what they did – who were instrumental in bringing it to pass. 'Christ will at length justify himself,' Richard Sibbes promised. 'This is a ground of faith.' And what justified Christ himself also vindicated his downtrodden but faithful followers:

As Christ will justify himself, so he will justify his church and children . . . . His children are now accounted the offscouring of the world. They are trampled and trod upon, they are the objects of scorn and hatred . . . . Will Christ endure this? No. He that 'justified' himself . . . will he not 'justify' his church, his mystical body, to be as they are indeed? Certainly it shall appear to the world that he will justify them, to be kings and priests, to be heirs, to be glorious, to be so near and dear to him . . . . The time will come that all this shall be 'justified' . . . . Therefore in our eclipses and disgraces let us all comfort ourselves in this. Let the world esteem us for the present as the refuse of the world, as persons not worthy to be acquainted with, not worthy to be regarded. We shall be 'justified' and cleared and glorified, especially at that day 'when Christ shall come to be glorious in his saints'.[85]

5

THE CHURCH

The godly are generally poor, but sometimes God raises them up to power and authority.

John Warren, 1655

While the preachers always insisted upon the need to save as much of England as possible, they and their theology also recognized that many, perhaps most, would never exhibit the level of commitment required to be counted among 'God's people' and that some would actively oppose them. 'Remember that though Jesus Christ be King of all the world in a providential way,' said Francis Cheynell, 'yet he is King of Saints only in a spiritual and saving way. Such immortal honor have all his saints, and none but saints . . . whose consciences Christ hath purged from the guilt . . . of sin . . . by a lively faith that they may serve the living God.' The idea of an elite corps of 'saints' who alone could be entrusted with the honor of serving God faithfully did not mean that the preachers necessarily drew the line between the saved and the damned so as to correspond precisely to the partisan division at any given time in the civil war. 'When I say "saints", I mean no one party of men,' claimed Thomas Goodwin in 1646. 'And it were the highest sacrilege in the world to engross that title of "saints" and the "godly party" to any one.' Still, that the godly could be identified with a specific 'party', a kind of vanguard of the elect, and that the party did have some special role in political as well as religious affairs was becoming recognized with increasing openness, even if the fear of its being hijacked by sectarian tendencies led some to insist that 'the godly party is of a larger extent than to be appropriated or confined within any one sect or faction'. The continued possibilities of hypocrisy and apostasy, betrayal, or merely insufficient zeal, as well perhaps as the chance of converting some of the apparently wicked or indifferent, prevented the preachers from simply identifying those who fought for Parliament at any particular moment with those who fought for God; this was not, however, to deny the underlying assumption that, as Thomas Palmer suggested in 1644, 'the Parliament's cause is God's cause and those which join with them are more God's people than on the other side'.[1]

While the division between souls might not always correspond precisely to that which had opened up in the kingdom therefore, it did define even as it transcended it, and it was a division that rendered all other divisions – and all other kingdoms – meaningless. 'All the world . . . is divided into two kingdoms,' declared Stephen Marshall, 'the kingdom of Christ, which is his church, and the kingdom of Satan, which is the rest of the world.' The world was thus split into two antagonistic camps – 'two kingdoms, two seeds, two contrary dispositions that pursue one another' – and God (or at least the ministers) recognized only two allegiances. 'All therefore that are not in the kingdom of Christ, they must needs be shoaled under the other kingdom of Satan.' While the troubles of the world were often described in their impact on nations and kingdoms therefore, the solutions were more often cast in terms of a different kind of 'kingdom', one not subject to the mortality to which others without exception would in time succumb. 'It is with other kingdoms as . . . it is with the earth,' Marshall said. 'They all wax old, as a vesture they change, and rot, and come to nothing. But the kingdom of Christ, like himself, hath never any end.' The same could be said of its subjects, also in contrast to those of purely political kingdoms, who had no necessary claim to be included. 'There be subjects of this kingdom,' said Vavasor Powell, 'and those are called in the New Testament "believers", "saints", "Christians", "the redeemed and called of God", or "churches" of saints, all which words imply that they must be in Christ and have grace who are members of this kingdom and not all the riffraff (as we speak) of the world.' Who precisely were the elite saints of this kingdom might not always be readily apparent, at least not to the riffraff of the world, but as subjects – or, as the preachers were beginning to describe them, 'citizens' – they would somehow recognize themselves and one another as such, having a special status that marked them off from the profane multitude of a corrupted world. 'They are singled out from others by a powerful conversion, upon which ground they are saluted,' said Henry Hall. 'Here they are but strangers and pilgrims out of their own country, but . . . the saints which are members of the church, though they live in the earth, yet they are accounted in scripture the citizens and inhabitants of heaven.'[2]

In Puritan ecclesiology this constituted the first definition of 'the church' – not any particular place in the world, whether geographical or institutional or structural, but 'the people of God'. 'The church is one thing, the place of the church another,' said Anthony Burges. 'The one consists of unblamable men, the other of wood and stone.' The church then was not necessarily the Church of England or any other worldly church, much less any worldly state, but international or 'catholic' in the widest sense, 'consisting of all saints in heaven and earth', and even so long as they did live in the earth these pilgrims and strangers and citizens of heaven not only had little regard for the world at large but often refused to recognize the boundaries of kingdoms and the ties of nationality. 'The whole world is a Christian's country,' declared William Bridge. 'The blood of Christ knows no nations.' The church was scattered among all nations, from which it would be gathered without respect of any. 'The church of Christ under the gospel is to be gathered out of all nations,' said John Owen. 'The church or kingdom of Christ . . . shall be gathered out of all nations and all sorts of people.'

The church was indeed a response to the problems affecting all nations, but it had no unconditional attachment to any in particular. 'The church's cause concerns not a nation only but nations,' Humphrey Hardwick said. 'Her cause is like herself, catholic.'[3]

While the church might consist of pilgrims dispersed among the nations, it was not static or without purpose: it was something to be 'gathered' with a 'cause' to be furthered, and most urgently when the nations and kingdoms of the world were in turmoil. 'It is usual with God to carry on the work of raising and restoring his church in times of trouble,' said John White. 'In the mighty concussions and subversions of the empires and monarchies of the world God carries on the designs of his church's deliverance and enlargement.' God's special (and imminent) plan for his church was indicated by 'the general shakings and earthquakes of kingdoms'. 'When Christ doth do any notable things for his church . . . he shakes the foundations and pillars of states and kingdoms,' Henry Wilkinson observed. 'Certainly God hath some great work in hand; otherwise he would not thus shake the heavens and earth, as he now doth.' Moreover, God's plans for his church were not necessarily consistent with those of men and especially the great and powerful politicians of the world for their secular commonwealths but might include consequences they never intended or anticipated. 'These motions that are in Christendom, this rending of states and kingdoms is in order to some revolutions in the churches,' said Richard Vines, pointing to the modern use of the word. 'Whatsoever statesmen and politicians may aim at, it is the churches' interest which the eye of God is upon, though they neither know nor intend it. . . . God hath other ends and purposes in these shakings of kingdoms and provinces than politicians and statesmen have.' What precisely were these ends and purposes even the members of the church themselves could not know for certain; but regardless of what came to pass in the world God could be counted on to carry them forward for the welfare of his special people. 'In all the combustions and devastations wherewith the kingdoms of the earth are shaken it is the Lord's care to keep his church on foot,' said Thomas Carter. 'He delighteth more in his church than in all other societies.' God would govern the affairs of the church with a providence that was somehow 'special'. 'There is a special providence of God which clasps the church,' Obadiah Sedgwick said. 'It consists of . . . most tender vigilency for his people and against their enemies.' This made the church the 'Kingdom of Heaven'. 'In the church, and in it only, the heavens govern,' declared Henry Hall, 'not only in a general way of power and providence.'

> The church is under the rule and government of the heavens in another manner than the world is . . . . He reigns over the church according to his own heart's desire, by the scepter of his word and spirit.[4]

It was still recognized, albeit reluctantly sometimes, that the godly were intermingled with the rest of the world and that just as they shared the traumas and the guilt of their society, so others often shared the blessings bestowed for (though only for) the godly. 'If wicked men have anything they have it for the godly men's sakes, because they are mixed together.' Yet there was also an assumption that, aside from his own people, God had little affection for the world, that it existed solely as a transient abode for the citizens of heaven, and that at some point he would allow it to continue no more. 'The world is upheld for the saints,' declared William Sedgwick. 'If they were out of it, God would speedily ruin it.' And God seemed at some point in time to have just such an intention, the world existing solely for the purpose of calling the elect, after which God would have no further use for it. 'The very world continues that everyone that in God's decree belongs to the church should be converted and brought to repentance,' Herbert Palmer insisted. 'When once the number of the elect is complete, all that remains in the world shall be burnt with fire.'[5]

In the meantime, however, there remained limitations in discerning who were 'the elect' and who were not, and the preachers frequently admonished that before the final judgment isolated individuals could never be distinguished simply on the basis of their outward, passive condition. 'Various and promiscuous are the Lord's dealings with the godly and wicked in this life,' remarked Thomas Palmer. 'God doth not infallibly feed his choicest saints with the sweet meats of prosperity and let the wicked only lie under the lash of biting calamity, woe, and misery. No, for if prosperity did ever wait upon God's people and adversity attend the ungodly, then we might easily find out the ways of God and know perfectly who were his.' Especially with respect to adversity and suffering, a connection did exist between the eternal decree and the temporal contingency but such that it was the response to adversity, rather than the adversity itself, that determined one's final status; and while affliction was always the consequence of sin, it did not follow that temporal suffering was ever any indication of eternal reprobation. 'Beware of drawing sinful inferences from sorrowful premises,' John Bond warned, 'by concluding that such a man or people are wicked because they are wretched, sinners because sufferers.' Temporal fortunes and misfortunes were significant, but they were not eternal, and too much was not to be read into their vicissitudes. 'Judge neither better of prosperity, nor worse of adversity than God's word warrants,' Simeon Ash cautioned. 'Can any man say that prosperity is a sign peculiar unto truth?' The word, not the world, was the source of divine authority, and the scripture itself often warned that it was the godly who would suffer and the wicked who would prosper in this life. 'So far are afflictions and sufferings, even the most grievous trials, from being a sign of God's wrath and an argument that they are none of his because they suffer such things, that it is rather an argument of God's special favor and love towards them,' Thomas Mocket asserted. 'The scripture runs much upon this, to show that prosperity is a note of the wicked and afflictions a note of the godly.'[6]

If anything, then, it was the godly, who did their best to follow his precepts, who could expect to suffer most in a cruel and unjust world. 'The state and condition of God's children is to suffer,' said Richard Sibbes. 'In the best estate there will be suffering one way or other . . . either from without or within.' If one aim of religion was to help people put aside their personal feelings of victimization and persecution, as a collective experience shared among the godly these same emotions were generously indulged. 'The outward condition of God's people is most what mean and contemptible,' said Stephen Marshall. 'They have little countenance from men. Few of them are "wise, noble, or mighty", but they are the "foolish, weak, and base ones of the world".' That this should be the expected condition of the saints in this world offered solace and hope to those who had come to have such a view of themselves, while encouraging them to divert their attention away from their own personal afflictions to identify and sympathize with their fellow victims among the righteous. 'The state of God's church and children in this world for the most part is to be afflicted and poor in their outward condition,' said Sibbes. 'A Christian is a despised person and the church the meanest part of the world in regard to outward glory.'

It was not always clear whether these forlorn souls were godly because they were despised or despised because they were godly, but it was not really important; their lack of esteem in the world and their lack of self-esteem were mutually reinforcing. 'What is the church but a company of weak persons?' Sibbes asked. 'God will have a care of them, though they be never so weak and despised in the eye of the world.' It was this of course that created the necessity of feeling that they were loved and valued by God and, indeed, among the 'chosen'. 'For the most part they are the poor of this world that are the chosen of God,' said Samuel Rogers, 'a great comfort therefore it may be to the godly poor in time of the greatest want that for all this the Lord loves them nevertheless and that want is not evil but good for them.' What precisely the preachers meant by 'poor' and the difference between the 'godly poor' and simply the 'poor' was not often made clear; but whether or not the poor were always godly, the godly were usually poor. 'Generally the people of God are the poor among men,' said John Warren, 'trodden under foot and afflicted.' The godly were the poor and suffering of humanity – 'the poorest, the meanest, and the most despicable persons in the world' – and while they often insisted that the godly would be victimized precisely because of their godliness, the direction of cause and effect could just as easily be reversed. 'There are none in the world that are so vexed, afflicted, and tossed as those that walk more circumspectly and holily than their neighbors,' observed Thomas Brooks. 'They are a byword at home and a reproach abroad; their miseries come in upon them . . . one upon the neck of another, and there is no end of their sorrows and troubles.' But in the eyes of God those whose reproaches became reproaches for his sake, who could feel they were despised for their loyalty to his despised religion, were far more exalted than those who reproached and despised them. 'The saints may not prosper, and that in those things which they do according to God's will,' acknowledged John Preston. 'Though [the wicked] do prosper, and godly men do not so, yet their low estate, their imprisonment, their poverty, their obscurity, the disgrace which they are under – this is better to them than the honor and the pomp, the titles and the riches that evil men have.'[7]

While the preachers could go on at length in this way, bewailing themselves and their followers as the oppressed and downtrodden of the earth, these endless lamentations of collective self-pity, at once touching and slightly ridiculous, were nevertheless articulated in order to channel the energy into constructive effort and encourage a readiness for self-sacrifice; and however much they seemed almost to enjoy and thrive on their status as the victims of society, they always returned to the reminder that it was not that one suffered that made a difference so much as how one suffered. 'Simply to suffer is not to do the will of God,' said Nicholas Estwick, 'but the vigor and acting of our graces in our sufferings makes us to be acceptable to God and makes them to be comfortable and profitable for ourselves.' While the preachers repeatedly insisted that the godly could never be distinguished from the wicked, based on their passive suffering alone, they did assert with equal vehemence that the very troubles for which all were responsible would eventually differentiate people, and in the end the difference between the godly and the wicked was not passive but active. 'The beginnings of reformation are times of great discrimination of the complexions of men's spirits,' said Nathaniel Holmes. 'A discovering time shall come when God shall put a difference between those that serve him and those that serve him not.'

The ministers assisted with the discriminating and the discovering and yet were aware that they were guiding a tendency toward social division that had begun with adversity itself. 'The troubles that befall in this life are common to godly and wicked men,' observed George Gipps, who insisted, nevertheless, that there was a difference: 'However temporal troubles are for matter alike both to godly and wicked, yet for manner they are sanctified to the godly and not to the wicked.' This distinction was often described as a difference in the judgments themselves into two types: 'corrective chastisements on the godly' and 'vindictive punishments of the wicked'. The distinction was in the response of the recipient and whether the affliction was interpreted in a constructive way. 'There is [a] difference [between the godly and the wicked] when the same affliction falls upon both,' John Preston explained. 'In the one, his heart is made glad and light in God's countenance . . . whenas the other hath nothing to hold him up.' Those who had nothing to hold them up tended to grasp at whatever they could find, to shift in ways the preachers regarded as dangerous and destructive, exacerbating rather than alleviating the problem. 'Untowardly children are dulled by whipping,' Gaspar Hickes said. 'The rod makes them hate their master and their book and run away from both. It is an ill temper that grows hard and dead under God's strokes.' God's children, on the other hand, responded differently. 'Saints are of a tender constitution,' Hickes added; 'they are sensible of every stroke from God.' While godliness was a response to change and adversity, it was only one possible response, and there was no guarantee that the nation's problems would inspire godly ways among people whose natural proclivity was precisely the opposite – as evidenced by the fact that there were problems in the first place. 'Indeed, afflictions and troubles in their own nature drive men from God,' Thomas Mocket pointed out. 'If God follow a wicked man with grievous plagues and troubles, if they have their own proper work and effect they make him more impatient and raging . . . and the more grievous are the troubles, the more outrageous evil men are.' That some managed to choose a more positive course in answer to worldly problems was due not to any goodness within them but only to the grace of God. 'God makes them to work this good effect in his people,' Mocket added, 'contrary to their nature.' Shared problems thus tended to alienate some from religion at precisely the time others were cleaving to it with renewed determination, and as God led his own to respond to the call, and others responded in other ways, the effect of social change was to polarize society between the godly and the ungodly. 'The same times, and troubles in them, which make godly men better,' observed Stanley Gower, 'make wicked men worse.'[8]

The difference between the godly and the wicked, then, however it may have been appointed from before the beginning of time, nevertheless manifested itself as a response to immediate troubles as they emerged within it; and as the wicked did become worse the people of God could expect not only to suffer in common with the rest of the world, and in greater measure than others, but also to become the victims of persecution and 'oppression'. 'Oppression and trouble may be in this world the portion of God's children,' warned Simeon Ash. 'Trouble and oppression may be the condition of God's own peculiar people.' Oppression bore a close affinity with sin, as has been seen, and similarly had its 'representative persons'. 'It is as old as the world,' said Joseph Caryl. 'As soon as there could be oppression, oppression appeared. Cain oppressed Abel . . . . Nimrod . . . was the patron of oppressors.' Like sin, oppression was a form of 'bondage', and it was from this as well that Christ would bring 'redemption'. 'Oppression is bondage; deliverance from oppression is freedom,' Caryl said. '[A] great deliverance hath Christ obtained for us . . . redemption from the oppression of man.' In the meantime, however, those whom Christ had delivered from one form of bondage could expect more of the other. 'All that will live godly must expect their share in persecutions,' John Conant warned. 'God doth sometimes visit his own people by the hand of their enemies.' It was not easy to explain why God punished those whom he loved, especially using those whom, it was said, he hated; but that he did so the preachers went to great lengths to emphasize. 'It is no strange thing to be brought into straits and troubles, to be afflicted, yea sometimes to be brought into great extremity,' said Thomas Mocket. 'It hath often been so with the church of God in all ages, as well as with particular persons.'[9]

As Mocket indicates, not only did the godly as 'particular persons' suffer at the hands of the wicked, among whom they were dispersed as individuals, but 'the church', as the preachers referred to the saints collectively, was continually the victim of 'enemies'. 'The church of God hath from the beginning met with enemies,' said William Strong. 'The church of God ever had, and will have, enemies and haters.' Enemies posed an ever-present danger for the church, and vigilance was a watchword for its members. 'The great design of the enemies of the church is by craft or cruelty, or both, to hinder any work that tends to the establishment or promoting of the church's good,' warned Matthew Newcomen. 'By secret conspiracies and treacherous combinations against the church [they seek] to undermine and ruin it.' Enemies were not only external but could infiltrate into the very heart of the church, even among the ranks of the apparently godly. 'These enemies are of two sorts, from without or from within,' said Strong. 'She hath always found the worst enemies to proceed out of her own bowels.' Herbert Palmer, preaching in 1643, provided one of the more extensive catalogs of enemies, their plots and conspiracies, and the quarters in which they lurked. 'The church hath many enemies who do, and will do, their best against her and are specially encouraged and advantaged by our neglect,' he warned:

> enemies possessing the person of the King, abusing his mind by their wicked suggestions and counsels . . . these enemies having prevailed in many places to rob and spoil houses, villages, towns, countries, to carry away prisoners and use them with more than barbarous cruelty . . . these enemies being in themselves many in number and of great strength, in diverse places apparently stronger than we, in all kind of strength (except spiritual) and in the whole powerful enough to put all into exceeding hazard by force and fraud (witness Bristol and the late damnable plot against the Parliament and City), specially considering the multitude of secret enemies, seeming but neuters, intermingled everywhere with us . . . (the City is not, the Parliament itself hath not been free) and not a few, even almost professed enemies, let alone and suffered . . . besides multitudes of professed neuters, ready to fall to the enemies wherever they shall appear stronger and in the meantime affording as little help as they possibly can.[10]

This paranoia regarding enemies thrived on a sense of victimization, and they were most susceptible to the message (and to the widespread alarm about conspiracies that was pervasive throughout this time) who felt most disadvantaged and most powerless to control their lives. 'We have enemies greater than ourselves . . . and therefore if we had not a better above us what would become of us but to be totally subjected under the power of enemies?' suggested Sibbes. 'Christ hath all the authority in heaven and earth . . . over our enemies, that they shall not do us harm.' But while enemies were everywhere, not all enemies were the same, nor were they to be equally regarded. 'We must distinguish of the persons of our enemies; some be private enemies, some public,' said William Perkins. 'Private I call those which be enemies of some particular men . . . yet are not enemies of God or of his truth. Public are those which are not only our enemies but the enemies of God . . . and religion.'

While a primary purpose of Puritan piety was to encourage people to put away the malice and resentment they felt for wrongs inflicted by their private enemies and even, in the spirit of Christian charity, to love those who had done them most harm, the mechanism by which this was itself effected was by channeling that same enmity into the collective hatred of public enemies and especially the enemies of God, religion, and the church. 'When they are our enemies only . . . then Father, forgive them, they know not what they do . . . Lord convince them, Lord convert them, is becoming language for Christians,' Thomas Case maintained. 'But when . . . they make it apparent to all the world that if there be a God in heaven they hate him, if a Christ and a gospel they are sworn irreconcilable enemies to both . . . then O Lord God of Hosts be not merciful to them . . . . Let them be confounded and troubled forever . . . and prepare them for the day of slaughter.' The saints did have to be careful that the hostility they directed against their enemies was indeed for the sake of God and not merely to settle their own personal quarrels. 'When they be God's enemies . . . then such expressions as these will be no breaches to the law of charity,' Case insisted.

> Provided that we look to our hearts . . . and that the enmity that these men bear . . . against God affect us more than the slaughter and persecution they breathe out against ourselves. If God see us pretending his wrongs but intending our own, cursing them as his enemies but hating them only as our own, we shall translate their curse upon our own heads.

How to be certain one's motives were pure was by no means left wholly to the discretion of the individual, since the determination of whether one's enemies were also God's enemies was impersonal and collective: God's enemies were the enemies of (all) the saints. 'They that are enemies to God's people . . . are they not enemies to God himself?' Case asked. 'They that thus hate the saints, do they not hate also the God of the saints?' Only as the saints comprised the collective church could their common enemies safely be said to be the enemies of God. 'The church's enemies are God's enemies,' Case declared. 'They that hate the church hate God.'[11]

The malice and enmity the preachers themselves so often observed pervading English society and decried as contributing to high levels of instability and violence were not eliminated by religion, then; they were merely channeled away from private quarrels into an alliance with God and his saints, so that now they had the same common enemies and friends. 'The Lord and his people are so conjoined,' asserted Stephen Marshall, 'that their friends are his friends and their enemies are his enemies.' The comparison could work both ways, but the point was to promote a collective response to these mutual enemies and direct it into cooperation and vigilance on the part of friends. 'God is rising for the help of his poor oppressed people in England,' Case announced. 'And if so, here is a word of terror to enemies . . . so also here is a word of exhortation to all you that are his friends.' All of this was more than simply a convenient excuse for villifying one's enemies, since one might well be required to repress hatred of private enemies to join with God's friends, and to know that one was truly among God's people it was necessary to ask oneself sincerely if one really did have the same allies and adversaries. 'A true trial of sociableness is when men will joy to sort themselves with those whom formerly they have been most unsociable and whose company they most loathed,' said Sibbes, noting that such 'sociableness' might not come easily to many previously solitary souls. 'When you love the Lord . . . then you will love those that are like the Lord, whosoever they are, though perhaps they are not so sociable, nor of so fair a natural disposition . . . now you have common friends and common enemies.' Together, the hatred of enemies and the love of friends became mutually reinforcing ways of coping with the hostility in one's heart, and both animosity and affection would be controlled so as to be restrained and released as needed. 'That you may discern this,' Preston suggested, 'consider whether you love all those that fear the Lord and hate all those that are enemies to the Lord.'

While the church may have originated as a means of controlling the hatred of enemies, following from this it was also a bond of association demanding an unswerving and unquestioning allegiance from its friends: a loyalty based on 'faith' or 'love' that by its nature could never be said to exist in the isolated individual but only in relation to the group. 'No man will ever be faithful to the saints but he that is himself a saint,' asserted William Strong. 'No man can love a saint, as a saint, but a saint.' Sainthood was a collective designation, a status reflected from the faith and love of other saints and expressed in fidelity and affection towards them; and the surest way to know if one was a saint was to inquire into the depth of one's commitment to the saints. 'Let us seriously consider . . . whether we count the godly the only excellent ones or not,' Richard Kentish urged. 'Wicked men may love the godly so as to show some kindnesses to them. But there are others that they love better . . . . Those that are godly indeed, they love the saints above all others . . . . The household of faith are the most precious in their esteem . . . . In these their souls chiefly do delight.' The ministers did subscribe to a concept of 'charity', meaning not toleration of ungodliness, but patience in winning those not yet of this 'household of faith', not yet fully capable, or worthy, of 'love'. 'Add to your brotherly love charity,' Thomas Hill urged. 'Lay not out all your love to the saints. There is a love due to them as members, but when you delight in the people of God, the household of faith, yet withal pity them that go astray and be charitable to them, and try all conclusions how you may win them on and engage them in the good way.' Still, while basic humanity to one's neighbors, like natural love to one's kindred, was never to be completely denied, there were appeals urging that special affection be directed toward those in the 'family of God'. 'Let us do good to all men,' urged Samuel Rogers, 'but especially to them who are of the household of faith, which is the multitude of all true believers, dispersed throughout the whole earth, known by the name of the church militant which is called God's family or household.'[12]

The church and its godly members were thus mutually and self-defining in the sense that a total commitment to it was effectively the criterion for inclusion within it. 'Who are the true godly?' asked Nathaniel Holmes. 'They are persons . . . [who] look for and expect whatever God hath promised to them, singly to their persons or collectively to them in their relation to the church.' Conversely, the wicked were not simply those who sinned, but those who failed to manifest sufficient zeal and self-denial for the good of the church: they might profess to uphold their own idea of the faith or of what constituted the church, but ultimately they would be ensnared to other affections and loyalties; the collective church was not their only concern. 'They do not hope for the good of the church as if they were of the church,' Holmes continued. 'They hope not as if they and the church had one Christ, one faith . . . one hope of glory. And so they show plainly that they are . . . not in a state of salvation.' Increasingly the church became the only allegiance a true member was to have, the only concern being to help the church. 'It is the end of all a man's life, next unto a man's immediate attendance upon God and taking care of his own salvation, to promote the church's good in building and restoration,' Herbert Palmer said. 'God did not bring any of us into the world to enjoy honors or pleasures, or to live to ourselves, but to be serviceable to the church of God.' For the true saint, such a care came to be virtually inseparable from that over 'his own salvation'. 'Such a frame of spirit as this will be the best evidence of your own safe condition, of your peace with God,' Stephen Marshall assured prospective saints. 'When the soul comes to enquire, What shall I do that Christ may be glorified, that his church may be edified? – to know no cross but the church's cross, to prefer the joy of the church before all his own peace and welfare – this is not only an argument of a man looking heavenward but one that hath proceeded far in the way.'[13]

The preachers had little concern for purely personal piety, and the true Christian would have little interest aside from the welfare of the church. 'If the voice of every Christian should thus resolve with itself, I desire to enjoy no liberty, no mercy of God myself which I do not enjoy in common with the church of God,' said Henry Burton, 'this is that makes every blessing to be indeed a blessing, when we do enjoy it, not alone with ourselves in particular, but with the church.' To think and act in solidarity with the saints and see the church's blessings and sufferings as one's own was to sit at the right hand of the Almighty, even in this world. 'What is it to walk with God but to observe which way God goes in the passage of his providence in those special works of providence towards his saints, and to suit our hearts accordingly?' asked Jeremiah Burroughs. 'To mourn with those that mourn . . . and to rejoice with them that rejoice.' This feeling of being part of a larger group with which one was expected to identify, a solidarity within which all emotions of sorrow and joy were to be shared, inspired a camaraderie and a readiness for total devotion and unhesitating self-sacrifice, and there were times when personal piety seemed little more than a preparation for the commitment that would eventually be demanded by the church. 'So long as men are in their unregenerate condition . . . there is not in them a substratum of real usefulness to the church,' Marshall explained. 'To do him service, first humble your souls deeply before God for your sins . . . and when you have . . . given yourselves first to the Lord then ye are fit to give yourselves to the church for the Lord's sake.'[14]

The 'life', then, which the godly received from the sacrifice of Christ, was itself measured by the capacity for selfless dedication and might be required to be

returned to him, especially given circumstances during the 1640s. 'The exigence of the church at this present time requires from you many . . . things,' Marshall warned the House of Commons. 'It may be some of you may be called as soldiers to spend your blood in the church's cause. If you knew the honor and the reward that belongs to such a service, you would . . . venture . . . all in the church's cause.' This was the attitude of the Almighty himself when he offered his son as a human sacrifice and that which imparted the divine image to his people. 'To lay down our lives for the brethren, as Christ laid down his life for us . . . this makes us (more than anything else) like unto God himself,' Marshall declared. 'They partake most of God's nature and most eminently bear his image who are his most useful instruments in doing good to his church and people.' As Marshall indicates, the model for this system of collective self-sacrifice was Christ himself. 'The brethren, the church, have a right to our utmost endeavor, with what hazard soever,' Herbert Palmer demanded.

> We owe it to them, we ought to venture our lives, and when the pinch comes actually part with them . . . . Christ, God and man both, laid down his human life for his church . . . . This ought to be reason sufficient to us to hold ourselves obliged to the same hazard in our measure in thankfulness to him and imitation of him and to testify the truth of our love which we profess to bear to the church . . . . All Christ's members must suffer after his example, even for the church's good, not meritoriously or satisfactorily (which was only proper to him the head), but by way of conformity to him, and testimony to him, to seal hereby the truth of the doctrine of Christianity, of faith and holiness, and proclaim it worth suffering for.

So intimately were Christ and his church conjoined in suffering and persecution that the church effectively was Christ. 'The church . . . is one with . . . Christ, in respect whereof its sufferings are called the sufferings of Christ, and Christ's sufferings called the church's sufferings,' said John Ellis. 'In reference to the church's necessities, Christ and the church are one.' Such unshakable solidarity carried especially ominous consequences for any who dared to inflict suffering on either. 'Let the wicked take heed how they meddle with the saints,' warned Thomas Palmer. 'They that put the saints in prison put Jesus Christ in prison; make the saints suffer, and you make Jesus Christ suffer.'[15]

By identifying it with Christ and with selfless devotion to other members, suffering was transformed from an isolated, passive, and demeaning experience into a cooperative, active, and ennobling duty, and in a sense the whole purpose of the church was to organize suffering. 'The church is a moving thing,' said Samuel Rutherford, 'in that change is part of suffering.' Because the church was conceived in suffering in the first place it would not only survive but even thrive on it. 'The sufferings of God's servants tend to the church's advantage,' said Simeon Ash. 'Now see how good it is to be imprisoned, beaten, tortured, burnt, and sawn asunder.' Suffering was redemptive, and in the church both suffering and redemption were shared. 'The excellent victory of suffering,' remarked Richard Sibbes. 'If anything overcome, this will do it, to suffer well. The church is a company of men that gain and overcome by suffering.' While the church would suffer extreme adversity, then, it could never totally or finally perish. 'It may indeed be sore assaulted and battered but cannot be overcome,' Henry Hall said. 'It may be endangered but not destroyed.' Like true faith, the true church could never be lost, and in fact faith itself gave the believer the assurance of 'the infallibility of the church's deliverance'. 'This use of faith the condition of the times wherein we live, so full of trouble and confusion, calls for at present,' John White said, 'whether we look upon the state of the church in general or our own in particular.' In that the church both consisted of the faithful and was that toward which they directed their faith and fidelity, its survival was ensured by the same decree as was the infallibility of saving faith. 'There is a difference to be made 'twixt the molestation of a church and the desolation of a church,' said Obadiah Sedgwick.

> What we maintain against the papists and Arminians concerning habitual faith, that same may as truly be affirmed of the church militant (the proper subject of faith) . . . she may be oppressed, but she shall never be suppressed . . . she may be shaken, but she cannot be shivered . . . . A Christian may die, but he cannot be overcome; so the church may often be disturbed, but it shall never be destroyed.

Faith was as efficacious for the church temporally as for the individual eternally, and likewise exerted its greatest power when all seemed hopeless. 'In the temporal saving of his people, God (frequently) carries matters after the manner as he doth in their spiritual salvation,' Sedgwick observed.

> When he intends to advance a soul as high as heaven then he seems to cast down the soul as low as hell, and he ushers in the dearest consolations (commonly) after the deepest humiliations and conflicts. This method he (many times) observes in the temporal deliverance of his church. Their salvation is (usually) . . . when there is nothing to be seen but their desolation.

There was no denying that within the membership of the church individuals would continue to suffer corporal death, but it was not that from which Christ had redeemed them. 'You must distinguish 'twixt a particular person and 'twixt a church,' Sedgwick added.

> It may oftimes so fall out that the cruel designs of wicked adversaries may prevail to the destruction of this or that individual person (if that may be styled a destruction which yet eventually redounds to the enlarging of the church, for seed when it is sown multiplies the more, and the blood of martyrs is the seed of the church), but they shall never prevail to the ruin of the church.[16s13]

The church, then, was immortal, unlike the temporal mortality of not only individuals but also entire nations, which could have no similar assurance. 'It cannot be said of any state as it is said of the church, God will establish it forever,' Richard Byfield asserted; 'this is true only of the church.' As such the church stood in sharp contrast with mortal kingdoms such as England whose claim to God's favor would always be conditional. 'England may be destroyed . . . and yet the church preserved, for the church is not confined to any place,' said Francis Cheynell. 'It concerns us then to be . . . such pilgrims on earth and citizens of heaven that it may appear that we seek a better country.' God in fact had little concern for secular states and nations and would not hesitate to wipe them from the earth if necessary for the benefit of his church. 'God for his church and people's sake will not spare to dash nations and kingdoms all to pieces in the day of his power and jealousy.' For those anxious to prove their citizenship of heaven, there could be little doubt as to where their allegiance was expected to lie. Stephen Marshall made it unambiguous: 'I go not about to determine what the event of these troubles will be to England as England is a civil or political state or commonwealth,' he told the House of Commons in 1643.

Christ breaks and molds commonwealths at his pleasure. . . . All kings and kingdoms that make war against the church shall be broken in pieces, and . . . in the end all the kingdoms of the world shall be kingdoms of our Lord and his saints, and they shall reign over them. But it is the cause of the church . . . which I hope is dearer to you than ten thousand Englands.[17]

The church, therefore, would not suffer forever; there would come a time of redemption. 'The troubles or afflictions of God's people are not perpetual,' John Conant promised. 'As they have a day of trouble, so also of salvation and deliverance.' Like any other salvation or deliverance of God's people, that of the church as a whole was not only desirable but inevitable, predestined in the counsels of the Lord from before the beginning of time. 'There he laid up the creation of the world from all eternity, and there he laid up the redemption of men,' said Joseph Caryl. 'There he laid up all the deliverances which at any time he hath wrought for his church.' Predestination, as the term itself perhaps suggests, thus applied as much to the 'temporal' salvation of the collective church as to the 'eternal' salvation of its individual members. 'The churches of Jesus Christ shall certainly be delivered from the wicked,' promised Thomas Palmer. 'The church's deliverance was determined by the counsel of heaven from all eternity, promised when the commission of persecution was first of all granted.'[18]

Once again the preachers can here be seen extending predestinarian theology from its other-worldly meaning into the political world with revolutionary consequences, encouraging their followers with the assurance of not only redemption from their sins but victory over their tormentors. 'The church's mercies and deliverance have their appointed season,' proclaimed John Owen. 'In the midst of the years it shall be accomplished. As there is a decree goes forth in its appointed season for the church's deliverance . . . so there is a decree bringing forth the wicked's destruction.' The 'double decree' of predestination was no longer limited to the next world (if it ever had been) but guaranteed an appointed time for both the deliverance of the church and the destruction of its enemies. 'The eminent rescues of the church have been and shall be conjoined with the eminent destruction of its adversaries,' announced Obadiah Sedgwick. 'God can make the bloodiest contrivances and hopefullest confidences of his church-destroying adversaries not only unprosperous, but also pernicious or hurtful to themselves.' In that this annihilation of the wicked would be brought to pass dialectically in the very course of executing their assaults upon the church, the kingdom of the devil contained the seeds of its own destruction. 'The destruction of the church's enemies shall be effected by their opposition against the church,' said William Strong. 'The church's enemies are destroyed in destroying, and she lives by dying.' That God chastened his own in no wise derogated from his commitment to punish his adversaries; on the contrary, it affirmed it. 'God will correct and punish his own people,' Thomas Mocket said; 'therefore much more the ungodly, and most of all the professed bloodthirsty enemies of his church.' Indeed, given that he did chasten his own people so grievously, such punishment was necessary to vindicate God's justice within this world. 'His justice appears . . . in the destruction and confusion of the enemies of the church,' Mocket continued. 'God sometimes suffers his people to be brought into great extremity and their incorrigible enemies to go far and prevail much for a time, but it is that his power and justice may be more clear and remarkable in their destruction.' By this measure, the more the enemies did prevail, the closer the church came to the hour of deliverance, which was increasingly seen as imminent. 'The time which the wicked set for the church's ruin shall be their own destruction,' Thomas Palmer declared in 1644. 'The church's deliverance shall not only certainly but shortly come; I mean not comparatively, but really within a little time.' In that the church was defined by its enemies as much as by its friends, God's hatred of the one expressed his love for the other. 'Much of the greatness and intenseness of his love to his own is seen in his enemies' ruin,' said Owen. 'The loving kindness of God to his church is seen . . . in the blood of the persecutors . . . . The properties he lays out in destruction are equally glorious with those he lays out in preservation.' Thus did the argument come full circle once again to the judgments of God, which continued to exist in dialectical interaction with his mercies, and both together manifested his 'glory' in the apprehension of the world. 'Let not our eyes in the late deliverance be always on the light side of the work, our own mercies,' Owen urged. 'The dark side of terror and judgment is not without its glory.'[19]

Moreover, the dialectic suggested that God would not only destroy the enemies of the church but he would do so using the church. 'God and his saints are in a league offensive and defensive,' said another. 'The people of God have a commission not only for a defensive but an offensive militia and posture of war.' The church itself existed in the world and was organized for military purposes. 'The church is the people of the Lord of Hosts,' declared Jeremiah

Burroughs. 'The church is called "the host of heaven". Howsoever despised by the world, yet this Lord of Hosts accounts his church "the host of heaven".' The 'special providence' governing war and that watching over the church were thus one and the same. 'God is the God of armies,' Burroughs announced. 'The providence of God is great in all wars, but especially those wars that concern his people, whether in a way of chastising them or defensive to save them, or offensive in avenging himself upon their enemies.'

Similarly, God's people were often described as 'soldiers', trained, drilled, and stationed for battle. 'God breeds up all his children to be soldiers,' Burroughs said. 'There are none in heaven but were bred soldiers, and as they grew up were brought up in military discipline.' The church was thus a kind of 'spiritual militia', as one said, armed with the citizens of heaven, stirringly decked out in martial regalia and marching to the cadences of the heavenly drummer, an army 'terrible with banners'. 'The church of Christ is an army with banners,' said another preacher. 'No weapon can prosper that is formed against it.' Those it employed, on the other hand, were destined to triumph. 'The weapons of the saints' warfare are as well offensive as defensive,' Thomas Coleman said. 'They have an effect on the enemy for destruction as well as on themselves for preservation.' While these weapons were often described as 'spiritual' – as in 'prayers and tears are the arms of the church' – it was not always clear where the spiritual ended and the corporal began. 'As he hath given a complete armor to every Christian wherewith to fight against the wiles and temptations of the devil, so he hath given a complete armor to his church wherewith to fight against all the errors and unsound doctrines of seducers,' Joseph Caryl said. 'Search the magazines of the gospel; bring out all the artillery, ammunition, and weapons stored up there . . . let them all be employed and spare not . . . . Christ hath formed and sharpened weapons for this war.' The church 'militant' as it existed on earth could have access to more material weapons as well, with which its members were also required to be drilled. 'All God's children are here members of the church militant,' Burroughs said. 'It is fit for them to be skillful, not only in the use of the spiritual armor, but of bodily also. Who so fit to be used in the battles of the Lord as they who have most interest in the Lord?' Again, the metaphorical usage was easily translated, and the spiritual and corporeal seemed to interact dialectically as mutually reinforcing means to the same appointed end. 'Though . . . the precise immediate means to set up the kingdom of Christ be spiritual,' acknowledged Nathaniel Holmes, 'yet . . . the removal of impediments, the overthrow of obstinate enemies that despise the word must be by the sword.'[20]

It was with this language that the preachers gave their otherwise diffident and dispirited disciples the confidence that victory over their adversaries was as certain as was the pardon of their sins. 'Whosoever may be the enemies and whatsoever may be the hazards, yet Christ and his church will be the conquerors,' promised Obadiah Sedgwick, 'him and his church and his cause.' Those who had risked everything in the cause of the church (and may from time to time have entertained thoughts of retreat) were assured that they and the cause to which they had dedicated their lives could not fail. 'The churches must be militant,' warned Thomas Hill, 'but however though their conflict be troublesome, yet their victory will be glorious and certain.' Martial and predestinarian rhetoric, therefore, and the certainty it provided to hesitant souls, did not simply describe action but promoted it. 'We should endeavor to serve providence to bring about the promised deliverance of the church,' urged John Strickland. 'We should also lay out ourselves freely in the church's cause . . . whether in our counsels, or in our estates, or in our persons . . . wherein God himself will be (nay, is) engaged for the event.' The 'cause' of the church would prevail because, like enemies themselves, it was the cause of heaven. 'The church's cause is God's cause,' Stephen Marshall announced. 'The church's relation to God is [such] that as their persons are nearly united to him, so their cause is his cause. As they account every cause of God to be their cause, so God accounts every cause of theirs to be his cause.' And being God's cause, it was a cause that could not but succeed. 'God's cause is a successful cause,' Marshall proclaimed. 'The church's cause is God's cause.' If the most formidable enemies in the spiritual warfare were fear and discouragement, the assurance of certain victory was itself the most powerful weapon, designed not to forestall action but to stimulate it. 'If our enemies be given into our hand, why should we fight?' asked Richard Sibbes. 'Yes; fight the rather, be encouraged to fight, because you shall be sure to conquer.' Once again, this came to be vindicated by the assurance it provided and the action which it promoted, and the prosperity of the wicked, however temporal or temporary, was itself an affront to God's 'truth' and therefore something in which he himself had a stake in defeating. 'When the enemy prevails against the church it does so far forth prevail against the truth which is professed and maintained by the church.' The cause of the church, the very survival and triumph of the church on earth, was intertwined with the cause of 'truth'. 'The quarrel [is] the truth,' declared Thomas Case.

> In [this] God is as much or more concerned than his people . . . . And therefore they that are enemies to God's people for the truth's sake hate God also whose truth it is. Look into all the battles of the church, since Christ's time to this day.[21]

Given this assurance (especially in the face of the most dire consequences for failure), there was no excuse for not joining the cause and standing alongside God in the battle. 'Surely then it is good being on God's side, to be of his party,' said Jeremiah Burroughs. 'This is the strongest side; this certainly will have the victory.' Moreover, those who failed to join God's side and help the church against its enemies in effect became its enemies. 'Cursed is he that keepeth back his sword from blood,' Thomas Horton quoted from Jeremiah, 'the blood of the church's enemies, which God ha[s] now commanded to be shed by the church's friends.' One's status with God was in the end determined by the depth of one's commitment to the church and its cause of prevailing against its enemies. 'All people are cursed or blessed according as they do or do not join their strength or give their best assistance to the Lord's people against their enemies,' declared Stephen Marshall. 'All are blessed or cursed according as they do or do not help the church of God in their need.' Marshall's most famous sermon, preached on the eve of the war, was perhaps the most extensive attack on those to whom the preachers referred as 'neuters'. 'It is not sufficient to do the people of God no hurt, but we must do them good,' said Henry Wilkinson. 'We must engage ourselves in Christ's quarrel, for he that is a neuter or indifferent, he is an enemy. He that is not with me, saith Christ, he is against me.' In the cosmic struggle between the church and its enemies all were of necessarity allied on one side or the other, and in the total war that was to ensue the preachers refused to recognize noncombatants. 'Whether you be soldiers of Christ in a militant way . . . or whether yet you be vassals of the devil, here are no neuters,' said Francis Peck. 'You are certainly every one of you militant either under Christ's or Satan's banner.' Once victory was secured, those who refused to share the danger and sacrifice would suffer the same vengeance as enemies. 'The sins of those that have neglected to help the church are no way lessened by God's overruling grace delivering his church another way nor by others' faithfulness whom he hath made use of to deliver it,' asserted Herbert Palmer. 'Destruction is owing to those that help not the church in danger, because they that forsook her in extremity are altogether unworthy to rejoice with her in prosperity.' There were, in short, no neuters in Christ's kingdom. 'Such as stand neuters are ordinarily crushed,' Marshall declared. 'The Lord acknowledges no neuters.'[22]

For all their concern with consensus, therefore, and with gaining as many supporters as possible, a point came when the preachers actively sought to polarize society, to promote conflict and division, and to force people to choose sides. 'Be not offended,' said Joseph Caryl, 'if in some cases where nature bids agree, the gospel bids divide.' Christ was an agent of conciliation, but this itself also made him a fomenter, or at least a catalyst, of conflict. 'Wheresoever Christ cometh there will be opposition,' said Sibbes. 'He breedeth division, not only between man and himself, but between man and man.' The two kinds of division were not unconnected and corresponded to two similar kinds of 'enemies', both of which would be vanquished together in the same battle. 'So long as we are here below . . . we have great conflicts with corruptions and temptations, with enemies within and enemies without,' Sibbes said. '[Christ] rules, and governs, and subdues all the enemies of his church, without and within.' The ministers did promote their own notion of 'peace', but harmony and peace could exist only in a dialectical relationship with conflict and war. 'Better have a holy and just war than an irreligious, dishonorable, and unsafe peace,' said Christopher Tesdale. 'Peace is nowhere to be found but in the true church.' And peace within often required conflict without: 'It is better for the church to be at peace with God rather than to be at peace with men.' With some men in particular it was apparently better to be at war: 'the enemies of our church and state', as Joseph Boden described them, 'that now [are] gone forth in battle against the godly party throughout these kingdoms'. 'Make peace with them now and they will soon make war with us and ours,' he warned. 'There is no peace with, as well as to, the wicked.' More often, therefore, the church was described as the church 'militant'. 'The state of Christ's church on earth, 'tis militant,' said Nicholas Lockyer, '. . . a militant church in a militant time . . . . Is not the church of Christ in England militant?' Because of the hostility of an evil and ever-threatening world, true believers were by necessity people of 'opposition' and 'violence'. 'It is the disposition of those that are the true members of the church of God to be eager and violent,' Sibbes asserted.

> Betwixt us and the blessed state we aim at there is much opposition, and therefore there must be violence. The state of the church here . . . is a state of opposition. Good persons and good things they are opposed in the world. Christ rules in this world 'in the midst of his enemies'. He must have enemies therefore to rule in the midst of; he must be opposed. And where there is opposition between us and the good things that we must of necessity have, we must break through the opposition, which cannot be done without violence.

This fascination with what were seen as the purifying effects of violence made it not only a means but increasingly something of an end in itself. 'The violent, and only the violent, and all the violent, do at length certainly obtain what they strive for,' Sibbes argued. 'Success is tied to violence . . . . We must use an holy violence . . . . Let us use violence, and violence will overcome at the last.'[23]

While the preachers never ceased to urge all to repress the lust for revenge against the wrongs and affronts inflicted by other individuals, implicit in this was the consolation that the day would come when the godly, as a group, would have their turn against the wicked and those who had made them the objects of scorn and derision (and perhaps this is why one pleasure for which the ministers gladly accepted postponed gratification was humor). 'The saints have their turn at last,' promised William Cooper. 'They shall laugh last.' The desire to settle scores emerged with special ferocity as the saints were organized collectively and rendered these meek and retiring souls capable of almost unbounded cruelty against those at whose hands they had suffered disgrace and humiliation: 'degradation for degradation, deprivation for deprivation, imprisonment for imprisonment, banishment for banishment, spoiling for spoiling, blood for blood' was the justice demanded by Joseph Boden – 'nay double to [them] according to [their] works'. 'Blood' in particular was given a special, almost mystical role in the terms of the church's deliverance. 'The church began in blood, hath grown up by blood, and shall end in blood,' Sibbes declared, 'as it was redeemed by blood.' A close connection existed between the 'blood' shed in sacrifice and that in vengeance, and those who may have long harbored a wish to purge the land with the blood of their enemies could see both come together in the blood of Christ, the 'blood of the lamb'. 'Get your robes washed in the blood of the lamb,' Stephen Marshall urged, '. . . redeemed with the same blood . . . . Willingly spend and be spent for the church's good.' The apocalyptic image of the 'lamb' conveyed meekness but also the strength that could be brought forth out of it when offered as a sacrificial atonement in the struggle against the powerful of the earth. 'He is a lamb, but such a one as can be angry,' argued Sibbes, who saw the lamb as a ferocious one:

> 'The kings and great persons of the world fly from the wrath of the lamb.' He that is so sweet, mild, and gentle, if we joint with him, on the contrary, if we come not unto him, we shall find the wrath of the lamb a terrible wrath, which the greatest potentates in the world shall desire to be hid from.

And as with the lamb himself, so for those gentle ones whose garments had been dipped in his blood. 'The mighty do frequently oppose the Lord,' Marshall warned.

> It is no new thing to find the mighty in strength, the mighty in authority, the mighty in wealth, the mighty in parts, in learning, in counsel, to engage all against the Lord, his church, his cause. The lamb's followers and servants are often the poor and offscouring of the world, when kings and captains, merchants and wisemen, being drunk with the wine of the whore's fornications, proceed to make war with the lamb and to give all their strength unto the beast, till the words of God shall be fulfilled.

'When the mighty of the world do oppose the Lord,' Marshall added, 'God's meanest servants must not be afraid to oppose the mighty.' Through the blood of this sacrificial lamb those who felt fearful and bewildered would know that they did not have to be afraid to oppose the mighty, because it was God who was fighting, and indeed had already conquered, for them. 'They have assurance that in the blood of the lamb they shall overcome,' Boden proclaimed.

> My brethren, who dares or can be a coward that hath it ascertained unto him upon unquestionable warranty that without doubt he shall get the better and overcome in the battle? That whether he kill or be killed, he shall be looked upon and honored as a conqueror? . . . This is the condition of all the faithful soldiers in the lamb's war against the beast and his party. For there is that blood already shed that hath overcome them all for us. Suppose those we are to encounter be kings: their strength is broken, crushed, and made weak, we have our feet upon their necks while we go forth to the war. . . . For he is King of kings and Lord of lords. The field is fought, and won; we only go forth to fetch in the trophies of victory.

Predestinarian motifs thus easily merged into apocalyptic to guarantee that the same blood that had redeemed the church before God would also redeem it from – and would demand that of – the wicked. 'The militant church's victories over the devil and his angels are obtained by the blood of the lamb Jesus Christ,' Thomas Hill declared.

> By the blood of the lamb divine justice is satisfied, God appeased, and the church reconciled to him. Her sins being done away which betray her to

her enemies, she becomes victorious . . . . By the blood of the lamb we obtain that grace which enables us prevailingly to resist the devil and his angels. For no pieces of the spiritual armor will be armor of proof unless they be dipped in the blood of Christ . . . whose blood hath an eternal efficacy. The church's victories are therefore ascribed to the blood of the lamb, because the . . . kingdom which Christ hath over his church . . . he possesses as the fruit of his bloody sufferings . . . . And his church likewise being a royal priesthood conquers through the blood of her King.[24]

As the decade unfolded it was increasingly this in which the preachers exulted. 'Ah! what a harvest hath hell had in our days of those who have engaged against the lamb and those that are called, chosen, and faithful!' exclaimed Thomas Brooks in 1652. 'Ah! how hath divine justice poured out their blood as water upon the ground! How hath he laid their honor and glory in the dust!' This cult of blood, as it might be described, decreed that the blood of a saint was sacred and that once it had been spilled God (and the church) would demand atonement. 'He will be revenged on all the persecutors of his church and take a strict account of every drop of blood that hath been shed,' promised Sibbes, 'for their persons are precious.' The sacramental value of blood turned even defeats into victories, as another 'king' would discover to his cost. 'The King loses by . . . the victories he gets over (his subjects but) God's saints,' Thomas Palmer announced in 1644.

The King had better to have a whole army of men against him than the blood of one saint. These saints which the King hath slain fight with him night and day. They are now with God in heaven, and they are continually hastening and moving God to fulfill his promises and avenge their blood.

Blood once shed, whether of the godly or the ungodly it seems, would be sanctified in the eyes of God, a kind of sacrificial offering that both atoned for the nation's sins and in the process cleansed and purified the saints. 'The blood thus shed shall be precious in the sight of the Lord,' Boden said. 'We may possibly kill God's enemies, and it is a mercy to the righteous to wash their feet in the blood of the wicked.' The thinly-disguised glee with which the ministers envisioned not only the indescribable torments of the damned but the agony in which the wicked would writhe, even within this world, poured forth from a hatred explicable only in terms of deeply repressed but also deeply harbored resentment, and the need to 'rejoice', to be glad and grateful to God, however horrifying his dispensations might appear to merely 'human' morality, could be pressed with a chilling single-mindedness. 'We are not this day rejoicing in the blood and ruin of men but in the justice of God upon them,' Joseph Caryl professed. 'We are not giving thanks because men are ruined but because Christ reigns . . . . And if Christ will set up his throne upon millions of carcasses of the slain, it well becomes [us] to rejoice and give thanks.'[25]

The warfare of the militant against the malignant church and its triumph thus came to acquire an almost sacramental aura – or so Stephen Marshall seemed to describe it, perhaps inversely: 'In one and the same day the spoiled church shall be rescued and they who oppressed her shall be fed with their own flesh and made drunk with their own blood.' Further, the system of collective atonement and self-sacrifice, sealed and sanctified in blood, could be institutionalized in the church in such a way as to threaten all that was sacred to the world and worldlings. 'The church treadeth down its enemies . . . for they do think and account of the wicked as a vile and abominable thing . . . and this the wicked do know, and this makes them hate God's children,' Sibbes observed. 'The church of God tramples on all things that rule wicked men, as riches, honors, and the like.' In place of what ruled the wicked the ministers would place their own rule, one that 'must be the only rule', and one that by its nature was dedicated to eliminating all others. The very virtue of this rule was that it permitted no deviation and tolerated no rivals; it demanded total dedication and unquestioning obedience, and all who failed to abide by this rule would be pursued and eradicated by those who did. 'The church of Christ is a terrible plague and vexation to all the rest of the world . . . because the laws and rules by which they walk do threaten nothing but ruin and destruction to all those that walk in other ways,' Marshall announced. 'The people of God do hold out that which must be the only rule, and they tell all the world that if they walk not according to their rule only, they will be damned, and destroyed eternally.'[26]

CONCLUSION

The rage of the disesteemed is personally fruitless, but it is also absolutely inevitable. This rage, so generally discounted, so little understood even among the people whose daily bread it is, is one of the things that makes history.

James Baldwin

The previous pages have set forth the ideology of revolutionary Puritanism much as it was set forth to popular and political audiences in its own day. Like the ministers, we have avoided becoming embroiled in dogmatic disputes or the daily ups and downs of secular politics. In presenting Puritanism in this way, there may be a danger of making it appear less problematic than any oppositional movement must inevitably be. The words in these pages have been those of ministers, intellectuals who saw ideas through to their logical conclusions. They encouraged the revolution and tried to shape it to their vision, yet with few exceptions it was not they who actually made it, and nothing has been said so far about the impact they made on those who did. A brief word, therefore, is in order to set these ideas in perspective.

There can be no doubt that the words spoken in these sermons and thousands like them did make a direct and significant impact on the minds of people and on the political events of the 1640s. Anyone who has browsed the letters and speeches of Oliver Cromwell, or any other of the politically active gentry, or read the proceedings against Charles I, will have found much of this rhetoric reminiscent of what was frequently expressed in both public and private to explain or justify concrete political action.[1] Yet it is also true that even after 1649 the Puritan ministers were never in a position to implement or enforce their godly program in its entirety and that the political world their disciples tried to construct was not necessarily precisely the one they envisioned. While it was the ministers who formulated and articulated ideas, they themselves at no time controlled any coercive apparatus and were wholly dependent on the sympathy of lay office-holders for its exercise. In more enthusiastic moments they might betray their aspirations to erect a 'theocracy' in England, but they were so far from exercising direct power in the state that they were not even granted exclusive authority over the church; Parliament was careful throughout to reserve for itself final say in all matters pertaining to both. Moreover, though the godly magistracy sought the ministers' advice and assistance as they asserted their new authority, many were already experienced in practical politics from years in Parliament or local government and also had considerable economic resources at their disposal. These allowed them a measure of self-confidence and leverage in public affairs as well as control over their clerical advisers, who were dependent largely on their patronage. Further, whatever the dimensions of their personal piety, the ideological purity of these lay saints was not always that of the ministers, and Calvinist religion was not the only form of discourse available to them for addressing social and political affairs.

The gentlemen to whom the ministers preached, Puritan as they may have been, were many other things as well. Many were skilled in the law; some subscribed to natural rights theories; a few were patrons of civic humanist and classical republican ideas; most were at least open to experimenting with all these systems of thought; all had a rich literary tradition on which to draw from classical antiquity, the continental renaissance, and the English common law. Together, these added up to a complex and sophisticated political culture with which the rather single-minded tendencies of radical Calvinism were forced to compete. Even some of the ministers, in their auxiliary role as propagandists, wrote resistance tracts that justified their rebellion more according to the principles of natural and common law than those of the Bible. Many of the sermons themselves, especially during the 1640s, are sprinkled with allusions to legal and political theorists as well as theologians. They were kept brief and to the point in order to avoid the appearance of ostentation, and I have tended to omit them altogether for the sake of space. But they were there – less to belie the preachers' professed intention to adhere strictly to the word and avoid 'human learning' than an indication of the complex level of education and understanding among their sympathizers. To recognize this is not to diminish the intensity of the emotions expressed by radical Protestantism; it is merely to acknowledge that it was not the only language available in which to express them.[2] These languages existed in a sometimes complementary, sometimes uneasy relationship with Calvinism, and while the ministers found casuistical methods for rendering them compatible with godliness, the fact that they felt compelled to do this indicates the extent to which alternative vocabularies were at hand to enunciate political principles. To detail precisely what difference this made to the course and outcome of the revolution would require another book, though it may be worth remarking that the social and economic as well as the cultural composition of the English revolution does contrast markedly with some apparently similar occurrences in our own time and suggests the problem of describing it simply as a 'war of religion'.[3]

The precise role and weight of Puritanism in the English civil war of the 1640s will perhaps always be a matter for debate. What is beyond debate is its impact on the politics of the modern world. Other modes of political discourse that have come down to us from the English revolution have also had a lasting and probably more visible impact on our own political culture, at least among those classes that dominate historical and constitutional scholarship. Yet virtually every major social and political movement in the English-speaking world has asserted itself on the popular level largely in the language of evangelical Protestantism. This is so not only of obviously religious revivals such as Methodism or the Great Awakening, but also of such seemingly 'secular' episodes as the American revolution and the abolitionist and labor movements. Behind a similar language, too, one might expect to find similar needs and drives, though scholars of these eras have found the persistence of Calvinism easier to observe than to explain.[4]

Like all history, then, the questions asked here were inevitably provoked in part by subsequent and contemporary experience. Today radical religion again commands serious attention from students of politics throughout the world, though so far this has inspired little re-examination of its role in seventeenth-century England. Religious fanaticism now appears among other, mostly non-European cultures; some people seem to become uncomfortable at the sight of it within the heart of liberal Anglo-Saxon Protestantism. The Whig view of history that is itself the legacy of that culture remains amazingly resilient, even among those who now claim to be doing valiant battle against it. But whether we continue to think of the civil war as one of the milestones on the highway of human and political progress, or as some dark and disturbing diversion we would rather pretend was never taken, it is still a part of our political world and of ourselves. I offer no judgments on the Puritans; too many elite historians from all parts of the political spectrum are quick to pronounce disapproval, often before they have begun. Even today intellectual ideologues, some of whom might well trace their pedigrees to Puritanism itself, seem more intent to establish distance than acknowledge affinity and to villify rather than to understand their predecessors – much the way Puritan historiography often villified its own and as revolutionaries have done ever since.[5]

But the Puritans are not the villains of history. They did not by themselves foment discontent and bloodshed where no disposition otherwise existed; neither are they responsible for the exploitative practices of modern industrial society. They were ordinary intellectuals trying to resolve agonizing moral dilemmas and find a way out of the turmoil of their world. That those who wage war against evil often become infected with it themselves is a familiar enough phenomenon in modern history and readily comprehensible by most people. Yet professional scholars seem to feel they must devise abstruse theories, discover arcane details, or locate historical scapegoats in order to understand what the prophets are shouting at the top of their voices. This study, I hope, has not become another example of the kind of revisionism-for-its-own-sake that now seems to have become almost obligatory in historical writing. My only aim has been to allow the prophets of the English revolution an opportunity to express to the modern world their own ideas in their own words, warts and all.

NOTES

In all citations the place of publication is London unless otherwise indicated.

INTRODUCTION

1. The preachers themselves expressed a similar concern: 'It is not fit, yea it is very hurtful, to make the pulpit a place for a continual and full handling of controversies in a common auditory,' said Richard Bernard, whose comments concerning some of his fellow preachers might apply to not a few modern scholars: 'They be much in controversies,' he remarked. 'The fruit of these men's labors is in . . . words, quiddities, and vain ostentation. These be the preachers full of discretion, but of little religion.' *The Faithful Shepherd* (1609), 18, 79. Like the preachers, I have generally avoided scholarly controversies, though historiographical essays abound in a field where historians now 'write not only for each other but about each other'. (Blair Worden, 'Revising the Revolution', *New York Review of Books*, XXXVIII, 1 and 2, January 17, 1991, 40.) See R.C. Richardson, *The Debate on the English Revolution Revisited* (New York, 1988). Puritan preaching has been discussed in Paul Seaver, *The Puritan Lectureships: The Politics of Religious Dissent, 1560–1662* (Stanford, 1970), and John F. Wilson, *Pulpit in Parliament: Puritanism during the English Civil Wars, 1640–1648* (Princeton, 1969).
2. Conrad Russell, *Parliaments and English Politics, 1621–1629* (1979), 8; quoted in Richardson, *Debate*, ch. 9, 171, where other 'revisionist' literature is cited. (See note 32, below.) For the resistance to Protestantism, see J.J. Scarisbrick, *The Reformation and the English People* (Oxford, 1984).
3. Lawrence Stone, 'Social Mobility in England', *Past and Present* 33 (1966), and *The Causes of the English Revolution, 1529–1642* (1972), esp. ch. 1 and 110–13; A.J. Fletcher, 'Honour, Reputation, and Local Officeholding in Elizabethan and Stuart England', and other essays in *Order and Disorder in Early Modern England*, ed. A. Fletcher and J. Stevenson (Cambridge, 1987).
4. J.T. Cliffe, *The Puritan Gentry: The Great Puritan Families of Early Stuart England* (1984).
5. Paul Slack, *Poverty and Policy in Tudor and Stuart England* (1988).
6. Kevin Sharpe, *Faction and Parliament* (1978), 42. For administration and government, see G.E. Aylmer, *The King's Servants: The Civil Service of Charles I, 1625–1642* (1961), and Anthony Fletcher, *Reform in the Provinces: The Government of Stuart England* (1986).
7. The conditions described in the preceding paragraph, no doubt overstated to make the point, have nevertheless all been documented in recent studies. For surveys, see Keith Wrightson, *English Society, 1580–1680* (New Brunswick, 1984), and J.A. Sharpe, *Early Modern England: A Social History, 1550–1760* (London and Bal-

timore, 1987). Rather different attempts to connect social change to religion include David Underdown, *Revel, Riot, and Rebellion: Popular Politics and Culture in England, 1603–60* (Oxford, 1985), esp. 22, 29f., and ch. 2, and William Hunt, *The Puritan Moment* (1983).

8. Lawrence Stone, 'The English Revolution', in *Preconditions of Revolution in Early Modern Europe*, ed. Robert Forster and Jack P. Greene (Baltimore and London, 1970); *Causes*, 98–9. This study concentrates on ideas about salvation or 'soteriology'; principles of organization or 'ecclesiology' will be saved for a later volume.

9. 'We cannot simply explain revolutions . . . in terms of hardships and inequities as perceived by an external observer. We need to know how such alleged hardships and inequities are perceived by those who experience them.' Henry Munson, Jr, *Islam and Revolution in the Middle East* (New Haven, 1988), 116.

10. Stephen Marshall, *A Peace Offering to God* (1641), 37–8. For the 'spiritual beggars' and 'spiritual vagabonds' of society, see chs. 2–3.

11. The term 'cosmic optimism' is from Perry Miller, *The New England Mind: The Seventeenth Century* (Boston, 1939), 38. William Perkins, *Works* (Cambridge, 1626–31), II, 303–4; Richard Sibbes, *Works* (Edinburgh, 1862–4, repr. 1978–82), , VI, 305.

12. John Langley, *The Mournful Note of the Dove* (1644), 28–9. These phrases are current among revisionist historians: e.g., Anthony Fletcher, *The Outbreak of the English Civil War* (1981), 418; but cp. Christopher Hill, 'A Bourgeois Revolution?', *Collected Essays* (Amherst, 1986), 117. Thomas Goodwin, *Zerubbabel's Encouragement* (1642), 52; Jeremiah Burroughs, *Zion's Joy* (1641), 2. Cp. Robert Zaller, 'Legitimation and Delegitimation in Early Modern Europe: The Case of England', *History of European Ideas*, X, 6 (1989), 655.

13. William Ames, *The Saints' Security* (1651), dedicatory epistle. Even Marx, whose characterization of religion has often been taken out of its more ambiguous context, paid tribute to the 'reality' of religious belief, perhaps in spite of himself, in terms the Puritans might have understood: 'Religious suffering is at the same time an expression of real suffering and a protest against real suffering,' he said. 'Religion is the sigh of the oppressed creature, the heart of a heartless world, and the soul of soulless conditions.' *Contribution to the Critique of Hegel's Philosophy of Law* (1844), introduction. Cp. Sibbes's recognition of the 'reality' of the popular opiate and spiritual fetishism against which his own religion contended: 'Imagination, though it be an empty, windy thing, yet it hath real effects,' he acknowledged. 'Superstition breeds false fears, and false fear brings true vexation.' *Works*, I, 180.

14. Sibbes, *Works*, I, 383. Christopher Hill, *God's Englishman: Oliver Cromwell and the English Revolution* (New York, 1970), 231.

15. See W.D.J. Cargill Thompson, *The Political Thought of Martin Luther*, ed. Philip Broadhead (Brighton, 1984), 9–10. The explanation of ideology as an emanation of social 'strain' has been likened to 'a spontaneous "damn!" of frustration'. Clifford Geertz, 'Ideology as a Cultural System', *The Interpretation of Cultures* (1973), ch. 8. Such vagaries might be avoided by allowing the preachers to speak in their own words. For a survey of theories as to 'why men rebel' as they relate to early modern revolutions of Europe, see Perez Zagorin, *Rebels and Rulers, 1500–1660* (1982), I, part one and *passim*; also Stone, *Causes*, ch. 1.

16. Michael Walzer, *The Revolution of the Saints: A Study in the Origins of Radical Politics* (Cambridge, Mass., 1965), ch. 1; cp. also Sheldon Wolin, *Politics and Vision* (Boston, 1960), 193–4.

17. Lawrence Stone, 'The Educational Revolution in England, 1560–1640', *Past and Present*, 28 (1964), 77. In his pastoral manual Richard Baxter suggested that a systematic catechistical indoctrination of listeners beforehand would facilitate the absorption of the applied commentary of the sermon. *The Reformed Pastor* (1656,

repr. 1983), 174–5ff. The modern reader interested in the technical points of Calvinist orthodoxy should consult the *Westminister Confession of Faith* (repr. Glasgow, 1983), as well the catechisms printed with it, which might be called the Calvinist Manifesto.

18. In themselves Puritan ideas were seldom original or unique. Puritanism at this time should not be seen as a fixed partisan grouping or body of doctrine but as a tendency to emphasize, popularize, and above all apply certain aspects of Calvinist doctrine in response to changing circumstances. That many of these ideas were widely shared and paralleled among the less militant and those not readily identifiable as hard-core 'Puritans' makes them all the more worthy of attention – not, as is too often the case, dismissed as unoriginal, commonplace, or biblical. See Patrick Collinson, 'A Comment: Concerning the Name Puritan', *Journal of Ecclesiastical History*, XXXI, 4 (1980). No succinct definition of Puritanism will be offered here; this study aspires to be what every good work on Puritanism is, an extended exercise in definition. Martin Luther, in *Discourse on Free Will*, ed. Ernst F. Winter (New York, 1961), 109.

19. Thomas Wilson, *Jericho's Downfall* (1643), 26–7; Samuel Hieron, *The Dignity of Preaching* (1615), 11; Francis Cheynell, *The Man of Honor* (1645), 44; Stephen Marshall, *The Right Understanding of the Times* (1647), 9–10; John Preston, *The Breastplate of Faith and Love* (1634), II, 224–6.

20. Bernard, *Faithful Shepherd*, 12–13; John Wilkins, *Ecclesiastes* (1647), 18 (citing Acts 13:15).

21. Cp. Michael Walzer, 'The Revolutionary Uses of Repression', in *Essays in Theory and History*, ed. Melvin Richter (Cambridge, Mass., 1970). William Jenkyn, *The Policy of Princes* (1656), 35; Bernard, *Faithful Shepherd*, 2; Lazarus Seaman, *Solomon's Choice* (1644), 20–1, 27–8; Francis Peck, *The Good Fight of Faith* (1645), 4; Stephen Marshall, *A Two-Edged Sword* (1646), 22.

22. Historians who seem to agree on nothing else when it comes to a definition of Puritanism usually agree on the importance of the word: Patrick Collinson, 'The Elizabethan Church and the New Religion', in *The Reign of Elizabeth I*, ed. Christopher Haigh (1984); Seaver, *Puritan Lectureships*. Sibbes, *Works*, VII, 545. Stone, 'Educational Revolution'; Mark H. Curtis, 'The Alienated Intellectuals of Early Stuart England', *Past and Present*, 23 (1962); David Cressy, 'Levels of Illiteracy in England, 1530–1730', *The Historical Journal*, XX, 1 (1977). cp. Bacon's essay 'Of Seditions and Troubles'.

23. Hieron, *Dignity of Preaching*, 2, 13, 18; Perkins, *Works*, II, 671; Edmund Calamy, *The Doctrine of the Body's Fragility* (1655), 16; Baxter, *Reformed Pastor*, 85.

24. Joseph Boden, *An Alarm Beat Up in Zion* (1644), sig. A3v; Wilkins, *Ecclesiastes*, 72–3; Richard Kentish, *The Way of Love* (1648), sig. A1r, 17; Perkins, *Works*, II, 670; William Ames, *Conscience* (1639), IV, 26; Baxter, *Reformed Pastor*, 70, 115–16, 117; Hieron, *Dignity of Preaching*, 15–16. Even for the citations they often felt the need to apologize. 'Let not the marginal quotations offend any,' Kentish said. 'They were not set down for ostentation.' The reader of modern scholarly literature too might do well to heed Milton's advice: 'Be not deceived, readers, by men that would overawe your ears with big names and huge tomes that contradict and repeat one another, because they can cram a margin with citations,' he warned. 'Do but winnow their chaff from their wheat, ye shall see their great heap shrink and wax thin past belief.' *The Complete Prose Works of John Milton*, I (New Haven, 1953), 358. See Victor Morgan, *Godly Learning* (1984), for Puritan attitudes.

25. John Brinsley, *The Preacher's Charge* (1631), 20–1, 29–30; Francis Cheynell, *A Plot for the Good of Posterity* (1646), 41.

26. A point illustrated by a stricture of William Perkins: 'Human testimonies . . . are not to be alleged . . . unless they convince the conscience . . . and then also it must be done sparingly, and with leaving out the name of the profane writer.' *Works*, II, 664.
27. Hieron, *Dignity of Preaching*, 2–3; Brinsley, *Preacher's Charge*, 4.
28. Bernard, *Faithful Shepherd*, 36, 65–6, 342; Cornelius Burges, *Agreement with God* (1645), 29; Cheynell, *Plot*, 27 (quoting Hos. 12:10).
29. Wilkins, *Ecclesiastes*, 20–1.
30. Those printed in defiance of parliamentary order being the exceptions that prove the rule. William Dell's *Right Reformation* (1646) made no pretense at being anything other than a blistering attack on what he called the 'carnal' reformation of the Presbyterians. The principles to which he appealed, however, were at least professed by all the preachers. Similarly, the defense of 'Erastianism' appended to Thomas Coleman's *Hopes Deferred and Dashed* (1645), even assuming it was delivered orally, was tolerated by the House for perhaps obvious reasons. Even so, Coleman made no attempt to disguise the point where the sermon left off and the polemic began.
31. Richard Byfield, *Temple-Defilers Defiled* (1645), sig. A4r; William Reyner, *Orders from the Lord of Hosts* (1646), sig. A2v.
32. The exception being Walzer, *Revolution*, a brilliant work to which the present study is indebted throughout. For the fast sermon program itself, see Wilson, *Pulpit*; for its precursors, Seaver, *Puritan Lectureships*. That the sermons did in fact exert an important impact on their audience and on political events is now generally accepted, even (perhaps especially) by the conservative 'revisionist' school: 'The role of religion in creating and sustaining the parliamentarian movement cannot be overestimated.' John Morrill, *Reactions to the English Civil War* (1982), 15. Contemporary conservatives certainly had no doubt about the central role of Puritan preaching in fomenting the revolution. See Hobbes's *Behemoth* (1889), 24 and *passim*, and Clarendon's, *The History of the Rebellion and Civil Wars in England* (Oxford, 1888), II, 319–22. For only a few of the most recent examples of political historians of various sympathies who have emphasized the importance of religion in general and Puritanism in particular in the political conflicts of the seventeenth century, see the following: John Morrill, 'The Religious Context of the English Civil War', *Transactions of the Royal Historical Society*, fifth series, 34 (1984), and 'The Attack on the Church of England in the Long Parliament', in *History, Society, and the Churches*, ed. D. Beales and G. Best (Cambridge, 1985); J.T. Cliffe, *Puritan Gentry* and *Puritans in Conflict* (1988); Jacqueline Eales, *Puritans and Roundheads: The Harleys of Brampton Bryan and the Outbreak of the English Civil War* (Cambridge, 1990); Conrad Russell, *The Causes of the English Civil War* (Oxford, 1990). A fascinating study which reveals much of the same language as this one on a more popular level is Paul Seaver, *Wallington's World: A Puritan Artisan in Seventeenth-Century London* (Stanford, 1985). A sampling of recent counter-revisionist scholarship can be found in Richard Cust and Ann Hughes (eds.), *Conflict in Early Stuart England: Studies in Religion and Politics, 1603–1642* (1989). Oddly however, 'the greater the respect historians of politics demonstrate for the religious convictions of the seventeenth century, the less interest they show in accounting for them.' (Worden, 'Revising the Revolution', 40.) As things now stand, the revisionists have effectively exposed the limitations of the 'Whig' and 'Marxist' approaches, though neither they nor their opponents have shown much interest in providing a positive alternative.
33. Edmund Calamy, *The Nobleman's Pattern* (1643), 30. Though conservative scholars are generally most dismissive of the Puritans' claim to be the voice of the oppressed, they are now often joined by those who themselves adopt the pose of speaking for the 'poor people and silly [i.e. simple] women', as if rivals must be eliminated. As will be seen, Puritan attitudes toward the poor and women were not always politically

correct by the light of today's academic left, though those who draw attention to this have trouble accounting for the fact that Puritanism drew a high proportion of its supporters from precisely these groups, whereas the sects so romanticized and overstudied today had a meager following in their own time. See Chapter 3. Robert Bolton, *Mr Bolton's Last and Learned Work . . . with His Assize Sermon . . . at Northampton* (1635), 210–2; Sibbes, *Works*, IV, 139, 194; Thomas Hill, *The Good Old Way* (1644), 11–12.

1. PROVIDENCE

1. Francis Cheynell, *The Man of Honor* (1645), 21; Edward Corbet, *God's Providence* (1642), 1–3; John Rowe, *Man's Duty in Magnifying God's Work* (1656), 1–2; Thomas Manton, *Meat Out of the Eater* (1647), 40. Recent scholarship on the impact of religion in the civil war has focused almost entirely on the controversies to which Corbet alludes. Nicholas Tyacke, *Anti-Calvinists: The Rise of English Arminianism, c. 1590–1640* (Oxford, 1987), has provoked a raging academic pamphlet war over the role of religious policy in the growing dissatisfaction with the regime of Charles I. Without denying their importance, these exchanges have been fully treated by others, and the focus of this study will be rather different.

2. Gaspar Hickes, *The Advantage of Afflictions* (1645), 6; William Gouge, *The Progress of Divine Providence* (1645), 16; Richard Sibbes, *Works* (Edinburgh, 1862–4; repr. 1978–82), I, 205; VI, 148; Corbet, *God's Providence*, 10.

3. Joseph Caryl, *England's Plus-Ultra* (1646), 38–9; Corbet, *God's Providence*, 25.

4. Gaspar Hickes, *The Glory and Beauty of God's Portion* (1644), 16; Corbet, *God's Providence*, 24–5; Thomas Hodges, *A Glimpse of God's Glory* (1642), 36–7; Samuel Rutherford, *A Sermon* (1644), 62.

5. John Owen, *A Vision of Unchangeable Free Mercy* (1646), 7–8; Corbet, *God's Providence*, 4, 11.

6. William Perkins, *Works* (Cambridge, 1626–31), II, 669; John Cardell, *God's Sovereign Power over Nations* (1648), 4; William Pemberton, *The Charge of God and the King* (1619), sig. A6r–v.

7. John Wilkins, *The Beauty of Providence* (1649), 8, 10, 16, 35, 49–50, 63, 82. For the affinities between Puritan providentialism and modern science, see Charles Webster, *The Great Instauration: Science, Medicine, and Reform, 1626–1660* (1975), ch. 1.

8. Jeremiah Burroughs, *The Rare Jewel* (1648), 94–6; Rowe, *Man's Duty*, 13.

9. Sibbes, *Works*, VI, 83–4, 241, 523.

10. Thomas Palmer, *The Saints' Support* (1644), 1; John Warren, *The Potent Potter* (1649), 14. The 'rule' is scripture (not 'conscience' alone, as Warren may seem to be but is not saying). 'In the carrying on of God's providential will, do not swerve from God's preceptive will, for it is not providence but the word that is your rule,' Thomas Jacomb said. 'Providence without the word is doubtful, but providence against the word is dangerous.' *The Active and Public Spirit* (1657), 45; quoted in Blair Worden, 'Providence and Politics in Cromwellian England', *Past and Present*, 109 (1985), 91. Both conservative and leftist historians, in their eagerness to demonstrate Puritan hypocrisy, either ignore such statements or suggest they must not have been sincere. See Chapter 3. Sibbes, *Works*, I, 206–7.

11. Burroughs, *Rare Jewel*, 94; Nicholas Lockyer, *England Faithfully Watched* (1645), 119–20; William Bridge, *Works* (1845), I, 484–5.

12. Samuel Rutherford, *The Trial and Triumph of Faith* (1645), 4; Wilkins, *Beauty of Providence*, 72–3; Sibbes, *Works*, I, 207; VI, 83–4, 241; Bridge, *Works*, I, 470; Jeremiah Whitaker, *The Christian's Hope Triumphing* (1645), 30.

13. Nathaniel Holmes, *God's Gracious Thoughts* (1647), 7–8; Thomas Carter, *Prayer's Prevalency* (1643), 5; Thomas Case, *God's Waiting to be Gracious* (1642), 6; Thomas

Hill, *The Militant Church* (1643), sig. A3v. Time as a theme in the political and historical thought of early modern England has been fruitfully explored in the work of J.G.A. Pocock, especially *Politics, Language, and Time* (New York, 1971). Oddly, students of Calvinism seem not to have applied it to the paradoxes of predestination.

14. Rutherford, *Sermon*, 49; Sibbes, *Works*, VII, 501; George Hughes, *The Woe-Joy Trumpet* (1647), 12–13; Hodges, *Glimpse*, 20, 37–9; Keith Thomas, *Religion and the Decline of Magic* (New York, 1971), 427. Thomas rightly points to the way political and legal writers tried to disguise their own innovations, but see Chapter 3. The argument pursued here in itself is not novel; all the best studies of Puritanism have suggested it: William Haller, *The Rise of Puritanism* (New York, 1938); Michael Walzer, *The Revolution of the Saints* (Cambridge, Mass., 1965); John S. Coolidge, *The Pauline Renaissance in England* (Oxford, 1970).

15. Thomas Valentine, *A Sermon* (1644), 47; Jeremiah Whitaker, *The Christian's Great Design* (1645), 19; Sibbes, *Works*, II, 471, 474 (also I, 342); IV, 215, 436–7; V, 216, 234, 290; VII, 37; Richard Vines, *The Hearse of the Earl of Essex* (1646), 22.

16. Vines, *Hearse*; William Jenkyn, *A Sleeping Sickness* (1647), sig. A2v; Sibbes, *Works*, IV, 51–3; VI, 45; Rutherford, *Sermon*, 53–4; Edmund Calamy, *The Nobleman's Pattern* (1643), 15; William Strong, *The Right Way to the Highest Honor* (1647), 2–3; Whitaker, *Christian's Great Design*, 6.

17. Obadiah Sedgwick, *Christ the Life and Death the Gain* (1650), 18; John Whincop, *Israel's Tears* (1645), 13–14; William Greenhill, *The Axe at the Root* (1643), 25–6.

18. Joseph Caryl, *Joy Out-Joyed* (1646), sig. A2v; Nathaniel Holmes, *A Sermon* (1650), 45; Jeremiah Burroughs, *The Glorious Name of God* (1643), 5–8, 11–12, 15, 19.

19. Burroughs, *Glorious Name*, 11–12, 24, 26–7, 83.

20. Stephen Marshall, *A Divine Project* (1644), 18–19; Burroughs, *Glorious Name*, 5, 82–3, 115, 117; Thomas Hill, *The Season for England's Self-Reflection* (1644), 6. Compared with theories of legal resistance, Puritan ideas on war have received little attention from modern scholars. See the following: Roland Bainton, 'Congregationalism and the Puritan Revolution from the Just War to the Crusade', *Studies on the Reformation* (Boston, 1963); Timothy George, 'War and Peace in the Puritan Tradition', *Church History*, LIII, 4 (1984); Walzer, *Revolution*, ch. 8.

21. Stephen Marshall, *A Sermon* (1652), 13–14; Jeremiah Burroughs, *Irenicum* (1646), 4; Samson Bond, *A Sermon* (1646), 29.

22. Burroughs, *Irenicum*, 1; Lazarus Seaman, *A Glass for the Times* (1650), 8, 14–15, 18–19; Lockyer, *England*, 211–15, 274; Sibbes, *Works*, II, 89; VI, 247 and *passim*; John Preston, *The Breastplate of Faith and Love* (1634), II, 111–12 and *passim*; Thomas Valentine, *A Sermon* (1643), 40; John Owen, *Works* (Edinburgh, 1862), VIII, *passim*; William Bridge, *A Lifting Up for the Downcast* (1649), *passim*; Burroughs, *Rare Jewel, passim*; Thomas Brooks, *Heaven on Earth* (1654; repr. 1982), 92 and *passim*. Max Weber has described the 'feeling of unprecedented inner loneliness of the single individual . . . through the Calvinist faith', though he seems to hold Calvinism somehow responsible for this rather than simply confronting what already existed. *The Protestant Ethic and the Spirit of Capitalism*, trans. Talcott Parsons (1958), 104, 108. Recent historians too, often under Weber's influence, have assumed the preachers simply created something called 'religious despair' and somehow imposed it on people, especially poor people. My argument (and I think theirs as well) is that they expressed and exploited feelings, stemming from poverty and other material conditions, that were already there. For other views, see Thomas, *Religion*, 521, and Christopher Hill, *The World Turned Upside Down* (1972), 136f.; cp. Walzer, *Revolution*, ch. 9.

23. Perkins, *Works*, I, 755; William Sclater, *Civil Magistracy by Divine Authority* (1652), 6; Obadiah Sedgwick, *The Best and the Worst Magistrate* (1648), 18 (echoing James I); Anthony Burges, *The Magistrate's Commission* (1644), 2 (on politics as a calling,

cp. Walzer, *Revolution*, ch. 7); Richard Vines, *Subjection to Magistrates* (1656), III, 18–20; Cheynell, *Man of Honor*, 7.

24. Cheynell, *Man of Honor*, 32–5; Strong, *Right Way*, 2–3, 41.
25. Strong, *Right Way*, 12, 24, 33, 34, 38–9. Mervyn James, 'English Politics and the Concept of Honour, 1485–1642', in *Society, Politics and Culture: Studies in Early Modern England* (Cambridge, 1986).
26. Cheynell, *Man of Honor*, 41; Warren, *Potent Potter*, sig. A3v; Jeremiah Burroughs, *A Sermon* (1646), 10–4. This sense in which the Calvinist God leveled hierarchy on earth as well as in heaven has been described by Walzer, *Revolution*, ch. 5.
27. Burroughs, *Sermon*, 5, 14; Sibbes, *Works*, V, 45–6; VI, 52–3.
28. Thomas Watson, *A Plea for Alms* (1658), 13–14. The point was considered an effective incentive to poor relief. ''Tis wisdom to consider the poor,' Watson continued. 'Remember how soon the scene may alter; we may be put in the poor's dress, and if adversity come it will rejoice us to think that while we had an estate we did lay it out upon Christ's indigent members.' Burroughs, *Sermon*, 43; Lockyer, *England*, 181f.; Burroughs, *Rare Jewel* (1651), 22.
29. Samuel Rogers, *The Poor's Pension* (1644), 16; Sibbes, *Works*, VI, 238; Burroughs, *Rare Jewel* (1651), 139. Paul Slack, *Poverty and Policy in Tudor and Stuart England*, (1988). For Puritanism in the poor sections of London, see Tai Liu, *London Puritanism* (1986), esp. 202. R.H. Tawney described the Puritan as one who 'sees in the poverty of those who fall by the way not a misfortune to be pitied and relieved but a moral failing to be condemned and in riches not an object of suspicion . . . but the blessing which rewards the triumph of energy and will.' The hunt for historical villains continues among some of the most elite scholars today, despite the fact that this assertion has never been documented for the period before the civil war and is diametrically opposed to what the Puritans themselves actually go out of their way to insist in countless sermons. 'I do not know any one thing that the scripture does more frequently or earnestly press than this,' John Cardell said of poor relief, 'or that we had more need to press in these hard times wherein abundance of poor people are even ready to starve for want of necessaries.' More to the point is how facile the Weber–Tawney thesis looks when it is seen that the appeal of Calvinism sprang precisely from a need to compensate for the loss or insecurity of worldly status. On this view, it is entirely understandable that Calvinism and anxiety over status should coexist within the same individuals; it hardly follows that Calvinism was the cause. *Religion and the Rise of Capitalism* (1922; repr. Harmondsworth, 1938), 229–30; cp. Christopher Hill, 'Protestantism and the Rise of Capitalism', in *Essays in the Economic and Social History of Tudor and Stuart England*, ed. F.J. Fisher (Cambridge, 1961), and *World Turned Upside Down*, ch. 16. See also Michael Walzer, 'Puritanism as a Revolutionary Ideology', *History and Theory*, III, 1 (1963), whose lead I prefer to follow. Another corrective can be found in Michael Mullett, *Radical Religious Movements in Early Modern Europe* (1980).
30. Rogers, *Poor's Pension*, 11, 28; Sibbes, *Works*, VI, 238–9; VII, 225; Perkins, *Works*, III, 5; Richard Greenham, *Works* (1601), 251, 784; William Jenkyn, *The Policy of Princes in Subjection to the Son* (1656), 16. Greenham's admonition was a frequent one, conspicuously passed over by the expositors of the 'Protestant ethic' thesis. Again the point here is poverty as only the most extreme manifestation of problems affecting the wider society and is not to endorse the wholesale idea of a 'culture of poverty'; cp. Slack, *Poverty and Policy*, esp. 104–7.
31. Sibbes, *Works*, VI, 241; VII, 216. The Puritans may have had a keener understanding of dialectics than many self-styled Marxist historians; however the view against which I am arguing is no longer confined to the Marxist notion of 'bourgeois revolution' but is now readily endorsed by conservative scholars as well. Cp. Hill, 'Protestantism and the Rise of Capitalism'.

32. Sibbes, *Works*, VI, 151; Rowe, *Man's Duty*, sig. A3v, 2–4, 17. That God (or at least the ministers) should be similarly insecure about his worldly status, and even in danger of losing it if not 'praised' by his more ardent followers, was further indicated by Rowe: 'It is fit that some should stir up themselves to give him praise, that so God may not altogether lose his honor in the world.'

33. Peter Sterry, *The Comings Forth of Christ* (1650), 45; John Owen, *The Steadfastness of Promises* (1650), 30–1.

34. Thomas Brooks, *The Hypocrite* (1650), 13, 19; John Owen, *A Sermon* (1652), 22; John Owen, *God's Work in Founding Zion* (Oxford, 1656), 20–1, 33; John Owen, *The Advantage of the Kingdom of Christ* (1651), 11, 30; Burroughs, *Sermon*, 12; Cheynell, *Man of Honor*, 41; Corbet, *God's Providence*, 2; Burroughs, *Glorious Name*, 120.

35. Warren, *Potent Potter*, 13–14; John Owen, *The Laboring Saint's Dismission to Rest* (1651), 348; Owen, *Works*, VIII, 461; John Warren, *Man's Fury Subservient to God's Glory* (1656), 31; Brooks, *Hypocrite*, sig. A3r.

36. Owen, *Advantage*, 18; Burroughs, *Rare Jewel* (1648), 95; Sibbes, *Works*, I, 416; Corbet, *God's Providence*, 5; Edward Reynolds, *Self-Denial* (1645), 23.

37. Reynolds, *Self-Denial*, 14; Burroughs, *Rare Jewel* (1648), 221; William Bridge, *Two Sermons* (1643), 12, 16; Marshall, *Divine Project*, 43; Owen, *Advantage*, 221; Cheynell, *Man of Honor*, 35.

38. Strong, *Right Way*, 39; Joseph Caryl, *The Works of Ephesus* (1642), 55; Francis Woodcock, *God Paying Every Man* (1646), 22.

2 SIN

1. Thomas Case, *The Quarrel of the Covenant* (1643), 71–2; Thomas Goodwin, *The Aggravation of Sin* (1643), 6; Nicholas Lockyer, *England Faithfully Watched* (1645), 182–3, 160; Richard Sibbes, *Works* (Edinburgh, 1862–4; repr. 1978–82), IV, 499.

2. Thomas Brooks, *Precious Remedies* (1654), *Works* (Edinburgh, 1866), I, 152 (quoting Matt. 15:19); Stephen Marshall, *The Right Understanding of the Times* (1647), 32–3; Stephen Marshall, *Reformation and Desolation* (1642), 45. England had a severe problem with alcoholism at this time; see Peter Clark, *The English Alehouse* (1983).

3. Robert Bolton, *Two Sermons Preached at . . . Assizes* (1639), I, 10; William Jenkyn *The Policy of Princes* (1656), 37. Cp. Michael Walzer, *The Revolution of the Saints* (Cambridge, Mass., 1965), ch. 9; Anthony Fletcher, *Reform in the Provinces* (1986).

4. Joseph Caryl, *The Works of Ephesus* (1642), 32; Sibbes, *Works*, I, 244, 385–6, 397–8; II, 88; Arthur Dent, *God's Providence* (1611), sig. C3r; John Preston, *The Breastplate of Faith and Love* (1634), I, 283.

5. Preston, *Breastplate*, 283–6; Sibbes, *Works*, I, 385–6, 397–8; Marshall, *Reformation and Desolation*, 16–17.

6. Sibbes, *Works*, I, 150, 179, 299; III, 339, 485–6; IV, 280; Robert Bolton, *Assize Sermon . . . Preached at . . . Northampton*, in *Mr Bolton's Last and Learned Work* (1635), 228.

7. Thomas Carter, *Prayer's Prevalency* (1643), 3; Bolton, *Two Sermons*, I, 3, 11; II, 71, 75–6, 87; Samuel Ward, *Jethro's Justice of the Peace* (1618), 11, 13, 47; Thomas Pestell, *The Churl's Sickness* (1615), 4, 16; Samuel Garey, *Breakfast for the Bench* (1623), 64; Bolton, *Assize Sermon*, 187. For office-holding, see G.E. Aylmer, *The King's Servants* (New York, 1961). That the ministers complained that rewards were not being bestowed according to 'merit' does not necessarily mean their solution was that they should or could be; their theology categorically refused to recognize any concept of merit, perhaps for reasons indicated here. See Chapter 4.

8. R. Bolton, *Two Sermons*, II, 68–9, 89–90, 187; Ward, *Jethro's Justice*, 8–9.

9. Sibbes, *Works*, I, 109; II, 492; V, 21; William Perkins, *Works* (Cambridge, 1626–31), I, 105; II, 469.

10. Perkins, *Works*, I, 205; II, 334–5; III, 267; William Dickinson, *The King's Right* (1619), 21; Sibbes, *Works*, I, 405; Bolton, *Assize Sermon*, 235–6, 238. The preachers' assessment is borne out by modern research. See A.J. Fletcher, 'Honour, Reputation, and Local Officeholding in Elizabethan and Stuart England', in *Order and Disorder in Early Modern England*, ed. A. Fletcher and J. Stevenson (Cambridge, 1987), and references cited there.

11. Nathaniel Holmes, *Demonology* (1650), 35; Sibbes, *Works*, I, 134; Perkins, *Works*, III, 608–9. In studies of European witchcraft and popular magic it is now respectable and even fashionable to consult anthropological studies of Africa: Alan Macfarlane, *Witchcraft in Tudor and Stuart England* (1970); Keith Thomas, *Religion and the Decline of Magic* (1971). Yet not so political ones; cp. Perkins's anthropology with that of Frantz Fanon in *The Wretched of the Earth* (New York, 1963).

12. Joseph Caryl, *The Oppressor Destroyed* (1662), 5–6, 7; Nicholas Lockyer, *England*, 409–11.

13. Charles Richardson, *A Sermon against Oppression* (1615), 10; Robert Harris, *David's Comfort at Ziklag* (1640), 37–9.

14. John Moore, *The Crying Sin of England* (1653), 21; Thomas Watson, *A Plea for Alms* (1658), 11–12; Thomas Jacomb, *God's Mercy for Man's Mercy* (1657), 40. Watson succinctly captured the difference between the medieval and Puritan attitudes toward poverty: 'Consider how sad a condition poverty is,' he remarked. 'Though Chrysostom calls poverty "the highway to heaven", yet he that keeps this road will go weeping thither.'

15. Jacomb, *God's Mercy*, 38–9; Richardson, *Sermon against Oppression*, 7; Perkins, *Works*, II, 99; III, 191, 360. The accuracy of Perkins's view has recently been challenged by Paul Slack, *Poverty and Policy in Tudor and Stuart England* (1988). However this well-known passage is worth quoting here only to demonstrate that it will bear a somewhat different interpretation from that usually assigned it. W. Crashaw in Perkins, *Works*, III, sig. Sss3r, 360. John Gore allowed of the 'common beggars' that 'there may be some that belong to the election of grace among them'. *The Poor Man's Hope* (1635), 21–2. Moore, *Crying Sin*, 7.

16. Watson, *Plea for Alms*, 65; William Whately, *The Poor Man's Advocate* (1637), 111; Richard Greenham, *Works* (1601), 643, 783–4; Jeremiah Burroughs, *A Sermon* (1646), 24; Samuel Rogers, *The Poor's Pension* (1644), 23–4.

17. Jacomb, *God's Mercy*, 18, 25–6; Moore, *Crying Sin*, 24; Richardson, *Sermon against Oppression*, 8; Lockyer, *England Faithfully Watched*, 413–14.

18. Edmund Calamy, *England's Looking Glass* (1641), sig. A2v, 24–5.

19. Stephen Marshall, *God's Masterpiece* (1645), 32; Thomas Case, *God's Rising* (1644), 29, 38; Carter, *Prayer's Prevalency*, 2–3; Edward Corbet, *God's Providence* (1642), 12–13.

20. Nathaniel Hardy, *The Arraignment of Licentious Liberty and Oppressing Tyranny* (1647), 24; Marshall, *Reformation and Desolation*, 29.

21. Jeremiah Whitaker, *Christ the Settlement of Unsettled Times* (1642), 1, 7–9, 15, 22–4, 32, 34; Samuel Rutherford, *A Sermon* (1645), 58. The simple notion that the preachers believed unequivocally that 'God had chosen England above all other nations for his special favor' is much too easy. William Haller, *Foxe's Book of Martyrs and the Elect Nation* (1963), 226 and ch. VII, *passim*. The only instance of Haller's term I have ever encountered is when the Scot Robert Baillie said that 'the sins of many persons remove not the favor of God from an elect nation', but even this was not in itself an endorsement of the assumption that England was one. *Errors and Induration* (1645), 4.

22. John Arrowsmith, *The Covenant-Avenging Sword Brandished* (1643), 4, 7, 10–11; Nicholas Proffet, *England's Impenitency* (1645), 35; William Carter, *Israel's Peace with God* (1642), 33. The Irish rebellion has received considerable attention recently; see Keith Lindley, 'The Impact of the 1641 Rebellion upon England and Wales, 1641–5', *Irish Historical Studies*, XVIII, 70 (1972). George Gillespie, *A Sermon* (1644), 19; Cornelius Burges, *Washing the Heart*, in *Two Sermons* (1645), 30; John Ley, *The Fury of War and the Folly of Sin* (1643), 9; Stephen Marshall, *A Sermon* (1647), 9, 11–13.

23. Nathaniel Holmes, *God's Gracious Thoughts* (1647), 2; Nathaniel Hardy, *Justice Triumphing* (1646), 11; Pestell, *Churl's Sickness*, 4–5; Baillie, *Errors and Induration*, 8–9, 10–11, 19; John Cardell, *God's Sovereign Power over Nations* (1648), 14–15; Peter Smith, *A Sermon* (1644), 38–9; John Owen, *Ebenezer* (1648), 25; Charles Herle, *Ahab's Falls by His Prophets' Flatteries* (1644), 7; Thomas Case, *A Sermon* (1645), 7; Hardy, *Arraignment*, 33–4; Edward Corbet, *God's Providence* (1642), 24.

24. Jeremiah Whitaker, *The Christian's Great Design* (1645), 25; Jeremiah Burroughs, *The Glorious Name of God* (1643), 102–3; Jeremiah Burroughs, *The Rare Jewel* (1651), 115; Sibbes, *Works*, I, 417; II, 395; Cornelius Burges, *Another Sermon* (1641), 55; Stephen Marshall, *A Divine Project* (1644), 2; Proffet, *England's Impenitency*, 11–12, 21; Henry Scudder, *God's Warning to England* (1644), 33; John Strickland, *God's Work of Mercy* (1644), 19; Thomas Mocket, *The Church's Troubles and Deliverance* (1642), 34–5; Thomas Valentine, *A Sermon* (1643), 7; Nicholas Estwick, *Christ's Submission to his Father's Will* (1644), 18. Marshall related this 'idolatry' to the more symbolic and controversial form: 'The not having learned this lesson is the cause of most of that sinfulness that is found in our ill-bearing of crosses.' *A Peace Offering to God* (1641), 11–13.

25. Anthony Burges, *Public Affections* (1646), 21; Scudder, *God's Warning*, 32; William Sedgwick, *Zion's Deliverance* (1642), 37; Obadiah Sedgwick, *Haman's Vanity* (1643), 31; John White, *The Troubles of Jerusalem's Restoration* (1645), 47; Thomas Manton, *Meat Out of the Eater* (1647), 40; Robert Harris, *A Sermon* (1642), 45. That all this was a preparation, rather than a substitute, for action can be contrasted with C.V. Wedgwood's precisely opposite assessment of religious symbolism in the royalist resistance of the 1650s. *A Coffin for King Charles* (New York, 1964), 200.

26. Sibbes, *Works*, I, 81; V, 403; Burroughs, *Rare Jewel*, 81, 157, 164; Corbet, *God's Providence*, 6; Burges, *Public Affections*, 21. Cp. Michael Walzer, *Exodus and Revolution* (1985).

27. Watson, *Plea for Alms*, 2; Edward Reynolds, *Israel's Petition* (1642), 34; Manton, *Meat*, 52; Scudder, *God's Warning*, 10; Samuel Torshel, *The Palace of Justice* (1646), 21; Carter, *Israel's Peace*, 13; Holmes, *God's Gracious Thoughts*, 2.

28. Sibbes, *Works*, I, 145; Thomas Case, *True Spiritual Thankfulness* (1646), 22; Thomas Case, *Jehoshaphat's Caveat* (1644), 8; Whitaker, *Great Design, passim*; Francis Cheynell, *The Man of Honor* (1645), 35; Thomas Hill, *The Good Old Way* (1644), 28; Obadiah Sedgwick, *England's Preservation* (1642), 11–13.

29. Sibbes, *Works*, I, 160; Burroughs, *Rare Jewel*, 91–2; John Maynard, *A Shadow of the Victory of Christ* (1646), 15; Samson Bond, *A Sermon* (1646), 47–8.

30. Stephen Marshall, *The Sin of Hardness of Heart* (1648), sig. A2v, 8, 12; John Owen, *The Advantage of the Kingdom of Christ* (1651), 21, 23; Sedgwick, *England's Preservation*, 22; Baillie, *Errors*, 29–30; Proffet, *England's Impenitency*, 22–3.

31. John Ward, *God's Judging among the Gods* (1645), 56; James Nalton, *Delay of Reformation* (1646), 6; Thomas Watson, *God's Anatomy* (1649), 4; Cornelius Burges, *A Heart Unwashed*, in *Two Sermons* (1645), 3; Matthew Newcomen, *A Sermon* (1644), 18; Matthew Newcomen, *The All-Seeing Unseen Eye of God* (1647), 29; Thomas Horton, *Sin's Discovery and Revenge* (1646), 21–2.

32. Richard Vines, *Caleb's Integrity* (1642), 34; T[homas] F[ord], *Reformation Sure and Steadfast* (1641), 13; Joseph Caryl, *Joy Out–Joyed* (1646), 15; Alexander Henderson, *A Sermon* (1644), 33; Sedgwick, *England's Preservation*, 31, 34, 36–8.

33. Carter, *Prayer's Prevalency*, 24; Calamy, *England's Looking Glass*, sig. A2v–3r, 29, 40; Edmund Calamy, *England's Antidote* (1645), 14; Burges, *Washing the Heart*, 37.

34. Sibbes, *Works*, VI, 188; Scudder, *God's Warning*, sig. A1v; Owen, *Ebenezer*, 7; Herbert Palmer, *The Glass of God's Providence* (1644), 31. Such statements were prompted by the threat from antinomianism.

35. Francis Roberts, *A Broken Spirit* (1647), 28; Sibbes, *Works*, I, 382; Horton, *Sin's Discovery*, 3; Caryl, *Works of Ephesus*, 39; Burges, *Washing the Heart*, 25–6; Alexander Henderson, *A Sermon* (1644), 11.

36. Bolton, *Two Sermons*, II, 96–7; Elidad Blackwell, *A Caveat for Magistrates* (1645), 37; Thomas Hill, *The Right Separation* (1645), 18; William Bridge, *Babylon's Downfall* (1641), 22. Note that Independents such as Bridge were just as concerned with sin as a 'national' problem as were Presbyterians; nor was the theme limited to parliamentary sermons, for it appears in many local ones as well. Thomas Case, *God's Waiting to be Gracious* (1642), 95; Burges, *Washing the Heart*, 38; Thomas Case, *Two Sermons* (1641), II, 23; Samuel Fairclough, *The Troublers Troubled* (1641), 21–2.

37. Christopher Love, *England's Distemper* (1646), 16; Blackwell, *Caveat*, 8; Anthony Tuckney, *The Balm of Gilead* (1643), 23–4; Calamy, *England's Antidote*, 27. For the emergence of a sense of political office as public service among local government officials at this time, see Fletcher, *Reform in the Provinces*, esp. 115.

38. Calamy, *England's Looking Glass*, 45; Burges, *Washing the Heart*, 19–20, 34, 37.

39. Herbert Palmer, *Utmost Venturing* (1643), 19; Burges, *Washing the Heart*, 35; Calamy, *England's Antidote*, 25; John Greene, *Nehemiah's Tears and Prayers* (1644), 13; Case, *Two Sermons*, I, 24. The ministers had some success in seeing legislation enacted to suppress these sins, though it was not always enforced; see Joan Kent, 'Attitudes of Members of the House of Commons to the Regulation of "Personal Conduct" in Late Elizabethan and Early Stuart England', *Bulletin of the Institute of Historical Research*, XLVI (1973). Similarly, for their impact on the personal conduct, or at least the consciences, of the members themselves, see J.T. Cliff, *The Puritan Gentry* (1984), chs. 1 (esp. 8–12) and 3. The point of course is that the members were receptive to the message and professed to honor it, not that they themselves necessarily always lived up to it.

40. Sibbes, *Works*, I, 149; Thomas Coleman, *Hopes Deferred and Dashed* (1645), 5; Francis Cheynell, *A Plot for the Good of Posterity* (1646), 15–17; Humphrey Chambers, *Peace and Love* (1648), 9. See Gordon J. Schochet, *Patriarchalism in Political Thought* (1975), esp. ch. 6.

41. Fairclough, *Troublers*, 20–1. The ethic of collective guilt was amply illustrated in the Old Testament, from which the preachers derived numerous examples; the story of Achan, used by Fairclough, was perhaps the favorite. See H. Wheeler Robinson, 'The Hebrew Conception of Corporate Personality', *Werden und Wesen des Alten Testaments; Beiheft zur Zeitschrift für die alttestamentliche Wissenschaft*, ed. J. Hempel (Berlin, 1936). Fairclough's celebrated sermon has been credited with directly influencing the Strafford trial; see H.R. Trevor-Roper, 'The Fast Sermons of the Long Parliament', in *The Crisis of the Seventeenth Century* (New York, 1968), 301–3, and John F. Wilson, *Pulpit in Parliament* (Princeton, 1969), 44–6. For legal principles involved in the trial that often paralleled Fairclough's theology, see Conrad Russell, 'The Theory of Treason in the Trial of Strafford', *English Historical Review*, LXXX (1965).

42. Fairclough, *Troublers*, 16; Palmer, *Utmost Venturing*, 16–17.

43. Henderson, *Sermon* (1644), 7; Palmer, *Utmost Venturing* 27–8; Calamy, *England's Antidote*, 27; Burges, *Washing the Heart*, 39–41. For the theme of blood feud in contemporary literature and politics, see H.A. Kelly, *Divine Providence in the England of Shakespeare's Histories* (1970). The reality was particularly acute in Scotland; see Jenny Wormald, 'Bloodfeud, Kindred, and Government in Early Modern Scotland', *Past and Present*, 87 (1980), esp. 93–5. Accusations of blood guilt were directed against royalists during the trials of the King's ministers, such as the Earl of Strafford and the Archbishop of Canterbury, and eventually against the King himself. See Patricia Crawford, 'Charles Stuart, That Man of Blood', *Journal of British Studies*, XVI (1977).

44. Burroughs, *Glorious Name*, 14; Oliver Bowles, *Zeal for God's House* (1643), 39; Palmer, *Utmost Venturing*, 39.

45. Palmer, *Glass*, 36; William Reyner, *Orders from the Lord of Hosts* (1646), 7–8, 9, 13; Thomas Case, *The Root of Apostasy* (1644), 9–10; Henry Hall, *Heaven Ravished* (1644), 29.

46. Marshall, *Divine Project*, 42; Anthony Burges, *Judgments Removed When Judgment is Executed* (1644), 3; Palmer, *Glass*, 50. The demand for justice even preceded that for religious reform, for reasons indicated by the sacrificial and sacramental tone of such injunctions. 'Your neglect of justice will provoke God to throw down all your religious services as dung in your faces,' Thomas Brooks warned. 'What is the reason? Your hands are full of blood.' *God's Delight in the Progress of the Upright* (1649), 16.

47. Case, *Jehoshaphat's Caveat*, 5, 13–15; Blackwell, *Caveat*, 21–2. For this theme, see Walzer, *Revolution*, ch. 7.

48. Case, *Jehoshaphat's Caveat*, 8–9, 11–12, 23–4; Blackwell, *Caveat*, 25. Joel Hurstfield, 'Political Corruption in Modern England', in *Freedom, Corruption, and Government in Early Modern England* (1973); Linda Levy Peck, 'Corruption at the Court of James I', in *After the Reformation*, ed. Barbara C. Malamant (Philadelphia, 1980). The preachers' exhortations clearly had an impact. Wilfred Prest dates the beginning of 'increasingly stringent ethical sensibilities' among common law judges from this time. 'Judicial Corruption in Early Modern England', *Past and Present*, 133 (1991).

49. Garey, *Breakfast for the Bench*, 41; Thomas Scot, *God and the King* (1631), 3; William Est, *The Judge's and Jury's Instruction* (1614), 11–12; William Pemberton, *The Charge of God and the King* (1619), 65, 66–7, 76–7; Ward, *Jethro's Justice*, 21, 24, 69; Richardson, *Sermon against Oppression*, 13.

50. Lazarus Seaman, *The Head of the Church* (1647), 14; Vavasor Powell, *Christ Exalted* (1651), 81–2; Jeremiah Burroughs, *Gospel Conversation* (1648), 319; Burroughs, *Sermon*, 29; Robert Harris, *A Sermon* (1642), 25–6; William Sclater, *A Sermon Preached at the . . . Assize . . . at Taunton* (1616), 12–13.

51. Thomas Scott, *Vox Dei*, (1623); Burges, *Judgments*, 9; Case, *Jehoshaphat's Caveat*, 13; Joseph Caryl, *David's Prayer for Solomon* (1643), 18; Brooks, *God's Delight*, 15; Ward, *Jethro's Justice*, 53–4.

52. Blackwell, *Caveat*, 34–7. The offenses Blackwell enumerates did become the focus of draconian (though seldom enforced) legislation by the Long Parliament. Keith Thomas, 'The Puritans and Adultery: The Act of 1650 Reconsidered', in *Puritans and Revolutionaries*, ed. D. Pennington and K. Thomas (Oxford, 1978). Puritan ministers and magistrates were also at the forefront of innovative schemes of social reform at the local level in the years leading up to the revolution, especially poor relief and problems associated with poverty. Margo Todd, *Christian Humanism and the Puritan Social Order* (1987), ch. 5, and Slack, *Poverty and Policy*, esp. 148–56.

53. Case, *Jehoshaphat's Caveat*, 9, 12–13; Richard Byfield, *Temple Defilers Defiled* (1645), 22.

54. Proffet, *England's Impenitency*, 45–6; Caryl, *Works of Ephesus*, 41, 43; Burges, *Judgments*, 5; William Strong, *The Trust and the Account of a Steward* (1647), 8.

55. Brooks, *God's Delight*, 19; Burges, *Judgments*, 4, 11; Case, *Jehoshaphat's Caveat*, 14–15.

56. William Greenhill, *The Axe at the Root* (1643), 33; Calamy, *England's Antidote*, 27; Case, *Jehoshaphat's Caveat*, 13; John Strickland, *Emmanuel* (1644), 32; Cornelius Burges, *Agreement with God* (1645), 39; Caryl, *Works of Ephesus*, 40.

57. Sibbes, *Works*, VI, 190; Ley, *Fury of War*, 13–14. Note the more aggressive use of this text in sermons than in resistance tracts, where it was merely something to be explained away. Sidrach Simpson, *Reformation's Preservation* (1643), sig. A3r–v; Caryl, *David's Prayer*, 27–9; John Lightfoot, *A Sermon* (1645), 28; Newcomen, *Sermon*, 24.

58. Palmer, *Glass*, 48; Case, *God's Waiting*, sig. A4r; John Cardell, *The Danger of Self-Seeking* (1649), sig. A2v; Robert Ram, *A Sermon* (1646), 3–4, 15; Case, *Jehoshaphat's Caveat*, 9–10.

3 COVENANT

1. Jeremiah Burroughs, *Gospel Worship* (1647), 195; William Bridge, *Works* (1645), I, 432–3. Cp. Blair Worden, 'Providence and Politics in Cromwellian England', *Past and Present*, 109 (1985).

2. Richard Sibbes, *Works* (Edinburgh, 1862–4; repr. 1978–82), I, 144; V, 306; VI, 215. The line between religion and law was not always clear during this period; for the Puritans it was almost nonexistent. Cynthia B. Herrup, *The Common Peace: Participation and the Criminal Law in Seventeenth-Century England* (Cambridge, 1987), and Wilfred R. Prest, *The Rise of the Barristers: A Social History of the English Bar, 1590–1640* (Oxford, 1986).

3. Thomas Hill, *The Good Old Way God's Way* (1644), 14, 18–19, 28; Samuel Rutherford, *A Sermon* (1644), 12; Thomas Watson, *God's Anatomy* (1649), 17. Since the persistent notion that Protestantism set the 'private conscience' against the authority of the church is still one of the principal supports for the conventional wisdom about Puritan 'individualism', perhaps one more passage is worth quoting to make clear their precise position on this:

> To make conscience the final judge of actions is to wipe out the handwriting of the word of God, which doth condemn many times those things which conscience justifies . . . . If conscience be warrant enough for practices and opinions, and liberty of conscience be a sufficient license to vent or act them, I cannot see but the judicatories either of church or state may shut up their shop and be resolved into the judicatory of every man's private conscience.

   And just to drive home where a creed of 'liberty of conscience' alone could lead: 'And put the case that the magistrate should conceive himself bound in conscience to draw forth his authority against false teachers or their damnable heresies.' Richard Vines, *The Authors, Nature, and Danger of Heresy* (1647), 60.

4. Anthony Burges, *A Reformation* (1643), 4–5; Alexander Henderson, *A Sermon* (1645), 12; Joseph Caryl, *The Works of Ephesus* (1642), 56–7.

5. Henry Archer, *The Personal Reign of Christ upon Earth* (1642), 30; Sibbes, *Works*, VII, 197; Nathaniel Hardy, *Justice Triumphing* (1646), 6, 8; Thomas Case, *Spiritual Whoredom* (1647), 18; Nicholas Estwick, *Christ's Submission to his Father's Will* (1644), 6–7.

6. Bridge, *Works*, III, 43; Samuel Bolton, *The True Bounds of Christian Freedom* (1645), 69, 76–7, 98–9, 400; John Owen, *A Sermon* (1652), 33 (quoting I John 3:4); Joseph Caryl, *David's Prayer for Solomon* (1643), 11; Peter Sterry, *The Comings Forth*

of Christ (1659), sig. aa3r. This chapter will address the popular and political understanding of covenant. It is not intended as an exhaustive technical treatment of what has come to be known as 'the covenant theology'. Nor will it be concerned with the oaths or 'covenants' required of partisans of the parliamentary cause; though an important extension of the covenant idea into secular politics, these were quasi-sacramental exercises and will be more appropriately discussed elsewhere. The standard works on covenant theology are by Perry Miller, 'The Marrow of Puritan Divinity', in *Errand into the Wilderness* (Boston, 1956), and *The New England Mind: The Seventeenth Century* (Boston, 1939). They have received considerable criticism however, the most important of which is John S. Coolidge, *The Pauline Renaissance in England* (Oxford, 1970), esp. 12–13. For citations of other recent literature, see Michael McGiffert, 'From Moses to Adam: The Making of the Covenant of Works', *The Sixteenth Century Journal*, XIX, 2 (1988).

7. Sibbes, *Works*, VII, 131; Bolton, *True Bounds*, 108–9 (quoting I Tim. 1:9), 111–12; Herbert Palmer, *Utmost Venturing* (1643), 14. For the enactment of the Mosaic law, see P.D.L. Avis, 'Moses and the Magistrate: A Study in the Rise of Protestant Legalism', *Journal of Ecclesiastical History*, XXVI, 2 (1975).

8. Bolton, *True Bounds*, 105–6, 109–18, 119–20 (quoting Rom. 4:15); Sibbes, *Works*, IV, 340.

9. Sibbes, *Works*, I, 171, 173–4; VII, 400, 409. It has been suggested that the Puritans 'were among the first to face the problems of developmental psychology'. C. John Sommerville, 'English Puritans and Children: A Social-Cultural Explanation', *Journal of Psychohistory*, VI, 1 (1978). Nicholas Lockyer, *England Faithfully Watched* (1645), 2; Anthony Tuckney, *The Balm of Gilead* (1643), 36–7; Jeremiah Burroughs, *A Sermon* (1646), 11; Francis Cheynell, *The Man of Honor* (1645), 30–1.

10. Sibbes, *Works*, I, 132; William Strong, *The Right Way to the Highest Honor* (1647), 1; William Perkins, *Works* (Cambridge, 1626–31), I, 134.

11. Samuel Fairclough, *The Troublers Troubled* (1641), 20; Perkins, *Works*, I, 160; George Cokayn, *Flesh Expiring* (1648), 23. Cokayn was preaching just before the regicide.

12. Richard Heyricke, *Queen Esther's Resolves* (1646), 22–3; Obadiah Sedgwick, *Haman's Vanity* (1643), 2; Thomas Case, *God's Rising* (1644), 33.

13. Thomas Valentine, *A Charge against the Jews* (1647), 26; John Cardell, *God's Sovereign Power over Nations* (1648), 16.

14. Jeremiah Burroughs, *The Rare Jewel* (1648), 35, 100; Sibbes, *Works*, III, 47–8; V, 262.

15. Thomas Goodwin, *The World to Come* (1655), 42–3; Edmund Calamy, *God's Free Mercy to England* (1642), 2, 29, 36, 42; William Greenhill, *The Axe at the Root* (1643), 12; Edmund Calamy, *England's Antidote* (1645), 17; Burroughs, *Gospel Worship*, 117; Richard Byfield, *Temple-Defilers Defiled* (1645), 1–2.

16. Obadiah Sedgwick, *England's Preservation* (1642), 7–9; Ralph Cudworth, *A Sermon* (1647), 73–4, 76–7.

17. Thomas Case, *Spiritual Whoredom* (1647), 23; Peter Sterry, *The Teachings of Christ* (1648), 30–1; Robert Baillie, *Errors and Induration* (1645), 33.

18. Sibbes, *Works*, VI, 3; Bolton, *True Bounds*, 26–8 (quoting Gal. 2:19); William Sclater, *Civil Magistracy by Divine Authority* (1652), 44; Robert Gell, *Noah's Flood* (1655), 19.

19. Sibbes, *Works*, II, 467; Francis Roberts, *A Broken Spirit* (1647), 11, 14, 16–17, 26–9.

20. Roberts, *Broken Spirit*, 18; Sibbes, *Works*, I, 166, 249; II, 467, 484; VII, 342.

21. Lockyer, *England Faithfully Watched*, 164; Sibbes, *Works*, I, 249; II, 475; V, 296, 310, 360–1; VII, 404, 406–7.

22. Humphrey Chambers, *Paul's Sad Farewell* (1654), 110; Sibbes *Works*, IV, 256; VII, 192; Robert Harris, *A Sermon* (1642), 17; Edmund Calamy, *The Great Danger of*

Covenant-Refusing and Covenant-Breaking (1645), 22; Burroughs, *Gospel Worship*, 267–8. The distinction between 'intercessor' and 'example' has been used to describe the roles of Imam Hussein in radical Shiism. Mary Hegland, 'Ritual and Revolution in Iran', in *Culture and Political Change*, ed. Myron J. Aronoff (1983).

23. Burroughs, *Gospel Worship*, 267–8; Sibbes, *Works*, I, 73; IV; 503; VII, 100, 361; Peter Sterry, *The Clouds in which Christ Comes* (1648), 10; Vavasor Powell, *Christ Exalted* (1651), 14; Fulk Bellers, *Jesus Christ the Mystical or Gospel Sun* (1652), 21; Estwick, *Christ's Submission*, 23; Burroughs, *Rare Jewel*, 45–6; Thomas Brooks, *Precious Remedies* (1652; repr. 1984), 222–4.

24. Sibbes *Works*, IV, 503, 506; V, 262 (paraphrasing II Cor. 12:10).

25. *Ibid.*, IV, 240; VII, 498, 499, 503–4.

26. *Ibid.*,I, 384; II, 231, 318; V, 85; VI, 48; John Preston, *The Breastplate of Faith and Love* (1634), I, 66.

27. Sibbes, *Works*, II, 318; Brooks, *Precious Remedies*, 223–4.

28. Preston, *Breastplate*, I, 59–60; Sibbes, *Works*, II, 181; VII, 411, 537; Lockyer, *England Faithfully Watched*, 428–9; Cheynell, *Man of Honor*, 56.

29. Cheynell, *Man of Honor*, 11–12, 39–40.

30. Sibbes, *Works*, VII, 121–2, 191, 286, 356.

31. Perkins, *Works*, III, 4–6, 360–1. For a very different view, see Christopher Hill, 'Puritans and the Poor', *Past and Present*, 2 (1952); cp. V. Kiernan, 'Puritanism and the Poor', *ibid.*, 3 (1953). Some of the physical deprivations of poverty could also have 'spiritual' significance. 'To be poor in spirit . . . is to see . . . that we are beggars and bankrupts and have no means to pay or satisfy,' said Sibbes, 'and this stirs up . . . "hungering and thirsting after righteousness".' *Works*, VI, 243.

32. Perkins, *Works*, III, 192, 284; Samuel Rogers, *The Poor's Pension* (1644), 5; John Cardell, *The Danger of Self-Seeking* (1649), 36–7.

33. Cardell, *Danger*, 35; Obadiah Sedgwick, *The Best and the Worst Magistrate* (1648), 22, 28. Preaching at an election (an increasingly popular occasion for sermons), Sedgwick went on to insist that similar responsibilities were incumbent on those who chose officials: 'You who are (this day) to choose a magistrate . . . be very serious,' he urged. 'I think it is (almost) an equal weight of difficulty to choose a good magistrate as to be a good magistrate . . . God looks upon every one of you in this work and considers what you intend or act.' *Ibid.*, 17–18. It has been argued that the civil war and interregnum marked a turning point in the process of choosing public office-holders from one of 'selection', based on personal status and loyalty, to 'election' on the basis of issues and appealing to an informed and conscientious electorate. Whether or not the issues were necessarily religious, it is reasonable to suggest that religion had something to do with this change. Mark Kishlansky, *Parliamentary Selection: Social and Political Choice in Early Modern England* (New York, 1986).

34. William Spurstowe, *The Magistrate's Dignity and Duty* (1654), 12; Cokayn, *Flesh Expiring*, 5; William Carter, *Israel's Peace with God* (1642), 15.

35. John Ellis, *A Sound Peace* (1643), 59; Perkins, *Works*, II, 214–15; Sibbes, *Works*, III, 417–18.

36. Bridge, *Works*, II, 133, 152. Cp. C. Hill, 'Covenant Theology and the Concept of "A Public Person",' *Collected Essays*, III (Amherst, 1986).

37. William Ames, *Saints' Security* (1651), 15; Burroughs, *Rare Jewel*, 124; John Brinsley, *The Saints' Solemn Covenant* (1644), 7; Sibbes, *Works*, I, 9, 22; VI, 342; VII, 295 (Michael Walzer, *The Revolution of the Saints*, Cambridge, Mass., 1965, has stated the point about choosing this way); Thomas Goodwin, *Works* (Edinburgh, 1861–6), I, 70. In the twentieth century, as in the seventeenth, these matters have aroused venomous academic disputes; recent work, much of which is highly arcane, is cited in McGiffert, 'From Moses to Adam'. A more technical study seems to reach

a similar conclusion to that offered here: John von Rohr, *The Covenant of Grace in Puritan Thought* (Atlanta, 1987).

38. Sibbes, *Works*, V, 394; VII, 483; Brinsley, *Saints' Solemn Covenant*, 28–9.

39. Preston, *Breastplate*, II, 144; Sibbes, *Works*, I, 59; V, 394. The emphasis on 'sincerity' may have been in contrast to the perceived ideals of court, where dissembling and deceit were seen as the advantageous traits. It was certainly in opposition to 'hypocrisy', a major concern of Puritan theology; see Chapter 4. Brinsley, *Saints' Solemn Covenant*, 30; Calamy, *Great Danger*, sig. A4v.

40. Nathaniel Holmes, *God's Gracious Thoughts* (1647), 13–14; Thomas Mocket, *The National Covenant* (1642), 26; Thomas Case, *The Quarrel of the Covenant* (1643), 97; Burroughs, *Rare Jewel*, 62–3; Sibbes, *Works*, IV, 260. I would hope this would help demonstrate why doctrinal disputes were so emotive; see Nicholas Tyacke, *Anti-Calvinists* (Oxford, 1987).

41. Goodwin, *World to Come*, 16, 25–6; John Lightfoot, *A Sermon* (1645), 18; William Gouge, *The Progress of Divine Providence* (1645), 9.

42. Sibbes, *Works*, IV, 213, 257, 259; Cheynell, *Man of Honor*, 13.

43. Cheynell, *Man of Honor*; Stephen Marshall, *A Sacred Panegyric* (1644), 13–14; Owen, *Sermon*, 9; Burroughs, *Rare Jewel*, 58, 124; Samuel Rutherford, *A Sermon* (1644), 59; Stephen Marshall, *A Sermon* (1652), 19.

44. Sedgwick, *Best and Worst Magistrate*, 4, 10; Sibbes, *Works*, IV, 521; Spurstowe, *Magistrate's Dignity*, 44–5.

45. Sibbes, *Works*, VI, 190, 301; Samuel Bolton, *The Sinfulness of Sin* (1646), 33 (Heb. 9:22); Cornelius Burges, *Washing the Heart*, in *Two Sermons* (1645), 39; William Price, *Man's Delinquency* (1646), 19; Carter, *Israel's Peace*, 33. This point is suggested in Rene Girard, *Violence and the Sacred* (Baltimore, 1972). Lockyer, *England Faithfully Watched*, 47–8, 54.

46. Carter, *Israel's Peace*, 33–4. The ministers showed little interest in the historical Jesus as depicted in the gospels; see Boyd Berry, *Process of Speech: Puritan Religious Writing and Paradise Lost* (Baltimore and London, 1976). James Nalton, *Delay of Reformation* (1646), 22; Bolton, *Sinfulness*, 33; Lazarus Seaman, *The Head of the Church* (1647), 1–2. 'Religion is nothing other than [an] immense effort to keep the peace . . . . If religious man worships violence it is only insofar as the worship of violence is supposed to bring peace; religion is entirely concerned with peace, but the means it has of bringing it about are never free of sacrificial violence.' Rene Girard, *Things Hidden since the Foundation of the World* (Stanford, 1987), 32.

47. Edmund Calamy, *England's Looking Glass* (1641), 7–8, 28; Francis Cheynell, *Zion's Memento* (1643), 39; Thomas Hill, *The Militant Church* (1643), 13–14; Thomas Case, *God's Waiting* (1642), 159; Cheynell, *Man of Honor*, 13, 61.

48. Tuckney, *Balm*, 11; Jeremiah Whitaker, *Christ the Settlement of Unsettled Times* (1642), sig. A4v; Case, *God's Waiting*, 81–2; Nicholas Lockyer, *A Sermon* (1646), 22; Bolton, *True Bounds*, 341–2.

49. Hill, *Militant Church*, 16; Jeremiah Burroughs, *Zion's Joy* (1641), 42; S. Bolton, *Sinfulness*, 36; William Cooper, *Jerusalem Fatal to her Assailants* (1649), 28–9; Edmund Staunton, *Phinehas's Zeal* (1645), 24; Stephen Marshall, *A Sacred Panegyric* (1644), 21–2; Lockyer, *England Faithfully Watched*, 196.

4 FAITH

1. Richard Sibbes, *Works* (Edinburgh, 1862–4; repr. 1978–82), V, 209, 365; Jeremiah Whitaker, *Christ the Settlement of Unsettled Times* (1642), 31; Thomas Case, *A Sermon* (1645), 14.

2. Samuel Bolton, *The Sinfulness of Sin* (1646), 32; Richard Vines, *Caleb's Integrity* (1642), 16; Thomas Valentine, *Christ's Counsel* (1647), 7–8; John Owen, *The Branch*

of the Lord (1650), *Works* (Edinburgh, 1862), VIII, 301; Ralph Cudworth, *A Sermon* (1647), 19, 21.

3. Sibbes, *Works*, IV, 224–7.

4. Henry Hall, *Heaven Ravished* (1644), 39, 53; Joseph Caryl, *Heaven and Earth Embracing* (1646), 4–7; Edward Reynolds, *Israel's Petition* (1642), 3–4.

5. John Whincop, *God's Call* (1645), 3; Thomas Hill, *The Good Old Way* (1644), 3, 7, 25–6, 27; Thomas Brooks, *God's Delight in the Progress of the Upright* (1649), 2.

6. Matthew Barker, *A Christian Standing* (1648), 31; Obadiah Sedgwick, *Military Discipline* (1639), sig. A3r–v, 1–3. For 'wayfaring and warfaring' and 'the eternal images of the pilgrim and the warrior', see William Haller, *The Rise of Puritanism* (New York, 1938).

7. John Marston, *A Sermon* (1642), 27; Thomas Brooks, *Precious Remedies against Satan's Devices* (1652; repr. 1984), 56–9; John Ellis, *A Sound Peace* (1643), 14; Cornelius Burges, *Washing the Heart*, in *Two Sermons* (1645), 27; Edmund Calamy, *England's Looking Glass* (1641), 2–3.

8. Francis Roberts, *A Broken Spirit* (1647), 16; Edmund Calamy, *Two Solemn Covenants* (1647), 5; Joseph Caryl, *A Sacred Covenant* (1643), 36. Despite being the central tenet of Protestant religion and the most extensive theme in Puritan preaching, including the sermons of the 1640s, the doctrine of faith has received little attention from historians of Puritanism. A thorough history of reformed doctrine is contained in Dewey Wallace, *Puritans and Predestination* (Chapel Hill, 1982).

9. Ellis, *Sound Peace*, 17; Sibbes, *Works*, V, 391, 404, 460.

10. Cudworth, *Sermon*, 43; John Preston, *The Breastplate of Faith and Love* (1634), I, 9; Sibbes, *Works*, I, 100; Christopher Love, *England's Distemper* (1646), 34; Edmund Calamy, *The Nobleman's Pattern* (1643), 26; Sedgwick, *Military Discipline*, 68; William Price, *A Sermon* (1642), 19–20. Peter Lake has noted the process by which 'the truths of right doctrine were fully internalized by the individual believer'. *Moderate Puritans and the Elizabethan Church* (Cambridge, 1982), chs. 6–7.

11. Thomas Watson, *God's Anatomy* (1649), 2; George Walker, *A Sermon* (1645), 36; Hill, *Good Old Way*, 16. Paradoxically perhaps, Hill was preaching against heresy. 'As in philosophy, so in divinity,' he said, 'credulity hath bred many heretics.' Simeon Ash, *Religious Covenanting* (1646), 7; Samuel Rutherford, *A Sermon* (1645), 25; Thomas Manton, *Meat Out of the Eater* (1647), 38; Preston, *Breastplate*, I, 47–8. Note the word 'consent', which was being increasingly employed in a different (though related) sense in political tracts. John Maynard, *A Sermon* (1645), 15.

12. Sibbes, *Works*, III, 397; V, 306, 312; VII, 415, 438.

13. Barker, *Christian Standing*, 30; William Bridge, *Works* (1845), II, 253; John Lightfoot, *Elias Redivivus* (1643), 44; Joseph Caryl, *The Arraignment of Unbelief* (1645), 15, 17, 24; Bridge, *Works*, II, 82–3, 128.

14. Francis Cheynell, *A Plot for the Good of Posterity* (1646), 23; Sibbes, *Works*, I, 23; V, 12–13; VI, 342; Obadiah Sedgwick, *An Ark against a Deluge* (1644), 7, 11, 14–15, 17; William Jenkyn, *The Policy of Princes* (1656), 44; Samuel Bolton, *The True Bounds of Christian Freedom* (1645), 119–20; Caryl, *Arraignment of Unbelief*, 28; John Bond, *Grapes among Thorns* (1648), 12.

15. Thomas Carter, *Prayer's Prevalency* (1643), 4; John White, *Jerusalem's Restoration* (1645), 20 (quoting Heb. 11:1 and II Cor. 4:18); Bridge, *Works*, II, 266; Stephen Marshall, *A Two-Edged Sword* (1646), 11.

16. William Jenkyn, *Reformation's Remora* (1646), 20–1.

17. Walter Cradock, *The Saints' Fullness of Joy* (1646), 9; Jeremiah Whitaker, *The Christian's Hope* (1645), 51; William Reyner, *Babylon's Ruining Earthquake* (1644), 59; Bridge, *Works*, II, 261–2; Cheynell, *Plot*, 22.

18. Sibbes, *Works*, I, 203; III, 383; Preston, *Breastplate*, I, 229; Thomas Brooks, *Heaven on Earth* (1654; repr. 1982), 281–2.

19. Thomas Valentine, *A Sermon* (1643), 40; William Perkins, *Works* (Cambridge, 1626–31), I, 378, 463; Nicholas Lockyer, *England Faithfully Watched* (1645), 278; Richard Greenham, *Works* (1601), 9.

20. Bridge, *Works*, II, 161; Sibbes, *Works*, I, 48, 157–8, 217; Perkins, *Works*, I, 365, 705; V, 374; VI, 164, 256.

21. Sibbes, *Works*, I, 65; V, 273.

22. Rutherford, *Sermon*, 37, 54; Preston, *Breastplate*, I, 56–8; Jeremiah Burroughs, *The Rare Jewel* (1648), 47–8; Francis Cheynell, *The Man of Honor* (1645), 12.

23. Sibbes, *Works*, I, 157; II, 183; V, 405; VII, 458; Joseph Caryl, *The Saints' Faithful Acclamation* (1644), 16; Preston, *Breastplate*, I, 231, 234.

24. Cheynell, *Man of Honor*, 5–6; White, *Jerusalem's Restoration*, 23–4; Anthony Burges, *A Reformation* (1643), 6, 14; Cheynell, *Plot*, 22–3; Caryl, *Arraignment of Unbelief*, 42.

25. Caryl, *Arraignment of Unbelief*, 33; Sibbes, *Works*, I, 212; White, *Jerusalem's Restoration*, 8; John Owen, *Ebenezer* (1648), 42; Thomas Palmer, *The Saints' Support* (1644), 8.

26. John Cardell, *The Danger of Self-Seeking* (1650), 21; Charles Richardson, *A Sermon against Oppression* (1615), 16; Sibbes, *Works*, I, 412; III, 410; V, 412.

27. Jeremiah Burroughs, *Gospel Worship* (1647), 102; Sibbes, *Works*, I, 411–13, 415; III, 410–12, 419–20.

28. Sibbes, *Works*, III, 388; Caryl, *Arraignment of Unbelief*, 42–3.

29. Ellis, *Sole Path*, 15–16; John Strickland, *A Discovery of Peace* (1644), 12.

30. Bridge, *Works*, II, 135, 266; William Sedgwick, *Scripture a Perfect Rule* ([1643]), 33, 37; John Owen, *The Steadfastness of Promises* (1650), 28–9; Owen, *Ebenezer*, 28–9.

31. Owen, *Steadfastness*, 28–9; Caryl, *Arraignment of Unbelief*, 13, 18–19, 21; Thomas Case, *God's Waiting* (1642), 125–6.

32. Owen, *Steadfastness*, 10, 12–13, 23, 48; Owen, *Branch*, *Works*, VIII, 307–8.

33. Burroughs, *Rare Jewel*, 64; Sibbes, *Works*, III, 391; Owen, *Steadfastness*, 51; Simeon Ash, *Religious Covenanting* (1646), 11 (quoting Deut. 7:9); [Jeremiah Burroughs,] *A Glimpse of Zion's Glory* (1641), 23.

34. Thomas Mocket, *The National Covenant* (1642), 6–7, 36; Case, *Two Sermons*, II, 55; Sibbes, *Works*, II, 183; VII, 483.

35. Sibbes, *Works*, V, 18; VI, 4 (quoting Heb. 9:22); Burroughs, *Gospel Worship*, 270.

36. Owen, *Steadfastness*, 22; Owen, *Works*, X, 358; Thomas Goodwin, *Works* (Edinburgh, 1861–6), IV, 27; Thomas Case, *The Quarrel of the Covenant* (1643), 97–9.

37. Owen, *Steadfastness*, 23–4, 25, 52; Bridge, *Works*, II, 65, 183, 187; Strickland, *Discovery*, 14; Thomas Brooks, *The Glorious Day of the Saints' Appearance* (1648), *Works* (Edinburgh, 1866), VI, 329.

38. Henry Scudder, *God's Warning to England* (1644), 15; Caryl, *Arraignment of Unbelief*, 33; Robert Harris, *True Religion* (1645), 13.

39. Strickland, *Discovery*, 24; Stephen Marshall, *A Peace Offering to God* (1641), 18; Thomas Brooks, *The Hypocrite* (1650), 12; Reynolds, *Israel's Petition*, 5; Owen, *Ebenezer*, 4–5.

40. Owen, *Ebenezer*, 8 (quoting Is. 28:21); Reynolds, *Israel's Petition*, 38; Nathaniel Holmes, *God's Gracious Thoughts* (1647), 12; Burroughs, *Rare Jewel*, 92.

41. Burroughs, *Rare Jewel*, 101f., 103–4 (irregular pagination); Reynolds, *Israel's Petition*, 4; Robert Baillie, *Errors and Induration* (1645), 38; William Spurstowe, *England's Eminent Judgments* (1644), 15.

42. Spurstowe, *England's Eminent Judgments*, 10, 16; Jenkyn, *Reformation's Remora*, 14; Owen, *Ebenezer*, 26, 49; Brooks, *Hypocrite*, 13; Matthew Newcomen, *The Craft*

and Cruelty of the Church's Adversaries (1643), 52; Strickland, *Discovery*, 31; Caryl, *Arraignment of Unbelief*, 34.

43. Baillie, *Errors*, 37; William Gouge, *Mercy's Memorial* (1644), 18; Palmer, *Saints' Support*, 26–8.

44. Edmund Calamy, *God's Free Mercy to England* (1642), 17–20. See James C. Spalding, 'Sermons before the Parliament (1640–1649) as a Public Puritan Diary', *Church History*, XXXVI (1967).

45. Owen, *Ebenezer*, sig. A4r, 13, 32, 44f.

46. *Ibid.*, 51, 54, 56; John Bond, *Salvation in a Mystery* (1644), 30; Ash, *Religious Covenanting*, 5; Joseph Caryl, *The Oppressor Destroyed* (1662), 10–11.

47. Sibbes, *Works*, I, 259; John Bond, *A Dawning in the West* (1645), 13–14; Greenham, *Works*, 251.

48. Calamy, *God's Free Mercy*, 17–20. Francis Cheynell, *Zion's Memento* (1643), sig. A3v; Case, *God's Waiting*, 127–8. For the controversial literature, see Nicholas Tyacke, *Anti-Calvinists* (Oxford, 1987).

49. Peter Sterry, *England's Deliverance* (1652), 20; Stephen Marshall, *The Right Understanding of the Times* (1647), 40–1; William Strong, *The Commemoration and Exaltation of Mercy* (1646), 14; Joseph Caryl, *England's Plus-Ultra* (1646), 7, 17; Thomas Coleman, *The Christian's Course* (1643), 8, 26, 27; John Strickland, *Mercy Rejoicing* (1645), 27–8.

50. Caryl, *Arraignment of Unbelief*, 22; Case, *God's Waiting*, 81; Holmes, *God's Gracious Thoughts*, 12; Sidrach Simpson, *A Sermon* (1643), 31.

51. Obadiah Sedgwick, *A Thanksgiving Sermon* (1644), 7; T. Carter, *Prayer's Prevalency*, 22; Stephen Marshall, *A Divine Project* (1644), 22; Caryl, *Heaven and Earth*, 14.

52. Spurstowe, *England's Eminent Judgments*, 7; Samuel Bolton, *Deliverance in the Birth* (1647), 16; Bridge, *Works*, II, 51, 115–16; Caryl, *Heaven and Earth*, 16. Cp. Keith Thomas, *Religion and the Decline of Magic* (New York, 1971), ch. 5.

53. Caryl, *Arraignment of Unbelief*, 43; Jeremiah Burroughs, *Gospel Worship* (1647), 277; Jeremiah Whitaker, *The Danger of Greatness* (1646), 32; Stephen Marshall, *The Strong Helper* (1645), 46–7; Henry Wilkinson, *A Sermon against Lukewarmness* (1640), 15; Peter Smith, *A Sermon* (1644), 22; Stephen Marshall, *Meroz Cursed* (1642), 54–5.

54. Carter, *Prayer's Prevalency*, 21, 23, 30–2.

55. Jeremiah Burroughs, *The Glorious Name of God* (1643), 86–7, 89; Rutherford, *Sermon*, 38; Simeon Ash, *The Best Refuge* (1642), sig. A3r; Thomas Case, *A Sermon* (1645), 11.

56. Christopher Tesdale, *Jerusalem* (1644), 24, 42; Lazarus Seaman, *The Head of the Church* (1647), 17; William Gouge, *The Saint's Support* (1642), 19, 28–9; Sibbes, *Works*, VII, 476; Caryl, *England's Plus-Ultra*, 40; Hall, *Heaven Ravished*, 30–1.

57. William Sedgwick, *Zion's Deliverance* (1642), 30, 33; Thomas Hill, *The Militant Church* (1643), 12.

58. George Gillespie, *A Sermon* (1644), 39; Sibbes, *Works*, V, 6, 261; VII, 204; Burroughs, *Gospel Worship*, 109. Though Sibbes could speak of Christianity as a 'trade', I prefer to follow Michael Walzer, *The Revolution of the Saints*, Cambridge, Mass., 1965, chs. 6–7, in emphasizing the political rather than the economic nature of the work ethic, though the latter continues to dominate modern literature. Cp. Christopher Hill, *Society and Puritanism in Pre-Revolutionary England* (1964).

59. Sibbes, *Works*, IV, 250; Preston, *Breastplate*, I, 69, 172–3; Thomas Watson, *A Plea for Alms* (1658), 23, 25.

60. Thomas Mocket, *The Church's Troubles and Deliverance* (1642), 10; Preston, *Breastplate*, I, 157; II, 76, 229, 234. For suffering persecution as the means by which Protestants had previously testified their faith to the world, see Maria Dowling and Peter Lake (eds.), *Protestantism and the National Church in Sixteenth Century*

England (1987), especially the essays by Catharine Davies, Joy Shakespeare, and Jane Facey.

61. Preston, *Breastplate*, II, 18; Joseph Symonds, *A Sermon* (1641), sig. B4r–v, C1r; John Whincop, *God's Call* (1645), 46. Puritan 'hypocrisy' is a favorite cheap shot of historians; one recent book contains seven index references to 'the hypocritical godly'. Christopher Hill, *A Tinker and a Poor Man: John Bunyan and his Church, 1628–1688* (New York, 1989), s.v., 'hypocrisy'. That the Puritans themselves not only recognized the inevitability of hypocrisy but made it a central theological issue, often directing the accusation against themselves, is typically passed over in silence; see *The Westminster Confession of Faith* (1646; repr. Glasgow, 1983), 75–6, 198–204.

62. Joseph Caryl, *The Works of Ephesus* (1642), 19–20; Owen, *Steadfastness*, 42; Stephen Marshall, *A Sermon* (1640), 12; Sedgwick, *Zion's Deliverance*, 46–7.

63. Edward Corbet, *God's Providence* (1642), 28; Caryl, *Works of Ephesus*, 20, 21–2; Sibbes, *Works*, I, 139; Bridge, *Works*, II, 209; Thomas Watson, *The One Thing Necessary* (1656), 42; Barker, *Christian Standing*, 51; William Strong, *The Right Way to the Highest Honor* (1647), 17.

64. Perkins, *Works*, II, 750–9; reprinted in *Puritan Political Ideas, 1558-1794*, ed. Edmund Morgan (Indianapolis and New York, 1965), ch. 3. Unless otherwise indicated, quotations from Perkins in the next four paragraphs are from this passage.

65. Obadiah Sedgwick, *The Best and the Worst Magistrate* (1648), 18. The two most eminent callings interacted in society much as the two types of callings did in the individual. See Patrick Collinson, 'Magistracy and Ministry: A Suffolk Miniature', in *Reformation Conformity and Dissent*, ed. R. Buick Knox (1977). This symbiosis culminated in the fast sermon program itself. Bridge, *Works*, V, 74–5f; Perkins, *Works*, III, 512.

66. Sibbes, *Works*, V, 293; Thomas Jacomb, *God's Mercy for Man's Mercy* (1657), 38–9. Some of these statements were evidently missed in Christopher Hill's attack on the Puritan 'lenience towards usury' in 'Puritans and the Poor', *Past and Present*, 2 (1952). Sibbes, *Works*, V, 293; VI, 521; VII, 457, 497.

67. Perkins, *Works*, II, 750–9.

68. Burroughs, *Rare Jewel*, 176–7. Cp. C.H. and K. George, *The Protestant Mind of the English Reformation, 1570–1640* (1961), 169–73.

69. Barker, *Christian Standing*, 51; Watson, *Plea for Alms*, 21–2; Watson, *One Thing Necessary*, 43, 70; Roberts, *Broken Spirit*, 16–17; Jacomb, *God's Mercy*, 13; Sibbes, *Works*, III, 191; V, 16; Preston, *Breastplate*, I, 27. This was, perhaps, the main social as well as theological objection to the old religion, that it provided justification for the pride of the powerful and successful of the earth. 'Popery is compounded of spiritual pride: merit . . . desert . . . free will, and the like, to puff up nature,' Sibbes argued. 'Is not nature proud enough?' *Works*, II, 272.

70. Preston, *Breastplate*, I, 71, 266; Sibbes, *Works*, V, 601; Burroughs, *Rare Jewel* (1651 edn), 121; White, *Jerusalem's Restoration*, 19; Cheynell, *Zion's Memento*, dedicatory epistle.

71. Calamy, *Nobleman's Pattern*, 35; Bridge, *Works*, II, 121–2; John Owen, *The Laboring Saint's Dismission to Rest* (1651), in *Works*, VIII, 358; Lazarus Seaman, *Solomon's Choice* (1644), 18–19; Barker, *Christian Standing*, 51.

72. Thomas Valentine, *Caleb's Integrity* (1642), 41–2; Preston, *Breastplate*, II, 19, 29, 93–4, 201, 212, 216; Calamy, *God's Free Mercy*, 21; Calamy, *Nobleman's Pattern*, 36. In the omitted phrases Preston emphasized that the whole point of love was to distinguish the soul's relationship with God from precisely the kind of commercial bargain some modern scholars have tried to detect: Love, he said, 'doth not play the huckster with the Lord (as we say); it doth not bring things to an exact account, but when a man loveth . . . he doth not stand to look for an exact recompense (for that is

to make a bargain with God). . . . You will not stand half penny-worthing.' The use
of such analogies to bring theology down to the level of everyday experience may
indeed have reflected the response of Puritan religion to an increasingly commercial
society, but it can hardly be described as a sympathetic one.

73. Daniel Evance, *The Noble Order* (1646), 16; William Carter, *Israel's Peace* (1642), 6,
7, 19; Henry Wilkinson, *The Gainful Cost* (1644), 15.
74. Evance, *Noble Order*, 15; Caryl, *Sacred Covenant*, 42; Gaspar Hickes, *The Life and
Death of David* (1645), 14; Sibbes, *Works*, I, 97; VII, 174; John Geree, *Judah's Joy*
(1641), sig. D2v.
75. Wilkinson, *Lukewarmness*, 29; Sibbes, *Works*, I, 5–7; IV, 216–17.
76. Oliver Bowles, *Zeal for God's House* (1643), 44; Anthony Burges, *Public Affections*
(1646), 4; Edmund Calamy, *An Indictment against England* (1645), 35. Michael
Walzer, *Exodus and Revolution* (1985).
77. Strong, *Right Way*, 14–18, 20.
78. Burges, *Public Affections*, 4; Sedgwick, *Military Discipline*, 82; Whitaker, *Christ the
Settlement*, 60; Brooks, *God's Delight*, 27, 31; Caryl, *Arraignment of Unbelief*, 26–7;
Barker, *Christian Standing*, 30.
79. Sibbes, *Works*, II, 321; III, 308, 468; IV, 343; Brooks, *Heaven on Earth*, 10–11, 37.
See Edmund Calamy, *A Pattern for All* (1658), 17–19, 21–2; John Von Rohr,
'Covenant and Assurance in Early English Puritanism', *Church History*, XXXIV, 2
(June 1965).
80. John Preston, *A Sermon* (1633), in *The Saints' Qualification* (1634), 285, 289, 290–2;
Cheynell, *Man of Honor*, 62; Thomas Valentine, *A Charge against the Jews* (1647),
28; Marshall, *Divine Project*, 27, 37–9; Wilkinson, *Lukewarmness*, 5, 13, 21–2, 30–1,
38–9; Thomas Wilson, *David's Zeal for Zion* (1641), 31; Preston, *Breastplate*, II, 236–
7.
81. Preston, *Breastplate*, II, 236–7, 241.
82. Sedgwick, *Zion's Deliverance*, 34; Thomas Case, *God's Rising* (1644), 42; Whitaker,
Christ the Settlement, 59; Owen, *Steadfastness*, 47; Thomas Case, *Jehoshaphat's
Caveat* (1644), 14; William Goode, *A Public Spirit* (1645), 7; Hill, *Militant Church*,
10; Cheynell, *Zion's Memento*, 11; Caryl, *Sacred Covenant*, 37.
83. Thomas Wilson, *Jericho's Downfall* (1643), 19–20, 28; Hill, *Militant Church*, 10, 12;
Francis Peck, *The Good Fight of Faith* (1645), 4–5, 9–10; Case, *God's Waiting*, 125–
6.
84. Elidad Blackwell, *A Caveat for Magistrates* (1645), 24; Brooks, *Glorious Day*, in
Works, VI, 325; Philip Nye, *An Exhortation* (1643), reprinted in James Reid,
Memoirs of the Westminster Divines (1811), II, 381; Case, *God's Waiting*, 159–60;
Stanley Gower, *Things Now-a-Doing* (1644), 26; Owen, *Laboring Saint's Dismission*,
in *Works*, VIII, 347, 355, 361; Goode, *Public Spirit*, 1; Strong, *Right Way*, 23, 25.
85. John Goodwin, *Ireland's Advocate* (1641), 4, 12–13; Price, *Sermon*, 24; Sibbes,
Works, V, 490–1.

5 THE CHURCH

1. Francis Cheynell, *The Man of Honor* (1645), 54; Thomas Goodwin, *The Great
Interest of States and Kingdoms* (1646), 53–4; Thomas Manton, *England's Spiritual
Languishing* (1648), 15; Thomas Palmer, *The Saints' Support* (1644), 12–13.
2. Stephen Marshall, *A Sermon of the Baptizing of Infants* (1644), 32; Richard Sibbes,
Works (Edinburgh, 1862–4; repr. 1978–82), IV, 217; VII, 389; Stephen Marshall, *A
Sacred Record* (1645), 11; Vavasor Powell, *God the Father* (1651), 49–50; Henry Hall,
Heaven Ravished (1644), 12–13. The precise definition of the church had long been
one of the central problems of the Reformation, second only to doctrine and in some
ways more contentious, especially in England; see Maria Dowling and Peter Lake

(eds.), *Protestantism and the National Church in Sixteenth Century England* (1987). 'The church' as discussed in Puritan sermons, and as something decidedly different from the Church of England, has been noticed by John F. Wilson, *Pulpit in Parliament* (Princeton, 1969), ch. VI, esp. 169, and Tai Liu, *Discord in Zion* (The Hague, 1973), ch. 1. Yet the ministers seldom used their pulpits to promote a particular form of church organization, and when they did their sermons were usually not authorized for print. 'These and the like questions are fitter for a thorough debate elsewhere than for a pulpit,' said one, expressing the consensus that the matter was to be decided collectively. Jeremiah Whitaker, *The Danger of Greatness* (1646), 38. They did preach concerning the principles of church 'government', and very real and ultimately irreconcilable differences did come to emerge between the two main groupings on the specific application of those principles; but larger issues were involved. Perhaps the best defense of treating the sermons as a group, without respect to ecclesiological 'party', was provided by Powell himself when he said 'the difference between Presbytery and Independency is not so great in their principles (though they differ in several circumstantials) as it is in their practices.' *God the Father*, 133.

3. Anthony Burges, *A Reformation* (1643), 26; Joseph Symonds, *A Sermon* (1641), sig. C3r; William Bridge, *Two Sermons* (1642), II, 19; Matthew Newcomen, *Jerusalem's Watchmen* (1643), 11; John Owen, *The Branch of the Lord* (1650), *Works* (Edinburgh, 1862), VIII, 286; Stephen Marshall, *A Peace Offering to God* (1641), 27; Humphrey Hardwick, *Zion's Deliverance and Reformation* (1644), 26. Cp. William Haller, *Foxe's Book of Martyrs and the Elect Nation* (1963).

4. John White, *Jerusalem's Restoration* (1645), 31; Thomas Case, *A Sermon* (1645), 8; Henry Wilkinson, *Babylon's Ruin* (1643), 20; Richard Vines, *The Posture of David's Spirit* (1644), 19–20; Thomas Carter, *Prayer's Prevalency* (1643), 18; Obadiah Sedgwick, *Haman's Vanity* (1643), 15–16; Hall, *Heaven Ravished*, 19.

5. Daniel Cawdrey, *The Good Man* (1643), 11; William Sedgwick, *Zion's Deliverance* (1642), 19; Herbert Palmer, *Utmost Venturing* (1643), 8; William Goode, *Jacob Raised*, (1647), 24.

6. Palmer, *Saints' Support*, 1; John Bond, *Job in the West* (1645), 12; Simeon Ash, *God's Incomparable Goodness* (1647), 3; George Hughes, *The Woe-Joy-Trumpet* (1647), 34; Thomas Mocket, *The Church's Troubles and Deliverance* (1642), 42–3. The same was true of entire churches: 'Outward prosperity is no mark of the true church,' Richard Sibbes insisted. 'Abundance of temporal blessings is no sign that we are in God's favor.' *Works*, V, 269.

7. Sibbes, *Works*, I, 401–2; II, 295, 515; VI, 296; VII, 99; Marshall, *Peace Offering*, 7; Samuel Rogers, *The Poor's Pension* (1644), 11; John Warren, *Man's Fury* (1656), 14; Thomas Brooks, *Precious Remedies* (1652; repr. 1984), 79, 127; John Preston, *The Breastplate of Faith and Love* (1634), I, 284, 288.

8. Nicholas Estwick, *Christ's Submission* (1644), 11; Nathaniel Holmes, *A Sermon* (1650), 29; Palmer, *Saints' Support*, 3; George Gipps, *A Sermon* (1645), 21; Nathaniel Hardy, *Justice Triumphing* (1646), 6; Preston, *Breastplate*, I, 290; Gaspar Hickes, *The Advantage of Afflictions* (1645), 8, 17; Mocket, *Church's Troubles*, 12; Stanley Gower, *Things Now-a-Doing* (1644), 8.

9. Simeon Ash, *The Best Refuge* (1642), 4; Joseph Caryl, *The Oppressor Destroyed* (1662), 2, 6; John Conant, *The Woe and Weal of God's People* (1649), sig. A3r, 8; Mocket, *Church's Troubles*, 32–3.

10. William Strong, *The Vengeance of the Temple* (1648), 8–9; Matthew Newcomen, *The Craft and Cruelty of the Church's Adversaries* (1643), 3, 14; Stephen Marshall, *Meroz Cursed* (1642), 7; Palmer, *Utmost Venturing*, 10–12.

11. Sibbes, *Works*, V, 308–9; William Perkins, *Works* (Cambridge, 1626–31), II, 65; Thomas Case, *God's Rising* (1644), 2, 6–7, 8, 9–11. The well-known hatred of

Catholics and the Catholic Church, by no means limited to Puritans, can be seen largely as such an attempt to create a single, ideologically-defined public enemy as an alternative to a myriad of private ones. See Robin Clifton, 'Fear of Popery', in *The Origins of the English Civil War*, ed. Conrad Russell (1973), and 'The Popular Fear of English Catholics during the English Revolution', *Past and Present*, 52 (1971); William Lamont, *Richard Baxter and the Millenium* (1979), ch. II, and Peter Lake, 'Anti-Popery: The Structure of a Prejudice', in *Conflict in Early Stuart England: Studies in Religion and Politics, 1603–1642*, ed. R. Cust and A. Hughes (1989).

12. Marshall, *Meroz Cursed*, 7; Case, *God's Rising*, 37; Thomas Case, *Deliverance-Obstruction* (1646), 10; Sibbes, *Works*, VII, 133; Preston, *Breastplate*, II, 118; Strong, *Vengeance*, sig. A2v; Richard Kentish, *A Sure Stay for a Sinking State* (1648), 9; Thomas Hill, *The Good Old Way* (1644), 37; Rogers, *Poor's Pension*, 36; John Moore, *The Crying Sin of England* (1653), 4–5.

13. Nathaniel Holmes, *The New World* (1641), 26, 75; Herbert Palmer, *Church Restorers* (1646), 16; Marshall, *Meroz Cursed*, 27.

14. Henry Burton, *England's Bondage* (1641), 7; Jeremiah Burroughs, *Zion's Joy* (1641), 21; Marshall, *Meroz Cursed*, 33–4.

15. Marshall, *Meroz Cursed*, 28–9, 53–4; Palmer, *Utmost Venturing*, 5, 8; John Ellis, *A Sound Peace* (1643), 17; Palmer, *Saints' Support*, 42.

16. Samuel Rutherford, *A Sermon* (1645), 14; 75; Ash, *God's Incomparable Goodness*, 2; Warren, *Man's Fury*, 32–4; Sibbes, *Works*, I, 406; Hall, *Heaven Ravished*, 11; Sedgwick, *Zion's Deliverance*, 4; Sedgwick, *Haman's Vanity*, 6–7, 8; Obadiah Sedgwick, *A Thanksgiving Sermon* (1644), 16.

17. Richard Byfield, *Temple-Defilers Defiled* (1645), 29; Francis Cheynell, *Zion's Memento* (1643), 42–3; Thomas Case, *A Sermon* (1645), 8. Note that just as the 'national' consequences of sin concerned the Independents as well as the Presbyterians, so the separation of 'the church' from 'the nation' was central to the rhetoric of Presbyterians such as Cheynell and Case as well, however much more reluctant they may have been to act on the distinction in practice. Stephen Marshall, *The Song of Moses* (1643), 47. This passage and others like it seem to have been missed by the numerous proponents of the persistent 'elect nation' thesis. See Haller, *Foxe's Book of Martyrs*.

18. Strong, *Vengeance*, 46; Conant; *Woe and Weal*, 28; Joseph Caryl, *England's Plus-Ultra* (1646), 27; Palmer, *Saints' Support*, 43.

19. John Owen, *Ebenezer* (1648), 9, 30–1; Sedgwick, *Haman's Vanity*, 18–9; Strong, *Vengeance*, 22; Palmer, *Saints' Support*, 6, 10, 43; Mocket, *Church's Troubles*, 17, 19. This interpretation of predestination – that 'the triumph of the saints was foreordained' – has been suggested by William Haller, *The Rise of Puritanism* (New York, 1938), 90, also 168–9, and again by Michael Walzer, *The Revolution of the Saints* (Cambridge, Mass., 1965), *passim*.

20. Strong, *Vengeance*, sig. A2v.; Joseph Boden, *An Alarm Beat Up in Zion* (1644), 15–16; Jeremiah Burroughs, *The Glorious Name of God* (1643), 5–6, 76, 92; Cheynell, *Man of Honor*, 64; John Arrowsmith, *A Great Wonder in Heaven* (1647), 41; Jeremiah Burroughs, *A Glimpse of Zion's Glory* (1641), 21; Thomas Coleman, *Hopes Deferred and Dashed* (1645), 12. This 'offensive' posture distinguishes Puritan sermons from the more legalistic arguments employed in resistance theory. 'I know many have taken great pains . . . to prove it lawful, in the present cause of God, the kingdom, and Parliament, to take up and make use of arms in the defense of religion, the church, and the truths of God,' said Joseph Boden.

> But . . . I shall make bold to go one step further and . . . press the saints to . . . use manfully weapons of offense against the beasts of Babylon. And I shall hence and here boldly affirm that he who now startles and staggereth, delayeth, and refuseth with the Parliament and their party to bear and use

arms against the prelates, papists, and atheists with all the fry of antichristian factors and panders is no other than a rebel and traitor against God.

Cp. Quentin Skinner, 'The Origins of the Calvinist Theory of Revolution', in *After the Reformation*, ed. Barbara C. Malamant (Philadelphia, 1980). Caryl, *England's Plus Ultra*, 24–5; Nathaniel Holmes, *A Sermon* (1650), 5–6.

21. Sedgwick, *Haman's Vanity*, sig. A4v; Thomas Hill, *The Militant Church* (1643), 6; John Strickland, *A Discovery of Peace* (1644), 38; Marshall, *Meroz Cursed*, 15, 17; Sibbes, *Works*, VI, 380; Thomas Horton, *Sin's Discovery and Revenge* (1646), 11; Case, *God's Rising*, 7.

22. Burroughs, *Glorious Name of God*, 123; Horton, *Sin's Discovery*, 9; Marshall, *Meroz Cursed*, 9, 12, 22; Henry Wilkinson, *A Sermon against Lukewarmness* (1640), 23; Francis Peck, *The Good Fight of Faith* (1645), 12; Palmer, *Utmost Venturing*, 28–9. Neutralism has figured prominently in recent scholarship; see John Morrill, *The Revolt of the Provinces: Conservatives and Radicals in the English Civil War, 1630–1650* (1980). Yet the notion that neutralism indicates the civil war was somehow imposed on an unwilling population by an extremist minority is simply preposterous. At least in the case of the educated and articulate, neutrals shared the (largely religious) values of both sides. 'Both sides had sworn to uphold the Protestant religion, the Shropshire gentleman Jonathan Langley remarked, "What reason have I therefore to fall out with either?"' Quoted in David Underdown, *Revel, Riot, and Rebellion: Popular Politics and Culture in England, 1603–60* (Oxford, 1985), 2. One need only imagine for a moment the response among this silent majority had a group of Roman Catholic clergymen used their pulpits to promote armed insurrection against the King.

23. Joseph Caryl, *David's Prayer* (1643), 30; Sibbes, *Works*, I, 97; VI, 300, 306, 310, 340, 381; Christopher Tesdale, *Jerusalem* (1644), 10; Strickland, *Discovery of Peace*, 27; Boden, *Alarm*, 18; Nicholas Lockyer, *England Faithfully Watched* (1645), 419–21.

24. William Cooper, *Jerusalem Fatal to her Assailants* (1649), 4; Boden, *Alarm*, 11–12; 20; Sibbes, *Works*, I, 132; II, 144 (quoting Rev. 6:16); Marshall, *Meroz Cursed*, 8, 33, 38; Hill, *Militant Church*, 10–12, 16.

25. Brooks, *Precious Remedies*, 191; Sibbes, *Works*, V, 311; Palmer, *Saints' Support*, 11, 44; Boden, *Alarm*, 31–2; Joseph Caryl, *The Saints' Faithful Acclamation* (1644), 16, 46.

26. Stephen Marshall, *God's Masterpiece* (1645), 28; Sibbes, *Works*, VII, 177; Stephen Marshall, *Emmanuel* (1648), 10.

CONCLUSION

1. William C. Abbott, *Writings and Speeches of Oliver Cromwell* (Cambridge, Mass., 1937–47). For other references, see the Introduction above, note 32.

2. J.G.A. Pocock observes a similar qualification in his study of classical republicanism during the same period, pointing out that Calvinist religion was the leading alternative. *The Political Works of James Harrington* (Cambridge, 1977), 23.

3. John Morrill, 'The Religious Context of the English Civil War', *Transactions of the Royal Historical Society*, fifth series, 34 (1984), 178.

4. The republicanism of the American revolution has been described as a 'secularized version' of Puritanism. Gordon S. Wood, *The Creation of the American Republic, 1776–1787* (New York, 1969), 418. See also Alan Heimert, *Religion and the American Mind from the Great Awakening to the Revolution* (Cambridge, Mass., 1966), and Lewis Perry, *Radical Abolitionism: Anarchy and the Government of God in Antislavery Thought* (Ithaca, 1973).

5. Cp. William Lamont, 'The Left and its Past: Revisiting the 1650s', *History Workshop*, 23 (Spring 1987).

INDEX

SUBJECT INDEX

NAME INDEX